The Haitian Revolution in the
Early Republic of Letters

OXFORD STUDIES IN AMERICAN LITERARY HISTORY

Gordon Hutner, Series Editor

The Haitian Revolution in the Early Republic of Letters

Incipient Fevers

DUNCAN FAHERTY

OXFORD
UNIVERSITY PRESS

Great Clarendon Street, Oxford, OX2 6DP,
United Kingdom

Oxford University Press is a department of the University of Oxford.
It furthers the University's objective of excellence in research, scholarship,
and education by publishing worldwide. Oxford is a registered trade mark of
Oxford University Press in the UK and in certain other countries

Published in the United States of America by Oxford University Press
198 Madison Avenue, New York, NY 10016, United States of America

British Library Cataloguing in Publication Data

Data available

Library of Congress Control Number: 2023935843

ISBN 978-0-19-288915-7

DOI: 10.1093/oso/9780192889157.001.0001

Printed and bound in the UK by
Clays Ltd, Elcograf S.p.A.

Acknowledgments

This book has long been in the making, and across the time I have been working on it I have accumulated far more debts than these acknowledgments can ever hope to repay. First among these overdue drafts is belated thanks to my students at Queens College who never blinked when I asked them to read neglected early-nineteenth-century American texts; who never faltered in their willingness to ask tough questions about these texts and of me for having assigned them; and for teaching me again and again that canonical devotions are always already twice told tales. To attempt to catalog all their names only underscores that a faulty memory is among my many limitations as a teacher, but I am forever grateful to have shared a classroom with: Ugo Eze, Farah Goff, Aniqa Islam, Scott Cheshire, Hijira Abdul Kareem, Dalia Davoudi, Cheryl Spinner, Amya Summerville, Shawn Brown, Adeloa Adeyinka, Isma Hasan, Fredia Burke, Javier Crooks, Evangelina Rizou, Brian Nemeth, Tarek Sobhy, Roger Smith, Andrea Papp, Syaed Karmini, Ahona Islam, Alex Huynh, Labiba Khurshid, Kaitlynn Lee, Alexander Diaz, Zaid Matta, Adam Mizrahi, Margaret Neubauer, Albert Antigua Javier, Wedline Chalestra, Eliana Spector, and most especially Guadalupe Martinez, Tenisha McDonald, Mariel Rodney, Sharon Tran, and Frances Tran.

I am equally indebted to my colleagues at Queens for all of their generosities and solidarities. In particular I am grateful to Lindsey Albracht, Ala Alryyes, Sara P. Alvarez, Ryan Black, Barbara Bowen, Glenn Burger (our stalwart and ever supportive chair!), Jeffrey Cassvan, Seo-Young Chu, Annmarie Drury, Miles P. Grier, Carrie Hintz, Caroline K. Hong, Briallen Hopper, Steven Kruger, Cliff Mak, Rich McCoy, Hillary Miller, Wayne Moreland, Marco Navarro, William Orchard, Sameer Pandya, Megan Paslawski, Vanessa Pérez-Rosario, Roger Sedarat, Siân Silyn Roberts, Amanda Torres, Andrea Walkden, Amy Wan, Karen Weingarten (the world's greatest interim chair twice over!), John Weir, Christopher Williams, and, of course, the irreplaceable Kim Smith.

At the Graduate Center, I have had the privilege of thinking with and learning from a wide range of emerging scholars. Many thanks to Param Ajmera, Sari Altschuler, Jacob Aplaca, Talia Argondezzi, Onur Ayaz, Courtney Chatellier, Luke Church, Anahi Douglas, Michael Druffel, Diana Epelbaum, Chris Eng, Tonya Foster, Margaret Galvin, Sean Gerrity, Sharifa Hampton, Kristina Huang, M.C. Kinniburgh, Lauren Klein, Jenny LeRoy, Stefano Morello, Kristin Moriah, Justin Rogers-Cooper, Danica Savonick, Jesse Schwartz, Sara Jane Stoner,

Maria Stracke, Frances Tran, Wendy Tronrud, Elly Weybright, Chelsea Wall, Simone White, and Dominque Zino.

I am deeply grateful to all of my colleagues in English at the Graduate Center, and most especially to Siraj Ahmed, Kandice Chuh, Matthew Gold, Carrie Hintz, Eric Lott, Joan Richardson, Robert Reid-Pharr, and Joe Wittreich. One of intellectual joys of the Graduate Center is the ability to think with comrades in other disciplines and I am grateful for all my interactions with Louise Lennihan, Patti Myatt, Rachel Sponzo, David Olan, Josh Brumberg, Matt Schoengood, Kendra Sullivan, Vin Deluca, Polly Thistlethwaite, Zee Dempster, David Humphries, Alyson Cole, David Waldstreicher, Michelle Fine, Ruthie Gilmore, Luke Waltzer, Jenny Furlough, Lisa Rhody, Claire Bishop, Gary Wilder, Uday Mehta, Herman Bennett, and Cindi Katz.

It has been an honor to spend almost every Tuesday morning across the last several years in the company of the Committee on Globalization and Social Change. The benefits of all those conversations spill across the pages of this book, and for all that I have learned from them (collectively and individually) I am forever indebted to Gary Wilder, Anthony Alessandrini, Siraj Ahmed, Herman Bennett, Claire Bishop, Susan Buck-Morss, Kandice Chuh, Collette Daiute, Grace Davie, David Joselit, Uday Mehta, Joan Wallach Scott, Linsey Ly, Gemma Sharpe, Sheehan Moore, Jesse Schwartz, Max Toomba, and Julie Livingston.

I have been lucky enough to haunt the plenary sessions and seminars of the Futures of American Studies for the last nine years for which I will always be beyond grateful to Don Pease. Among the many delights of early mornings and late nights in Hanover is the chance to be in the company of Don Pease, James E. Dobson, Colleen Boggs, Soyica Diggs Colbert, Elizabeth Maddock Dillon, Donatella Izzo, Cindi Katz, Eng-Beng Lim, Eric Lott, Israel Reyes, Sandy Alexandre, Kimberly Juanita Brown, and Patricia Stuelke for a few days every summer. And I think everyone involved in Futures would agree, the undeniable gift of every assemblage of the Dartmouth Institute is the chance to learn from and think with Hortense Spillers. My thanks to all of them and to all the plenary speakers and seminarians I have had a chance to learn from!

I am grateful to have had the chance to present portions of this work and develop my thinking about it at a variety of conferences and seminars. Many thanks to the Bavarian Academy of American Studies Summer School, The Center for the Humanities Atlantic Studies Research Group at the University of Miami, the Leeds University Research Symposium, the Manchester American Studies Seminar at the University of Manchester, the Columbia University American Studies Seminar, and the Network of American Periodical Studies at the University of Nottingham. I have also been lucky enough to find home spaces at a number of scholarly organizations and I am deeply indebted to the Charles Brockden Brown Society, The Society of Early Americanists, C19, BrANCA, and the ASA. Without question the best gifts of these conferences is the chance to learn from people like Melissa Adams-Campbell, Mary Grace Albanese,

Jesse Alemán, Sari Altschuler, Dale Bauer, Philip Barnard, Ben Bascom, Robert Battistini, Bridget Bennett, Sarah Blackwood, Anna Brickhouse, Hester Blum, Michelle Burnham, Ed Cahill, Hamilton Carroll, Jim Casey, Heather Chacon, Michelle Chihara, J. Michelle Coghlan, Aly Corey, Daniel Diez Couch, Pete Coviello, Jacob Crane, Elizabeth Maddock Dillion, Mary J. Dinius, Jeb Dobson, Kathleen Donegan, Sari Edelstein, Bert Emerson, Hilary Emmett, Kimberly Engber, Paul Erickson, Benjamin Fagan, Maria Farland, Molly Farrell, Gordon Fraser, Rod Ferguson, Brigitte Fielder, Fritz Fleischmann, Gordon Fraser, John Funchion, Theresa Strouth Gaul, Jared Gardner, Reed Gochberg, Phil Gould, James Greene, Laurel V. Hankins, Glenn Hendler, Beth Hewitt, Keri Holt, Kristina Huang, Helen Hunt, Toni Wall Jaudon, Mark Kamrath, David Kazanjian, Thomas Koenigs, Chris Looby, Christopher Lukasik, Sarah Mesle, Katie McGettigan, Jennifer Morgan, Kristin Moriah, Jarvis McInnis, Hannah Murray, Molly O'Hagan Hardy, Matthew Pethers, Yvette Piggush, Liz Polcha, Ashley Rattner, Ashley Reed, Peter Reed, Martha Elena Rojas, Cécile Roudeau, Marion Rust, William Ryan, Johnathan Senchyne, Stephen Shapiro, Kate Simpkins, Michelle Sizemore, Sam Sommers, Laura Stevens, Patricia Stuelke, Brian Sweeny, Kimberly Takahata, Kyla Wazana Tompkins, Lisa West, Karen Weyler, Caroline Wigginton, Kelly Wisecup, Ivy Wilson, and Xine Yao.

I once, to his face, compared Gordon Hutner to a heavy weight champion, and that hardly does him justice. His faith in this project and his continual good counsel was always sustaining and his insights helped me better conceive of its opening and closing frames. Thanks as well to the two anonymous readers for all of their time and attention, and thanks to everyone at Oxford University Press and most especially to Hannah Doyle, Emma Varley, and Saranya Ravi.

I had the good fortune to be able to call on Herman Bennett, Michael Drexler, Andy Doolen, David Humphries, Sean Gerrity, Miles Grier, Eric Lott, Uday Mehta, Lisa Rhody, Siân Silyn Roberts, Justin Rodgers-Cooper, and Jesse Schwartz to read portions of this book at various stages, and it is no doubt all the better for their insights and suggestions. Jacob Aplaca did yeoman's work across one long summer by copyediting my draft manuscript that I never would have finished without all his time and attention. Stefano "1516" Morello, more than once, helped me think about patterns of digital circulations and that is just yet one more reason I am in his debt.

Michael Drexler generously allowed me teach his edition of Sansay's Secret History while he was still working on it, and while neither of us knew it as the time the seeds for this project were planted in our initial formative conversations about teaching and canonical omissions for which I am eternally grateful.

I am not entirely sure where I would be without Andy Doolen's unwavering comradeship - not only has he talked me off the ledge more than once, but he had an accurate scouting report ready to go on Immanuel Quickly as soon as the pick was in! I am still looking forward to our getting into the Old Welbeck business.

I owe no thanks, at all, to the Bodacious Cowboys but will send them some anyway for sharing my petty interest in posts about Fred & the Gallaghers! And E "more soon"—even if it's a cold, cold winter or its springtime and you were just a boy. Maybe this is the year we actually drive out to Stone Canyon before the lights on all the Christmas trees go out.

Without question, one of the great joys of my career has been co-conspiring with Ed White to launch the 'Just Teach One' project, and all of that collaborative work has always made my thinking better because he more than anyone else understands that what we teach matters in defining the kinds of critical work we can do.

Across several decades now, I have treasured my friendships with Ingrid Epperly, Darren Fried, and Karen Lemmey—the gifts of those relationships are unrepayable. Thanks as well to Matt, Jack, and James "Bobby" Epperly who despite their penchant for rooting for the wrong sports teams always buoy my spirits.

My deepest thanks of all is to Mary-Ann Faherty whose wisdom and love has always nurtured, guided, and supported me.

Contents

Introduction

Haiti in the Early American Republic of Letters

The climax of the anonymously published *Zelica, the Creole* (1820) is among the most abstruse of any American novel.[1] The scene unfurls during the late stages of the Haitian Revolution on a plateau outside Cape François, with a frenetic muddle of thrusting blades and indistinguishable combatants; it culminates with two murders, a suicide attempt, and the arrival of a "thousand" diasporic Africans marshaled by an "enchantress" wielding a "magical image" (3:290–1). In the short span of a few paragraphs—housed in the last of the novel's lengthy three volumes—the central axioms governing the plot suddenly rupture beyond repair. The bulk of the novel charts the struggle of contending entities and ideologies vying for control over the future of St. Domingo, but the abrupt entrance of a Black army intent on ordering the chaotic scene seemingly settles any lingering uncertainties. Still, in the wake of this insurgent claiming of authority, *Zelica's* sounding out of operant early-nineteenth-century debates about race, citizenship, freedom, and belonging quickly begin to vibrate in different frequencies. The echoing reverberations of this unexpected shift resonate well beyond the final pages of the novel as the remaining protagonists depart St. Domingo bearing their colliding histories and ideologies with them. In this sense, while the future of Haiti appears stabilized by the novel's end turn, the rest of the circum-Atlantic world stands on the verge of importing its potentially incendiary revolutionary legacies.

The first victim of *Zelica's* jumbled hillside violence, De la Riviere, was a wealthy French plantocrat turned revolutionary. To instantiate his devotion to the insurgency, De la Riviere undergoes a "chemical preparation" to become phenotypically Black (3:201). Even more than the radical alteration of his ideological commitments, Da la Riviere's dyeing of his epidermis haunts the narrative as an embodiment of the dangers of Black Jacobinism. The second victim, Clara St. Louis, was the wife of a Creole planter and the most prominent U.S. citizen in the novel. Throughout the text, Clara serves as a proxy for American sensibilities, and her inability to comprehend the complexities of the events unfolding around her embodies the Republic's aversion to fully reckoning with diasporic African struggles for freedom. Yet, whatever Clara's Americanness signified remains entombed in Haiti as the Black enchantress commands her followers to transform Clara's grave into a shrine of liberty for the emerging Haitian Republic. Instead of her

The Haitian Revolution in the Early Republic of Letters: Incipient Fevers. Duncan Faherty, Oxford University Press.
© Duncan Faherty 2023. DOI: 10.1093/oso/9780192889157.003.0001

nationality shielding Clara from danger, the novel frames her narrative trajectory as a means of stressing the susceptibility of American bodies—and its body politic—to the deadly contagions of misrepresentation and misappropriation. In essence, *Zelica* insists that the primary martyrs in St. Domingo include an American whose citizenship provided her no sustainable protection and a Frenchman in perpetual Blackface. By casting free white Euro-Americans as the victims of Haitian struggles for liberation, the novel reduces diasporic African emancipation to mere afterthought. Moreover, in abandoning its earlier narrative investments in Black perspectives, *Zelica* effectively overwrites them amid the culminating monochromatic focus on U.S. American futurity.

After the revelations on the craggy ridge, the novel concludes with the titular protagonist Zelica (De la Riviere's mixed-raced daughter and Clara's erstwhile protector) rescued from her suicidal plunge by British sailors intent on transporting her to the United States. Shrouded in mystery for much of the plot, Zelica remains an indecipherable figure of hybridity even as she emerges as the only principal figure to venture northward. Opposed to both systems of enslavement and of revolutionary bloodshed, Zelica advocates for new forms of freedom while simultaneously hoping that securing them will not upend Enlightenment structures of power. Her inability to maintain this ameliorating function—given form by her failure to protect Clara as she had pledged—suggests this centrist position was no longer viable. Thus, the question of just what Zelica would transport with her into the United States remains unanswered. Finally, in an act of ardent punctuation, the concluding paragraphs depict Zelica as ravaged by a mysterious "incipient fever" which renders her incoherent during her voyage to the United States (3:304). Plagued by her complex histories and pushed forward by contending circum-Atlantic tides, Zelica functions as an amalgamation of revolutionary signifiers: an infected mystery in motion, a contagious personification of fractious Black Atlantic relations. The text ends in this liminal oceanic space, pregnant with anticipation and on the brink of arrival.

Despite all its apparent strangeness, *Zelica, the Creole* was not an anomaly. Indeed, the novel's uncanonical status reveals a fundamental and enduring problem with American literary history. The early nineteenth-century print public sphere was awash with distress over sympathetic attachments to revolutionary Haiti drifting northward. The plot of *Zelica* only appears alien to traditional accounts of American literature because of how our scholarly and pedagogical praxis continually marginalizes this urgent preoccupation with Haiti.[2] *The Haitian Revolution in the Early Republic of Letters: Incipient Fevers* aims to counter this tacit disavowal by registering just how obsessed early American readers were with the seismic force of the Haitian Revolution and its capacity to produce aftershocks in the American domestic sphere. When resituated within the early American Republic's ecosystem of Haitian intrigue, the figure of the pyretic Zelica on the verge of an American arrival resonates with considerable force. By disinterring these once popular texts and their neglected narrative patterns, *Incipient Fevers* restores the nascent Haitian Republic's influence on early American national development. In so doing, this book delineates how American writers mobilized a variety of fantasies about Haiti to debate the parameters of the delimited forms of freedom that had established their own republic. Moreover, it charts how these multifaceted discourses about Haiti so often positioned it as the illiberal antithesis of U.S. American democracy. Such discourses were abetted by an American foreign policy that minimized Haitian autonomy as well as through the racialized definitions of belonging taking root in the nascent American Republic's culture and society.

In reckoning with how traditional literary historiography has silenced certain contexts around race, citizenship, representation, and freedom from orienting the field, *The Haitian Revolution in the Early Republic of Letters* recuperates lost textual objects while redressing a crucial blind spot in American literary history. My subtitle (*Incipient Fevers*) echoes the acute anxiety conjured in the figuration of Zelica's possible infiltration of the American ethnoscape while ravaged by an indeterminable disease. Across the period examined in this book, a range of texts contended that any interaction with refugees from Haiti (Black or white) would precipitate radical unsettlements. The connotations of 'incipient', in other words, resonate with an array of meanings concerning the significance of Haiti for the early United States. This tendency to ignore the function of Haiti effectively endorses the incipient project of liberal modernity which (as Lisa Lowe persuasively argues) self-consciously embraced discourses of emancipation and belonging while muting discourses of dominion and expulsion.[3] Thus, a secondary ambition of this book aims at cultivating additional scholarly interest in the early nineteenth century by attending to how and why Haiti figured so prominently in shaping national development during an era so often imagined as a fallow period of cultural production. Our canonical notions of inclusion and progressive enfranchisement nurture a belief in a whiggish liberal modernity, but can only do so—consciously or not—by excommunicating narratives and eras that trouble the nationalist paradigm. Texts that articulate a vision of the United States as a white ethno-state and which advocate for rigid definitions of belonging could not (and cannot easily) be accommodated by the field's hereditary attachment to liberalism without exposing the limitations of such a reliance.

Concerns about Haiti saturated the early American print public sphere from the outbreak of the revolution in 1791 until well after its conclusion in 1804.[4] The gothic, sentimental, and sensationalist undertones of openly speculative periodical accounts accelerated within the genre of fiction, where the specter of Haiti was a commonplace trope. Haiti was not an enigma occasionally deployed by American writers, but rather the overt bellwether against which the prospects for national futurity were imagined and interrogated. The hauntology of Haiti operated as a habitus, a structuring structure which consistently served (to modify a phrase of Avery Gordon) as "the thing behind the things."[5] Ideological representations of Haiti infected the imaginations of early American readers and this sickness, this excitement, and this shared furor has yet to be fully acknowledged within American literary history. Outlining how Haiti haunts U.S. cultural production, *Incipient Fevers* maintains that these two revolutions were so interanimating that it should be impossible to conceive of them separately.[6] The sheer volume of information about Haiti that circulated in the early American print public sphere—with reports appearing in newspapers on a quotidian basis for almost two decades—forms a quantitative challenge to these efforts at erasure. Likewise, the centrality of depictions of Haiti within the formation of early American aesthetic practices underscores the necessity of understanding this impact qualitatively. Unfortunately, scholars have long occluded how early Americans understood their nation as entwined with Haiti. To correct this misuse, we need to consider how and why the futurity of the United States was deliberated over and against a Haitian Republic, which itself was (almost) simultaneously struggling for articulation. Finally, to reestablish this Haitian obsession necessitates recovering and more carefully examining the intricacies of non-canonical texts like *Zelica* since they form a central part of this early American Haitian archive.

Early-nineteenth-century American writers consistently figured Haiti through what Elizabeth Maddock Dillon has theorized as "discourses of intimate distance."[7] For Dillon, intimate distance functions as a spatial designation, a marker of interpersonal dependence, and an indicator of the fluency between bodies concurrently coded as dissimilar. The suggestiveness of this descriptor, its ability to draw attention to both literal bodies and social-political ones, encapsulates how unspoken affiliations can quickly drift into being a source of intense anxiety as these contending (and often oppositional) demands for recognition asserted themselves. Objects or subjects that are intimately distant still enact definition onto one another, even as the space between them also belies their distinctiveness. In Dillion's accounting, the phrase embodies tensions inherent in a system designed to perform two tasks: first, bridging the Atlantic and asserting kinship across oceanic dislocation, while second and conterminously maintaining an irreconcilable division between white and non-white bodies (or in this case, between white and non-white New World Republics). As economic networks conjoined distant sites ringing the Atlantic basin—and rendered them legible and bound to one another by the promotion of white supremacy—the forcibly transported people that generated wealth for settler colonial capitalism were simultaneously and violently estranged from the social compact. Intimate closeness and intimate separation are, in other words, central to the formation of European incursions into the Western hemisphere. For myriad writers in the early Republic, Haiti was both unambiguously familiar and categorically incompatible. Reminders of the dangers of an economic dependency on enslavement, these multi-generic treatments of Haiti also depicted its cultural order (both pre- and post-Revolution) as counterparts to U.S. democracy. Synchronously held fast and rejected, Haiti was the ever-present index of the United States: a distorted reflection of the Republic's past, a troubling echo of its present, and a nightmarish harbinger of divisive futures. As early Americans were well aware, given the frequency with which news and opinions about the Haitian Revolution filled the pages of American periodicals, the production of Black freedom in St. Domingo betrayed the limitations of American democracy. The formation of an independent Haitian Republic, in short, called into question the obscuring work that "all men are created equal" enacted and which American literary history has for so long copiously resisted confronting.

Across the last two decades, a crucial attention to the Caribbean's sociopolitical impact on the development of the emerging United States has revitalized the field of early American studies by moving it away from its isolationist origins.[8] Concomitantly, within literary studies, so much of this work remains grounded in readings of Leonora Sansay's *Secret History; or, The Horrors of St Domingo* (1808) that the field has replicated a version of intimate distance while attending to the importance of the Haitian Revolution.[9] As I will explore in more detail in Chapter 4 of what follows, all too frequently Sansay's *Secret History* stands privileged as a singularity, one that allows for a consideration of the Haitian Revolution as an external event. Framing Sansay's text as the solitary repository of U.S. reactions to Haiti surreptitiously reinscribes them as a *secret* history. Such a practice enables recognition and containment of the Haitian Revolution within literary historiography. Sansay's novel terminates with the American sisters returning to the United States after divorcing themselves from foreign connections; given this conclusion, readers can still imagine the inchoate American Republic as psychosomatically feverish, but, perhaps, not literally infected by alien revolutionary contagions. In contrast, the narrative trajectory of *Zelica* renders such a fantasy of immunization unsustainable by recasting the identity of the refugee from that of white women intent on reclaiming their natal citizenship to the feverish daughter of an enslaved woman and a radicalized former French planter.[10] Instead of ending with a gesture of willful foreclosure, *Zelica* emphasizes the contingencies involved in deciphering the meanings of Black Atlantic mobility and revolutionary migration by culminating in the titular protagonist's possible, and indecipherable, entry into the United States. Given that *Zelica* was published twelve years after *Secret History* (even as they both are set in 1802), its insistence about possible infiltration registers how American writers working in a variety of genres and across several decades understood Haiti's impact as compounding rather than dissipating well after it declared independence in 1804.[11]

For all its promiscuous roaming across the Caribbean basin, Sansay's novel charts a roundtrip voyage to Philadelphia. Shaken, but not infected, by revolutionary fervor, Sansay's white American sisters presumably reintegrate into

U.S. society without altering the domestic order. The circularity of the text's geographical imagination provides one explanation as to why the text has so easily been accommodated into the canon. *Secret History*, in other words, concludes with a return to a familiar space, one easily housed with the field's relentless privileging of an East-West axis for charting national development. The texts explored in *Incipient Fevers* undercut the solidity of this residual trans-Atlantic compass by routing ideological questions along latitudinal lines of influence rather than longitudinal ones. In other words, I argue that our traditional sense of the political geography of the nineteenth century remains distorted by an inveterate privileging of the wrong nodal point as the prime meridian.[12] Focusing on Cape François rather than Greenwich to accurately map how the early Republic of Letters plotted its own socio-political stability, this book asserts the primacy of Haiti within American culture across the first two decades of the nineteenth century.[13] *Incipient Fevers* refigures the importance of early-nineteenth-century cultural production by charting how its geographical imagination strayed beyond the ostensible teleology of an Anglophilic trans-Atlanticism. As such, I aim to complicate our understanding of how western frontiers came to animate American culture by considering national expansion, via the Louisiana Purchase, as an underexamined byproduct of Haiti's struggle for emancipation. Contending with how domestic anxieties about social and cultural reproduction coalesced in response to the birth of an independent Black Republic reveals how questions of diasporic African freedom were consistently indexed through Haitian liberation.

In *Incipient Fevers* Haiti becomes the locus for interrogating conceptions of U.S. national futurity by decoding how U.S. writers deployed Haiti to pose crucial questions about the limitations of American versions of Republican ideologies. In so doing, I explore serialized texts from the era's robust periodical culture, and then move to contextualize my readings of them by attending to how these same periodicals editorialized their reportage about events in Haiti. Selected, in part, for the way they collapse any spatial distinction between the U.S. south and Caribbean plantations these texts routinely emphasize the economic commonality of these divergent spaces via projected fantasies about quasi-labor-less northern agrarianism.[14] For many northeastern Federalists, Jefferson's election created the conditions of possibility not only for renewed political turmoil, but also for the licentious and undemocratic mores of southern planters to upend the domestic social order across the entire nation. In the wake of their dismissal from political authority, a loosely affiliated Federalist intelligentsia labored to reassert their influence by blurring the boundaries between Monticello and Cape François. Essentially, these Federalist writers depicted these capitals of the corrupt plantocracy as counterformations to American national stability (past, present, and future). Others, perhaps less venomous in their distaste for Jeffersonianism, advocated for economic circuits of exchange that would reduce dependency on enslaved labor to protect the U.S. against the fluctuations of circum-Atlantic trade. Hardly anti-racist or even necessarily abolitionist in tenor, these texts sought to secure the profits garnered by Black Atlantic capitalism by promoting new avenues of resource extraction in response to the problem of Haiti. *Incipient Fevers* surveys these various narrative iterations as a textual archipelago: a cluster of independent but still allied formations open to examination both for their particularities as well as for how the currents between them register submerged ligatures of connection.

Treating the Haitian Revolution as a singularity fails to account for the protracted duration of the struggle (which lasted from 1791 to 1804), while depreciating the complexities of its unfolding. This critical redaction further condenses the import of Haiti to a universalized sense of fear across the entirety of the United States.[15] These residual habits of reading gloss over how American writers responded to shifting events in St. Domingo in tactical ways, fluidly reworking their emphasis depending on reflecting regional political affiliations or evolving economic visions for the United States. These corollary reactions necessitate a deeper consideration, one only made possible by moving away from treating these rhizomatic influences as predictably linear. Recovery of the extent of early American fixations with Haiti requires, in short, scrutinizing the fluctuations of a multi-directional attentiveness instead of recursively adhering to teleological presumptions. Therefore, this project engages the fluctuating import of Haiti on the American imagination both during and after the Revolution.

Given that so many early-nineteenth-century American texts overflowed with concern about Haiti, it has been easier to ignore cultural production from this period altogether than to cherry-pick objects easily accommodated within the confines of a progressive canonicity. Or, to put it another way, many of the texts published during this early-nineteenth-century interregnum present a constitutive challenge to a liberal canon formed around a progressive conception of national development. *Incipient Fevers* inventories the shortfalls of our canonical formations by focusing attention on the first two decades of the nineteenth century, when an obsession with Haiti was paramount in the U.S. print public sphere and when the specter of Haiti was acutely present in the white American imagination. Despite this intensity of interest for American writers and readers alike—or more likely because of it—the period from 1800 to 1820 has remained largely unexplored. To address these larger questions about field formation, the following section probes the place of the early nineteenth century within American literary history.

"Colonial Period, Revolutionary Period, Knickerbocker Period...and so on"

From its earliest formations, American literary history has declared the first two decades of the nineteenth-century devoid of cultural merit; more bluntly, this era remains pigeonholed as a textual wasteland.[16] Addressing one of the most pronounced temporal gaps in U.S. literary studies, *Incipient Fevers* argues that this neglect springs in part from Haiti's centrality in this period's cultural imagination. By dismissing textual production from this era, scholars have consistently avoided acknowledging how early American writers depicted the Haitian Revolution as a counter to U.S. democracy. These representations of Haiti as an American antithesis expose the xenophobia and white supremacy within the early American Republic that extends to the literary canon designed to manufacture a national tradition.[17] One genesis for this project stems from my belief that our discipline's canonizing impulses have not actually been guided by aesthetic concerns but rather by a tacit commitment to disavowing extra-national associations—especially when those connections undercut the supremacy of whitewashed American definitions of freedom. The solitary exception to this habitual repudiation has been the overemphasis on associations with England, a critical doxa that often results in the uncritical grafting of American culture onto English literary movements.[18] This reductive sense of literary genealogies negates latitudinal lines of influence on the development of the United States. Therefore, part of the exigency of *Incipient Fevers* arises from a commitment to registering the role of American literary history as animating the nationalist project of anti-Blackness, a tendency which comes into clearer focus through attention to the archive of early American Haitian narratives.

Without question, the initial generation of American literary historians embraced an isolationist imaginary that in turn shaped the foundation of the discipline. Such enclosure was understandable for these foundational figures, given their location within the constrictive framework of English departments and the prevailing critical attachment to independent national traditions as repositories of value. In other words, a focus on domestically isolated textual production was likely the only available avenue for field formation. Nevertheless, the lingering presence of this impulse within the field's infrastructures ironically deterritorializes our understandings of the temporal and spatial dimensions of early U.S. cultural production. One reason why such public history projects as, for example, 'The 1619 Project' have appeared to some as radical reinterpretations of American cultural history stems from the traditional attachment to New England, above all other spaces, as the ideological birthplace of the United States.[19] In framing Plymouth Rock, and not Jamestown, as *the* primal scene, the progenitors of American Studies grounded the field in configurations of migrations for freedom without fully decoding just who those freedoms were for or how they were produced.[20] A failure to acknowledge this retrograde attachment to a monochromatic origin myth obscures how texts and contexts uneasily accommodated by this regionalist arbiter remain exiled beyond the pale. This ideology produced an American literary history plotted to celebrate freedom and inclusion, but one undisturbed by the realities of the limitations of those concepts across time.

Fully comprehending why the importance of Haiti exists only at the peripheries of American literary history requires a reappraisal of shopworn patterns of periodization. More specifically, as I will argue below, the ossification of the subdivisions of American literary history occurred almost at the same time that they were initially conceived in the early twentieth century. While the terms for these periods have changed over time, the demarcations they superimposed continue to buttress American literary history. Evidence of this inertia fueled the lamentations within, arguably, the earliest sustained critique of the field. Crafted by the first "Professor of American Literature," a title bestowed upon Fred Lewis Pattee by Pennsylvania State University in 1895, a "Call for a Literary Historian" bemoans the torpid state of U.S. literary studies. Published in the June 1924 edition of H.L. Mencken's *American Mercury*, Pattee's jeremiad was not a closet drama intended to provoke an academic coterie; rather, it was a public-facing denouncement of a field by one of its most prominent founders. Tellingly, Pattee began with a charged confession of intellectual exhaustion. "I have nearly a hundred histories of American literature on my shelves, and I am still adding more," Pattee declared, "a hundred volumes to tell the story of our literary century, and all of them alike, all built on the same model!" These volumes surveyed identical terrains, Pattee observed, promoted the usual suspects as canonical, and consistently adopted the same constraining rubrics—"Colonial Period, Revolutionary Period, Knickerbocker Period, New England Period, and so on"—to guide their endeavors. Anxious that his contemporaries rehashed old formulas instead of forging new interpretative pathways, Pattee warned that the field would soon choke on its own reiterations.[21]

My intention is not to lionize Pattee as a literary augur capable of prophesizing the limitations of future critical turns; nor am I advocating for a return to his restricted pantheon of white male authors. Still, despite these considerable limitations in terms of who and what might constitute our objects of study, Pattee's polemic provides an opportunity to take stock of the undeviating history of periodization of American literature. Even as Pattee chipped away at the habituated use of these cemented classifications a century ago, his categories remain resoundingly familiar. Pattee's first two periods (Colonial and Revolutionary) endure as the contemporary subfield of Early American literature. Likewise, the latter two descriptors mark familiar canonical signposts. His use of Knickerbocker signals the rise of Washington Irving and James Fenimore Cooper post-1819, and his label of a New England period reveals how what has more familiarly been called the American Renaissance has always been (as Pattee understood) a predominately regional formation disguised as a national one.[22] Arguably, the categories that Pattee diagrammed as determining the orbits of American literary studies in 1924 continue to map our canonical constellations.[23] More importantly, many of the periods that Pattee's contemporaries eschewed have remained typecast as unworthy of attention.

Most major anthologies of American literature reflect an unwavering sense of periodization by cleaving to the very categories Pattee critiqued for their ossification. Even as various iterations of American literature anthologies have marketed themselves as increasingly inclusive, the temporal categories they embraced have barely shifted across the last half century. For example, since its inaugural publication in 1979, the *Norton Anthology of American Literature* (still the most popular classroom anthology in the United States) has paid scant attention to the first two decades of the nineteenth century. While the *Norton* has deployed 1820 as an important dividing line, for all intents and purposes the various editorial teams have curated early American literature as if it went dormant in 1801 before resuming production in the 1830s.[24] Aside from selections from Washington Irving's *The Sketch Book* (1819), selected entries from the Lewis and Clark journals (1804/5), and sporadic publication of William Cullen Bryant's "Thanatopsis" (1811 and 1816), few texts from the early nineteenth century ever appear in any edition of the anthology. As the impressive digital humanities project 'Early American Literature Anthologies' spearheaded by Abram Van Engen vividly demonstrates, the *Norton* has held a regional predisposition since its inception.[25] This provincial editorial fixation has sculpted a canon in which New Englanders are overrepresented and thus their rightful place in American literary history has continually been overemphasized.[26] Rival anthologies seeking to compete with the primacy of the *Norton* have correspondingly framed their presentations of the early nineteenth century through implied absence rather than considered engagement.[27] My privileging of periodization is not intended to circumnavigate questions related to inclusion, diversity, geography, and canonicity that undoubtedly vex the editorial teams of every anthologizing project; rather my interest resides with highlighting this shared attachment to glossing over the first two decades of the nineteenth century.[28] Without question, these contending visions of American literature have built on important work in the field and helped alter the terrain of knowledge production for both students and scholars alike. Yet, regardless of all this work, the temporal taxonomies that form the spinal columns of American literature anthologies have seldom wavered.[29]

The lone scholarly publishing initiative which attended to the first two decades of the nineteenth century was the short lived Oxford University Press's *Early American Women Writers* series.[30] While this project recuperated two volumes from the early nineteenth century, Tabitha Gilman Tenney's *Female Quixotism* (1801) and Rebecca Rush's *Kelroy* (1812), unfortunately neither text elicited sustained critical or pedagogical engagement. The overall impulse of this Oxford series was to restore the importance of early American women writers (including Susanna Rowson and Hannah Foster in the 1790s) for the field. Many of these recovered volumes plot the lack of social mobility for white women in the early Republic, detailing how the American Revolution failed to rescript misogynistic conceptions of citizenship and gender. While these crucial feminist interventions reshaped prevailing conceptions of early American literature and recuperated the importance of several early American women writers, they did not dramatically push the field to take up questions of race, dislodge the dominance of trans-Atlantic Anglophone affiliations, or redraw the temporal subdivisions of American literary history.[31]

In a poignant meditation on recovery projects in early American studies, Theresa Strouth Gaul diagnoses the causal relationship between scholarship and teaching. While digital access to databases has opened up new lines of inquiry, Gaul appropriately maintains that what is "*in print*" generally "determines what is read and taught in classrooms and receives analysis in dissertations, scholarly journals, and monographs." In charting the ebb and flow of recovery, Gaul details how many of these reclaimed texts (including many in the Oxford series) fell back out of print because "nationalist frameworks" could not easily account for their incongruous narrative "elements." Even as she remained optimistic that "Transnational approaches" in early American studies might rectify this scholarly apathy, Gaul nevertheless deplores how the prominence of "nationalist paradigms" dislodge recovery efforts which cannot easily be accommodated by such a restrictive fixation. Without question the field has changed in the decade since Gaul's essay was published, but her survey still registers some stunning information about the temporal orientation of American literary history. For example, she catalogs how of the 498 articles published during 2007–8 devoted to American women writers in the field's "eight top journals," only "six" focused on pre-1800 authors. To this staggering statistic, I would add only that the vast majority of those essays focused on the nineteenth century examined post-1820 texts. Gaul's accounting exposes that even as the transnational turn has sparked innovative work, it has not significantly altered the temporal canonical categories that Pattee warned about a century ago.[32]

Further complicating this torpidity around periodization remains the tendency to frame textual production from the immediate post-Revolutionary period as progressive. For example, "among the significant legacies of Cathy Davidson's *Revolution and the Word*," Ed White has pointedly argued, "is the default characterization of the early U.S. novel as generically and socially radical: the word is part of the revolution."[33] This privileging of supposedly progressive commitments has produced a distorted sense of the early Republic's print public sphere. In response to this overamplification of the revolutionary elements in post-Revolutionary canonical objects, White advocates for a wider investigation of the variety of ideological discourses inflecting cultural production in the early American Republic. While a redacted vision still defines the first formative U.S. literary period, the counterrevolutionary elements of early American Haitian fictions appear more incongruous than they actually were. Recursively, many early-nineteenth-century American texts use the occasion of the Haitian Revolution to argue for tighter regulation of the social, economic, and cultural forces within the United States. The texts considered in this book, such as "The Story of Makandal" and *The Black Vampyre*, were selected for the way they respond to the new forms of freedom enacted by the Haitian Revolution by strategically positioning these emergent freedoms as an existential threat to U.S. American stability. And, arguably, only by returning to these registers of conservative thought can we begin to understand fully the intensity of interest in Haiti as an archive of revolutionary potential.

Conservative strains of cultural production seldom anchor Americanist work, in part because they unsettle the foundational conjunction of canonization with liberalism. The archive of early American Haitian narratives explored in this book catalogs overt fears about Black freedom so directly that it reveals how white supremacy resonates within that liberalism. Indeed for much of Euro-America, and especially for white people in the United States, the Haitian Revolution, as Tyler Stovall argues, "came to symbolize the racial parameters of freedom," defining "liberty for whites" through "independence, order, and prosperity," whereas "for Blacks it meant massacre and lawlessness."[34] In their conservative assertions of U.S. hierarchies of value, texts such as Martha Meredith Read's *Monima; or, The Beggar Girl* are captivated both by fears about French Jacobinism and by the more terrifying prospect of racialized revolution in the Caribbean. In dramatizing these anxieties, narratives like Isaac Mitchell's *The Asylum; or, Alonzo and Melissa* deploy aesthetic strategies of alienation and estrangement in order to bind citizens to an imaginary isolated nation immunized from connections to external spaces. Presenting the Haitian Republic as a nightmarish inverse of the United States produces a vision of U.S. American whiteness severed from any possible associations with creolization. While the term creole had across the eighteenth century been understood as defining anyone born in the New World with European ancestry, during this period the term evolves to take on the more modern connotation of noting linkages to the French Caribbean.[35] Those possessing these early-nineteenth-century anti-revolutionary ideologies yearned to distinguish American whiteness from New World whiteness more generally to suggest that the problems of racialized belonging which had unsettled Caribbean colonization could be forestalled in North America. Central to these efforts at reconfiguring white supremacy was a loosely choreographed articulation of an American democratic identity grounded in a nationalized version of whiteness divorced from the dubious morality of Creole planters. Attempts at reasserting a redacted American whiteness were driven by mid-Atlantic Federalists who sought to distinguish themselves from both colonial Creoles and enslavers in the southern United States. Disingenuously framing themselves as detached from the structuring violences of enslavement, northern Federalist writers sought to consolidate questions of citizenship and freedom by insinuating that the mid-Atlantic region was less imbricated in the horrors of the Black Atlantic than other spaces in the hemisphere.[36] One strategy deployed by Federalist writers to accomplish this reterritorialization was to resurrect ideologies about New World declension and reconstitute them as issues of morality. White people directly connected to enslavement, regardless of their geographical location, were declared degenerate and therefore incapable of full participation in a Republican society. This notion of a direct link between enslavement and the erosion of moral capacities was simultaneously extended to condemn the enslaved, and thus was also used to reify racist anti-Black ideologies.[37] This prejudicial thinking allowed Federalist writers to avoid contending with the implications of Black liberation, since they had already predetermined that any connection to enslavement rendered one unfit for democratic citizenship.

Fueled by conservative methodologies, operant configurations of whiteness congealed in response to the Haitian Revolution. These attempts to constrictively define Americanness were produced as a counterformation to the more expansive definition of freedom that the Haitian Republic made a tangible political possibility. Attending to narrative manifestations of American freedom as defined by whiteness in the early nineteenth century brings into relief how this political agenda circulated throughout the early post-Revolutionary period. Resituating early American Haitian narratives within the history of literary production at the beginning of the nineteenth century produces a more nuanced understanding of previous textual production, highlighting how anti-revolutionary propensities transformed into a dominant mode of discourse. While new narrative forms and techniques came into being to advance what I describe as a constrictive vision of American belonging, its origins were as old as the Republic itself. Given how the Haitian Republic produced a new political reality, these reactionary techniques were forced to respond to the actualities of Black freedom in ways that earlier texts had not. As early-nineteenth-century American writers reaffirmed coded strategies for promulgating anti-Black ideologies, they simultaneously struggled to create new methods that could account for the establishment of a second republic in the hemisphere. Haiti's emergence, in other words, undercut American exceptionality by exposing the limitations American democracy's foundational myths.

The works examined in *Incipient Fevers* foreground how disquietude over the future of domestic enslavement pervaded American cultural production well before the ameliorating compromises of 1830 or 1850. While Americanists have long scoured mid-century cultural production for evidence of the preliminary drum-taps of the Civil War, the divisive clamor of sectionalism beat even before the formal adoption of the Constitution. American literary history's reliance on the chronotope "antebellum" displaces cultural objects from their own temporal contexts to figure them as progenitors of a crescendo that too many scholars still surreptitiously treat as an inevitable event. Consider, for example, how one of the first critics to seriously attend to the importance of the Haitian Revolution for American culture, Eric J. Sundquist, figures this influence as landing in middle of the nineteenth century. In his illuminating reading of Herman Melville's *Benito Cereno* (1855), Sundquist argues that while the novella "does not prophesy a civil war" it still "anticipates, just as plausibly, an explosive heightening of the conflict between American democracy, Old World despotism, and Caribbean New World revolution."[38] Slippages between prophesy and anticipation allow Sundquist to position Melville's text as predictive, even as it obscures *Benito Cereno*'s investments in decoding the legacies of events from fifty years in the past.[39] Although Sundquist rightfully discerns how Melville narrativized the tectonic collision of American political ideologies, European conceptions of sovereignty, and Caribbean struggles for freedom, he erroneously suggests that Melville feared a reckoning had not yet already occurred. Arguably, the enduring force of *Benito Cereno* resides in its understanding of the rupture produced by the Haitian Revolution in the early nineteenth century. Much can be gained from moving beyond reading *Benito Cereno* as a harbinger of future conflicts, to understanding it as a deep dive into neglected archival materials detailing how the specter of Haiti rescripted the cultural order of the United States in the early nineteenth century.

Sundquist's interpretation represents, perhaps even paradigmatically, the practice of reading *antebellum* texts as anticipating future cultural upheaval. While the Civil War was unquestionably an important cultural cataclysm, the field's overreliance on it as *the* determining event oversimplifies the evolutionary trajectories of economic, political, social, and cultural debates (as well as frequent armed skirmishes) over enslavement and freedom. Our collective fixation on *antebellum* as noun creates a chronological inconsistency about when the contending ideologies of America's democratic visions, Europe's colonial endeavors, and diasporic African struggles for emancipation first forcibly collided. Reading *Benito Cereno* as a speculative warning rather than as a historical fiction has long obscured how fears about Black insurrection as a threat to national cohesion were a perpetual source of concern in the early Republic. Orienting American literary history toward 1865 silences the past by muting how Haitian liberation had six decades earlier caused the United States to redefine its democratic infrastructures to impede Black freedom. *Incipient Fevers* addresses the erasure of Haiti from early American literary history by foregrounding the urgency with which early American writers interpreted the meaning of Haiti. Moreover, this project undertakes this recovery by attending to a period all too often dismissed for its charged affective partisanship.

Prior to the celebrated bilateral harmony and shared national purpose associated with the election of James Monroe, petulant intolerance (both regionally based and not) persistently threatened the unity of the American Republic. The figuration of this period as "the era of good feelings," a phrase inaugurated by Benjamin Russell in Boston's *Columbian Centinel* in 1817, captures how the collapse of what political theorists term the First Party System in the United States was understood as healing the divisiveness of the proceeding years.[40] Monroe's efforts to become the first president to travel to each state in the union was in many ways a public relations campaign designed to heal the damage enacted by the disastrous gathering of New England Federalists at the Hartford Convention in 1815. Dismayed at the direction of the nation, including the possibility of the growth of enslavement because of the Louisiana Purchase, New Englanders at the Convention openly contemplated seceding from the union to form a new independent nation.[41] Arguably, the Hartford Convention was one capstone event of an era of *un*good feelings—that fractious period preceding Monroe's efforts at national reconciliation.[42] Haitian liberation loomed large in these partisan political and cultural debates, fueling animus on every side. The chapters that follow depict emblematic flashpoints within the era of ungood feelings—a moment permeated with tensions around the futurity of the early Republic—in order to address the period's neglect in American literary history. In so doing, these chapters argue that Haiti animated early nineteenth-century conceptions of American democracy in that it was the structuring structure for concerns about enslavement and emancipation in the fractious partisanship of the period.

Continuing to ignore how Haiti haunted the early American imagination means misapprehending how the imperial ambitions of the United States grew out of the machinations of the era of ungood feelings. The belief that the United States needed to secure its own safety and economic prosperity by asserting a larger influence on extra-national territories in the Americas initially coalesced in the early nineteenth century. What would retrospectively be termed the Monroe Doctrine, the idea that the United States would view any European intervention into the politics of the hemisphere as a hostile act, was partially born out of America's complex reactions to the incipient fevers which infected the United States during and after the Haitian Revolution. European colonial authorities, bent on treating the territories in the New World as inexhaustible sites of extraction, had produced (in the minds of many observers in the United States) the conditions of possibility for the Haitian Revolution. In its efforts to quarantine itself from domestic revolutionary outbreaks, Americans increasingly sought to differentiate U.S. enslavement from the practices of European empires. The specter of Haiti haunts these fictional, quasi-fictional, and non-fictional attempts to discern variations in a horrifying system. Thus, it remains crucially important to consider how these myriad fantasies about Haiti shaped burgeoning ideas about globalization and comparative internationalism in the early American print public sphere. Habitually neglecting the era of ungood feelings obfuscates America's growing belief that self-preservation required policing the hemisphere, an impulse profoundly tethered to early-nineteenth-century fears about Black liberation. *Incipient Fevers* corrects this mispractice by exploring emblematic artifacts from the significant archive of American narratives about Haiti published in the early nineteenth century. And, finally, by uncovering the import of this interstitial period, this book aims to foster increased transit between the work of early Americanists and U.S. Americanists by emphasizing the figurations of unfreedom which permeate cultural production in both subfields.[43]

"What's Past Is Epilogue"

The Haitian Revolution in the Early Republic of Letters progresses chronologically to register the evolving reactions of early American writers, politicians, and concerned citizens to the unfolding events of the Haitian Revolution. This organizational scheme allows me to account for shifting circumstances produced through new discursive responses to altering political conditions. While the book does not argue for literal lines of influence between the various texts under examination, it does explore how later texts exhibit a keen awareness of the rhetorical strategies deployed in of earlier productions. Since the early American Republic of Letters was inundated with information about Haiti, thinking about recursivity and adaptation exposes how the writers examined in this book labored to capture the attention of a reading public habitually attuned to events in the Caribbean. Even as many of the texts considered here enjoyed a degree of contemporaneous popularity, or at least notoriety, they have since received scant critical attention. At the same time, many of the literary conventions of the canonical interregnum are at odds with the typical Americanist benchmarks for critical analysis. The majority of the texts studied in what follows first appeared either anonymously or pseudonymously, and almost of them were first published in serialized form in the era's thriving periodical press. As such, my analysis scrutinizes publication contexts as well as variations in operant perceptions about developments in Haiti. Moreover, *Incipient Fevers* takes seriality not simply as a mode of publication but as an aesthetic strategy paradigmatic of an ecosystem of information recursively put forward about Haiti in manifold publication formats, including newspaper reports, political and promotional pamphlets, public and private correspondence, novels, sketches, and opinion pieces.[44] These innumerable multi-generic accounts about Haiti were interanimating and shaped the ways in which readers' recursively blurred the boundaries between fictional accounts of Haiti and supposedly factual ones. Even a cursory environmental scan of this era's print public sphere reveals how Haiti formed both quantitative and qualitative challenges to the self-perceptions of American citizens about their own future trajectory. The early American Republic of Letters was, in other words, habitually tethered to Haiti as the key codicil, one capable of explaining, altering, or revoking foundational premises of America's own revolutionary legacies.

    Chapter 1, "'Not an End': Seriality, Revolution, and 'The Story of Makandal',"
investigates the widespread U.S. reprinting of a short narrative published under a variety of different titles. The text originally appeared in the September 1787

edition of the *Mecure de France*, but was soon translated into English and published in British periodicals; it quickly migrated to the United States, where no less than seven reprintings appeared in American periodicals in such places as Boston, New York (twice), Philadelphia (twice), Salem, NY, and Norwich, CT between 1793 and 1823. Ostensibly, the narrative presents a fictionalized biography of François Makandal, an actual 1750s maroon rebel who attempted to poison the white colonial population of Saint-Domingue in order to liberate the island. Yet the text curiously transmutes Makandal's insurgency into petty jealously, narratively downscaling his actions from the realm of international politics into personal emotion. In so doing, the narrative disavows Makandal's ideological commitments to large scale emancipation by rendering him a figure of unhinged appetite. By depoliticizing historical events, Makandal figures not as a theorist of new forms of freedom, but as a singular being forced to flee the tyranny of an exceptionally bad overseer. In essence, the narrative presents this moment of insurgency—one of the largest and most organized eighteenth-century rebellions against enslavement—as a meditation on how aggressive mismanagement enkindles resistance.

The chapter repositions the biographical sketch as a fulcrum for late eighteenth- and early nineteenth-century American readers to consider events in Haiti and those closer to home. In particular, the chapter explores the tale's rumination on systems of enslavement, indexing of diasporic African knowledge, and fantasizing about the causes of rebellious behavior. By ending with Makandal's execution, the narrative culminates in a restoration of white supremacist colonial control. In presaging Black resistance as doomed to failure, "The Story of Makandal" provided an object lesson for readers concerned about the consequences of Haitian unrest. As the chapter argues, the serial reanimation of this narrative was intended to predict a restoration of white supremacist power abroad while reifying it at home. Thus, the chapter interrogates how the resuscitation of a narrative about failed resistance may have been used to offset anxieties produced by current events published within the same issue of a periodical. This methodology allows me to explore the impetus for American editors to return to this text as a means of explicating contemporary circumstances. How, why, and when, in other words, did American periodical editors turn to this text to supplement their larger interests in Haiti? What was the work they hoped it would accomplish? In addressing these questions, the chapter focuses specifically on an 1802 reprinting of the text in a Philadelphia newspaper, which appeared as many of the Creole refugees who had flocked to the city during the outbreak of the Revolution were preparing to return amid Napoleon's campaign to recolonize the island. Using the 1802 reprinting as a test case, the chapter speculates about the role of serialized publications in forging structures of feeling around events in Haiti while also considering the place of this seemingly foreign text in the development of early American literature.

Chapter 2, "'Sympathy' in the Era of Ungood Feelings: Martha Meredith Read's City of Unbrotherly Love," explores the hauntology of Haiti by focusing on how early American fiction figured the Republic as hermeneutically, temporally, and ontologically disjointed by the arrival of French, Creole, and enslaved refugees in the United States. Extracted from the middle of Martha Meredith Read's 1802 novel *Monima, or the Beggar Girl*, the titular question orienting the chapter accentuates how the ghostly indecipherability of foreign connections endanger the domestic realm. Read's novel blurs the boundaries between the foreign and the domestic through a focus on formerly elite refugees who arrive in Philadelphia hoping to escape the revolutionary turmoil. Unfortunately, these figures find no succor in the United States, as the residents of Philadelphia almost universally remain hostile to their plight. In depicting an American social scene bereft of networks of sympathetic support, Read draws linkages between radicalism in the Francophone world and the rise of Democratic-Republican politicians in the United States.

Often called the Revolution of 1800 by historians, Jefferson's election as president upended Federalist power in the United States and created a legitimation crisis for those displaced from authority. A range of Federalist writers, including Read, responded to their predicament by flooding print networks with sensationalized representations of the dangers of Jeffersonianism. Federalist depictions consistently intimated strong connections between Monticello and a pre-Revolutionary Cape François as sites of moral corruption defined by their dependent connections to enslavement. Linking the futurity of the United States with contemporary unrest in Haiti, displaced Federalists asserted that improper leadership would enkindle radical counterreactions. In essence, Federalist fictions seized upon fears about bad plantation management (explored in the previous chapter) as prognosticating what a Jeffersonian abandonment of foundational principles would mean for the early Republic. Read's *Monima* routes anxieties about displacement through her exploration of how revolutionary unsettlement elsewhere has displaced formerly elite figures and rendered them destitute beggars in Philadelphia. As she stages her fears about the future course of the United States, Read considers how the displacements enacted by the Haitian Revolution were transforming domestic conceptions of sympathy, fraternity, republicanism, and equality. Using Read's novel as a point of departure, the chapter maps ways Federalist writers resurrected previous understandings of ideologically charged terms of belonging as a defense against Jeffersonian radicalism.

Chapter 3, "'Free of Every Thing which Can Affect Its Purity': Maple Sugar, Caribbean Cane, and the Futures Past of Laborless American Development," examines a nascent economic nationalism intended to immunize the United States from the uncertainties of foreign trade. After the outbreak of the Haitian Revolution, the price for cane sugar skyrocketed. In the wake of the surge, a range of concerned northern politicians, amateur economists, and wealthy property owners (in private letters, in pamphlets, in tracts, public planning documents, and in agricultural treatises) promoted the "laborless" enterprise of maple sugaring as a means of redeeming the U.S. from foreign dependence. These writers promoted maple as a counter economy to cane, one which could divest the United States from dangerous connections to revolutionary plantations. Central to these efforts was an attempt to dissociate Jeffersonian notions of agrarianism away from an unspoken reliance on enslaved laborers by championing a new praxis of laborless resource extraction. Simmering amid all these maple sugar materials was a keen understanding of how the economic fallout of the Haitian Revolution should drive the U.S. to alternative modes of production to forestall racialized revolution at home.

The final portions of Chapter 3 consider the function of a lengthy subplot about the economic and political gains of maple sugaring within the most popular American gothic novel of the nineteenth century, Isaac Mitchell's *The Asylum; or, Alonzo and Melissa* (1804/1811). Mitchell's novel features a detailed consideration of a persecuted and penniless European couple who migrate to Connecticut. By virtue of their maple husbandry, the couple becomes financially independent and serves as a model of companionate marriage for Mitchell's titular star crossed lovers. An astonishingly lengthy footnote (covering the better portion of four pages in the earliest editions of the novel) parallels the text at a crucial juncture, allowing Mitchell to detail the ease of maple sugaring and its attendant economic generativity. This footnote stages the praxis of maple sugaring as emblematic of American Republican identity by recording that "during the American revolution" such products as "molasses, spirits, and sugar" were domestically produced from corn, carrots, beets, and maple sap. Reading Mitchell's novel alongside a range of other ideologically sympathetic materials, this chapter reveals how the promotion of maple sugaring came to symbolize national economic independence and advanced an explicitly anti-plantocracy political agenda.

Chapter 4, "Transmitted to America: Zelica's Incipient Fever and the Legacies of the Haitian Revolution," contemplates two American novels with plots that unfold in Cape François during the 1802 French expedition to recolonize St. Domingo. The first, Leonora Sansay's *Secret History; or, The Horrors of St. Domingo* (1808), has been the primary touchstone for early Americanist attempts to read the significance of Haiti for the early Republic. The second text, the pseudonymously published *Zelica, The Creole* (1820), reworks the plot of Sansay's earlier novel to gauge how the function of Haiti in the U.S. American imagination shifted across the decade separating their publication. Despite scant evidence, *Zelica* has often been attributed to Sansay and thus glossed over as loose baggy monster sequel to *Secret History*. Instead of focusing on the authorship issue, a rabbit hole without end, this chapter argues that more can be gleaned from thinking about how these texts divulge contradictory conceptions of revolutionary contagion than by teasing out some linear causal relationship. Moreover, the chapter seeks to detail the inherent problem of simply using Sansay's solitary 1808 novel as a means of thinking about the importance of the Haitian Revolution for American literary history.

The divergent interpretations of the meaning of Haiti curated by these two texts reflect how the legacies of the Revolution shifted across the first two decades of the nineteenth century. In this regard, the chapter marks how earlier apprehensions about the socio-political effects of the Haitian Revolution (which drive the plot of *Secret History*) evolved into more intimate fears over how it potentially subverted American whiteness itself. Written a decade after Haitian Independence, *Zelica* openly questions how Black freedom made visible longstanding American assumptions about the relationship between whiteness, citizenship, and freedom. Both texts revolve around a failed marriage between an American citizen and a Creole refugee; each, in turn, highlights how the stability of U.S. social reproduction could be dislodged by these West Indian connections. Emphasizing the vulnerability of female protagonists to dangerous foreign influences, *Zelica* and *Secret History* rethink the tenets of American whiteness in juxtaposition to that of other peoples of European descent in the hemisphere. Even as both texts trace how U.S. history and sociality stem from its participation in a circum-Atlantic world predicated on excessive mobility and exchange, *Zelica* reflects how by 1820 such fluidity was understood as unwarranted. While Sansay's 1808 novel expressed muted unease over a northern migration of radical contagions, by 1820 (as *Zelica* vividly records) poignant fears about domestic infiltration were palpably widespread. Using *Zelica* and *Secret History* as measures of cultural restlessness in the face of an independent Haiti, this chapter argues that cultural unease over Black freedom aggregated across the second decade of the nineteenth century. In charting this compounding attention to the function of Haiti for American national self-fashioning, the chapter moves to register the damage caused by fixating on this impact as a *secret* history.

Chapter 5, the final chapter, "'UNIVERSAL EMANCIPATION!' New York's Print Public Sphere and the Haunting Legacies of the Black Atlantic," further surveys the increased trepidations over Haitian connections in the late 1810s. The chapter positions New York as a microcosm of national anxieties by examining how rapidly the local press connected accounts of domestic insurrection to rumors of Haitian influence. Fears about revolutionary infection permeated New York's own local political debates about enslavement. Beginning in 1799, the New York legislature enacted a series of gradual emancipation acts that finally "freed" all enslaved people in 1827. Crafted to recompense enslavers for their loss of future income, deferred emancipation acts meant that New York was sporadically debating the consequences of African American liberation for close to three decades. Unsurprisingly, racism within the state concurrently increased as white citizens openly questioned what it would mean for formerly enslaved people to become citizens. At the same time, New York politicians sought to export their local model for emancipation to the national stage, hoping its compensating measures might help curtail the push of enslavement into the Missouri territories.

The chapter culminates in a reading of the first American vampire tale which was itself born from the pages of New York's periodical press. The pseudonymously published *The Black Vampyre: A Legend of St. Domingo* (1819) openly riffs on a multiplicity of discourses about the emergence of African American emancipation and fears about international Black solidarity. While ostensibly a satiric reworking of John Polidori's *The Vampyre* (the first Anglophone vampire tale published just a month before), *The Black Vampyre* expressed more extensive interest in global systems of exchange than its predecessor. In addition to relocating the origins of vampirism away from eastern Europe and to Africa, the novella deploys the vampire to critique the bloodsucking exploitations of Black Atlantic capitalism. As part of this criticism, the text highlights the connections between the exploitations of Caribbean plantations, the rebellious intent of enslaved people, and the New York region. Considering the text alongside the anxiety about foreign infiltration circulating in the New York press, the chapter unpacks how the domestic implications sensationalized in *The Black Vampyre* parallel contemporaneous periodical accounts as a means of grounding its otherwise outlandish plot.

Finally, the coda to *Incipient Fevers*, "What's Past Is Epilogue," explores how early nineteenth-century African American writers and African American print networks repurposed the history of the Haitian Revolution as precursor for their own struggles for freedom. As such, this chapter returns (with a decidedly different inflection) to the questions of serialization that framed the opening chapter. More particularly, the coda investigates how figurations of Haiti played a pivotal role in the editorial direction of the first African American newspaper, the *Freedom's Journal* (1827). As some of this reportage began to encourage a migration of African Americans to Haiti, a reworking of the cultural meanings of the revolution was a necessary corollary to the project of creating affinities between African Americans and the Haitian Republic. The coda offers a brief reading of "Theresa—A Haytien Tale," perhaps the earliest extant piece of fiction written by a diasporic African in the United States, which was serialized in the *Freedom's Journal* in 1828. The sketch displays the struggles of a free woman of color and her two daughters as they attempt to flee the marauding French army and warn Toussaint of an impending ambush. In so doing, "Theresa" positions bourgeois free people of color, a class similar to the audience that *Freedom's Journal* tried to cultivate, as central in upending white supremacist authority. In short, the tale stages a free diasporic African population as essential to establishing national freedoms. Linking a reading of "Theresa" to the larger discursive contexts out of which it emerged, the coda gestures toward how African American print networks reconfigured the meaning of Haiti for the larger American print public sphere. As a measure of the afterlives of these contending interpretations of the meaning of Haitian freedom, the coda scrutinizes the surfacing of references to Haiti in signs fashioned by demonstrators at contemporary Black Lives Matter protests. These allusions sparked a racialized panic among the contemporary alt-right, underscoring how an age-old white supremacist vision of Haiti as the antithesis of U.S democracy continues to infect the American imagination.

1

"Not an End"

Seriality, Revolution, and "The Story of Makandal"

> Jack was, in a sense, a proxy—he was Makandal, he was Gabriel, he
> was perhaps even Toussaint Louverture—a character who could be
> displayed, observed, even briefly admired, before being dispensed
> with and the slave order returned to its regularity.
>
> Laurent Dubois, *The Banjo: America's African Instrument* (2016)

As his title announces, Edward W.R. Pitcher's path-breaking *Fiction in American Magazines Before 1800: An Annotated Catalog* sought to tabulate the massive amount of eighteenth-century fiction published in "major" "American" magazines into a single index.[1] Like the majority of his scholarly generation, Pitcher privileged materials published in English in framing the contours of American literature. In amassing his data, he retrospectively surveyed all the territories that would become, by the dawn of the nineteenth century, the United States as a coherent imagined community. Despite the inherent limitations in mapping the continent as a national inevitability, Pitcher's compendium remains a crucial, yet underutilized, resource for thinking about where and how an eighteenth-century English-speaking North American reading public would have encountered fiction. While her landmark work focused on the later Jacksonian-era print public sphere, Meredith L. McGill's conceptualization of how promiscuous reprintings and unattributed pirating defined the work of magazine editors still largely holds true of the early U.S. national period as well.[2]

Imported short fiction circulated alongside domestically authored productions, indiscriminately filling the pages of early American magazines with a cornucopia of styles and forms. These magazines offered readers a variety of ways of thinking about the relationship between fact and fiction. While critics have privileged the dozens of domestically authored novels published in the last two decades of the eighteenth century as the defining canon of U.S. literary production, Pitcher's compendium draws attention to the thousands of pieces of serialized fiction printed in U.S. magazines during this same period. Although his charting was incomplete (as he underscores in his volume's opening pages), Pitcher's formative plotting of print networks discloses the rhizomatic nature of eighteenth-century North American print culture for its producers, compilers,

The Haitian Revolution in the Early Republic of Letters: Incipient Fevers. Duncan Faherty, Oxford University Press.
© Duncan Faherty 2023. DOI: 10.1093/oso/9780192889157.003.0002

and readers.[3] Texts appeared, disappeared, and reappeared across time and space through print networks that rang along both domestic and international lines.

Instead of focusing on the importance of novels (often printed just once and in a single city), Pitcher gestures toward rethinking American literary history by embracing periodicals as the dominant print medium in the early Republic. Such praxis would also necessitate considering the serial form's attendant issues of miscellany, generic confusion, fragmentation, circulation, anonymity, and pseudonymity. Yet these remain literary tropes all too often neglected by early Americanists. As Jared Gardner persuasively argues, the "magazine and novel 'rose' together in eighteenth-century America," and while the novel became the dominant form in the 1820s for the "previous generations, the outcome was by no means certain."[4] These early American readers consumed the "vast and disparate array of anonymous texts" that filled the pages of early national periodicals at an astonishing rate.[5] Indeed, these readers routinely encountered in magazines "an output many times greater (both in terms of quantity and quality) than that produced by all the novelists of the period."[6] Early American readers navigated oceans of short fiction and often did so without any charting of authorial histories or national traditions to guide them. While we have privileged authorial biography and natal origins in our canonical configurations, these indices do not reflect the actual reading experiences of early Americans.

Critical understanding of the early American periodical archive, and its impact on the construction of alternative models of political and social formation, remains fragmentary.[7] Similarly, we have barely scratched the surface of the complexities of the composition of periodicals. Magazines frequently juxtaposed reportage of current events alongside literary renderings of the same occurrences, and such generic abutment unsettled the supposed distinctions between these rhetorical modes. To return to the pages of an early American magazine as an index of literary development requires not only a suspension of familiar critical signposts as the primary inroad into interpretation, but also a movement beyond the novel as the privileged genre for literary study. Coterminously, such a turn requires countering habitual investments in national literary traditions and the explanatory classifications that have evolved in service of that framework. While novelists may have marketed themselves as part of a developing domestic literary scene, magazine editors did not always have the same restrictive focus in selecting materials for publication. Moreover, they could often only fill their issues by coopting foreign productions and passing them off as domestically authored pieces.[8]

In this chapter, I want to explore how the rhizomatic networks of literary production that Pitcher sketches intersect with the early American Republic's obsession with enslavement and racialized revolution. While current scholarship has shifted the dial away from nationalizing narratives of literary production toward seriality and fragmentation, we have yet to account fully for the role such fiction played in matters relating to race and the period's pervasive paranoia about plantation violence. Item number 2,465 in Pitcher's catalogue dexterously navigates this conceptual convergence. At first blush, the seemingly unremarkable entry entitled "The Story of Makandal" surreptitiously resides within its surroundings; nothing about it marks it as unique among the strings of titles Pitcher collected, nor registers the Haitian setting of the tale. Scores of the other entries stand identified by titular protagonists with decidedly non-Anglo appellations and with similar introductory generic markers serving to anchor their exoticness. Even a cursory perusal of Pitcher's ledger reveals how early American periodicals routinely featured tales set in Africa, the Middle East, and the Caribbean.[9] Sometimes taxonomized (no matter their actual geographical settings) by contemporary critics as "Orientalist" tales, these narratives often promised fantastical entry into non-European forms of sociality by depicting spaces populated by harems, sultans, mountains of specie, threats of divine retribution, and brutal violence.[10] As Len Tennenhouse has observed, many of these seemingly outlandish tales operated as sublimated mediations on the Caribbean plantation system that defined the economic structure of the eighteenth-century circum-Atlantic world.[11] But such a focus on transatlantic relations distorts the fact that these decidedly non-Anglo-American protagonists also functioned, to borrow Laurent Dubois' term from the epigraph to this chapter, as proxies: as figures that could be observed (even momentarily) before a reader returned to the regularity provided by the other materials lodged within any given periodical order.[12] Like apparitions demanding attention, these serial proxies reappeared long enough to disquiet, but did not loiter to unsettle, normative conceptions of the domestic social order.

Pitcher's annotations on the text may be somewhat cursory, but they do indicate a wanton and complex circulation history. According to Pitcher, "The Story of Makandal" was first printed in the U.S. in the January and February 1793 editions of The Massachusetts Magazine; or Monthly Museum. The text subsequently appeared under the title "An Account of a Remarkable Conspiracy Formed by a Negro in the Island of St. Domingo" in the August and September 1796 issues of The New-York Magazine, or Literary Repository. Fourteen months later, The American Universal Magazine published it in its January 1798 issue. In recording the text's genealogy, Pitcher references a note unearthed in the February 1788 issue of London's Universal Magazine of Knowledge and Pleasure, which states that it was "reprinted from a story, said to have been translated from the French of the Mercure de France."[13] Despite his best efforts, Pitcher failed to locate the source referenced by the Universal Magazine, confessing, "no French original has been located."[14] This fleeting, but suggestive, acknowledgement of a more complicated textual history of "The Story of Makandal" concludes Pitcher's cursory annotations concerning the tale and its wanton circulation.

Essentially, "The Story of Makandal" simply abides as one of the nearly 3,000 entries compiled in his volume. Yet, to reiterate Pitcher's description of the incompleteness of his own cataloging efforts: "This is a beginning, not an end."[15] Taking up Pitcher's challenge, this chapter functions as a "beginning" in the sense outlined by the chapter's opening epigraph. In his study of the banjo's rootedness in diasporic African culture, Laurent Dubois characterizes the Caribbean slave rebellion leader Jack Mansong (also known as Three-Fingered Jack) as a serial proxy (or fungible cypher) "who could be displayed, observed, even briefly admired, before being dispensed with and the slave order returned to its regularity."[16] This claim emerges from the ways in which a variety of representations of Mansong (from folk tales to whispered rumors, to popular staged versions and panto-mimes, to William Earle's novel *Obi or, The History of Three-Fingered Jack* (1800)) circulated across the Anglophone world in the aftermath of his uprising. Dubois's study offers a compelling history of musicology and race, but for my purposes, the episodic haunting of Mansong underscores how an endless return to beginnings without ends short-circuits the linear trajectory of progressive conceptions of American literary history. By attending to the orbits of this serial versioning, we can more fully engage with the critical legacies of enduring repetitions and habitual erasures in circum-Atlantic textual production. Specifically, I argue, the recursive surfacing of "The Story of Makandal," and the other figures and texts it echoes, exhibits the ways in which the specter of Haiti prompted American readers to think about their own rebellious beginnings and to indulge in fanta-sies about their own possible ends. In what follows below, I explore how "The Story of Makandal" haunted the American cultural imagination by tracing how serialized versions of Makandal appeared in American periodicals as means of adjudicating how racialized unrest in Haiti potentially impacted U.S. stability. More specifically, I want to consider how a broadly circulating narrative about Makandal functioned as a textual revenant, one that consistently reemerged—in French, English, and German—beginning in the late 1780s and continuing until the 1840s.[17]

Accounting for Makandal

To borrow a well-worn phrase from early American literary culture, "The Story of Makandal" is a fiction founded in facts. In March of 1758, the maroon leader François Makandal was burned at the stake in the middle of the public square in La Cap. According to contemporary accounts, plantation owners from the sur-rounding districts forced enslaved people to watch the horrifying spectacle. In delaying the execution until a large crowd could bear witness, French authorities staged the event to reassert their supposedly unshakable control. Makandal was sentenced to death for conspiring to poison Cape François's water supply and plotting to overthrow the white colonial regime. The historian Carolyn Fick suggests that Makandal had planned his revolution "with extraordinary audacity" over the course of twelve years.[18] Surprisingly, even the unreliable colonial records, which habitually underestimate the capabilities of enslaved diasporic Africans, describe his organization as large and highly structured. Indeed, one colonial French authority reported, "one would almost be tempted to admire" Makandal's "constancy and ingenuity" in plotting to liberate the island.[19] Historians often describe Makandal's efforts as "the first real attempt in the long history of slave resistance at disciplined, organized revolt" and the first sustained effort to reimagine the racialized hierarchies that governed Europe's colonial holdings.[20] Makandal, in other words, represented (and continues to represent) a seemingly never-before-recorded collective agency on the part of enslaved people. And, while he was interpreted as possessing exceptional leadership abilities, the more acute danger he embodied stemmed from his ability to organize potential resistance which exceeded the scale of a localized insurgency. The circulation of information connected to Makandal routinely foregrounded his capacity for network building, turning him into a symbolic representation of the dangers of diasporic African collectivity.[21]

Makandal's success as an insurgent was aided by his self-promotion in messianic terms. He proclaimed his knowledge of poisons a divinely inspired gift and part of his capacity to prophesize the future. Despite French efforts to solidify their dominance by publicly dramatizing his execution, contemporary accounts reveal that witnesses later declared that Makandal magically escaped the flames.[22] These persistent rumors only fueled speculations about Makandal's prophetic powers, including his supposed immortality. In the aftermath of his gruesome execution, Makandal remained a major inspiration for resistance to white supremacy and a ghost in the machine of the colonial imaginary.[23] Starting roughly thirty years after Makandal's unsuccessful plan to emancipate St. Domingo and continuing for the next six decades, magazine and newspaper readers in both Europe and the United States sporadically encountered narratives about his history. This is "The Story of Makandal" registered in Pitcher's index, the same text he cataloged as fiction and figured as another instantiation of widespread patterns of literary redistribution.

Since Pitcher's ambition resided in collating bibliographic information about the sheer volume of short fiction published in American periodicals, it seems disingenuous to fault him for not offering fine-grained stylistic differentiations across the text's numerous iterations. Still, while Pitcher designates "The Story of Makandal" as a work of fiction, this baggy generic classification hardly serves as an adequate descriptor. To put it another way, we need to reanimate the fluidity of eighteenth-century understandings of generic taxonomies to comprehend this text as a fiction. Part historical sketch, part biographical portrait, part meditation on the proper treatment of enslaved laborers, part racist depiction of the knowledge of diasporic Africans, and part imaginative fantasy about the ritual triumph of the colonial regime in the face of rebellion, the text (like many eighteenth-century magazine pieces) strains any attempt at conventional literary taxonomy. Moreover, a French source does exist: a beginning that hints at the more complex ends of the textual history of "The Story of Makandal." For Pitcher, the French origins of the tale proved the dead end that prevented any further exploration of its publication history, but digitalization allows us to travel where he could not. The September 1787 edition of the *Mecure de France*, which was called "the most important literary journal in prerevolutionary France" by the historian Jeremey D. Popkin.[24] Within the pages of the *Mecure de France*, the text appeared under the title "Makandal, Histoire véritable," and was attributed to a "M[onsieur] de C..." By November of the same year, it had appeared in at least one other French journal, *L'Esprit des Journaux*, and in the next few months, it began to appear outside of France. By February of 1788, it was reprinted in the *Universal Magazine of Knowledge & Pleasure* (London) as "The Negro Makandal, an authentic History"; by April *The Gentleman's and London Magazine* had printed it, and later that year it was published in the German journal *Olla Potrida* (Berlin). Another German version, in the *Neue Litteratur und Völkerkunde* (Dessau and Leipzig) was printed in 1790. In January of 1789, the text emerged in another British journal, the *Literary Magazine & British Review*, with the title "Account of a Conspiracy in St. Domingo" and again in the 1794 *New Wonderful Magazine and Marvellous Chronicle*.[25] So popular was the tale in Britain that an extended drama inspired by the narrative, "King Caesar; or, The Negro Slaves," was produced in 1801. This brief script reproduced the bulk of the first half of the *Mercure*'s narrative as King Caesar / Makandal's backstory, before spinning the details into a melodrama that projects the story into a decidedly different direction.[26] The drama capitalized on the currency of Makandal as a figure of performative interest by scripting him as a villainous figure intent on destruction. This stage version of Makandal appears as a misguided figure who casts himself as an aristocratic figurehead of a perverted social order.

Soon after this (assuredly incomplete) textual circulation in Europe, the text arrived in the United States with many printings following the translation reproduced in London's *Literary Magazine & British Review* (*LMBR*), a version which took editorial liberties with the French original. While the earliest English translations preserved a title close to the French—"The Negro Makandal, an Authentic History"—the editors of the *LMBR* altered the title to an "Account of a Conspiracy in St. Domingo." A paragraph musing about Zami's love for Samba was removed, and sentences linking Makandal's history with a broader conspiracy of race war were inserted.[27] These changes were central to the text's reprintings in the United States, where the story found most of its English-language printings commencing in the 1790s, beginning with its initial U.S. publication in the January 1793 edition of the *Massachusetts Magazine*. U.S. interest in the text lasted at least as late as its final extant printing in the January 1846 edition of the *New York Illustrated Magazine*. In between these two printings, the text also appeared in several other U.S. magazines, including *The New York Magazine, or Literary Repository* in August of 1796; in the *Philadelphia Repository* in March of 1802; and in *The Minerva* in June of 1823. It also appeared in a few northern newspapers—in the *Washington Patrol* of Salem, New York, in September of 1795, and in the *Chelsea Courier* of Norwich, Connecticut, in 1797, for instance.[28]

More printings than charted above probably occurred, both in the United States and in Europe, but even this preliminary textual history exposes something about the text's unrestrained circulation across borders and decades. In sum, the textual history of the "The Story of Makandal" registers a cartography that respects no conception of state-sanctioned precincts, of national literary traditions, of linguistic siloes, or of regional boundaries. Rather, it evinces a quixotic, revenant-like quality in its spatial and temporal durability, serving as a spectral presence waiting reanimation by periodical editors as a dire reminder of the dangers of enslavement. In *Ghostly Matters*, Avery Gordon articulates how the present remains haunted by unreconciled social forces that haunt the margins of cultural formations. Following Gordon, we might then think about how and why the text functioned as something that needed to be reckoned with, as a cultural object that editors redeployed to ground rising fears about both international and domestic unsettlements.[29] We might, to put it another way, think of the text as a ghostly familiar imbued with the power of reframing contemporary affairs.[30] For editors and readers alike, the stylized portrait of Makandal served as an object lesson from the past, one intended to draw a consistent line from the inevitable success of past white supremacist assertions of power into the present.

By the time of the first U.S. appearances of "The Story of Makandal," American readers would have been familiar—through innumerable newspaper accounts— with the 1791 burning of Cap François and the disruptions to French colonial power in Saint-Domingue. By the time of the 1796 publication, U.S. readers would have read about or, depending on their location, encountered the thousands of refugees who had fled the revolution for the safer confines of the United States, many of them Creole planters who brought enslaved people along with them to such havens as Philadelphia and Charleston. By this time as well, the term "French Negro" had entered the popular U.S. lexicon as a marker of a potentially doubly disruptive figure, one who carried with them the uncertainties of both the French and Haitian revolutions.[31] The attempted British invasion of Saint-Domingue, well underway by 1796, was also a source of daily fascination for U.S. newspapers. Readers likely monitored these reports with a dual skepticism that was almost as concerned about the effects of a successful revolution of enslaved peoples as it was by the prospects of British control over even more of the West Indian trade. American readers were never far from news about events in Haiti; indeed accounts registering the import of the Revolution proliferated at a boundless rate. As Haiti became the locus for European imperial ambitions in the hemisphere, as Spain and England both openly plotted invasions and the French desperately sought to bring its most prosperous colony back under their control, American observers grew accustomed to thinking about how the future of Haiti would rescript their own circum-Atlantic connections.

Haiti was consistently on the minds of U.S. periodical editors and readers across the last decade of the eighteenth century in ways almost impossible to exaggerate. For example, as Elizabeth Maddock Dillon argues, after reading an advanced notice advertising tickets for sale published in 1794, the mayor of Charleston prohibited a production of Thomas Southerne's play *Oroonoko* over fears that it was "too welcoming of the egalitarian politics of the racial revolt on display in the Haitian Revolution (and by extension, welcoming the racial revolt against slavery in the United States)."[32] Just six months prior to this, as Dillon exhibits, Charleston had enacted a legal prohibition preventing free Black people from Haiti from entering the city for fear of the revolutionary contagions they might bring with them. These legal machinations were partially fueled by how the city's newspapers had drawn parallels between local stability and foreign influence.[33] The news of Caribbean unrest—as it was broadcast in the periodical press—was, in other words, actively structuring domestic legal procedures and entertainment possibilities across the Republic.

As coverage of the protracted struggle spread, it was understood as potentially influencing a wide variety of domestic issues. Local security, national stability, westward expansion, and continued access both to foreign commodities (especially refined cane sugar) and to enslaved labor were all understood as intimately connected to events in Haiti. By associating the antecedents of domestic slave unrest with (Black) Jacobinism, fantasies about a docile U.S. slave population remained intact, even as an easy scapegoat for turmoil was displaced onto a foreign existential threat. The lines between fact and fiction were consistently blurred in this coverage, and indeed the distinction might only be accurately parsed by the retroactive desires of historians. Across the 1790s and 1800s, reports continually appeared, detailing rumors of invasions or the spotting of secret agents being dispatched to incite the domestic slave population to rebel.[34] Periodicals seldom retracted erroneous speculations; instead, they remained undercurrents within the continual tides of information emanating from and about the Caribbean. Unhinged rumors drifted indistinguishably alongside accurate reports, and this intermingling only increased the appetite for information about turmoil in the former French colony.

This generic confusion between biography and gothic sensationalism might account for the popularity of "The Story of Makandal," which announced itself as a reconfiguration of events from the middle of the eighteenth century. While there were cursory mentions of Makandal's attempted rebellion in the late 1750s, the reprintings of "The Story of Makandal" that appeared in domestic periodicals neglect this earlier correspondence. Instead, they cast the text as an object lesson concerning an earlier moment, one that likely served as a way for readers (as for historians later) to think about the consequences and causes of revolutionary actions as well as their potential to unsettle the white supremacist order of the circum-Atlantic world. Consider, for example, this prefatory frame accompanying the March 27, 1802, reprinting of "The Story of Makandal" in the *Philadelphia Repository and Weekly Register*:

> The following remarkable story may perhaps give some general idea of the character of negroes of St. Domingo,—those principal actors in the late horrid scenes transacted on the ill-fated island. The facts are supposed to have happened about forty years ago.[35]

The headnote's reference to the "late horrid scenes" exhibits a pronounced faith in the 1802 French plans to recolonize the island. Indeed, this Philadelphia printing—carried in three installments from the end of March to the middle of April of 1802—occurred just two months after General Leclerc's expeditionary forces entered Cape François and concluded just two weeks before an optimistic Bonaparte would decree the restoration of enslavement on the island.[36] The *Philadelphia Repository*, which likely counted refugee Creole planters (and certainly their American neighbors) among its readers, disinterred the narrative to affirm that while the struggle for self-emancipation had been cyclical, so too might be the reassertion of colonial exploitation. The past might function as prologue, and by thinking about how horrible scenes had been rewritten over four decades ago, the headnote implies that a restoration of white European order might be imminent. By casting "the character of the negroes of St. Domingo" as unevolved despite this passage of time, it also surreptitiously cordons them off in the past to deny them any further generative agency in the present or the future.

This reissuing of "The Story of Makandal" was intended for a reading public that might have been as optimistic as they ever would be about the French efforts to retake the island since the Haitian Revolution had begun eleven years earlier. It surfaced, in short, during a window in which the French, the exiled Creole refugees who had fled the island and the citizens of Philadelphia who had sheltered them were anticipating the success of Napoleon's ongoing invasion efforts. Moreover, it arrived amid rampant accounts prognosticating that the self-emancipated diasporic Africans would be reenslaved and their challenge to white supremacy extinguished. In March of 1802, Toussaint's forces were in retreat.[37] He would surrender to French authorities two months later and, for a fleeting moment, Euro-Americans fervently believed that a white supremacist regime would imminently reconquer St. Domingo. Considered in this light, this 1802 redistribution and its prefatory proclamation about "principal actors" who had lately "transacted" horrifying violence might best be understood as proof of the impossibility of successful Black resistance. Like the French colonial attempts to stage Makandal's execution to performativity reaffirm their imperiled authority, the headnote in the *Philadelphia Repository* positions the narrative in an evidentiary way. The editors cast Makandal as an antecedent to contemporary Black Jacobins as if to underscore that these rebels would face the same fate as their predecessors. And, like the 1758 efforts to curtail Makandal's symbolism, this 1802 attempt at circumscription failed to bottle the revolutionary excesses that Makandal embodied and continued to represent. Still, the attempt to resurrect "The Story of Makandal" as a paradigmatic example of the character of enslaved people struggling for self-emancipation registers the currency of the narrative for editors (and their presumptive readers) in the early Republic. The fact that it culminates in the execution of a rebellious enslaved person speaks to the possible intentions behind its import in the United States as well.

In *Freedom as Marronage*, Neil Roberts draws a prescient distinction between silence and disavowal that speaks to the function of this intermittent seriality. Perhaps, as well, Roberts provides a way to understand the intent of the prefatory explanation offered by the editors of the *Philadelphia Repository*. "Disavowal centrally requires," Roberts argues, "what I take to be a simultaneous *double movement*: an acknowledgement *and* a denial."[38] Disavowal, thus, requires recognition as well as refusal, and it does both simultaneously. Roberts's concept of disavowal registers the duality inherent in the more familiar frames (silence, unthinkable, secret history) by which critics have charted how news about revolution in the Caribbean manifested in the early Republic. One cannot silence anything, as Michel-Rolph Trouillot so deftly argued in his path-breaking *Silencing the Past: Power and the Production of History* (1985), unless one hears its potential to make a sound; one cannot conceive of something as unthinkable without being cognizant of it; one cannot suppress a secret history unless one knows its existence.[39] For Roberts, this twinned awareness and renunciation needs to be central to our critical work. Indeed, his call for us to take seriously "the implications of the disavowal of slave agency" evinces how the sporadic serialization (at later moments of crisis) of a narrative about an ultimately unsuccessful rebellion performs this double movement.[40] It does so because reprintings of "The Story of Makandal" both acknowledge the long history of struggles for liberation while concurrently denying them any possibility for success. The narrative works didactically by affirming the supremacy of colonial order even in the face of resistance. Considered in this vein, the reigniting of Makandal's history provided a benchmark for white readers during later moments of resistance by enslaved peoples. The reproduction allowed for a contextualized admission of previous moments of unsettlement while simultaneously refuting the viability of any present or future act of resistance. By republishing the text, editors could imply (at least through 1804 and the declaration of Haiti's independence) that recovery (from destabilization) functions as a constitutive element of the same cyclical pattern.

In "History Hesitant," Lisa Lowe reflects on the paradox of recovery, the difficulties of imagining that archival work can function as a means of "recuperation" or "repossession."[41] In surveying how such projects aim to register "a full humanity and freedom" for enslaved peoples, she also cautions how they might also unintentionally reinscribe the idea that enslavement remains a "*past condition*," a "historical object that is completed or overcome, from which recovery is possible."[42] In place of this, and building on a range of thinkers from the Black radical tradition, including C.L.R. James, Frantz Fanon, Cedric Robinson, Angela Davis, Achille Mbembe, and Robin D.G. Kelley, she defines a critical practice that remains hesitant, echoing W.E.B. DuBois's 1905 figuration of a hesitant sociology, wherein one would not "move immediately toward recovery or recuperation."[43] In place of conclusion, she urges that we "pause to reflect on what it means to supplement forgetting with new narratives of affirmation and presence."[44] For Lowe the act of hesitating enables a comprehension of how "the archive of liberalism"—the texts, contexts, and objects that "perform the important work of mediating and resolving liberalism's contradictions"—reenacts the violences of enslavement.[45] At its core, "The Story of Makandal" articulates itself as a narrative of unfreedom, a text that manifests how Makandal—framed by the text as an exemplary enslaved worker pushed too far—can be held at a distance from operant definitions of liberal humanity (in a variety of times and spaces) while still serving as evidence of what Lowe calls "the safekeeping and preservation of liberal society."[46] Indeed, "The Story of Makandal" functioned so well that it could routinely be activated as a reminder of the failures of enslaved peoples, even exemplary ones, to achieve self-liberation. Such recursivity exhibits how this deceptively simple text crystalized a broadly shared figuration of liberal humanism that might prompt a tear for the abuse Makandal suffered while still provide comfort through cyclically performing his supposedly just execution. In essence, the text distills how the contradictions of liberalism, as Lowe argues, were often mediated though textual fantasies about the exceptionality of marginalized individuals. In so doing, the narrative disinters a past liberation struggle not to affirm progressive possibilities, but to reinscribe how structures of unfreedom could endure, remix into a new form, and ultimately prevail.

Fictional Truths, Truthful Fictions

Before proceeding, I want to offer another potential beginning for thinking with "The Story of Makandal." Since its initial publication, C.L.R James's *The Black Jacobins* (1938) has been a keystone of the Anglo-American scholarly tradition of the Haitian Revolution. Intriguingly, his description of François Makandal as having "revelations" like "Mahomet" echoes one of the preliminary lines from "The Story of Makandal."[47] Moreover, James's brief treatment reproduces other specific details from the *Mercure* narrative as central facets of Makandal's biography. Across the twentieth century, the majority of the critical treatments of the actual Makandal rely on the *Mercure* narrative, or one of its reprisals, as historical evidence. For example, Carolyn E. Fick discusses the *Mercure* piece in her description of the scope of Makandal's conspiracy, reading the French narrative as part of a retroactive whitewashing campaign "to interpret such acts [of resistance] purely in terms of individual interest: vengeance, jealousy, reduction of the workload, infliction of economic loss on a master" in order to erase Black sovereignty from interpretations of "slave revolts."[48] Similarly, David Geggus describes the widespread influence that "a novelette-like story published in a Paris paper" had on late eighteenth-century conceptions of Makandal.[49] Finally, Laurent Dubois notes how the text and its popularity operated in the last two decades of the eighteenth century to "set in motion a cycle of paranoia and violence that continued" across the circum-Atlantic world for decades.[50] Many other historians, building on the citational practices of their predecessors, have framed portraits of Makandal through the looking glass of the *Mercure* narrative. Arguably, more than any other document, the *Mercure* narrative has suffused critical thinking about Makandal and his 1758 struggle for freedom.

In her path-breaking book *Servants of Allah*, Sylviane Diouf crafts one of the most authoritative accounts of Makandal in part to refute the validity of the *Mercure* narrative. In sum, she moves to separate historiography from the delusory influence of this fiction. According to Diouf, colonial authorities habitually embellished the scale of Makandal's conspiracy, noting that his "reputation was such that a French document of 1758 estimates—with much exaggeration, no doubt—the number of deaths he provoked at 6,000 over three years."[51] Whatever hyperbole resides within that estimation, it represents a staggering number; especially given that in the middle of the eighteenth century, the entire population of St. Domingo was estimated at fewer than 170,000.[52] By this calculus, Makandal was believed to have killed one approximately out of every twenty-eight people on the island over a three-year period. Just as it remains difficult to verify the outsized scale of Makandal's actions, the facts of his actual life remain difficult to corroborate and, for Diouf, are undermined by the popularity of the *Mercure* narrative. She observes that "many scholars" have relied on the *Mercure* narrative (or one of its reiterations or translations) for information about Makandal, and she decries how it records "obvious fantasies, inaccurate names, and other literary licenses."[53] Diouf concludes that this text presents a "grossly fictional narrative" that clouds the historical record and obscures understanding of Makandal's actual life, his political ambitions, and his vital legacies.[54] No doubt Diouf's observations about the glaring inaccuracies contained within "The Story of Makandal" are correct, but the text's veracity may be one of its less interesting dimensions. For the majority of Euro-American eighteenth- and nineteenth-century periodical readers, the distinction that Diouf draws between fantasies and facts may not have mattered at all, especially in regards to Haiti. Given how many times, at such crucial moments, these literary licenses were reanimated, they clearly provided periodical editors an important prism for refracting possible connections between foreign Black rebellion and U.S. stability. As such, perhaps "The Story of Makandal" can tell us more about the structures of thought and feeling operant for white Americans in the early Republic than any accurate biographical account ever could.

Yet, what it would mean to embrace the fictionality of this narrative as a means of understanding the development of U.S. literary culture? Put slightly differently, what would it mean to consider this text as a work of eighteenth- and nineteenth-century U.S. fiction? Such a consideration need not detract from importance of the actual Makandal, but would rather position this short piece as a telling fiction. Instead of dismissing it as inaccurate, the text might be examined for how it registers that even decades after Makandal's execution this version of his history was still being consumed by readers in the United States. Many of the American reprintings neglected to signal that the text was not an original or that it was a translation. Moreover, even the presence of such a gesture might not indicate anything about how it would have been received in a print culture where so many texts were introduced by such rhetorical frames. The trope of presenting a text as "discovered" was commonplace in early American periodicals, even when the text itself was a fabrication. The presentation of ostensible fictions as "founded on facts" was another convention deployed in a wide range of fictive texts, including specifically the three most canonical early American literary texts—Susanna Rowson's *Charlotte Temple* (1791), Hannah Webster Foster's *The Coquette* (1797), and Charles Brockden Brown's *Wieland* (1798).[55] Much critical ink has been spilled over the cultural work of these texts, and the idea that they (albeit loosely) took inspiration from actual events guides many of these readings. Early American readers, in short, were accustomed to reading stylized depictions of historical events and possessed less rigid investments in generic distinctions. Although the rapid increase in the partisan nature of our own contemporary information culture, marked by the virulent circulation of such terms as "fake news," suggests that we may well be dwelling within a similar moment in which generic classifications are understood as inherently fluid.[56]

Clear-cut separations between fact and fiction were far from concretized in the long eighteenth century.[57] Arguably, these blurred generic lines give rise to the very obscuring history which Diouf rails against. The number of reprintings of some version or another of "The Story of Makandal" means that, in all likelihood, more early American readers would have encountered some version of this fiction than would have read any of the traditionally canonized novels from the period. Consider these numbers by way of example. Scholars have estimated that somewhere between "750 and 1,000" copies of the *Wieland* were printed in Brown's lifetime.[58] The estimated number of subscriptions for the *American*

Universal Magazine was 1,696; and the front pages of the *New York Magazine, or Literary Repository* lists sales agents across New York and New Jersey, into Danbury, Philadelphia, Boston, and Charleston, and advertises as among its subscribers such notable figures as George Washington, John Adams, John Jay, and Richard Varick.[59] However, these numbers and names tell at best an incomplete story. As Cathy Davidson long ago demonstrated, it is impossible to accurately tally the number of readers who encountered a piece of printed matter.[60]

More recently, Nazera Sadiq Wright (writing about the circulation of newspapers and periodicals in African American communities) demonstrates how a single copy of a periodical would have been shared among several literate readers, but also likely read aloud to others.[61] Wright further exhibits how periodicals highlighted this sense of themselves as multifunctional by routinely featuring varied scenes of reading within the pieces comprising a single issue. The size of the print run serves as one questionable measure by which to trace encounters with a text, and given how magazines and newspapers were imagined as more ephemeral, it seems fair to imagine that a single copy of a novel would survived longer than an issue of a magazine. At the same time, particularly since the digitization of eighteenth- and nineteenth-century periodicals and newspapers remains far from complete, it is possible that more readers encountered some version of "The Story of Makandal" than any of the foundational texts around which we craft metanarratives about the development of American literary culture. Somehow, between 1797 and 1802, an attachment to the narrative persisted in the United States. Between 1802 and 1823 and then between 1826 and 1846, it remained dormant but ready to be reactivated. Even if we cannot fully reconstruct or explain this survival, it still evinces that "The Story of Makandal" endured, in a variety of guises and forms, to be resurrected as a meditation on present conditions. As such, the text functioned as a revenant memory for periodical editors who wanted to resuscitate a narrative about failed diasporic African resistance to provide contextualization for their contemporary readers.

"Reprinting," as Dalila Scruggs argues, "had the potential to empty an article or a fictional story of its original intent and meaning to the point where they come to stand for the very inability to testify."[62] Such a figuration privileges the ungraspable meaning of original intent that runs counter to the anonymous and fluid norms of periodical culture in the long eighteenth century. Scruggs aims at mapping instances of African American intent; her mission, in other words, resides in recovering traces of self-assertion concerning a group of writers and readers habitually uncounted and underdocumented by critical practices. In contrast, my attention to the circulation and animation of "The Story of Makandal" argues it served as a set piece redeployed by a variety of white editors precisely because they believed that current contexts could frame the "original intent" for their readers in some engaging way. Kyla Schuller (building on the work of Stuart Hall and Lisa Lowe) has argued that "cultural texts" can be understood as functioning "to reconcile the contradictions between labor and capital, capital and nation."[63] Following Schuller, I want to stress that issues of translation and authorial intention fail to fully account for how the reissuing of "The Story of Makandal" framed arguments about labor and capital that, while displaced into the historical past of St. Domingo, spoke to contemporary circumstances. While no doubt the transmission of the text does cut it loose from its original contexts, the geographical and temporal breadth of its circulation registers how editors embraced its significance.

One way to think about this serial attachment to the text would be to consider how it created the conditions of possibility to redress contradictions between labor and capital. The recurrent interest in the text belies a concern with attending to the space between freedom and unfreedom by charting the unevenly framed subjects of the colonial relation that formed the basis of racial capitalism in the circum-Atlantic world. The text captivated editors enough that it—across a lengthy period—remained readily accessible. "The Story of Makandal" cyclically returned to the American public sphere despite what we think of as the ephemerality of periodical publications. It persisted as a means of asking readers to think about the possibilities of the resistance of ehslaved peoples to the dictates of a white supremacist regime of power by way of recalling a precedent which demonstrates how such endeavors were inevitably failures. The story of Makandal, in effect, proves the eventual reassertion of the very power structures that the historical Makandal had struggled to unsettle. A seemingly unremarkable item in Pitcher's index of titles, "The Story of Makandal," or rather the story of "The Story," reveals the text as an archive of possibility for instructing readers about failed resistance and the durability of racial capitalism.

The History of Illustrious Villains

Readers of the *New-York Magazine, or Literary Repository,* who encountered "An Account of a remarkable Conspiracy formed by a Negro in the Island of St. Domingo" in August and September of 1796, would have understood this meditation on "the history of illustrious villains" as prescient (4).[64] The print environment surrounding these serial installments had been intermittently saturated with news about Haiti across the previous several years. Given this thick context, the narrative's function as a proxy capable of commenting on contemporary events needed no signposting for readers all familiar with the dangers of a revolutionary French Caribbean. Instead of effacement, the text offers a detailed account of Makandal as a means of pathologizing his behavior, exposing his "depravity," and diagnosing the root causes of his rebellion (4). The reprinting offers up a terrifying past moment of insurrection that culminates in a restoration of colonial authority during endless accounts of the failures of European powers to reassert control over Haiti. Such a move assuredly substituted Makandal for contemporaneous rebels, even as it rehearsed the suppression of their endeavors. By suggesting that the unreasonable abuses of his overseer—and not an innate resistance to enslavement—sparked Makandal's actions, the text manifests a sense that French mismanagement fueled the Haitian Revolution. As such, it implies that the situation in Haiti was not hopeless and that a restoration of proper management systems might forestall future problems. By presenting readers a chance to reflect on earlier ruptures, reprintings of "The Story of Makandal" affectively conjoined contemporary events to a previous unsuccessful rebellion to remind them of previous challenges to white supremacist control, while also reassuring them that these efforts had always been unsuccessful. In this sense "The Story of Makandal" is a twice-told tale (perhaps even with a plot that was vaguely familiar to early American readers), but one believed to be capable of relieving current anxieties through its insistence on Makandal's failures to enact lasting structural change.

The narrative mutes Makandal's political commitments to self-determination by depicting his motivations as a decidedly less radical, more personal form of protest. Instead of large-scale political revolution, Makandal's resistance appears totally self-reflective. The text's preoccupation with Makandal's early exceptionality as a model enslaved worker structures the feelings that it seeks to activate. By establishing his archetypal nature at the outset, the narrative heightens the dramatic reversal staged in his transition into an emergent threat. This focus further establishes questions about plantation management as a substratum of the overall text itself. From a white supremacist point of view, the story of Makandal reads as tragic, in part, because it represents the potentiality of a collective Black radical tradition to resist the deprivations of enslavement. Additionally, and perhaps more potently, the narrative figures this situation as avoidable since Makandal's rebelliousness springs not from concerns about systemic injustice but directly from the misguided actions of one bad overseer. Given how this text was recursively called upon to teach readers the same object lesson amid evolving contextual circumstances, early American editors apparently highly regarded the ideological work that it could perform. As such, it seems important to trace how the structure of its plot functions to allow for a brief sympathetic attachment to Makandal while he remains enslaved, even as it then invests enormous attention to disavowing his potential as a political actor. The popularity of this text registers its importance in laying out a pattern that would inflect future texts similarly concerned with fictionalizing the import of the Haitian Revolution. One cultural legacy of "The Story of Makandal" emerges from how its narrative orbit begins with a small-scale critique of the plantation system but which quickly spins into a discursive register aimed eventually at propping up both white supremacist authority and what it imagines as more humane versions of enslavement. Following the unfolding of the narrative itself, in other words, reveals the ways in which this pattern of depicting Haitian rebellions as apolitical and devoid of merit functioned in the early American print public sphere.

The narrative draws on conventional racist tropes found across contemporary accounts of enslavement to present Makandal as both exceptional and the inevitable consequence of bad colonial management. Presented to readers as simultaneously smart, industrious, and hardworking, and overly sexual and immature, the text imagines Makandal as the ideal enslaved person that is nonetheless easily ruled by base appetites and impulses. His keen intelligence, his ability to "read and write the Arabian language," and a talent for "music, painting, and sculpture" (4) bolster his exceptionality, but it is in ethno-medicine that Makandal most excels. Despite his young age (he was "only twelve years of age when carried to the West-Indies") he was already "well acquainted with the medicine of his own country, and with the virtue of plants" (4–5).[65] Makandal's homeopathic skills indicate his value (both to his enslavers and to his fellow enslaved laborers) and his potential as an agent of subversion, since "knowledge" of the medicinal properties of plants proved "so useful, and often so dangerous in the torrid zone" (4). Sold to a planter on the outskirts of Cape François, Makandal quickly distinguishes himself as an invaluable asset to his enslavers for his "knowledge and industry" (4). Moreover, he is "respected" by the other enslaved Africans because of his ability "to cure their disorders, after they had baffled the skill of the European physicians" (5). His reputation as a healer soon spreads, and within a short period of time, "from one end of the island to the other, the sick who were deemed incurable, invoked the name of Makandal, sending to ask from him the leaf or root of some herb, which for the most part relieved them" (5). Carefully articulating how Makandal's mastery of botanicals surpassed that of colonial officials, the text highlights his abilities even as it denigrates the source of his knowledge as homeopathic instead of academically professional.[66]

Makandal sustains the steady function of the plantocracy by restoring the health of the colony's enslaved diasporic Africans. His abilities as a musician and dancer further promote communal belonging and evince another way in which Makandal is implicated early on in the preservation of the plantocracy. But the narrative does not let go of the fact that his knowledge and his performative popularity prove a double-edged sword, and this precarious positionality makes him a figure of revolutionary potential. In this sense, the very talents that make Makandal an exceptional figure in propping up the colonial regime become the means by which he threatens its stability. Just as he spends his early years maintaining the health of enslaved laborers, the capacity for him to do otherwise consistently haunts the margins of the text. "Happy! had he always employed his talents for innocent purposes," the narrator interjects early on, "but they soon became the source of the greatest crimes" (5). This telling admission emphasizes how the plantation system depended so deeply on what Elizabeth Maddock Dillon has called "bare labor."[67] Dillon coins this term as a pointed reworking of Giorgio Agamben's conception of bare life that has all too often been erroneously applied to the plantation system. As Dillon argues, enslavers sought not to eradicate enslaved peoples, but rather more insidiously to manipulate their social behaviors to extract as much labor out of them as possible.[68] Makandal's artistic skills raise morale even as he restores other enslaved laborers—beyond the care of white doctors—back to harvesting. As such, Makandal's surplus labors repair disruptions to the colonial relation and insure profitability.

In the logic of the text, Makandal's life consists of three parts: his boyhood in Africa where he learns Arabic and botanical medicine; his early years of enslavement, during which he assists the systemic exploitation of enslaved peoples; and finally, the sequel to this existence wherein he commits (according to the colonial order) monstrous crimes. The judgment to the third act appears before the texts narrates the events of the first temporal stage. This structure undoubtedly reassured readers that while the events of "twenty-five years past" may still haunt St. Domingo, they did not obliterate larger structures of white supremacist power (4). As such, the narrative evinces how insurrection—no matter how calamitous it might appear—failed to disorient white authority. The rhetorical framing of the possible erasure of Makandal's name at the threshold of the narrative underscores the potentiality of this fiction as a pedagogical tool; readers can imagine what he might have done while comfortably knowing he failed. Considered alongside the daily accounts of the violent unrest in St. Domingo, these reminders about an unsuccessful revolutionary figure from the past (as terrifying as he might have been) likely alleviated insecurities: especially so because of how the text exhibits that Makandal was forced by circumstances into dissent.

Around "the age of 15 or 16," Makandal becomes sexually active, as "love began to inflame his breast and to rule with the most astonishing impetuosity" (5). But Makandal was not interested in heteronormative coupling as "all those that possessed more than ordinary attractions, participated in his homage, and inflamed his desires" (5).[69] A typical racist depiction of an overly sexualized Black male, Makandal's inability to select a single object of desire becomes a compounding problem: "his passion acquired energy and activity in proportion as the objects which inspired it were multiplied" (5). In a slowly increasing (but still subtle) way, the narrative casts Makandal as a creature of unhinged desire; the more potential partners he encounters, the more he wants. At least in terms of his sexual proclivities, Makandal appears ravenous. Makandal was not filled with "satiety and indifference" after "enjoyment"; instead, he became more attracted to his partners and possessed with a "proud jealously" that "defended the empire of his love" (5). Covetous and acquisitive, Makandal epitomizes delusory narcissism.

Interestingly, this figuration mirrors operant representations of Caribbean planters as embodiments of consumptive appetite. The characterization also echoes the tenets of widespread oriental tales, populated by caricatures of rapacious deys, avaricious sultans, and thinly veiled voyeuristic fantasies of harems, which suffused the same circum-Atlantic print networks as "The Story of Makandal." In effect, this fictive Makandal matches the immorality of other predatory eroticized figures so familiar in the eclectic terrain of eighteenth-century periodical fiction. Coterminously, this depiction of Makandal as pure appetite replicates racist configurations of diasporic Africans as licentious. Moreover, Makandal has his own textual doppelganger who serves a crucial function in the plot. The "overseer of the plantation to which he belonged" develops the same lustful attachment for "a beautiful young negro girl, who had attracted the notice also of Makandal" (5). Following this admission, resides a curious accounting of the women's desire:

> The reader may readily imagine how much embarrassed such a female must be, to fix her choice between a rigorous and despotic master, and the most distinguished of all the negroes in that part of the country: her heart, however, inclined towards her equal, and the offers of the overseer were rejected. (5)

The rhetoric here mockingly links the woman's choice of a lover as a debased process of enfranchisement—she inclines toward her equal, and the narrative presents her decision as definitive. This potential sexual rivalry furthers the text's construction of the overseer as abusive and arbitrary, even as it whitewashes the systemic brutalities of enslavement.[70] More specifically, the threat of sexual violence vanishes in this fantasy scenario. Unbelievably, the overseer does not menace or attempt to rape the young enslaved woman, and her ability to consent remains unviolated. By representing this enslaved woman as immune to sexual coercion—by disavowing the possibility of sexual violence against her—she functions as an obscuring cover for the violence of the intimate distance of the plantation system. In effect, the narrative obscures the racist strictures that denied enslaved women any agency over their own body. In so doing, it doubles down on the idea that, aside from this overseer, the conditions of the plantation system were reasonable, a distortion that further renders the overseer an anomaly. Effectively, this framing both hints at and obscures the realities of sexual exploitation against enslaved women in such a way that allows readers to gloss over the endemic dehumanizations of eighteenth-century racial capitalism.[71] While the text does not afford her a name, instead identifying her only as "a beautiful young negro girl," it does dwell, at least momentarily, on this issue of her imagined choice (5). Indeed, the narrative goes as far as to ask the readers to sympathize with her struggle to choose "between a rigorous and despotic master, and the most distinguished of all the negroes in that part of the county" (5). Suggesting that "the reader may readily imagine how much embarrassed such a female must be," the narrator posits this act of transference as easily undertaken, as if this enslaved woman and the presumptive universal reader share the same levels of free will (5).

"Her heart," this brief episode concludes, "however, inclined towards her equal, and the offers of the overseer were rejected" (5). Given how the text has fashioned Makandal's exceptionality, marking her as his equal is a curious flashpoint. On the one hand, it indicates their shared mutual condition of enslavement; on the other, it also conveys some semblance of the woman's self-worth in that she considers herself equivalent to the unrivaled Makandal. Either way, her actions indicate that she has no affinity for her unequal, the overseer, whether that disparity stems from racial difference or from his "despotic" behavior. Overall, this brief aside triggers Makandal's transformation from paradigmatic enslaved laborer to revolutionary. Moreover, the concision of the trigger for Makandal's conversion into a rebellious figure serves the formal function of stripping him from having any political commitments or ideological opposition to the colonial order, instead it reduces his dramatic alteration into a seemingly rapid reaction to being pushed too far. Furthermore, the passage highlights that this unnamed woman's choice would be the same decision the presumptive reader would make after they acknowledged embarrassment over this sympathetic connection. Given the option of a kind of companionate relationship (perhaps only in the most literal meaning of that term) and a potential union with a despot, who would choose otherwise? Her choice, and the overall tenor of the passage, cast the overseer as an undesirable option, one whose behaviors render him disagreeable despite his elevated status. The scene encapsulates a portrait of what enslavement was like for beautiful, young diasporic African women, unencumbered in this imaginative recasting by the realities of systemic sexual violence. In so doing, the paragraph renders the colonial relation as liberated from the very exploitative and violent oppressions that actually defined it.[72]

The overseer stands in for any number of avaricious white people even as his actions disassociate him from the presumptive reader. Thus, while the overseer represents white supremacist authority within the text, he remains non-normative as his attempted courtship of an enslaved woman distances him (on the public surface at least) from genteel white readers.[73] Additionally, the text belabors the point about his bad leadership to stress how he fundamentally represents unhinged rapaciousness over whiteness itself. Given how the quasi-romantic triangle deviates from the abusiveness of the slavocracy, it is worth attending to the work that the fictive courtship performs. The fabrication of this love plot stands as one of the most purely fictive elements in the story: in terms of the plot itself, and also given the tale's larger concerns about freedom and the systems of management. Rebuffed, the overseer becomes "enraged," and he attempts to find any possible justification to punish Makandal (5). This proves difficult, since Makandal, despite his "nocturnal peregrinations," still "discharged his duty with so much punctuality and zeal, that he was never exposed to the least chastisement" (5). The narrative emphasizes the rarity of the unpunished enslaved person, noting that this was "a circumstance rather astonishing in a country where the lash is continually lacerating the bodies of the unhappy negroes, and where the soul of the European not yet inured by custom to the most horrid spectacles, is filled with both terror and pity" (5). Still, even as the overseer "redouble[s] his vigilance" and polices Makandal's behavior with an unprecedented zeal, he never finds an acceptable justification (5). Exhausted by his inability "to invent a pretext," the overseer—in the middle of the planting of sugarcane—orders Makandal "to be stretched out on his belly, and to receive fifty lashes" (5).

In seeking to inflict a brutal punishment because of his bruised ego, the overseer exposes his barbarity. Likewise, his decision to implement such a debilitating penalty—on one of the hardest working enslaved people under his watch—during the height of agriculture work registers how unsuited he is for a leadership role. As such, the overseer's umbrage exhibits substandard judgment and poor economic policy, a double critique of the deprivations of his mismanagement. Indeed, this episode registers the damages to social stability enacted by malfeasance, given how the overseer undermines economic productivity and turns an exemplary enslaved worker into a rebellious figure. While far from being an abolitionist text, the narrative depiction of the petty overseer underscores how the plantocracy relies of a pretense of justice in order to maintain stability even as it exposes the fragility of this social dominance when its own warped standards are violated.

"The pride of Makandal," the narrative declares, "revolted at this act of injustice"; "instead of humbling himself," he refuses compliance (5). Makandal "disdainfully cast his implements of husbandry at the feet of his rival, telling him, that such a barbarous order was to him a signal of liberty" (5). Since the overseer breaks the normative rules governing enslavement, Makandal understands himself as emancipated and lights out for freedom. Yet, the overall effect of this representation delimits Makandal's political agency into that of a solitary disgruntled worker; his actions arise not from a commitment to altering the insidious system he was forced to inhabit, but rather spring from a refusal to consent to an unjustifiable corporeal punishment. Liberal consent resurfaces to imply that accord was somehow possible despite the racialized hierarchies of New World settler colonialism and enslavement. This question of some sort of governing rational accord between the enslaved and their enslavers lingers in how the narrative registers that overseer's orders to capture Makandal are only half-heartedly followed by the other diasporic Africans on the plantation.[74] Given the trajectory of the plot, and the larger-than-life threat to white supremacy that Makandal embodied (both in the middle of the eighteenth century but also every time the text resurfaced), the cause of Makandal's refusal to abide this rescripting of the conditions of enslavement are revelatory. Makandal's abnegation, in this characterization, does not occur because of a rejection of enslavement (a condition he is not born into, meaning he has some experience of freedom) but rather from an objection to an unwarranted sentence. This figuration registers the text's political investments in naturalizing and affirming the durability of the institution of enslavement by recasting rebellion as idiosyncratic acts of individual Black resentment. Moreover, the popularity of this text (presumably because of its distillation of these very political ideologies) suggest the ways in which its structuring of the limitations of Black resistance struck a chord with a wide spectrum of early American periodical editors and evinces how in some ways it instantiates a set of generic expectations for American Haitian fictions.

Despite the rage of the overseer who orders Makandal hunted down, he escapes and unites "himself to the maroons; that is to say, runaway slaves; and twelve years elapsed before he could be apprehended" (6). As he continues in the area, he maintains "a correspondence with his former companions"; and notwithstanding repeated attempts, nothing could persuade any of the still enslaved Africans "to betray their friend, their comforter, and their prophet"; (6). In so doing, the text records a sub rosa society of enslaved Africans in St. Domingo—a place apart from surveillance, but still within the precincts of the plantation society. His rejection of enslavement, then, betrays white fantasies about how fragile the line between self-determination and subjection was within a plantation society so disproportionally populated by diasporic Africans. Makandal takes advantage of this porousness to carve out a new social position for himself, rechanneling his botanical abilities to fashion a cult of personality around his rumored mystical powers. This serves as another way in which the text denigrates diasporic Africans, by stressing their supposed superstitions. The diasporic Africans do not understand that Makandal's magic arises from his superior botanical knowledge. This thread of the narrative functions as another disciplinary turn intended to reassert the validity of white supremacy. The existence of maroon societies thriving as paracultural orders outside of the legal ambit of planter control becomes reflective not of a counterculture but of a byproduct of the imagined primitive behavior of diasporic Africans.[75] Rather than mark the resistance that the other enslaved Africans enact by their collective refusal to turn Makandal in, their activity has to be ascribed to fear rather than solidarity. The text carefully navigates between these poles of resistance and enslavement without unsettling the ideologies of power that underwrite racial capitalism. While the text does not dwell on how Makandal simply throws down his tools and avoids capture for twelve years, it nevertheless registers this act even as it curtails its implications by magnifying Makandal's exceptionality. By presenting the oppressive regimes of enslavement as somehow tolerable under normal conditions, the text highlights how the aftermath of Makandal's flight to freedom could have been avoided if only the overseer had behaved appropriately.

Here for the first time the text presents Makandal's curiously engraved staff, his fetish. Rather than describe Makandal's *obeah* practices as religious, the narrative positions him as a charlatan preying upon the naïve beliefs of diasporic Africans. Dismissively figuring a scared object as a mere prop, the text casts Makandal as a swindler claiming power over life and death. As such, the narrative circles back to the promised transformation marked in the opening paragraph: the alteration in Makandal's use of botanical knowledge. The healer becomes the poisoner to reconsolidate his privilege. Makandal becomes a kind of puppet master, as he establishes a network of associates who travel across the island on his behalf. "The negroes in general," the narrator declares, "are very fond of commerce" (6). Because of this propensity, it was commonplace for numbers of "pedlars" to "go about with European goods to the different plantations" (6). This deceptive countereconomy (predicated on moving European goods among a captive population) provides another feigned release valve by affording the enslaved the capacity to exchange goods and services. Makandal exploits this existing system to provide cover for his agents who pretend to be peddlers to make their movements permissible.

While the real Makandal plagued St. Domingo's colonial government by using a network of rebels to organize large-scale resistance, the serialized portrait of Makandal conjures him as only motivated by petty jealousies. The text notes how "he assembled a number of maroons" upon an "almost inaccessible" mountain summit, where they formed a para-society with "their wives and children, with well cultivated plantations" (7). Still, even as he commands "armed troops" to "sometimes" descend and "spread terror and devastation in the neighboring plantations" or to "exterminate those who had disobeyed the prophet," Makandal's rebelliousness remains muted (7). Perhaps the narrative strategy raises the idea of terror without giving it form as a means of shocking but not totally unnerving readers. Just as the opening of the text stressed that his opposition had been defeated, the representation of that resistance also prevents the actual damage he caused from being memorialized in print.

Whatever terror he may have fomented, Makandal's agenda had, according to the text, a minimal impact on the colonial order of St. Domingo. Instead of detailing Makandal's subversive potentiality, the narrative again overemphasizes his imagined sexual appetites. This doubling down draws deeper parallels between Makandal and the overseer. Just as the overseer failed to comprehend how the enslaved young woman chooses Makandal over him, Makandal cannot grasp (as I will discuss in more detail below) how another enslaved woman (the beautiful Samba) favors another. Like the despotic overseer, Makandal responds to being spurned with affronted violence. The text, in other words, returns to the question of female agency as a means of thinking about male rage. The narrative represents Makandal's acquisitive sexual impulses as overpowering his capacity for reason and overwriting any interest in solidarity. Failing the immediate gratification of his desire, Makandal selfishly lashes out at anyone who spurns him. The repetition of this plotline interestingly links Makandal to the overseer's disastrous model of leadership, and this twinning further undercuts Makandal's potential for political resistance. Just as the text refuses to recognize the Makandal's ideological opposition to the colonial regime, it also erases his commitment to freedom. For all its attention to the revolutionary potential of Black insurrection, the text forecloses the possibility that his struggle was collective or even driven by political motivations.

Makandal first meets Zami, one of the "young negroes" that he attached himself to and who provided him "an account of whatever passed upon the plantations to which they belonged," when he becomes part of his network of agents (7). Notable in his own right for his "spirit and courage," Zami falls in love with Samba after watching her dance (7). Samba has her heart "wounded with the same dart which had just pierced" Zami, and their mutual attraction circles back to the rhetorical framing of Makandal's own earlier trajectory (8). Here Makandal transmutes into the same narrative position as his earlier antagonist. Or, perhaps more accurately, this second version of unhinged jealousy stands as more damning as it registers a more intimate violation of kinship since Zami serves Makandal as a trusted lieutenant. Furthermore, he directs his vengeance against a woman, a further indication of Makandal's villainy as at home within the libertine tradition. The solidarity that Makandal should possess for one of his comrades and his appreciation for Samba's ability to choose her lover (like his earlier nameless love object) vanish in the face of presumed scorn. If the narrative contains a condemnation of power, then it does so by underscoring how Makandal becomes an inverted version of his former self during his marronage despite his own experiences with the violent capriciousness of enslavement. Ultimately, his leadership reveals itself as nothing more than a bad imitation of the despotic overseer. The text, in other words, labors to suggest that Makandal has a limited horizon of political possibility.

In order to pave the way for Makandal's villainy to clearly emerge, the narrative portrays the secret marriage of Zami and Samba in the overwrought language of an ornate eighteenth-century sentimental tale: "amidst a grove of odoriferous orange trees," they express their "affection" for one another, and soon after Samba "perceived that she was about to become a mother" (8). Unaware of their marriage or of Samba's pregnancy, Makandal plots to have her killed since she has "mortified me with continued refusals" (8). Dismayed that his advances are rebuffed, Makandal orders Zami to poison Samba—a command which betrays the source of his supposedly magical power. His previous machinations were disguised from view, as the narrative indicates that even his agents remained ignorant of their roles in his schemes. This moment marks the first time that Makandal does not accurately understand the situation he inhabits, since he has no comprehension of Zami's attachment to Samba. This further equates Makandal's ethical behavior with that of the overseer who spurred him to become a maroon in the first place, especially in the sense that his failure to properly understand consent causes him to violate social norms.

Outraged that a favored subordinate has Samba's heart, Makandal draws "his cutlass" with murderous intent; only the sudden arrival "of some Europeans, who were calling the slaves to their labor" stays his hand (9). Quickly fleeing the scene, Makandal abandons the poisonous powder he prepared to kill Samba. While Zami entertains thoughts of betraying Makandal "to the overseer," his dread of the power of Makandal's "image" keeps him in check (9). After another day of forced labor, the anxious Zami flies to meet Samba in their secret garden bower; when she fails to appear, he ventures to her house on another plantation. Here he finds her dying body surrounded by lamenting women. Zami soon learns that Makandal had sent "a female negro hawker" to poison Samba, a discovery which pushes Zami to turn Makandal over to the colonial authorities (9). In so doing, he hands over the white powder that Makandal had abandoned and soon "a chemist at Cape François" determines it "to be violent poison" (9). With this evidence, "it was then suspected what had been the cause of an immense number of sudden deaths which happened among the negroes," and suddenly, "people shudder at the thoughts of the danger which threatened the whole colony" (9). Quickly the Maréchaussées, or free Black people charged with capturing runaways, are dispatched to "seize Makandal" (9).[76] Recognizing the difficulties of this charge, Zami takes matters into his own hands and apprehends Makandal himself.

Several of Makandal's accomplices are simultaneously arrested. After they confess their participation in his schemes, they reveal that Makandal's ambition had been "to destroy privately the greater part of the planters, or to ruin them, by poisoning all their slaves who appeared to be attached to them" and exterminating "the whole race of white men by a general massacre" (10). For his own part, Makandal would never "confess anything" (10). Despite a death sentence, Makandal preserves his "audacity and fanaticism even in the midst of the flames" (10). "He declared hauntingly from the top of the pile," the narrative records, "that the fire would respect his body; that instead of dying, he would only change his form; and that he would always remain in the island, either as a large knat, bird, or serpent, to protect his nation" (10). Makandal's assertion causes "the ignorant negroes" to believe that his fetish "would save him." As the flames burn around him, Makandal's strength allows him to pull up "the stake" affixing him to the pyre and stagger forward "ten or twelve paces" into the gathered crowd. These witnesses momentarily become a unified chorus, shouting out "A miracle!" in response to this startling turn (10). However, this second flight from colonial violence proves short-lived, as "a soldier who happened to be near" fatally struck him with "a stroke of his saber." Thrown back into the burning pile, Makandal, the text declares, "suffered the punishment which he so justly deserved" (10).

Even though the French military had failed to apprehend Makandal for twelve years or even understand how he was responsible for disrupting colonial authority since his escape, it now belatedly asserts mastery over his fate. Yet the representation of the crowd as ignorant, after their brief transformation into a unified cohort invested in a miracle, aims at dismissing any unity this figuration avows. It is not superstition that motivates them now, but a momentary collective notion of a miracle of deliverance—a fleeting circumvention of colonial power. The text closes with a glimpse of Makandal as an individual potentially delivered from immolation by a supernatural transformation. Perhaps something about this final representation encodes his resistance in a lasting (albeit fragmentary) way, if for no other reason than the heroic dimensions of his stoic refusal to submit. Yet, in the end, Makandal becomes a failed rebel safely entombed in the past, accessible for consideration after the fact but only as a figure of suppressed rebellion.

In reality, the actual Makandal had plotted to seize Cap François by poisoning the city's water supply. The resulting epidemic, Makandal hoped, would allow him to take the city (and then the colony) by force, once the French had either been wiped away or fallen too ill to defend themselves. The narrative's figuration of Makandal's actions significantly alters this practice by presenting his network of agents as attempting to poison his intended victims with doctored fruit, thus attacking them by disrupting their food supply. While primarily focused on the middle of the nineteenth century, Kyla Wazana Tompkins's generative work on what she calls "kitchen insurrections" provides a compelling framework to comprehend how threats to water or foodstuffs haunted white readers so dependent on diasporic Africans to cultivate, harvest, cook, and serve their sustenance.[77] U.S. Americans often had considerable anxiety over the security of their foodways, as Tompkins insightfully decodes, in part because of their dependence on enslaved laborers at every step from farm to table. For Tompkins, "the politics of food" was "indelibly" marked by concerns over "what was rapidly becoming the racial identity at the heart of the national project: whiteness."[78] Fears over ingestion were acute for U.S. Americans across the nineteenth century, and while "The Story of Makandal" does not overtly record Makandal as acting to poison the food supplies (or the water supplies) of French colonials, it nonetheless surfaces these vulnerabilities. Actually imprinting this dire susceptibility may well have been a terror too real to manifest in print; or this shifting away from imprinting white vulnerability—so central to the overall downsizing of the scale of Makandal's actions—might have been a precaution intended to forestall imitation. Considered in this vein, the text covers over white susceptibility to attacks from enslaved workers who were so intimately involved in manufacturing their domesticity. Whatever motivated this fictionalizing shift, the specter of an undetectable manipulation of social relations (as Tompkins enjoins us to consider) still seasons the heart of this narrative.

Resistance as Reaction

The narrative concludes by fossilizing the remaining plot threads into their own resolutions. Satisfied that he has "avenged the unfortunate Samba," Zami commits suicide in the hopes of joining her in the afterlife (10). Whatever had initially made him an agent of Makandal's designs evaporates with Samba's murder, as if the narrative can imagine no future for Zami beyond ossification. His death makes Zami transcendently sentimental; if he had lived, the text would have had to acknowledge how he had captured Makandal even as French colonial authorities could not. Alive, Zami symbolizes the superiority of diasporic Africans; martyred by a broken heart, he serves as a monument to generic heteronormative relations. The text, in other words, cannot imagine (or allow its readers to imagine) any of the diasporic African characters it features as socially reproductive: they function as cautionary tales to a white colonial order, but they cannot engender anything beyond tragic warnings. Neither Zami nor Samba nor Makandal can survive, as the ending effectively transmogrifies acts of resistance into serialized misfortunes.

Makandal's signification across the narrative perpetually shifts, and this protean figuration allows for him to be activated for different ends at various moments of unsettlement. Initially praised as an innately intelligent, industrious enslaved worker, his subsequent denigration reverses his exceptionality. After he resists an unwarranted punishment, he stands excoriated for being manipulative, exploitative, and insatiable. Finally, his stoic defiance and prophetic promise of return mark his final gestures. Although the text appears straightforward, Makandal's presentation remains a complex one. While the narrative closes with a restoration of white supremacist colonial order, Makandal's initial actions appear justified within the logic of the narrative. This central crux rests unresolved in the text, except through Makandal's duplication of the overseer's behavior. By harping on the inefficacies of enslavers, the text denounces the kinds of petty brutality enacted by the overseer (and subsequently Makandal himself) in how they structure power relations. While hardly anti-racist, the text nevertheless criticizes the uncertainties of the plantation system in such a way as to make some of its inherently destabilizing dependencies visible as fissures. By fictionalizing the historical record, the narrative frames resistance as reaction (and only reaction), and not as an attempt to imagine freedom otherwise. Within this fictionalized portrait, all of Makandal's revolutionary energy merely duplicates the same perversion of power that spurred his initial flight. Instead of struggling to reimagine operant political structures, the text reduces Makandal to just another serial rendition of a bad overseer.

While the text critiques the practices of slavery in St. Domingo, and presumably by extension on plantations more broadly, it also highlights the impossibility of effectively policing such spaces.[79] Makandal may have survived as a maroon rebel for twelve years; he may have disrupted normal practices, stolen untold goods, and poisoned countless victims; he may have even inspired others to briefly join his cause and fear him more than they did the agents of French power, but, in the end, he becomes consumed by anti-revolutionary fires. The text overwrites his ability to foster sustainable allegiances and attempts to curtail any sense that he might inspire future resistance. By figuring a diasporic African as centrally involved in his capture, the text also further reduces his capacity to serve as a symbol of collective diasporic African desires for freedom. He stands convicted by the narrative logic of the text as much for his crimes against other enslaved people as he does for his resistance to white supremacy. Such a narrative turn works to accentuate the improbability of diasporic African assemblage. In effect, it suggests that Black radicalism was (and could only ever be) a solitary endeavor; and, as such, perpetually doomed to self-consumptive failure.

Considered in this light, the narrative served to reassure periodical readers across the circum-Atlantic basin that despite what they were encountering about the instabilities and insurrections in St. Domingo, conflagrations like this had occurred before and had been suppressed. Short-term interruptions in white governance might have happened, but nothing that, ultimately, proved capable of unsettling the sovereignty of colonial power. While the text allows for a potential sympathetic attachment to Makandal because of the violence inflicted upon him early on, the concluding sections of the text dissolves that sympathetic relation by depicting him as menacing Zami and Samba with a mirroring retribution. The narrative linkage between the villainous overseer and Makandal fractures any sentimental affiliations readers might have held by implicitly suggesting his lack of proper feeling.[80] His own visceral reaction to the overseer's unjustified actions reroutes itself into the means of condemning him for the same behaviors. Instead of being a figure of social justice, the text recasts Makandal as an egotistical hypocrite.

Makandal's poisoning of a pregnant woman utterly shatters any shred of admiration that readers might have had for his flight from tyranny and subsequent parallel existence. The structure of the narrative corrects, in short, any possible attachment to Makandal by reasserting the racial hierarchies that underwrite the inequalities of Black Atlantic capitalism. In effect, Makandal's death restores the supremacy of the racialized plantation system that he sought to escape. In this caricature, Makandal does not struggle for freedom, but rather for personal pleasure. As such, the text archives him as a historical relic; in doing so, it avows his revolutionary commitments for white Euro-Americans as thinkable but uninspiring.[81] Makandal might produce shudders at the mention of his name, but this fictionalization denies any possibility of understanding him as a world-altering rebel. His motivations surface as personal, petty, and vengeful, not as heroic, communal, and revolutionary.

Cutting Makandal off from futurity—by robbing him of any motivation beyond mere appetite—effectively neuters him. Moreover, because of how the text parallels Makandal and the overseer as twinned bad managers, it further reduces readers' capacity to envision him as an emblem of Black radical possibility. Since Makandal appears so ill-equipped to cultivate solidarities, the text eradicates any possibility for him to inspire a large-scale movement for freedom. Stripped of political agency, the text pigeonholes its Makandal as a symbol of despotism. This reductive figuration polices the possibility of diasporic African agency by demonstrating that it cannot succeed since it lacks a coherent collectivity.[82] The narrative freezes Makandal into the past temporality of twenty-five years prior by disavowing his ability to speak to the present except as an object lesson about the repercussions of arbitrary force. Unable to see beyond his hunger for immediate gratification, this *story* of Makandal restricts his capacity to impact futurity.

While readers might "judge what he would have done" under different circumstances, they do so knowing full well that he had not been "placed in the same situation as" those "two ambitious fanatics," "Mahomet or Cromwell" (2). The power of Cromwell and Mahomet, from a certain Anglo-American eighteenth-century perspective, resided in their ability to inspire other people to their cause, and their legacies still shape the globe well after their own deaths. Neither a regicide nor the founder of a new religion (which was presumed to be a threat to white Christian authority), this tale's version of Makandal has his ability to unsettle a white supremacist order foreclosed by the text's narrative arc. He falls short of enacting any political action that would have protracted consequences. Yet the text still catalogs Makandal within this powerful list of names; presenting him as a nodal point in a tryptic of potentially seismic figures each capable of shattering the central tenets of traditional European order. Such a figuration hints that Makandal might yet possess a revenant-like ability to return to haunt the colonial imagination.

Serially presented and serially executed, the Makandal of the *Mercure* narrative (and its various resurrections) could not inspire radical solidarity. At the same time, this text and its distortion of Makandal remained an otherworldly presence in the archives of U.S. periodicals. "The Story of Makandal" loitered as a smoldering memory waiting to back burn any encroaching threats to the social order through the heat of its anti-revolutionary rhetoric. Somehow, the text was on hand; ready to recertify that a white supremacist order would eventually triumph over its opposition. The manifold emergences of the text suggest something entirely different from archival silence, something more akin to careful preservation. A variety of editors, across decades and across fragmented print networks, had access to the text so that they could repurpose the fictional history it encoded. Canonical enough for editors to recursively exhume it; the text persisted so it could structure resistance as futile. Typecasting Makandal as a symbol of defeat, this narrative framed him as a substitute rebel whose downfall at the hands of white power serially reasserted (at least in print) the reordering logic of racial capitalism. A substitute for the potential terror of domestic insurrections, the tale evinces an attachment to Haiti itself as a proxy for contending with the troubling legacies of Black Atlantic histories.

All too often, critics treat genre fiction (and shorter magazine fiction more generally) like "The Story of Makandal" as a massive conglomerate. This tendency to amalgamate without differentiation quickly dismisses the need to study any particular text on the basis of its presumed repetitions. According to this methodological logic, the whole seems much more important than any single part, even if some of those parts reappeared at divergent moments and across a variety of venues.[83] Such a critical practice ignores how these serial proxies functioned for readers of American periodicals; crucially, seriality needs to be understood in multiple registers when thinking about this archive of shorter fiction. Not only did these texts appear in serial publications, but these printings often spanned multiple issues, an experiential segmentation which demanded more of readers who needed to hold onto the plot between installments. Readers, in sum, spent considerable time (albeit sporadically) with periodical texts. Finally, they collectively constitute a protracted attention to the non-normative social horrors of enslavement underpinning all social relations within what would become the United States. We need to take more seriously, as Laurent Dubois' observation about proxies implies, the ways in which many of these rebellious Black figures habitually blurred into ever-present archetypes. In so doing, we can better comprehend how these episodic revenants served as iterative interruptions in the otherwise continued dominance of prevailing systems of exploitation. Nevertheless, the serial nature of this figure, its reoccurrence as a riptide within cultural memory, remains a relatively unexamined facet of early American literary studies. While "The Story of Makandal" itself falls outside of all the normative classificatory indexes used to define what constitutes an early American text, its persistence (across time and space) in U.S. American periodicals calls into question some of the residual tenets of our field imaginary. What would it mean to embrace this text as, following Pitcher's suggestion, a piece of American magazine fiction? What would it mean to invest more in genealogies of readers rather than authors? What would it mean to think of "Makandal" as a U.S. American proxy?

The sporadic currency of "The Story of Makandal" lays bare some of the complexities of operant American fantasies about enslavement. As a narrative both about companionate relationships and absent threats of sexual violence (but which also does not feature any white women), the text extends the issue of choice beyond the delimited frame that the field has long clung to as defining. It elides the horrors of enslavement by foregrounding bad management practices as unsettling the routinized exploitations of structural racism. This text emphasizes the dangers of unpoliced spaces of marronage for their capacity to shelter counterformations with the potential to disrupt the dominant paradigm. Yet even as "The Story of Makandal" registers fissures within the foundations of the plantocracy, it further moves to inter Makandal in "the history of illustrious villains," a gesture which entombs him within the annals of a Eurocentric history without undermining Euro-American power (2). For American periodical readers, long accustomed to seeing published accounts which linked domestic insurrections back to the Haitian Revolution, the story of Makandal's fate triggered both ideas about restoration and, after 1804, about unthinkable loss. By attending to Makandal's "depravity," these readers could distance themselves from the unsettlement he represented by disavowing any permanent connections to his ghostly matter.

Makandal's serial appearances within the American print public sphere reminded readers of this rebellious specter. Moreover, it should likewise prompt critics of American literary history to recall that our inherited notions of an isolationist imaginary forming the spinal column of U.S. cultural production was a fantasy enacted by a Cold War generation intent on framing American literary history as a beacon of whiggish stability.[84] Early American readers and editors hardly cared if "The Story of Makandal" was a text in translation, produced by a foreign author, or failed to mention the emerging Untied States when they habitually returned to it. For these early Americans, this story of Makandal crystalized a way for them to define American futurity by circulating a fictionalized version of Haitian history which insisted on differentiating the origins of the two Republics and the political orders that their founders had fought for.

2

Sympathy in the Era of Ungood Feelings

Martha Meredith Read's City of Unbrotherly Love

The Gazette of the United States published a three-column letter under the pseudonymous byline of Serranus on New Year's Day 1802.[1] Ostensibly addressed to Thomas McKean (the Democratic-Republican governor of Pennsylvania), the missive condemns McKean's vindictive behavior and implores him to change his ways. While the 1799 election had been a bitter struggle, McKean's subsequent purge of Federalist bureaucrats had no precedent in American politics. Indeed, his actions were so extreme that many historians have retrospectively labeled McKean the father of the spoils system.[2] Casting McKean as abhorrent, Serranus notes that even Thomas Jefferson, the nominal head of the Democratic-Republicans, had recently called—in his first inaugural address delivered just a few months earlier in March of 1801—for reconciliation. To make this point, Serranus cites Jefferson's declaration that "every difference of opinion is not a difference of principle" and his invocation that "We are all Republicans; we are all Federalists."[3] After his fractious campaign against John Adams, Jefferson used his inaugural address to denounce partisan wrangling and urged Americans "to regain the road [of unity] which alone leads to peace, liberty and safety."[4] While Serranus grants that the governor was not "bound by the President's concessions," he nevertheless sarcastically prompts McKean to "be enlightened by his rays."[5]

But instead of unifying contending parties, as Jefferson had at least symbolically pledged to do, Serranus accuses McKean of inflicting "ruin to the extent of [his] power," even though such behavior was both "destructive of republican principals" as well as "unjust and inhumane."[6] McKean was making political differences into personal (and personnel) matters by persecuting Federalists to such an extent that "many honest men with their families, are now groaning in poverty."[7] Serranus asserts that "neither your predecessor, nor his sect, was intolerant," to condemn McKean for subverting the "the right of suffrage" through pronounced intimation.[8] Comparing McKean to Cicero and Buonaparte, "the first Caesar of France," the epistle casts him as an inversion of the ethos of both the "ancien Regime" and of "seventy-six."[9] Considered together, these allusions exclude McKean from the realm of acceptable behaviors, suggesting that he had abandoned the stabilizing power of social norms. The allusion to the patriotic revolutionary generation (conjured by "seventy-six"), who had already by then become legendary, positions McKean's actions as extraordinary violations of

The Haitian Revolution in the Early Republic of Letters: Incipient Fevers. Duncan Faherty, Oxford University Press.
© Duncan Faherty 2023. DOI: 10.1093/oso/9780192889157.003.0003

foundational praxis.[10] The reference to the Ancien Régime reflects the Federalist strategy, as Courtney Chatellier has persuasively argued, for figuring the "French Revolution as marking an absolute break between tradition and modernity."[11] As Chatellier maintains, "the idea of Old Regime France as a bygone world of traditional values gained traction as a concept in Federalist writing precisely at the moment when" they believed "French Revolutionary ideology" had infected the Democratic-Republican party.[12]

In his biting invitation for McKean to alter course, Serranus implores him "to put yourself in imagination only, in the place of a discarded subordinate officer, unconscious of crime" who had been displaced by a new political party.[13] This summons questions McKean's capacity for sympathy, in a Smithian sense, by wondering if he could possibly comprehend the pain he inflicted. The rhetorical solicitation condemns McKean on two levels: both for his literal crimes and for his utter lack of a sympathetic imagination. In this regard, Serranus casts McKean as representative of Democratic-Republicans who "have been hungering and thirsting after power," but have no idea what to do with it after having "obtained it."[14] Bucking a traditional praxis of magnanimity, McKean reviles anyone who had opposed his election and does so at the cost of actually governing the state.[15] In short, the letter accuses McLean of destroying civic order and "this," the letter warns, "is the wish of the Jacobins."[16]

After surveying all the damage McKean had wrought, Serranus ends his open letter by reminding readers that "the Federalists are too conscious of their weight in the community" to ever be "cajoled or dragooned into disgraceful compliances." Claiming the high moral ground, given how McKean has rendered so many "honest men" into "martyrs to *their* principles," the letter reaffirms the Federalists' commitment to "the peace and welfare of their Country." Moreover, Democratic-Republicans should recall that "France holds out a double lesson," since it both presents "the tremendous power of Demagogues" while also showing "how they can be crushed." By staying true to traditional moral and political values, Federalists (even after being unseated from power) could preserve the foundational tenets of the Republic by continuing to resist McKean's (and Jefferson's) radical ideologies.[17]

While Serranus's jeremiad might appear a solitary cry in a pseudonymous partisan wilderness, the column represents but one wave in a floodtide of Federalist invectives against the dangerous liaisons between Jeffersonianism and Jacobinism. In the wake of the election of 1800, a wide range of Federalist writers responded to their displacement from traditional positions of authority by inundating the Republic's print networks with sensationalized accounts of what they understood as a burgeoning national crisis. Consistent in these figurations—in fact central to the emergence of a new Federalist aesthetics—was an overwhelming anxiety about the ways in which Democratic-Republicans were inspired by radical foreign ideologies.

While the specter of the *sans-culottes* suffused many of these texts, a much more consistent strategy animating these Federalist cautionary tales was the intimation of strong connections between Monticello and Cape François. By linking the futurity of the United States with unrest in Haiti, these Federalist writers sought to demonstrate how corrupt leadership would enkindle radical and violent counterreactions. In what follows, I chart the complex temporality and territoriality of this emerging Federalist aesthetics by attending to how they mobilized representations of the Haitian Revolution to locate their concerns about the fractured futurity of the American Republic.

In his formative study of the aesthetic dimensions of "literary Federalism," William Dowling argues that a loosely affiliated coterie of politically oriented writers embraced "language" as the means of fashioning "an alternative to the conditions of American social existence."[18] Dowling allows us to understand how Serranus hinted at a divergent trajectory for Pennsylvania, one protected from McLean's embrace of Jacobin precepts. Yet Dowling relies on a linear transatlantic temporality to chart the circum-Atlantic world and, as such, oversimplifies the complexities of the amalgamating vectors defining Serranus's aesthetic praxis.[19] As Serranus makes clear, Federalists understood France as the source of two strains of thought: both a radical Jacobin social leveling and the model of resistance encoded in the cultural mores of the Ancien Régime. Moreover, Federalists understood Jacobinism as possessing a more promiscuous geographical influence than Dowling maps. It was not just a ravaged Paris that Serranus lamented, but also a smoldering Cape François. By the early nineteenth century, the term Jacobinism, as Rachel Hope Cleaves maintains, was synonymous with a "multivectored" conception of "the revolutionary spirit of the late eighteenth century."[20] To continue to reduce these compounding anxieties as "a trialogue (between Britain, France, and the United States)" ignores their reverberations on global, national, regional, and local scales.[21] Part of this blurring of revolutionary spaces fueled Federalist depictions of Thomas Jefferson as both a radical Francophile and an enslaver. As such, for the Federalists, Jefferson not only demonstrated revolutionary appetites but also helped perpetuate the conditions of possibility for a domestic outbreak of racialized revolution. Jefferson was attached, in other words, to the wrong French influence. The Federalist press further promulgated these fears by intimating that Jefferson had fathered enslaved children, and while they never fully divulge the open secret about Sally Hemings, they do insinuate the connection as another indication of Jefferson's radical depravity.[22]

As one Federalist critic (writing under the pseudonym Burleigh) argued, if Jefferson was elected "the soil will be soaked with blood, and the nation black with crimes."[23] Fearing the havoc that would result from Jefferson's election, Burleigh deployed racist dog whistles (like the use of "black" to mark the forthcoming crimes) to demarcate the Republic's state of emergency. Mirroring larger Federalist patterns of representation, Burleigh understood Jacobinism as an international revolutionary force with as many connections to racialized unrest in Haiti as to the guillotines within the hexagon. The Federalists feared that the terrors of Jacobinism would root themselves into the American social fabric if Jefferson became president; as Serranus's columns exhibit, the only thing capable of opposing this infestation was the Federalist capacity to imaginatively maintain their steadfast commitments to traditional forms of belonging. As Chatellier establishes, this aesthetic Federalism was not simply anti-Francophone but rather fundamentally opposed to radical forms of "social leveling."[24] Indeed, Chatellier demonstrates how these Federalist writers took to the popular press to exhibit how they "believed that the trend toward egalitarianism that had started in France had allowed Americans to disavow the differences between the natural aristocracy and the 'swinish multitude.'"[25] Or again, these Federalist stalwarts bemoaned how a commitment to radical equality destroyed traditional praxis in France and threatened to inflict similar damage in the United States.

Federalists typically routed this anxiety about social disorder and destabilized hierarchies through the lens of an imperiled subject—a figure in need of suitably secure contractual protections. This trope furnished Federalist writers with a site of potential instruction for a culture they feared was adrift.[26] If democracy (as Adams prognosticated) was Lovelace and the people Clarissa, Federalist fictions of the early nineteenth century sought to tabulate the violations enacted on the seduced and abandoned social order.[27] Like the end turn of Richardson's novel, the protagonists of these Federalist fictions produced a corrective after their violation in an attempt to "undo" the damage rendered by misplaced trust and false associations.[28] Despite Jefferson's efforts in his inaugural address to curtail bitter partisanship, lingering tensions were only exacerbated by subsequent Democratic-Republican victories. Given the zealous saber rattling on both sides, describing the period as the era of ungood feelings might best encapsulate the heightened tension surrounding the election of 1800 and its aftermath.[29]

The charged affect which dominated the Federalist periodical campaign against Jefferson did not dissipate after his supposedly conciliatory inaugural address. If anything, as Serranus's citation evinces, Jefferson's gestures of reconciliation only sparked further derision. Typically historians have pointed to the absence of a physical aftershock as evidence of the strength of national democracy in the wake of the election of 1800. Yet in so doing, they have routinely neglected the uncertainties encoded in textual figurations of the era's cultural life. While these rippling tensions eventually attenuated, their force early in the century demonstrates an almost commonplace recognition of the tenuous state of the emerging Republic's social cohesion. The idea that the dyspeptic election had subverted national stability hastened apprehensions about whether Jefferson's victory was just a foreshock of change or the epicenter of a cataclysmic breach: was the election a harbinger of future ruptures or was it a ravaging singularity from which recovery might still be possible? These reservations helped structure an already prevalent urgency about the imbrication of the post-1800 nation in a world of empires, increasing global economic integration, racialized violence, and seemingly endless revolutions. From ongoing paranoia sparked by the Haitian Revolution, or the Burr Conspiracy, or the Louisiana Purchase, or abiding conflicts with Native Americans, or Gabriel's Rebellion, or the economic ramifications of the Embargo and Non-Intercourse Acts, the first decade of the nineteenth century was marked by widespread anxieties about the Republic's future.

The literary culture of the period, as I am arguing here, is the best record of the worries and fears of a Federalist intelligentsia that was becoming increasingly pessimistic about the future. While continuing to deploy its dystopian analytic in newspaper articles, political speeches, sermons, essays, and private correspondence, Federalists turned to the genre of fiction to coercively fashion new models of subjectivity for an electorate they believed desperately needed correction. What choice did they have? They had lost the capacity to legislate social interactions and in casting about for new forms of influence they soon discovered that the generic conventions of sentimental and sensational fiction offered them a new medium through which to explore the ramifications of political disarray. The novel (especially the serialized novel), accommodated a prolonged juxtaposition of properly ordered domestic relationships, socially anchoring marriages and parental relationships alongside their dangerous counterparts. As these writers staged the potential victims of misrule, they utilized traumatic disarray as a pedagogic exercise. In so doing, these "era of ungood feelings" Federalist writers turned to the themes of adultery, robbery, incest, economic ruination, and threats of sexual violence as tropes capable of charting how improper domestic relationships weakened social, cultural, and political stability.[30]

Displaced patriarchs, ruined by alterations in political authority, served as a key locus for such figurations by underscoring how the rise of Jacobinism had fractured the traditional household (the cornerstone, for them, of a healthy Republic). By depicting the threats to cultural stability as domestic dramas, these Federalist writers consistently interrogated the relationship between protean households and national stability. Fiction allowed these writers to explore the political dimensions of kinship relationships as well as model appropriate patterns of civic behavior. This often unrecognized agenda percolated in a range of literary texts published in the first decade of the nineteenth century—novels like Charles Brockden Brown's *Ormond* (1799), the pseudonymously published *Moreland Vale* (1801), and Tabitha Tenney's *Female Quixtotism* (1808). These novels explore the effects of radical social philosophies and consider the stabilizing potential of clearly defined social hierarchies; in so doing they personified the fears that Serranus and Burleigh had so ominously sketched.

By delimiting historical flashpoints as the spark for literary interpretation, early Americanists have relied on historians to define their objects of study. Yet just as literary critics have oversimplified the tenor of early-nineteenth-century textual production, so too have historians reduced the operant sense of Federalism into redacted notions of elite social hierarchy and/or a pragmatic sense of institutionalism. Such a critical tendency to privilege electoral politics and political writing (domains dominated by elite men) has undervalued how these early nineteenth-century Federalist writers (who were more often than not women) deployed a counterfactual narrative technique to privilege properly configured domestic relationships, to unfold a qualified but sympathetic attachment to England, and to underscore the dangers of even a passing connection to radical Francophone influences (even as they continued to pay homage to the Ancien Régime). Seizing upon a set of readily available rhetorical tropes, these texts transmogrify the seduction and gothic genres into a sustained campaign to restore a semblance of Federalist authority. But they do so from a nostalgic position, often investing significant narrative attention in returning to the initial moments of infestation to fantasize about ways in which the Republic might have been safely (and anachronistically) inoculated against a ravaging pandemic.

In the struggle to find a narrative strategy that could accurately reflect their longing for a superseded national future, many of these early-nineteenth-century Federalist writers blurred the boundaries between the French and Haitian Revolutions to register the global dangers of Jacobinism.[31] These neglected texts often deployed a conflated narrative temporality to figure the Jeffersonian ascension (what we now call the Revolution of 1800) as unfolding within a contiguous ambit of the French and Haitian Revolutions. Moreover, it is precisely this expansive sense of territoriality which has caused these texts to remain ignored because they are decidedly at odds with a canon delimited by a historiography which frames this period as one consumed with questions of national consolidation. As such, these neglected novels represent radical political change as a process of problematic aggregation, and they sought to use fiction to explore the effects (and affects) of these compounding breaks from traditional praxis. The rest of the chapter that follows explores an emblematic instance of these attempts to register the danger that circum-Atlantic Jacobinism posed to the emerging Republic. In so doing, I focus on the Federalist fixation with the literary public sphere as a space through which to restructure the feelings of the nation and to heal the breach opened up by the Revolution of 1800.[32]

Dispossessed Elites

Orbiting back to Serranus's polemics against Democratic-Republican intolerance, I want to stress his rhetorical choices register more than just hyperbolic political objections. His column appropriates a series of generic tropes to fashion a compelling, albeit alarmist, argument; as such, it exploits a wider array of Federalist aesthetic practices. Indeed, his attempt to have McKean imagine himself as one of those patriotic—but nonetheless displaced—men echoes the narrative strategies of Martha Meredith Read's *Monima; or The Beggar Girl* (1802). Crafted amid the aftershocks of the Revolution of 1800, Read's novel explored the ways in which a perceived loss of communal responsibility fractured the American social order. Centered on the tribulations of the eponymous heroine who finds herself forced to beg for alms to sustain her wrecked father, Read's novel charts how the rise of radicalism in France and Haiti combined to ruin a once proud, wealthy family. Yet, within the novel, the terror enacted by the unfeeling Philadelphians who prey upon Monima outstrips the horrifying specter of foreign intrigues. Indeed, Read diagnoses the lack of sympathetic domestic social attachments as an epidemic that stands desperately in need of a cure. Remarkably, the novel characterizes almost all of the American characters as unredeemable; instead of offering some figure who embodies a virtuous national ethos, the Philadelphians populating *Monima* range from illiterate pretenders to depraved scoundrels. Finally, in having Monima and her French heritage serve as a model of proper behavior, Read (just as Serranus before her) reminds her readers that France provides a double lesson for the United States: while it may be the wellspring of radical traumas, it also provides models of resistance. In essence, Monima's trials do not simply dramatize what a Jeffersonian ascendency had wrought, but rather stage ways to counter the effects of the declension of political culture.

While we know very little about Martha Meredith Read, she was no stranger to the lost authority of Federalists since most of her male relatives were shunted aside after Jefferson's election.[33] For example, Read's father, Samuel Meredith (1741–1817), was a decorated officer during the Revolutionary War, a member of the Pennsylvania Assembly, and the first secretary of the Treasury; he held this cabinet position from 1789 until 1801 when Jefferson's inauguration caused him to resign for health reasons. Read's uncle, Lambert Cadwalader (1743–1823), was also a decorated Revolutionary War veteran and a two-term Federalist congressman (1789–91 and 1793–5) from Pennsylvania. Read's father-in law, George Read (1733–98), was not only a close ally of Alexander Hamilton and signer of the Declaration, but also had served two terms in the Senate before becoming the chief justice of the Supreme Court of Delaware in 1793. Read's husband, John Read (1769–1854), was a confidant of John Adams, who appointed him the agent general of the United States for Jay's Treaty (a position he occupied until 1809); and he was among those few Federalists who retained influence during Jefferson's administration. In short, many of her male relatives suffered the very displacements that Serranus lamented. Given her familial history, it seems plausible that at least one of the unnamed exiles populating Serranus's complaints could have been a Meredith, a Cadwalader, or a Read.

In many ways, Read's *Monima* functions as a conservative response to the cacophonous cultural upheaval following the Revolution of 1800. The novel exemplifies Federalist strategies for fictionalizing what Joseph Fichtelberg calls the "legitimation crisis" facing the nation after the displacement of traditional authority.[34] While the novel grapples with operant instabilities in issues of national identity, it does so with an expansive cartographic imagination, placing circum-Atlantic physical mobility alongside questions about weakened domestic infrastructures of political and economic exchange. In so doing, Read traces broader hemispheric connections to catalog how U.S. American history and sociality stem from its participation in a fluctuating and porous circum-Atlantic world. Moreover, the novel charts how—from the French countryside to the plantations of Cape François to the streets of Philadelphia—the emergence of radicalism had replaced traditional practices (and the families that represent them) with unbridled self-interest. By domesticating issues of foreign unsettlement, Read emphasizes how the deracination of Federalist authority had eroded cultural cohesion. Moreover, it does so by suggesting how Jacobinism had first unmoored the Ancien Régime in France and subsequently bankrupted what the novel imagines as humane planters in the Caribbean.[35]

In *Monima*, Read figures the U.S. landscape as haunted by itinerant elite refugees in flight from nefarious conspiracies and racialized unrest. She represents these dispossessed figures—despite their exemplary commercial humanism—as victims of revolutionary excess. Their arrival in the U.S. forced American culture to renegotiate its own sense of national identity; and, while it would be easy to suggest that the destabilized social order depicted in the novel results only from foreign influences, Read sutures these fissures to the domestic social structures that these victims of political intrigue immigrate into. In essence, what had once been renowned as the city of brotherly love now hauntingly lacks any reservoir of public sympathy. The novel ambitiously tries to navigate these displacements amid the legacies of multiple revolutions—the American, the French, the Haitian, and the Revolution of 1800—by depicting them as operating within a complex webbed simultaneity. Read rejects plotting these revolutions as discrete events in a linear causal chain—the familiar figuration of a domino theory—in favor of conceiving of them as intimately connected facets of the circum-Atlantic crisis of republicanism dominating the tail end of the long eighteenth century.[36]

As the novel opens, Monima and her father arrive as strangers in Philadelphia after burying her mother and sister who have perished during a yellow fever outbreak. This loss comes on the heels of reports that both her brothers were killed during the family's retreat from revolutionary St. Domingo. The family had absconded to Haiti after suffering unjust persecution in France at the hands of a secretive conspiracy that had engineered the confiscation of their hereditary estates. With only her skills as a seamstress to rely upon, Monima wanders around Philadelphia in the hopes of trading piece work for sustenance. Thwarted at almost every turn, Monima eventually stands convicted of vagrancy and sentenced to the city workhouse. Later still, after both she and her father are kidnapped by a jealous American housewife, an uncaring Philadelphia magistrate commits Monima to a lunatic asylum. Malnourished and without any hope, Monima finally takes to the streets as a beggar. In this destitute condition, she finds the streets of Philadelphia populated, not by anyone willing to extend a friendly hand, but rather by wealthy white male sexual predators.

After being victimized by a disturbingly cruel U.S. society, Monima and her father are eventually rescued by a wealthy Frenchman named Sonnetton (a French refugee who had maintained his wealth and, thus, had managed to enter into the upper echelons of Philadelphian society). Despite Sonnetton's longstanding connection with her father, the two parties had failed to reconnect because of how Philadelphians had Anglicized his surname (mistakenly calling him Sontine), rendering it indecipherable to French ears.[37] Like ships passing in the night, Monima and Sonnetton/Sontine, while aware of each other's presence in the city, manage to narrowly miss one another several times across the novel. Various other abusive figures, including Sonnetton's adulterous American wife, actively conspire to keep them apart. Depicting a city utterly bereft of sympathy, the novel offers perhaps the most harrowing representations of poverty, food insecurity, and moral bankruptcy of any early U.S. novel. Without any elite American actors capable of extending aid, the dispossessed refugees from both the French Revolution and the Haitian Revolution enter a barren ethnoscape.

Read uses the same language to describe the mobs who cheer innocent victims in France as she does the crowds who jeer Monima for being incarcerated in a workhouse. Famished, exploited, and imprisoned, Monima is represented as slave-like, and indeed one of her tormentors delights in plotting to reexport her "to [her] French negro country" (50).[38] For more than a few of the white Philadelphians who interact with her, Monima's time in St. Domingo overwrites (or at least makes questionable) her claims to whiteness.[39] This blurring of her racial identity conjoins with her abject poverty to open Monima up to a series of threats of sexual violence, as a range of Philadelphian men falsely believe these social constructs reveal her promiscuity. Flummoxed by this unwanted attention, the virtuous Monima fails to fully comprehend these attempts at coercion. Worse still, Read depicts city authorities as utterly suspicious of the idea of a chaste but impoverished woman. Monima's position as a former member of the social elite has been so systematically dismantled that she is literally held in bondage by the machinations of the daughter of "an illiterate and vulgar family" (213). Across the novel, Philadelphia, once famous for its hospitality and sense of communal brotherhood, now stands as an inverted shell of its former self and home to the same cruel ideologies that had forced the family to flee France and Haiti.

Unwholesome Prejudices

A preface declaring the moral stakes of the novel precedes all the sensationalist threats Monima faces.[40] Writing under the byline "An American Lady" and casting herself as a supplicant to an "honored sir," the dedication positions Read as a figure "unnoted, unpatronized," and "without one smile from lenient friendship" (iii). Apologetic for all of the "original defects" of this first attempt at publication, Read plays with the notion of being "a stranger here" in "the literary world" to intimate parallels between the outsider status of the text's titular heroine and the author herself (iii). Foreshadowing the besieged plight of Monima, Read presents herself as "surrounded with many difficulties" and in need of "the fostering hand of friendship to support me under my present apprehension" (iii). Read further defines the "moral purpose" of the novel as twofold. First, she hopes that the text will "speak obedience, unbounded love, respect and veneration to the hearts of children for their parents" (iii). Second, she notes the novel aims to "be calculated to rouse a sentiment of charity in the opulent toward the oppressed and life-worn children of affliction" (iii). Casting herself as "a refuge from the pointed shafts of local criticism," Read confesses the hope that her efforts will elicit "friendship" from someone so well renowned "to be a father to the poor" (iv).

Still, Read's preface does more than establish the apologetic cover that appears in the front-matter of any number of other early U.S. American novels. While many authors presented themselves as supplicants to the reading public through preemptive excuses, Read's dedication also highlights how "An American Lady"— with all the privilege that such a social position entails—could find herself an estranged petitioner. This theme of the relationship between the figure of the author and the sympathies of the reading public continues in the two distinct prefaces that Read appends to the three different printings of the text. The novel was first published in 1802 in New York by T.B. Jansen & Co. Booksellers, who also printed a second edition in 1803. A slightly altered version was printed by Eaken & Mecum in Philadelphia in 1803, marked by a new preface that seemingly responds to recent critical reviews. While both prefaces stress the veracity of the novel as a text "founded on facts" (another familiar trope of early American novels), the Philadelphia preface presents a more antagonistic defense of the plot's being an accurate depiction of local conditions.

Included in both New York publications, the original preface harmonized with the dedication to accentuate how the novel sought to "display characters *as they are*" as a means of delineating "the pernicious...ignorance, prejudices and immorality" suffusing the Republic (v). Presenting her text as adhering "to truth and nature," Read condemns "NOVEL-TINKERS" who "arrogate to themselves the right of infringing in the limits of nature, by conjuring up scenes, images, and actions which *nature cannot boast*" (v). Such texts, Read continues, "answer no valuable purposes to the enlightened citizen" since their sympathies cannot be drawn out by "impossibilities"; worse still, these fictions "ingraft unwholesome prejudices" on "the minds of the uniformed, weak, or the youthful" (vi). Replicating a somewhat standard version of Federalist elitism, especially in regards to apprehensions about the anti-social possibilities of fiction, Read notes that her text has a didactic purpose.[41] By attempting to "speak to the heart," Read announces her intentions to impress "on the minds of children the incumbency of certain duties toward their parents" so as to awaken "in the thoughtless, compassion toward the sufferer of merit" (vi). Here Read frames her novel as a pedagogic exercise, marking *Monima* as a tool to edify impressionable readers about the necessities of charity, allegiance, and respect.

The preface appended to the solitary Philadelphia printing strikes a similar chord as that of the New York editions although it also doubles down on the accuracy of the novel's plot. Moreover, the preface boldly refutes accusations from *"men who*, it is my sacred opinion, *have never been at the pains of reading these pages*," but who have still disdainfully "called into question" the "truth of the following tale."[42] Read's Philadelphia preface reveals that the earlier New York edition had sparked some local debate and indicates that this revision rebukes these criticisms. Like Serranus before her, Read laments the questionable moral sense of these individuals as well as their penchant for offering partisan opinions on subjects they lack the capacity to understand. Read accuses this unscrupulous faction, openly parodied in the novel itself, of having "a total forgetfulness of the existence of adversity," leaving them unable to comprehend "a tale which speaks nothing but adverse vicissitudes" (iv). Principled readers will understand *Monima* as presenting "only a very plain picture of life," whereas "those who delight most in cabals of intrigue" will dismiss it as "insipid and uninteresting" (iv). Firing a shot at Democratic-Republicans, Read's Philadelphia preface mimics many of the tenets of Federalist unease about the erosion of social mores brought about by the influence of Jacobin thought.

Read's Philadelphia preface solidifies sentiments only implied in the earlier New York version by announcing her ambition to "teach" the "rising generations" the importance of "the sweet lessons of charity and heaven-borne benevolence."[43] Insisting that Monima represents a factual instance of a devoted child, animated by pure "filial love," Read announces her text as an antidote to the fractured state of operant structures of feeling. The novel itself plots out how these ruptures emerge from the destabilizing influence of radicalism in France and then Haiti. The plague of social leveling unhoused Monima's family from their rightful European and colonial estates, but the compounding horror stems from how they find Philadelphia to be equally alienating. Depicting the city as claustrophobically xenophobic, Read registers how these widely held prejudices emblematize an overall decline in the sympathetic attachments of the Republic's citizens.

Read's other extant novel, *Margaretta; or The Intricacies of the Heart* (1807), built upon *Monima's* concerns about the Democratic-Republican ascendency, indicating that the Revolution of 1800 remained a concern across her career. At the conclusion of this second novel, Read directly references the election by noting that the ill-educated farmer who raised Margaretta (her presumptive father for most of the narrative) had cast his vote "elated with a hope that the republican ticket would carry."[44] By having a bad patriarch (a man more invested in selling off his adopted daughter than in allowing her to find happiness) as a visible supporter of Jeffersonianism, Read accentuates how domestic surety was undercut by unfeeling heads of households (or states). While *Margaretta* directly considers the impact of the Haitian Revolution on American culture, it largely does so through a fantasy temporality which imagines a pre-Revolutionary Haiti as mirroring the social conditions of an increasingly Jeffersonian America.[45] It does this through an extended portrait of Margaretta's captivity on a plantation just outside Cape François where a French planter subjects her to a litany of threats of sexual violence. In some ways, the plot of Read's second novel mutes the idea of Haiti as an independent space, reflecting how conservatives sought to silence the impact of the Revolution. Or to put it another way, the outcome of the Revolution haunted the pages of this second novel through the linkages Read fabricated between the licentiousness of pre-Revolutionary Haiti and Jeffersonianism.

Published just a few years earlier, when many Euro-Americans still imagined the French would retake Haiti, *Monima*'s concerns about how foreign radical ideologies might infiltrate the United States were both more present and less open-ended than they were in Read's second novel. While *Margaretta* imagines a domestic household on the shores of the Susquehanna as a sufficient buffer against a corrupt political sphere, *Monima* remains much less sanguine about the Republic's futurity. It seems that by 1807, Read had abandoned any faith that the public sphere might resist social leveling; instead, she proposes a totalizing retreat to an elite domestic space—which could constellate a community of interdependent subjects around it—as the only anchor against further dissolution. *Margaretta* also features a withdrawal from international exchange and asserts that semi-seclusion provides the only buffer against the fluctuations which had previously plagued Margaretta. At the close of the novel, a fortunate discovery reveals Margaretta as the long-lost daughter of English aristocrats, although for much of text she understands herself to be the daughter of semi-literate subsistence farmers in Maryland. The end of the novel firmly reroots Margaretta through the revelation of her heritage, while simultaneously underscoring that if this had been clear at the novel's opening it would have prevented her from roaming around the Atlantic basin in search of security. In contrast, *Monima* revolves around an inverse set of national concerns and circum-Atlantic geographies: via its charting of how a European-born young woman finds herself forced into captivity by the citizens and the state apparatus of the American republic.

If *Margaretta* ends with some glimmer of hope for a restabilized American ethnoscape, one finally walled off from the disruptions of excessive mobility, *Monima* projects no such conviction in isolation. Indeed, in her earlier text, Read remains unsure that her fellow citizens can be saved from the predatory forces that have infected Philadelphia. As such, the earlier text more straightforwardly reveals Federalist fears about the intersections of Jeffersonianism and the damaging social upheavals of foreign revolutions. Read's *Margaretta* feels more like a proto-Cooper novel, such as his *Home as Found* (1838), which echoes Read's fantasy of a well-ordered household (built on the banks of the same river) providing protection against social leveling (albeit in Cooper's case its Jacksonian and not Jeffersonian democracy that he fears).[46] Still, rather than retroactively conjoin Read to the later insular nationalist writers that Fred Lewis Pattee called the Knickerbockers, it is crucial to understand how Read's work resonates with her own contemporaries like Charles Brockden Brown and Tabitha Tenney. If we think of *Monima* as a kind of capstone to the first iterations of the early American novel and its concerns about the unsettled state of the early Republic, then it becomes easier to comprehend how Read's first novel routes these lingering concerns about foreign contagions through a Federalist nostalgia. In short, the text longs for a moment before the disruptions of the French Revolution and the seismic effects of the Haitian Revolution had unsettled the cultural order of the United States.

Utter Strangers

Monima opens with the observation, voiced by Monima's father, that "this is a bleak morning" (13). As Monsieur Fontanbleu consumes their "last morsel," he questions his daughter about her prospects for procuring work (13). When Monima confesses that she has no viable leads, her father (who shows no readiness to work himself) begins to despair. Placing her "trust" in "providence," Monima reminds him that "the city is large" and that "heaven, no doubt" will somehow "supply us" with meals yet to come (13). On the brink of starvation, in a city in which they "are utter strangers," Monima takes on the dual roles of provider and comforter for her recently widowed parent (13). Prior to their arrival in Philadelphia, Monima's mother had "through, many almost unprecedented misfortunes" selflessly kept the family together and made "life desirable to Monsieur Fontanbleu" (14). By the conclusion of the second paragraph, Read establishes that Monima's three older siblings (two brothers and a sister) have all recently perished, reducing the once robust family into the destitute parent and child introduced in the opening line. Just "sixteen" years old, the "almost houseless" Monima wanders the streets of Philadelphia with "no resources," forced to hope for "mercy" from "merciless strangers" (14).

In part because of her youthful "inexperience," but also because she has little sense of the marketplace, Monima appears ill-suited to the situation she finds herself in (14). Hoping to find sympathy based on national affiliation, Monima returns to the house of Madame Sontine to ask for needlework to take home with her. Unbeknownst to Monima, as noted above, "Sontine" is actually the American-born wife of Sonnetton (a Frenchman who had once been her father's ward and would eagerly help his former mentor if he only knew where he was). Two plot devices forestall this reunion. The first obstacle to Sontine helping the Fontanbleus is that no one in Philadelphia appears capable of correctly pronouncing French words, so they remain comically alienated from one another because of the insular monolingualism of Americans. The second, much more insidious, hindrance becomes the primary means by which Read criticizes the distorted inversion of its former self that Philadelphia had become.

Upon his arrival in Philadelphia, Sonnetton made the misstep of marrying "an American" from "a low situation" (15). Although unaware of her husband's long-standing connection to Fontanbleu, Monima's natural grace sparks an insane jealously in Madame Sontine. Throughout all of their interactions, Madame Sontine maintains a "haughty" attitude to the supplicant while openly complaining in front of her about how "every French beggar" in Philadelphia arrives at her house because of her husband's natal origins (16). These xenophobic dismissals establish that Madame Sontine has only married because her husband affords her undeserved class mobility. Mistaking her husband's generous spirit for inconstancy, Madame Sontine does whatever she can to keep Monima's French heritage from him. When Monima passes Sonnetton on the stairwell after another crude dismissal, Madame Sontine rebukes her husband's concerns by denigrating Monima as "an Irish beggar girl" who shields her head with a handkerchief not because of the raging storm but because "rum pimples" cover her face (17). Sonnetton's initial unease over the "poor looking girl," quickly slips from his mind as a result of his wife's insinuation that she suffers the visible side-effects of alcoholism or venereal disease. As the episode closes, Madame Sontine takes pleasure in the success of her disambiguation, and Read figures the differences between the partners by noting that while Sonnetton felt that all of his countrymen held "a powerful claim on his pity," his wife was constitutionally "averse" to "charitable actions" (17).

This opening vignette, barely covering the first three pages, encapsulates much of the novel's plot by laying out the ambits of the four main characters. For much of the rest of the narrative, Fontanbleu maintains his dependent state, only reminding his daughter of their plight rather than acting to alter their condition. While he continues to suffer, he does so from the confines of secluded spaces as if his venerable age shields him from public shame. Madame Sontine continues to deride anyone approaching her for help while persistently taking pleasure in torturing Monima and deceiving her husband. Like a perverted puppet master, whose machinations include orchestrating the kidnapping of Monima and her father, Madame Sontine plots her various misdeeds from the confines of her drawing room. Sonnetton remains slightly naïve about the actual circumstances unfolding around him as he vacillates between abstractly wanting to help the dispossessed French citizens in Philadelphia and being distracted by other less important, but seemingly more immediate, business concerns. His wealth affords him certain privacies, and he bounces between his two estates and employs a proxy to carry out his limited charitable actions. Monima spends much of the rest of the text innocently (and almost heedlessly) scouring the city for work, even as she routinely fails to understand the sexual innuendo American men bark at her in public. Of all the prominent characters in the novel, Monima remains the only one without any tangible access to private space.

Forced to walk the streets as a beggar, Monima routinely suffers verbal abuse and unwanted sexual attention. Her inability to successfully read the precarious situations she inhabits, coupled with her estrangement from American law, results in her being sentenced (by the maneuvers of Madame Sontine) to the public workhouse.[47] Unable to persuade anyone of her innocence—as all the city officials remain convinced by her poverty that she stands in need of correction—Monima collapses after being beaten for not keeping up with the work thrust upon her. By depicting Monima as inhabiting the public sphere, Read condemns the supposedly charitable civic institutions that demand the city's most vulnerable residents forfeit their privacy. At the same time, she uses the workhouse episode to demonstrate that radical social leveling would result in the dire plummetting of elite figures. In this sense, Monima becomes a chaste, but presumptively, fallen woman who, despite never straying from her filial duty, suffers persecution from the very civil authorities designed to assist those like her.

The absence of a social safety net which might extend succor to friendless 16-year-old daughter caring for a superannuated patriarch highlights how *Monima* mirrors Charles Brockden Brown's more famous *Ormond* (1799) in several intriguing ways. While not set against the destabilizing force of a yellow fever epidemic like Brown's novel, *Monima* does feature the tribulations of a young woman struggling to sustain her father in the aftermath of economic ruin. Moreover, both of these fallen patriarchs have lost their fortunes as a result of nefarious former associates who have conned them. Yet Read's narrative treats the plight of Fontanbleu with a sympathetic tone utterly missing in Brown's treatment of Dudley. In essence, Read blames external radicalism for the Frenchman's downfall rather than presenting him as willfully blind to his own circumstances. Brown literalizes Dudley's lack of sight as the psychosomatic result of his failure to secure a future for his daughter, and his eventual utter dependence upon her reminds the reader that he fails to fully acknowledge his faults. Dudley retreats from reality in the face of deprivation; by contrast, Fontanbleu remains helpless but affectual toward his daughter and never loses concern for her futurity. Read remains more invested in the preservation of patriarchal authority (especially in creating the conditions of possibility for restoring the proper leaders to positions of influence) than Brown, and this divergence centrally animates each text.[48]

Even as both texts plot how radicalism has infected the United States, Brown charts this infiltration primarily through the figures of Ormond and his sister Marinette who openly proclaim their participation in foreign intrigues. While the bloody violence of the Jacobinism vividly stains the pages of *Ormond*, Read has no interest in sensationalizing such dramatic events. While it would be hard to call *Monima* a realist text, her narrative investments differ from Brown's most sharply in her attempt to navigate commonplace notions of politics and sociability without resorting to melodrama. Read's text avoids the paranoid offstage and barely articulated conspiracies that inflect Brown's plots, focusing her attention instead on the wider social impact of these emergent ideologies. This disparity arises not just from the generic differences between the sentimental and gothic modes, although these distinctions do account for some of the tonal dissimilarities. Brown evinces a fluid circum-Atlantic imagination, with his novels habitually charting the flow of information, bodies, and commerce across the Atlantic basin. Within this charting, the United States stands as a nodal point but not necessarily a unique one. Throughout her novel, Read's deep nostalgia for the exceptionalism of both a Federalist United States and the Ancien Régime of France (and the stabilizing effects they offered their respective nations) simmers across the plot and effectively privileges the idea of a properly ordered nation state as a social necessity.

Considered in a different way, Brown's *Ormond* never entertains the possibility of restoring the Dudley family to their lost position; to be sure, such a switchback would run counter to the questions he seeks to address. In contradistinction, *Monima* advances a strong sense that reinstatement remains viable. Indeed, her narrative aims at reestablishing the Fontanbleus, so much so that she even improbably reunites the two supposedly murdered sons (thought to have been killed by insurgents in Haiti) with their father and sister in Philadelphia. Read's ending features myriad acquittals and reversals to ensure that the Fontanbleus no longer occupy positions of precarity. Among the concluding events is the death of Madame Sontine, who wastes away after a final confrontation with her husband. During their final heated exchange, Madame Sontine admits to both her infidelities and her relentless persecution of Monima. Cleared of any doubts about her character, Monima marries the now widowed Sonnetton and, together, they forge a brighter future not just for themselves but for the others around them.

Monima concludes with a renewed faith that the fractured state of social reproduction has been healed to sufficiently allow for a return to traditional infrastructures of feeling. Sonnetton's marriage to an ill-born American woman has been childless in addition to deceptively loveless; as such, Madame Sontine does not leave any legacies behind to poison posterity. And, with Madame Sontine's removal, the novel culminates with the protagonists safely rehomed after weathering a variety of turbulent revolutionary storms. But Read still seems more interested in the eye of the storm than the happy outcome. Moreover, it is within this suffering middle section that the starkest differences between Read's and Brown's texts manifest. While both novels revolve around the idea of a secret witness, *Monima* imagines reparative justice through the mending of a superseded class-based order.

Of What Nation Are My Ghosts?

Chapter seven of *Monima* opens with an ostensibly comic exchange about the "unseasonable complaints" of starving ghosts (64). The episode unfolds at Sonnetton's manor on the outskirts of Philadelphia on the morning after a lavish dinner party. A sudden snow storm had forced the guests to remain overnight, and they reconvene for breakfast abuzz with hungover witticisms. One of these guests complains that he endured a fitful night as a pair of strange groaning voices that he describes as "airy boarders" kept waking him (19). Playfully mocking the generosity of his host, this sleepless guest declares: "It is strange [Monsieur Sonnetton] that a man of your liberality, should be cruel enough to starve your ghosts! for shure as I live, I have heard them complain of hunger" (64). Soon the conversation devolves into a playful mocking of the rambling sleeper and the host who refuses to nourish his haunting spirits. Amid all the jocularity, no one notices as a startled Madam Sontine clumsily spills "half a cup of coffee into the plate of poached eggs" (64). After suffering more feigned complaints about his hospitality, Sonnetton interjects with a question: "of what nation are my ghosts?" Sonnetton's "earnest" look of astonishment at hearing the response "French" quickly silences the "hilarity of his guests" (64). The scene ends with Sonnetton declaring that "after breakfast *I shall inspect my house*" (64).

Sonnetton's empathic pledge transmogrifies the "vivid hue" of his wife's complexion into "a livid paleness" (64). Her consternation over this impending inspection almost betrays her knowledge that the presumptively comic tale of ghosts arises from a tragic drama she had orchestrated. As part of her jealous campaign against Monima, Madame Sontine had ordered kidnappers to seize the Fontanbleus and lock them in the attic of the country house. Sonnetton's house is indeed haunted, not just by the starving prisoners but more crucially by his wife's "avaricious and narrow-hearted nature" (49). Lacking her husband's genuine benevolence, Madame Sontine delights in punishing precarity. This incongruence between the unhappily married pair mirrors another hard juxtaposition present in this scene. On the ground level of his country estate, Sonnetton has provided two lavish meals and overnight shelter for some of Philadelphia's elite citizens. Meanwhile, just above, his former savior (Fontanbleu) and eventual companionate wife (Monima)—upstanding moral figures made destitute by revolutionary upheaval—experience incarceration without food, water, or heat. If Sonnetton would actually inspect his house, he would find its priorities misaligned with his kinship commitments.

Weather shy elites shelter in place rather than hazard a snow squall while just a hair's breadth away the Fontanbleus shiver from exposure and malnourishment. The thin line between superabundance and deficiency fails to keep the groans of the latter from the bedrooms of the former. As the novel unfolds, Read stresses how this mismatch becomes a compounding problem as Sonnetton finds himself the duped master of a house divided not only against itself, but also against the very principles of social stability. Madame Sontine's misplaced jealously drives her to commit a series of crimes behind her husband's back but, nevertheless, financed by his estate.

While there are moments within the novel when Madame Sontine's illiteracy plays to a comic effect (such as when she writes a letter in broken phonetic English) her overall lack of sympathy and understanding betray her questionable moral character. Her failures to comprehend global politics, her inability to recognize the infectious complexities of the French and Haitian Revolutions, leads Madame Sontine to obliterate the differences between refugees from political turmoil and invasive radical insurgents. As such, she provides the perfect foil against which the Fontanbleus embody the importance of these distinctions. In effect, Madame Sontine exhibits the most flat-footed understanding of political turmoil, unable to differentiate between various groups of foreigners, and instead figuring them as an indecipherable amalgamation. While her husband and the Fontanbleus do have a shared history and a strong sentimental connection (which she knows little about), she reduces that tangible affinity to a simplistic sense that all French people gravitate toward one another only because of a shared Gallic heritage.

Despite the fact that her husband has migrated to Philadelphia because of instabilities in France and Haiti, she maintains a distorted sense that all immigrants are indistinguishable. Desperate to prevent any presumptive affinity from forming between her husband and Monima, Madame Sontine forcibly sequesters the distraught Fontanbleus until she can devise a way of reexporting them "to their French negro country" (15). As symbols of a dispossessed class of people associated with the Ancien Régime, the Fontanbleus represent displaced peoples urgently in need of American sympathy. Essentially, Read replicates the Federalist logic of proper social affinities by presenting the Fontanbleus as representative of the true American Republic. In other words, she defines the question of affiliation not via nationality, but instead through morality and social class. Cast adrift by the rise of radical ideologies, the Fontanbleus stand in for the self-imagined position of Federalists in the United States as much as for formerly elite French refugees. The same radicalism that twice unhomed the Fontanbleus, Read suggests, has infected the United States and could soon transform Federalist elites into friendless supplicants even in Philadelphia.

Madam Sontine lacks the sensitivity to nuance to read the realities before her, instead reducing migrants from revolutionary turmoil into commodities who can be shipped back to their port of origin. She fails to understand that her actions would expel a group of people who should be understood as the natural allies of a properly aligned American Republic, and that her co-conspirators represent the radical element (including the Frenchman responsible for stealing the Fontanbleus' ancestral estate) which should be expunged. Read takes pains to suggest that Madame Sontine's lack of morality stems from how unloving and irregular her early life was. Uneducated in the proper social codes, she thinks only of selfish accumulation. For Read, prominent social standing comes with a responsibility to order the public sphere and to provide for those in need of assistance. Imagining the Fontanbleus as criminals instead of victims reveals Madame Sontine's perverted sense of affinity. As such, the topsy-turvy ethnoscapes depicted in Read's novel vibrantly index Federalist concerns about the loss of coherence in the U.S. social order in the wake of the Revolution of 1800. Madame Sontine stands in for a kind of Democratic-Republican ascendancy in that she reflects a usurpation of traditional forms of belonging. Effectively, Madame Sontine works to eradicate traditional forms of communal care with petty jealousy and thus her actions destabilize the welfare of the entire community.

Madame Sontine actively creates a society at risk, as she torments the innocent and undercuts normative modes of behavior. In essence, she corrupts society by demanding that people attend to her misaligned desires. The query framed by Sonnetton about his own house—"Of what nation are my ghosts?"—synthesizes the questions that Read poses about the destabilized U.S. American social landscape by asking readers to consider the origins of the forces actually haunting Philadelphia. What does it mean for society if individuals who have the capacity to help others only scoff at the guiltless? What kind of privileged person bears witness to undeserved pain and refuses assistance? These are the very questions which animated Federalist critiques of Democratic-Republican praxis during the era of ungood feelings. Just as Serranus, and countless other pseudonymous Federalists writers, had railed against the uncaring practices of their opponents, so too does Read suggest that the Democratic-Republican ascendancy has transformed the United States into a heartless culture.

In posing these questions, Read's novel grapples with what such volatility means for the possibility of cross-cultural affiliation. By opening up the prospect that Sonnetton's house could be haunted by ghosts from several nations, the novel registers its investments in an expansive cartographic imagination. Read's surveying of this broader terrain enables her to speculate about how the ebb and flow of human traffic impacts the concretizing of an American ethnoscape.[49] While Madame Sontine blames the potentiality of foreign contagions as the source of her domestic uncertainties, Read labors to demonstrate that these problems actually stem from local conditions. What haunts Philadelphia are not the literal refugees from the French or Haitian Revolutions, but the lack of a legitimate domestic social hierarchy that could extend the proper sympathetic benevolence to these non-citizen sojourners. Within *Monima*, Philadelphia no longer serves as the city of brotherly love; rather it has become a space wherein those in need of assistance, as Henri petter notes, are "made to suffer by society for the very circumstance of their poverty."[50]

Petter's distillation of the Fontanbleus' plight echoes how they understand their own imprisonment. After being forced into an attic crawl space of the Sonnetton country house, Fontanbleu notes that "The North-Americans" are such "charitable creatures" that" they wish to spare us the pain of public starvation" (53). Interpreting the kidnapping as an American solution to poverty, Fontanbleu concludes that "we are confined here to die privately," rather than becoming a public spectacle (53). In his understanding of American charity as aimed at sweeping the misfortunate out of public view, Fontanbleu comprehends his plight not as the result of a singular vengeful individual but rather as emblematic of American character more broadly. Read doubles down on the implications of this critique by noting the number of servants (including her own brother) who carry out Madam Sontine's nefarious plot. By drawing attention to how easily the servants comply with her vile orders, to keep Monima and her father "for four successive weeks" in a state of perpetual "cold, hunger, and apprehension," Read stresses the cancer of domestic mismanagement (62). As Madam Sontine "lived gaily," with days "crowded with company" and "generally devoted to card-playing or dancing" amid the lower floors of the house, the Fontanbleus wither away (62). This tension between upstairs and downstairs exhibits how Madame Sontine's ill-gotten class mobility underwrites her capacity to inflict pain.

If we extend the logic of Fontanbleu's vision of American charity to Sonnetton's query about the national origins of the ghosts haunting his house, Read's multivalent use of "domestic scene" allows her interrogation of the current state of American stability to come into clearer focus. What now haunts Fontanbleu and Sonnetton does not originate in either Haiti or France, but instead springs from a domestically born threat. Given how Madame Sontine stands in for the inversions wrought by the Democratic-Republican evisceration of traditional structures of feeling, the entrance of the specter of foreign contagions suggested by Read functions as misdirection. Fearful of their being discovered by her husband, Madame Sontine orders the Fontanbleus removed to a new secret garret, and covers her tracks by inventing a story about a chambermaid with a secret lover whose tryst had produced the ghostly sounds. On the cusp of finding out the truth, news arrives that some of Sonnetton's valuable cargo has struck ice in the Delaware River. The fact that urgent commercial business distracts Sonnetton from attending to his own precarious domestic affairs, while understandable, accentuates the tensions between public and private responsibilities. Given how little Sonnetton would personally contribute to rescuing his cargo, the ease with which he turns away from the domestic sphere suggests his culpability in his wife's transformation of what should be public assistance into privatized torment. At the very least, it hints at the damage caused by the inattention of individuals who should know better.

To emphasize how the displacement of Federalist authority has damaged the Republic, Read weaves in a veiled reference to Jefferson just as Monima and her father return to Philadelphia after their attic imprisonment. A servant who feared that actual ghosts were in the house created a window for escape, and after finding their way out of the mansion, they walk the several miles (barefoot in the snow) back to Philadelphia. Seeking to catch their breath on the steps of one of the city's mansions, Monima and her father soon become a spectacle to the wealthy inhabitants of the neighborhood. In particular, Read fashions a vignette about one man, who "occupied the largest house in the neighborhood," and was renowned for extravagance (including the fact that "besides the incumbrance of his wife, kept a mistress at a princely expense"), who represents the consequences of extreme wealth being held by immoral people (82). This corrupt elite figure stares at the starving Fontanbleus and decries how "intemperance has ruined numberless families" (82). In the middle of this brief portrait of an unfeeling man, Read deploys the strange phrasing "whose annual income was little interior to the President's" to describe his opulent wealth (82). Why draw a connection between this man, whose "genteel appearance" belies his "harshly" judgmental behavior, and the president (83)? And why preface that allusion by noting that this wealthy man possesses openly questionable sexual morals since it is public knowledge that he keeps a mistress?

The unnamed man without feeling epitomizes corrupted patriarchs more generally, and his churlish behavior reveals a great deal. His only suggestion of aid takes the form of his begrudging offer to pay for someone to carry Monsieur Fontanbleu to the "Bettering-house," a reference to Philadelphia's Blockley Almshouse where the city's indigent were often exiled alongside orphans and the mentally ill (82). Faced with a social problem, the unfeeling man judgmentally offers only a resigned "shrug" (82). Convincing himself of the Fontanbleus' responsibility for their own poverty, this man demands them be removed from his neighborhood. The brief aside that references the president introduces this man's callous lack of sympathy, allowing Read a surreptitious but pointed critique of Democratic-Republican leaders. Despite having the means to allow for an extravagant lifestyle, this man remains unmoved by the plight of those in need. When a nearby "poor woman" observes that Fontanbleu "would die of cold before he could reach half way" to the almshouse, the confronted man simply contemptuously walks away (82). His final parting shot takes the form of remarking to Monima that she should prevent her father from getting "drunk" and that she should be "more industrious herself and not let the black rags she wore, run away with her!" (83).

Luckily the Fontanbleus do then receive kindness from a working class family, who take them in despite the marked disdain of a "genteel looking man" (83). This couple, Peter and Deb, offer Monsieur Fontanbleu a chance to recover; moreover, they agree to care for him as Monima ventures toward "their former abode" to speak with their landlord after their enforced month-long absence (83 and 84). Monima quickly discovers that the landlord has sold their meager possessions since he assumed they had absconded over past due rent. Stressing that "Monima, was not worth a single cent," Read compounds the dire circumstances of the Fontanbleus (84). While the impoverished Peter and Deb provide assistance as best they can, the elite denizens of the city assume, based on their surface appearance, that the Fontanbleus must be morally insolvent. This pointed disdain for people in need—from the very class of people that Read connects to Jefferson—affirms the moral corruption of Philadelphia's new-found elite.

As the Fontanbleus reach their lowest point, Read breaks the temporality of the novel's plot to detail the initial difficulties that ignited their migration across the Atlantic by describing events that unfolded "a year previous to the birth of Monima" (95). Resetting the stage of the text to pre-Revolutionary France (and then to pre-Revolutionary Haiti), Read registers what initially caused Fontanbleu so much misery. Despite the shifts in geographical settings, the force of this inserted backstory resonates with what has already occurred in Philadelphia. Moreover it manifests these connections by asserting that the radical forces which originated in France and then migrated to the Caribbean had decidedly infected American enthnoscapes. This prehistory details how a fraudulent usurper managed to unhome the Fontanbleus by disassociating them from the usual customary networks of connection. In effect, Read provides a precursor to Madame Sontine in the figure of Pierre de Noix, a former intimate of Monima's elder brother Ferdinand. Read's mirroring of Madame Sontine and de Noix reaches its climax in the later stages of the novel as the two become lovers and nefariously plot to murder the Fontanbleus and steal Sonnetton's wealth. Indeed, across the novels' last third these two villains become virtually indistinguishable. However, before this blurring occurs, Read exhibits how de Noix's jealousy has dislodged the Fontanbleus from their traditional estate and fractured the family to its core.

Both Ferdinand and de Noix had found themselves attracted to the same woman, Julia Frenton, who quickly confessed her attraction to Ferdinand. Enraged that he has been passed over, the covetous de Noix concocts a scheme to kidnap Julia and feign her murder. Casting suspicion on Ferdinand, de Noix arranges for his arrest and abusive interrogation. De Noix further plays a part in accusing Monsieur Fontanbleu of a crime he did not commit so that he too suffers partisan persecution. After Julia escapes de Noix's clutches, she manages to testify on behalf of Ferdinand, leading to his exoneration. In an effort to extract some justice for all that his family has suffered, Ferdinand demands a duel with de Noix. However, before the former can get off a shot, de Noix fatally wounds Ferdinand who dies in Julia's comforting arms. After the death of his son, Fontanbleu continues to languish in prison after a corrupt judicial system sentences him to death for a murder he had not committed. The sudden arrival and confession of the real murderer barely saves Fontanbleu from the gallows. Fearing how thoroughly French society has become corrupted by a radical break from what the text presents as the foundational sense of communal belonging, Fontanbleu then relocates to the Caribbean. In effect, the unjust circumstances that lead to the death of his son (and his own unwarranted imprisonment) serve as "a gnawing canker to his heart" and drive Fontanbleu to search for a better life elsewhere (208).

During his passage to St. Domingo, Fontanbleu meets a 16-year-old Sonnetton who is similarly undertaking the crossing because he too has been forced from his ancestral home. Orphaned at a young age, Sonnetton has had his birthright stolen by "fraudulent agents, and grasping guardians" (211). All of Sonnetton's "relations" were so envious of his "parent's prosperity," that soon after the latter's death they used a variety of illicit maneuverings to defraud Sonnetton of his inheritance (211). Robbed of his patrimony, Sonnetton has effectively become "an outcast, and little short of a beggar" (211). Embittered by what has happened to him, Sonnetton has come to believe that "the pursuits of man, are bounded by self gratification" and that "the love of wealth, is his first simulative" (210). Moved by Sonnetton's description of his suffering from the "duplicity of man," Fontanbleu decides to help the young man, thus serving as a model patriarch within Read's taxonomy.

Upon their arrival in St. Domingo, Fontanbleu immediately writes letters on Sonnetton's behalf while continuing to shelter the young man on his plantation. Over the course of two years, Fontanbleu's "trusty agents" restore Sonnetton's fortune, and the now wealthy young man returns to Europe for a "three year" tour of the continent to finish off his education (212). During this period of calm, the Fontanbleus settle relatively happily into their new life on a sugar plantation just outside of Cape François; but the increasing chaos of the French Revolution ruptures communication between Sonnetton and his benefactor. Fearing that a rise of radicalism will once again jeopardize his fortune, Sonnetton sets sail for North America. Shortly after his arrival, "with the rashness of a Frenchman," he soon falls in love with Ursala Mermitton whose "artful" masquerade disguises her "illiterate and vulgar" nature (213). Meanwhile, despite his self-described "humane treatment" of his enslaved laborers—which he hoped would "secure him from the fate that threatened his neighbors"—the struggle for liberation arrives at Fontanbleu's plantation (214). Read describes the tumult of the Haitian Revolution as equally dangerous to both "the good and bad" French planters, and after a clandestine raid of his estate (in which he presumes that his last two sons have perished) Fontanbleu and the rest of his family flee the island (214).

Rescued by a passing American vessel, the Fontanbleus arrive in Portsmouth where they spend the next five years in modest circumstances. Eventually, Fontanbleu decides to move his family to Philadelphia in the hopes of creating a partnership with a former associate to establish a "commercial line with" their remaining "little stock" (216). After a brief diversion to Baltimore, the family arrives in Philadelphia where "a contagious sickness" soon claims the lives of Fontanbleu's wife and two eldest daughters, leaving him and Monima as the only remaining members of the family. Grief stricken and almost penniless, Fontanbleu passes de Noix on the streets of Philadelphia and falls into an even deeper depression. This chance meeting returns the plot to the opening time frame of the novel, with Monima venturing out to find work and being directed to the house of Madam Sontine.

A return to the novel's opening temporal setting brings the novel full circle, with Read weaving together multiple versions of the same critique to accentuate how insidious behaviors have framed the experiences of both Sonnetton and Fontanbleu regardless of their geographical location. While the text's acknowledgment of the Haitian Revolution remains submerged, Read firmly links its origins to the same corruptions she registers as afflicting both France and the United States. In essence, she blames the outbreak of the Revolution, and the ensuing violence which destabilizes the hemisphere, on the unhinged appetite of avaricious capitalists. Read very carefully argues that capitalism does not inherently corrupt the social order, but rather this happens when immoral individuals ascend to positions of authority and then act to distort the socially regulating possibilities of commercial humanism. By implication, Read argues that the prevalence of a rampant extractive capitalism has engendered a counterreaction, one which was so swift that the formerly enslaved people could not properly distinguish between benevolent plantation owners (as if such an absurdity was possible) and corrupt ones.

While she dramatically oversimplifies the reasons formerly enslaved people embarked on the struggle to claim their own freedom, Read doubles down on asserting that a leadership crisis fractured the circum-Atlantic world. She locates this sentiment in Madame Sontine's designation of Monima as someone from a "French Negro country," a conjunction which, for Read, absurdly conflates Frenchness and Blackness. Again and again in the text, the inversion of social hierarchies is seen as a problem, creating conditions whereby vindictive usurpers have the possibility to damage innocent people. Read's suggestion is that it was uncompassionate planters who sparked the revolution in Haiti, intimating that if a different order (practicing "humane treatment," as had Fontanbleu) had governed the island then perhaps the costly violence which ensued might have been avoided (214). While Read's position might seem misplaced, it reflects one strain of Federalist thinking about the crisis of the Haitian Revolution (a state of emergency they feared would migrate to the United States), which blamed the corrupt management of the plantocracy and not enslavement itself for creating the conditions that would make revolution a possibility. In effect, Read presents the Haitian Revolution as a counterformation not to the violences of human trafficking and what Elizabeth Maddock Dillon calls "bare labor," but to senseless mismanagement.[51] Radical social leveling was a byproduct of improper leadership, and it was through this causal relationship that Federalists like Read understood events in Haiti as impacting the United States. The turn away from the benign commercial humanism favored by Federalists (marked by paternalistic management) toward unregulated self-gratification would in their minds produce an inevitable back-lash. Driven by a desire for self-gratification, this emergent class of bad leaders across the circum-Atlantic world had eroded social stability and routinely flouted the rule of law. In short, they cared as little about kinship as they did about politi-cal and social stability.

The end of the novel features Monima's near-rape and attempted murder. On top of these physical threats, Read overlays the problem of fraudulent witnessing (as de Noix bribes someone "to take a false oath" against her) as the novel repro-duces one last time the various distortions of the social order it has been charting (459). Yet when Monima and her father finally reunite with Sonnetton, "terror, poverty, and want receded in swiftest motion from" them (460). Shortly after-wards, one of Monima's missing brothers arrives from St. Domingo to disprove the erroneous report about his death. Here the text implies that some order had been returned to St. Domingo (perhaps mirroring an early-nineteenth-century Federalist hope for the renewal of French authority in light of Napoleon's 1803 invasion plans) as the newly arrived brother tells his father that "his former possessions on the Island" had been restored and "that Pierre, his brother, lived in St. Domingo, and was married to a very amiable woman" (463). Glossing over the idea that the Haitian Revolution could enact structural change, the novel intimates that it might yet be possible to undo radical notions of equality.

In turn, Monima (now happily married to Sonnetton) becomes the charitable presence she never found in Philadelphia. Madame Sonnetton serves as the antithesis of Madame Sontine, as Monima uses her husband's fortune to aid the poor and the dispossessed. She "became the soother of the afflicted, the mother of the orphan, the supporter of the oppressed, and the indulgent friend of the sufferer of sensibility" (464). Cognizant of her own suffering from "distressful poverty," she remains motivated by a "double compassion for the miseries of her fellow creatures" (464). With her husband's blessing, she transforms herself into a beacon of hope. In the absence of a return to a caring civil government, Read posits that a properly aligned wealthy household could provide a shield against the ravages of a Democratic-Republican rise to power.

Nostalgic Formations

Monima initially appeared in the late summer of 1801 as installments in *The Ladies' Monitor*, a New York-based journal to which Read frequently contributed. Several of these sections appeared alongside Read's attempt to remodel Mary Wollstonecraft's *A Vindication of the Rights of Woman: with Strictures on Political and Moral Subjects* (1792) for early-nineteenth-century Americans. Only two extracts of Read's "A Second Vindication of the Rights of Women" survive, printed in the August 22nd and September 5th editions of the *Monitor*. Reading the serialized portions of each project together (since they may have been written during the same period provides a way of thinking about how the proto-feminist ambitions of each text inform the other. As Joseph Fichtelberg has argued, while "Read professes to seek radical solutions"—just as "her model" Wollstonecraft had done previously—"A Second Vindication" remains notable for how it "swerve[s]" away from revolutionary thought.[52] In her reformation of Wollstonecraft for an American bourgeois audience, Read labored to tame the liberatory ambitions of the original. In this regard, Read's centrist approach to the question of women's rights mirrors the socially conservative ideologies suffusing *Monima*.

One example of this intertextuality can be found in what Fichtelberg has rightly called Read's attachment to "the paternal bond" as an "irreducible truth."[53] Obviously, as Fichtelberg notes, a devotion to patriarchal authority as the core element of cultural formation could not have been further from Wollstonecraft's philosophy. For Fichtelberg, Read's usage of sentimental discourses accounts for this difference, an attachment directly at odds with Wollstonecraft's rejection of mawkish distractions. Read's conceptualization of traditional forms of social hierarchy, both in *Monima* and "A Second Vindication," as the defining factor for cultural cohesion rejects Wollstonecraft's resounding anger with misogynistic strictures. But, perhaps more crucially, Read's reconfiguration of Wollstonecraft transmogrifies a radical praxis into a nostalgic formation aimed at preserving Federalist ideologies. Both of Read's texts, essentially, stress the importance of the bonds between fathers and daughters as providing the crucible for the proper education of women. Thus, Read's work in two distinct genres exhibits the primacy of the heteropatriarchy in her conception of moral development.

At its core, Read's "A Second Vindication" explores the relationship between "education," the "conduct of men," and the question of "courtship."[54] As such, Read's attachment to masculine authority as "natural" completely reverses how Wollstonecraft champions "the exercise of reason" as the fount from which "knowledge and virtue will flow."[55] Just as she had in *Monima*, Read arrays sentimental motifs in "A Second Vindication" to position the family as the only viable bulwark against "corroding" social practices.[56] According to Read, women's rights had not been suppressed by male domination but rather by society's abandonment of the examples of the natural world. It is the "misapplication of the properties of nature" that "stamps the man a villain" and turns him into "a corrupter of young women."[57] Read's argument in "A Second Vindication" parallels her intentions in *Monima* in that the novel similarly explores the moral implications of men attempting to coerce young women into premarital relationships. Read further cements these narrative connections by implying that vulnerable white women represent the imperiled American nation.

For all of Fichtelberg's attention to Read's nascent feminism, he does not fully comprehend how her vindication prefigures the limitations of second wave feminism. Fichetelberg, in short, undervalues the centrality of whiteness in Read's conception of women's rights. This attachment vividly surfaces in her use of incest as a recursive touchstone in the extant excerpts of her "A Second Vindication." In recounting a litany of the ways in which even "the young, the innocent, and the artless of the female sex," through the violent prevalence of men who use "an insinuating address," have "been reduced to the most degraded states of life," Read notes that even some "fathers have been guilty of it themselves toward some youthfully innocent daughters."[58] Neither the "institutions" of marriage or family have curtailed "the wicked oppression" nor the "diabolic injustice" of men who pursue their own gratification over and against normative social prohibitions.[59] By stressing that parents, and especially fathers, have a moral duty to secure their daughters' "welfare" by teaching them "to guard against flattery," Read defines her concerns as relying upon mappable connections.[60] To put it another way, Read's definition actively disavows the systemic problem of what Hortense Spillers has called "poppa's maybe."[61] This elision is notable given that Read's catalog of social problems—fractured families, extramarital sex, sexual violence and coercion, and (most vividly) incest—were (as she was aware) the very structuring violences against women endemic to enslavement.[62] Her focus on publicly recognizable genealogies predetermines whose hereditary connections matter and need to be accounted for. Or, again, by suggesting that publicly recognized patriarchal gene-alogies form the basis for natural kinship, Read disavows her own location in a culture in which maternal connection (and only maternal connection) defined the legal status of anyone with even an ounce of diasporic African blood and simultaneously defined who could and who would not be understood as a victim of sexual violence.[63]

As Brian Connolly persuasively argues, "to put it simply, in the discourse of slavery, incest was aligned with Blackness, and the incest prohibition with white-ness."[64] The liberal subject imagined by Read as occupying the natural center of social and political life in the early Republic was for her predicated on an overt acknowledgment of racialized biological kinship structures. Anyone incapable of establishing those connections, or any attempt to unsettle their surety, was for Read either a perpetrator or a victim of a devious force. By her embrace of "insin-uate" as the key term by which to label anti-social behavior, Read stresses the subtle and artful penetration of virtue denotatively corralled in the word. Thus the secret child, the byproduct of clandestine violence, always prohibitively stands outside the normative bonds of kinship. Saidiya Hartman has deployed the term the "ghost in the machine of kinship" to describe the social alienations of enslave-ment, the delusory ways in which the fracturing of familial relations shaped both the lives of the enslaved and the wider cultural formations in which they were forced to labor.[65] Hartman's figuration, as Judith Bulter suggests in building upon this observation, underscores the impossibility of separating "questions of kin-ship from property relations (and conceiving of persons as property)."[66] Following the thrust of Butler's assertion, we might think of Read's novel as circling around the relationship of kinship and property to sound out the contours of their inter-connectivity. This faith in the relationship between heredity and economics haunts Read's formation of the family unit within both *Monima* and "A Second Vindication," as each text measures the risks entailed by circulating female bod-ies. In so doing, Read emphasizes that the question of freedom cannot be disasso-ciated from property and kinship.

No longer in possession of the real estate which instantiated their status, the Fontanbleus attempt to hold fast to their kinship without any of its principal props. In this sense, Monsieur Fontanbleu echoes the delusory position that Serranus bemoaned was the fate of so many Federalist men exiled from power by McKean's partisanship. Yet, as Read's novel intimates, all hope was not lost because Monima still maintained the protection of her whiteness, which provided a defense against the actions of predatory men. So the darkest fears animating Serranus's concerns, that Federalist families would be fractured, surfaces in the novel only to be forestalled by what Read thinks of as the natural shield of pub-licly recognized kinship. For all the abuse that Monima suffers, her close proxim-ity to her father prevents her from actually becoming a public commodity. While Monima may be nearly figured as "expendable and defeated," to use another of Hartman's terms to describe the conditions of enslaved people, her white kinship underwrites her innocence and allows her to avoid actually becoming either of those things.[67] In the context of real expendability, Monima can stand proximate to this horror without succumbing. People may imagine her as nearly property, but they cannot actually strip her of the protections of whiteness. Part of the miraculous ending of the text emerges out of its two-pronged notion of resto-ration: first, the long-thought-dead sons' return; and, second, Fontanbleu's recov-ery of his real estate. In short, Read coterminously reinstates kinship and property, as if to evince how, for her, they are co-constitutive.

Read advances the idea that white fathers can insure their white daughters' access to the public realm without divorcing themselves from the protections afforded them by the private sphere. As Read understands it, fathers have a duty to teach their daughters how to cross (and recross) the boundaries between the public and private realms. Yet such a capacity for mobility remains predicated on the surety of an enduring private domestic space grounded (for Read) in a tradi-tionally imagined family unit. To put it another way, if Haiti haunts the plot of *Monima*, it does so in part through the specter of a racialized vision of incest. As Elizabeth Maddock Dillion has argued, incest registers the "concern with the cir-culation of persons and relationships in the shifting terrain of the global econ-omy" across the long eighteenth century.[68] In many ways, *Monima* reflects this concern, particularly when the starving Monima and her father are imprisoned above the elite party guests who mock their hunger pangs as ghostly whispers. In the serialized publication of the novel, these very chapters precede the first installment of Read's "A Second Vindication" in which she details the social consequences of inappropriate relationships between fathers and daughters."[69] This textual abutment imprints a fixation on the father as the chief moral pedagogue and fears about incestuous desire as literally bordering the plot of the novel itself.

While Monsieur Fontanbleu's dire economic circumstances force him to rely on Monima's public circulation, she never understands herself as a commodity. Even when Monima and her father are closely confined prisoners, the specter of incest never arises. Monima always remains protected by the presence of her white father (enfeebled as he is) since he embodies her definable connections. When Madame Sontine seeks to dismiss Monima as belonging to "her French Negro country," she attempts to override these very protections by connecting her to the unstable genealogies of planter societies and enslavement more generally. It is, in effect, an attempt by Madame Sontine to link Monima to what Russ Castronovo has argued are the ways in which enslaved children "issued forth not from" namable parents "but from a matrix of nonhistory, from a textual-sexual space that signified emptiness and absence, illegitimacy and silence."[70] Monima's white legibility safeguards her from actually being abused as a literal "French Negro." Read teases out the distinctions between these two categories by making Monima adjacent to violent exploitation and erasure but stops short of forcing her into an irreversible disavowal.

The final pages of *Monima* address the crisis of downward mobility for white citizens as Monima fashions herself a source of comfort for people with discernable histories. She feels compelled to help individuals who have emerged out of history (to lean on Castronovo's phrasing) to prevent them from sliding into an unnamable position. She aims, in effect, to make whole again people downtrodden by a society they are already a part of, but she betrays no intention to reimagine the social sphere. In short, Monima acts to conserve a fractured order from suffering further fissure and, if possible, to restore it to its former glory. In laying out the terms of white women's rights and giving them form in Monima's narrative journey, Read accentuates how publically recognized genealogical connections can forestall ruination. These anchoring privileges might need support in the face of radical ideologies, but they could be maintained provided something like a Federalist authority labored to keep them in place. As far as Read seems concerned, the best way to resist the displacements that Serranus railed against was through the surety of family connections since civic authorities did not seem invested in stabilizing the public sphere.

In both "A Second Vindication" and *Monima*, Read affirms the ability of fathers to educate their "natural" daughters and to guard them from insinuation. Her reliance on patriarchal connection foregrounds how the rights of women are really another way of shoring up the position of white citizens in the early Republic. Even a beggar girl can be restored to the upper class if her kinship connections remain legible during a period of crisis. Madame Sontine represents the dangers of Democratic-Republican social leveling because she seeks to obliterate the protections of whiteness by abandoning normative moral codes. As she moves to eradicate Monima, in effect to paint her Black, Madame Sontine attempts what for Read would represent an unnatural reclassification. The distorted moral sense of Madam Sontine means that she can imagine a way for a white woman to be transformed into a native of a "French Negro country" without any risk to the stability of the American social order. From a Federalist perspective, such a perversion of traditional praxis was deeply disconcerting, reflecting a hyperextended version of Democratic-Republican social leveling.

In positioning Madame Sontine as unredeemable, Read accentuates how she lacks the ability to comprehend the importance of the normative social protections afforded by class and genealogical connections. In this regard, Read dramatizes the concerns that pundits like Burleigh and Serranus had about the costs of Jeffersonianism; in effect, she imagines Fontanbleu's exile as a kind of test case of the consequences of Jacobinism. As the reversals in normative social behaviors that marked late-eighteenth-century France and Haiti migrated to the United States, what was at stake was a blurring of the boundaries between Black and white, and between the surety of tradition and the chaos of an unnatural order. The novel also echoes Serranus's suggestion that France might provide the solution as well as the problem to the uncertainties plaguing the United States. After all, the French-born Monima not only resists subjection, but she moves afterwards (with her husband's hereditary French wealth) to assist other white citizens faced with analogous predicaments. In a correspondingly haunting way, Read implies that there are two inheritances from Haiti that might also animate the present: that of the legacies of supposedly good managers and rapacious ones. Echoing the racist sentiments of texts like "The Story of Makandal," and its figuration of rebellion as sparked by an unjust overseer rather than as resistance to the structuring exploitation of the plantocracy, Read posits that what ignited racialized revolution were the transgressions of bad leaders. The Fontanbleu sons survive the revolution presumably because they represent better leadership and were therefore spared from retribution during the struggle for self-emancipation. Their return serves as a clarion call about the importance of proper management styles: bad leaders, just like bad patriarchs, engender chaos. Like Serranus and countless other Federalist writers, Read sought to indemnify the Republic's future by refurbishing the influence of properly feeling white fathers and the families that they acknowledged.

3

"Free of Every Thing which Can Affect Its Purity"

Maple Sugar, Caribbean Cane, and the Futures Past of Laborless American Development

In late February of 1791, a "respectable number of Citizens," gathered in the "Senate-Chamber, in the City of New York, for the purpose of instituting a Society for the promotion of Agriculture and Manufactures."[1] Among the distinguished New Yorkers in attendance was Robert R. Livingston, a former member of the "Committee of Five" responsible for drafting the Declaration of Independence. During his appointment as chancellor of New York, Livingston had administered the oath of office to President-Elect George Washington at Federal Hall in Manhattan in 1789. Another eminent attendee of the meeting was Ezra L'Hommedieu, a prominent Long Island landowner and active civilian leader during the Revolution. Like Livingston, L'Hommedieu had served as one of New York's delegates to the Continental Congress and had just narrowly missed being chosen as one of the state's inaugural U.S. senators. At the time of the meeting, Livingston and L'Hommedieu may well have been the two most influential men in New York State not currently holding elected office.

Either by prearrangement or by quickly realized consensus, L'Hommedieu was appointed to chair the meeting. Shortly after the deliberations began, Livingston was tasked, along with Simeon De Witt and Samuel L. Mitchell, to form a sub-committee to draft a governance document for the society.[2] With such eminent citizens involved in its foundation, it is hardly surprising that the Society's initial efforts received a great deal of local attention. Undeniably, the very masthead of the Society signaled that the issues they sought to address were of the highest order of public interest.[3] In part, the Society aimed to cultivate a set of recognizable and sustainable industries within the state in an effort to guide its future economic growth. Like many leading citizens of the early Republic, the members of the Society believed that New York would play a central role in shaping the future prospects of the United States. Indeed, this sentiment about New York's importance suffuses George Washington's famous christening of it as "the empire state" in an open letter thanking the city for honoring him for his wartime service.[4] Yet, if New York was seen as a harbinger of new forms of accumulation, it was in part framed as such because—even as late as 1791—the economic prospects of the

The Haitian Revolution in the Early Republic of Letters: Incipient Fevers. Duncan Faherty, Oxford University Press.
© Duncan Faherty 2023. DOI: 10.1093/oso/9780192889157.003.0004

state still remained untapped potentialities.[5] Through the publication of open letters, committee proceedings (like that of the Society for the Promotion of Agriculture and Manufactures), ideologically driven newspaper articles, and various other forms of reportage, elite New Yorkers flooded the print public sphere with a steady stream of their concerns about the region's future course. Again and again, these wealthy New Yorkers urged the state government to invest significant public funds in infrastructural improvements and to privilege certain forms of agrarian development in order to give a particular shape to the state's growth.

Unlike most of its neighboring colonies, large sections of the non-coastal areas of New York were essentially untransformed by Euro-American settler colonialism as late as the last decade of the eighteenth century.[6] Across New York's colonial history, settlements had hugged the shores of the Hudson River, the Long Island Sound, or the Atlantic. While these waterways were crucial commercial arteries for England's North American colonial holdings (as they had been for the Dutch before them), much of the state remained unsullied by Anglo-American terraforming incursions. Prior to the Revolution, much of the state's acreage was controlled by a handful of families who maintained dominion over their lands even as they left them relatively untransformed.[7] These landholding families sustained influence by refusing to portion off their estates to tenant farmers, and thus avoided subdividing their colonial allocations. As a result of these longstanding practices, the deforestation that marked settlements from Massachusetts to the Carolinas had rarely occurred within the interior portions of the New York colony.

Indeed, so much of colonial New York remained "wilderness," that the British planned to compensate officers for their wartime service with large land grants located in this region. The most famous example of this plan resulted in the formation of Cooperstown, built (by William Cooper) on a land grant which had been deeded to the steadfast loyalist, and illegitimate son of Ben Franklin, William Franklin.[8] Still, even as interior villages, like Cooperstown had sprung up, New York had yet to find its place as an agricultural powerhouse in the fledgling early American economy. Part of the ambition of the Society was to counteract this lagging development. Among their first actions was to circulate an open letter that contained a series of queries aimed at collating current trends and standards.[9] The queries marked the Society's motivation, in short, to ignite "the progress of Agriculture, Arts, and Manufactures in this state."[10] On the one hand, the open letter framed by this Agricultural Society mirrored efforts by similar civic-minded groups in other states and regions.[11] Yet, what made New York unique was the relatively embryonic stage of its economy. Colonial staples like tobacco and cotton did not thrive in the northeastern climate, so the kinds of harvesting infrastructures that had developed in more temperate states had never taken root. As a result, the Society aimed to shift the external perception of the state's commodities by establishing New York as a net exporter of agricultural goods in the early American marketplace. Given the ways in which eighteenth-century commodities were often advertised by point of origin—from Virginian tobacco to West Indian sugar, to Madeira wine—identifying a signature crop and creating a brand identity for New York's products was of paramount concern to the Society's officers. Since homesteaders were never likely to harvest enough of a surplus to engage in disparate trade networks, they essentially had little to gain from such a public relations campaign. But for large-scale landowners' intent on maximizing their profit margins, the promotion of a signature staple product or crop would help them nurture a regionally based plantation-like system in one of the least settled areas in the post-revolutionary United States.

This chapter explores how outsized delusions about maple sugaring emerged as one of the earliest fantasies about how to transform the uncultivated "wilds" of New York into a vast sea of laborless profit. It does so by first charting how nascent efforts to promote maple sugaring as the key to the state's growth widely circulated in the region's print public sphere. In ranging across this material, the chapter charts how these maple sugar promotional materials measured the lack of labor required to produce maple sugar against the costs of a dependence on foreign Caribbean cane. In the eyes of its proponents, maple sugar promised the incredible wealth of cane sugar production without either the costs of enslaved laborers or the potential disruptions of trade brought about by the resistance of enslaved people. Arguments about the bounty of maple sap, which emerged in the print public sphere in direct response to the Society's call for information and continued to circulate in a variety of forms in periodical culture for several years, openly advocated for New York maple sugar to replace West Indian cane for the American market. Less concerned with abolition and more invested in the production of wealth for New York landowners, these maple sugar advocates nonetheless routinely stressed how maple sugar would liberate the United States from further imbrications in Black Atlantic trade and the potential disastrous consequences of racialized revolution. This linkage of maple sugar and white freedom continued to linger in the cultural imagination well after the failure of the industry to take root in the state, and the second half of the chapter explores how this connection formed an important substratum of the most popular gothic novel of the nineteenth century, Isaac Mitchell's *The Asylum* (1804/11). In so doing, the chapter registers how Mitchell resurrected a by then defunct maple sugar fantasy to posit causal links between sugar harvesting, white settler freedom, and economic stability in the aftermath of Haitian liberation. In short, this chapter aims to register the ways in which the specter of unrest in Haiti gave birth to dreams about New York's capacity to somehow establish a plantation-like agricultural economy without the need for importing diasporic Africans into the unsettled frontiers of the region. How, in other words, might New York become an engine of New World accumulation and somehow still remain a largely post-revolutionary white settler society? Mitchell's novel blurs the temporalities of the

Age of Revolutions in his efforts to consider how post-revolutionary white settlers might establish themselves as independent amid the fluctuations of circum-Atlantic trade fractured by Caribbean unrest. Finally, the chapter turns to Kara Walker's contemporary theorization of the connections between New World expansion, enslavement, and a hunger for sugar that she staged on the shores of Manhattan as a means of underscoring New York's centrality in the cane sugar trade.

Refining on Common Sense

Among the first responses to the Society's open letter was one concerning the "manufacture of Maple Sugar," drafted and sent "by the Honorable Judge Cooper, Esquire."[12] A former wheelwright and shopkeeper in New Jersey, William Cooper's transformation to settlement founder and land speculator was a thoroughly post-revolutionary ascendency. As Alan Taylor details in *William Cooper's Town*, Judge Cooper (as he grew accustomed to calling himself) had acquired a relatively undeveloped tract of several thousand acres in the fluid real estate market that arose in New York after the Treaty of Paris.[13] His first, and most successful, endeavor was the founding of Cooperstown on the shores of Lake Otsego in the late 1780s. By the fall of 1790, Cooper had moved his family (including the infant James Fenimore Cooper) to the nascent settlement with an eye to transforming the area into a thriving agricultural district.

Cooper's rhetoric casts his letter as a selfless intervention aimed at accelerating the work of the Society. Although he had not, likely to his chagrin, been invited to join, he nonetheless urged them to take concrete action. As he makes clear in his second paragraph, he feared the Society would focus its attention simply on "refining on common sense," and he urged them instead to correct "errors now in practice, and deliver to the public rational principles for common use."[14] Instead of modestly advising the state's famers, Cooper wanted them to overtly shape the future development of the state. Never shy about his own capacity to correct commonplace misconceptions, as his son's immortalizing portrait of him as Judge Templeton in *The Pioneers* (1823) made clear, Cooper offered up a bold plan he hoped the Society would endorse.[15] His blueprint consisted of a wide-scale promotion of the cultivation and protection of maple trees to create a regional sugar industry that might rival that of the West Indies. Given the importance of this undertaking, Cooper maintained, the endeavor needed to be large enough so that it could prove effective. The scale Cooper had in mind precluded any individual landowner (no matter the size of their estate) from undertaking such a scheme independently, since its success required government intervention. The wealth of connections held by the board of the Society, Cooper implied, could insure the viability of his project if they cultivated a new kind of husbandry in the state.

Such a reorientation of land usage patterns could, Cooper maintained, insure that New York became a vital part of the larger circum-Atlantic economy. To do so, all the Society had to do was to embrace the bounty of maple sugaring and its delimited labor demands in order to promote peace and prosperity for the state.

Cooper simultaneously frames his argument as ecological, economic, and (to a lesser degree) anti-slavery. He does so by suggesting that a highly structured state-wide cultivation plan could shift the nation's relationship to the traffic in sugar from one of foreign importation to domestic exportation. Given how profitable European sugar plantations had proven for their respective empires, Cooper's ambitious strategy may have proven very interesting if for no other reason than the boldness of his claims. Cooper asserts that, "a full supply of that article of life may be manufactured within the boundaries of this State, for the consumption of the United States," if only some group would take an active hand in governing the area's development.[16] Pointing to what he describes as the large tracts of "unimproved land in the northern and western parts of the state" (including acres of land under his control), Cooper contends they are ripe for structured development.[17] Out of necessity, small farmers clear-cut their allotments to create grazing pastures or fields for planting. In place of this destruction of irreplaceable resources, Cooper argued that the upstate regions should be governed by an "overseer" who would orchestrate these spaces as "settled by families" who were supplied with "the utensils suitable for carrying on the manufactory" of sugaring.[18] Such a change would radically replace deforestation and tillage with preservation and tree tapping. Cooper's scheme depended on these laborers receiving credit in advance for "the returns of sugar at a price that will bear transportation," so that they could enter this contractual relationship with an assurance of profit.[19] In place of independent farmers, the territory would be comprised of maple sugar harvesters locked into a hierarchical relationship with overseers and landowners. According to Cooper, these tenant employees would surpass the profits realized by the production of other staple crops.[20] The vision of essentially laborless resource extraction that Cooper articulates also advances a particular vision for population control, and these ideological concerns (as I will argue in more detail below) animate much of the thinking around the possibilities of maple sugaring as they circulate alongside the birth of Haitian liberation.

Aware that his argument might be received with skepticism, Cooper produces evidence based on several years of "ocular demonstration." According to Cooper's "well founded calculations," it was fairly typical for "one man" to "procure from a tract of country less than ten miles square, fifty thousand pounds of sugar" per year. Given this, Copper argues, it would be possible to carve out a territory of "fifteen millions of acres" and designate it as a maple plantation. The sap produced from the trees on this preserve could be boiled into "upwards of eleven million pounds" of granulated maple sugar, "equal to eleven thousand hogsheads of a thousand weight each; a much greater quantity than has ever been landed in one season at all the ports of America." This sizable tract of New York forest, if properly managed, could surpass the sugar production of the West Indies. Moreover, Cooper argued, it would do so with scores of contractual employees instead of hundreds of thousands of enslaved people. Cooper's vision promised to realign New York's place within both a national and a global economy, while also liberating the United States from a dependence on the problematic fluctuations associated with foreign imports. Central to Cooper's vision of maple sugaring resides an idealized vision of population control, wherein small handfuls of independent but still supervised white employees could produce the same vast revenues as thousands of enslaved laborers without needing to bring larger numbers of diasporic Africans into the state.[21]

Positioning himself as an economic visionary, Cooper prognosticates that this industry would help prepare for a time "when slavery shall be done away."[22] Thinking about the connection between sugar and enslavement, he argued that abolition was something that "the present generation" looks toward and that "the succeeding one will no doubt put it in practice."[23] Such sentiment leads him to predict an inevitable rise in the price of sugar, since "the West-India planter" would have to "prepare more expensive provisions for his laborers, not to mention wages and other expenses that consequently attend the hireling."[24] While he does not envision altering landownership or the racialized hierarchies of capitalism, Cooper does foresee a time when the cost of "sugar will continually rise in that quarter" because of what he envisions as a shift in the governing labor relations in the Caribbean.[25] Pointing to the "blood and treasure which has been expended in protecting the sugar plantations of the West-Indies islands"—while failing to account for the blood and lives lost in its production—Cooper argues that these costs fly in the face of common sense and nature's bounty.[26] European "parliaments and kings" expend untold revenues upholding the violent regime of enslavement, while the State of New York possesses the natural resources that could, "without cultivation," yield a greater amount of sugar.[27] By embracing maple sugaring, and creating a profitable domestic industry out of an untapped resource, the leaders of the state had the opportunity to spare "the lash of cruelty" endlessly being struck "on our fellow creatures!"[28] While this sympathetic figuration appears opposed to racist violence, given how it is couched in a series of notations about the costs of importing and policing enslaved workers, it really functions as further evidence that Cooper's vision of an almost worker-free plantation is the superior economic system.

Cooper's abolitionism reads as a second order concern to his projections for a financial windfall. Still, the fact that it serves as a touchstone in his piece—which otherwise argues for creating a new kind of feudalism—exposes how the consumption of cane sugar and the enslavement of diasporic Africans were inextricably linked.[29] The shift from one sort of commodity harvesting to another—an overreliance on forcibly exploited human efforts to an endeavor fantastically framed as nearly labor-less—reduces one of the brutalist forms of enslavement to mere economic bad practice. Thus, Cooper's critique does not directly articulate a vision of liberation but it implies one better suited to insure the safety of white property owners. Indeed it reflects a certain liberal framing of enslavement as a foreign problem; one who's worst injustices might be undone by a structural alteration in processes of capital accumulation. Cooper projects New York as the engine of this new capitalist order because his strategy promises to yield renewable profits for large-scale property owners without tethering them to the problems inherent in the cane sugar production. In short, the expenses, dangers, and instabilities of Caribbean cane production haunt Cooper's articulation of maple plantations as a means of underscoring the peacefulness and surety of his preferred method of extraction.

William Cooper's audacious plans for maple harvesting may appear at first glance impractical. Yet, his schema also manifests his keen awareness of how global politics impacted the sugar market. Recent events had caused a spike in the price of sugar, an increased cost that likely made the kind of intervention Cooper advocated far more palatable than it might have been even a few years earlier. Beginning with the storming of the Bastille two years earlier on July 14, 1789, the French Revolution had further rescripted the operant meanings of *liberté, égalité, fraternité*, in the wider circum-Atlantic world. Even as the Declaration of the Rights of the Man and of the Citizen of 1789 (co-authored in part by Thomas Jefferson) had not explicitly mentioned the issue of enslavement, many French free people of color in Saint-Domingue and elsewhere had seen its passage as an occasion to lobby for abolition.[30] Just several months after the Declaration's adoption, there was the formation of the Colonial Assembly in Cape Francois, including such members as Vincent Ogé, Jean-Baptiste Chavannes, and Julian Raymong, who allied themselves with the Amis des Noirs to advocate for a reformation of the political order in the French Caribbean. As the revolution in France, which had almost entirely disrupted their economy by 1791, began to spread outside of the hexagon and to fuel the hopes of both free Black people and the enslaved people of the French colonies, it also led to fluctuations in France's participation in international trade markets. As Laurent Dubois notes, while Britain "consumed most of the sugar produced in its colonies domestically," the vast "majority of the products that arrived in French ports from the Caribbean were consumed outside of France."[31] American sugar bowls, in other words, were filled with French sugar, and much of that was produced in increasingly radicalized Saint-Domingue. This caused the cost of cane sugar to spike endlessly in the Age of Revolutions. As such, Cooper's attempt to read the tealeaves for the New York Agricultural Society was a timely intervention in regards to shifts in circum-Atlantic economies. While it was far from the first time he (and others) had actively sought to promote maple sugar as a means of freeing the United States from a tenuous foreign dependence, it marks a significant shift in terms of a public attempt to make the case by linking it to current events in Haiti.

The Hands of Freemen

A September 2, 1790, story in Providence, Rhode Island's *United States Chronicle* reveals the wide interest in Cooper's exploits when it reported that a sloop from Albany arrived in Philadelphia on August 18th bearing with it "40 hogsheads of MAPLE SUGAR, the property of William Cooper, Esq." The story notes that the sugar had been produced in Cooperstown and that a number of Albany's "respectable characters" had signed a "certificate" testifying to how it was "superior to the best Muscavado sugar." A similar notice appeared four days later in Portland, Maine's *Cumberland Gazette*, and it too underscored that Cooper had so improved on the refinement process, which had been for "more than thirty years" plagued by "inexperience, and the badness of the apparatus used in manufacturing it," that "it was never contemplated that it could be brought to its present excellent quality." More importantly, for both Cooper and his potential customers, this New York maple sugar cost less than imported Caribbean cane. Attempting to create a buzz for his frontier commodity, Cooper's minor foray into the Philadelphia market (given that his forty hogsheads would have drowned in a sea of West Indian cane) might not have even caused a splash in the city's marketplace if it had not tapped into the burgeoning economic nationalism of the post-revolutionary moment. As the story spread across the northeast it reflected a keen recognition of the importance of foreign sugar to the American diet and what such dependence meant for the early Republic. In his own way, Cooper conjoined these two factors to create a campaign for a domestic industry that he fervently hoped to launch. And he did so, in no small part because of the bounty of mature maple trees on his own landholdings.[32]

Continuing the presentation of maple tapping as a countereconomy to the questionable morality of Caribbean cane harvesting, further newspaper accounts about Cooper's foray into maple sugaring stress its moral purity. For example, a report in the *New-York Journal, & Patriotic Register* asserted that Cooper's commodity should also be esteemed since "it was made by the hands of Freemen, and at a season of the year when not a single insect exists to mix with it and pollute it."[33] Cane sugar was to be avoided since it was the byproduct of "the unwilling labor of slaves." Moreover, French sugar was also produced "in a climate and a season of the year in which insects of all kinds abound." These insects, the report continues, invariably "feed and mix with" the West Indian "Sugar," a description which defines it as tainted.[34] In contrast, New York maple sugar could be produced without these soiling imperfections. Since this American sugar was judged equal in quality but with an additional purity—both in material and ethical terms—spoke to the superiority of the domestic commodity. Cooper's gambit was, in effect, to market his sugar as free of the stain of enslaved labor and a host of other "foreign" containments. Indeed, many of the newspaper accounts that celebrate maple sugar as the product of freemen culminate in a coded racist fear of what Kyla Wazana Tompkins has called "kitchen insurrections" by raising the possibility that enslaved people might be attempting to defile the cane sugar they were forced to produce.[35] In addition to all the "West-India insects" which might besmirch cane sugar, the *New-York Journal* story ends with a crescendo by noting that "to these ingredients is added the *sweat* of" of the enslaved laborers, "and when they are angry, nobody knows *what* else."[36] This promotional logic casts racism and xenophobia as arguments for dietary health. Indeed, for many of the observers of Cooper's patriotic experiment to forge a domestic sugar industry, no refining fire could erase the potentially disease-carrying pollutants of West Indies cane.

Just as Cooper's maple sugar was arriving in the city to such performative fanfare, Philadelphia's own *The Federal Gazette and Philadelphia Daily Advertiser* printed another promotional tract entitled "Thoughts on the Importance of the Maple Sugar Tree." Singed with the initials "A.B.," it seems plausible that the piece was written by the Quaker abolitionist Anthony Benezet, who had long railed against "the brutalities of the slave trade." Perhaps even more curious than the identity of the author is that the byline is inscribed as being from "Coopers-Town," suggesting that in all probability the writer was in league with William Cooper. The piece argues that the cultivation of maple sugar, as a pointed countereconomy to foreign importation, was "a matter of such consequence to the whole of the United States." Decrying the "great expense of blood and treasure" that "the different powers of Europe" disburse "to defend" their holdings in the West Indies, for the sole purpose of harvesting "the juice of the cane," the missive implores Americans to cast their buckets into the forests of America for a sustainable solution. "The sugar of West-India islands cannot be procured but at an expense," A.B. maintains, "and by methods at which the enlightened inhabitants of this land of freedom should startle with horror."[37]

By comparison, the piece asserts—in a slightly veiled reference to Cooper (since it cites the "Albany gazette" as its source)—that "one man," in just a few weeks "without any other assistance than his own exertions," managed to produce "six hundred and forty pounds good grained merchantable sugar." For those with any knowledge of the bounty of the business, A.B. maintains, "this is not thought...to be an extraordinary quantity for one man in that time." Given the superior cleanliness of American farmers, they will be deeply attentive to keeping "free of every thing which can affect its purity." This limpidness renders American maple sugar "consequently more healthy than that imported from the West-Indies," which in another echo of Cooper's promotional materials was always already contaminated. Indeed, A.B. argues, "scarcely a spoonful of West-India sugar is used, but what is more or less mixed with dirt and filth, parts of insects, pieces of stone, sticks, &c." Since enslaved workers have no investment in the profits of West Indies sugar, they have no impetus to care about its cleanliness. Moreover, the cultivation of a domestic sugaring industry would also produce a "savings" to "this United States" of incalculable "cash, or cash articles which are at present sent to purchase sugar from aboard." Finally, "the probability of war" in the West-Indies (and the resultant "stoppage of importation" or shortages) would "raise the price of sugar intolerably as we have already experienced, unless we prepare in time, and not only preserve our trees, but immediately make use of the peculiar privilege which is granted us by Providence, and set about the manufacturing of American sugar."[38]

Given the echoes between A.B.'s passionate injunction and Cooper's own more bombastic figurations, it is tempting to read them as different threads of a larger attempt to equate maple sugar with economic nationalism. In essence, they emphasize that transforming the mid-Atlantic into a sugaring region would reverse trade imbalances while also immunizing it from a continued dependence on enslaved labor. By predicting how this region could become the sugar factory for the early Republic, these missives center on an ecological vision of limitless resources. Devoid of any real sense of the actual labors involved in maple sugar production, the letter writer remains wildly optimistic about the boundless yield from the average tree. Still the similarities between this account and Cooper's own report to New York's agricultural society suggest the appeal of this provisional accounting for landowners with large areas of undisturbed forest. The shared fantasy, in other words, tapped into (literally) a way to produce huge profits without the need to import a potentially rebellious labor force.

These sweeping projections about maple sugar were also usually predicated on fantasies of erasure as these plans to parcel out vast forest tracts for sugaring never accounted for the presence of indigenous peoples. Indeed, by reducing the requirements for land possession to just the simple insertion of a spiel into a single mature maple, these speculations could hasten the prospects for indigenous dispossession.[39] Central to the maple-sugar-as-economic-engine sensibility was, without question, a concrete notion of these uncultivated forests as a genuine *tabula rasa* a depiction which endlessly glosses over the violences of indigenous dispossession. This blank slate could be inscribed so as to avoid the horrors of enslaved labor that had marked every other large-scale European agricultural practice since the beginning of settler colonial incursions. So while these plans might appear abolitionist in nature, it is important to mark the fact that these promotional materials make clear that this is a second order concern. They are not so much anti-racist as they are offering an alternative model to maximize profits without incurring the potentially ruinous costs of resistance. While some prominent abolitionist groups did take up the mantle of maple sugar as a means of divestment from the plantocracy, it would be anachronistic to retroactively link the two issues as inseparable or even as equally motivating.

A few weeks before this report appeared in Philadelphia, New York's *Daily Advertiser* printed an open letter "To the Society of Friends, commonly called Quakers." This missive aimed to convince the Quakers that maple sugar might prove the most effective weapon in the sect's longstanding attempts to "suppress the commerce carried on for slaves with Africa." According to A.Z., the author of the open letter, the advancement of maple sugaring might "contribute more to the emancipation of slaves than all the laws of all the legislative bodies in America." The piece argues that since "it is well known that nine-tenths of all the slaves brought from Africa, are employed in the culture of sugar," if a rival industry made cane sugar unprofitable then enslaved labor might no longer be necessary. Once cane cultivation no longer realized immense profits, the "white inhabitants" of the Caribbean would have "little inducement" to remain in a "climate so prejudicial to their constitution." Without a guarantee of unrivaled profits, these planters would assumedly pull up stakes and leave these islands "to the blacks for whom providence originally designed them." Maple sugar, this writer maintained, could cultivate global economic change in ways that legislative acts could never facilitate.[40]

Attempting to persuade Quakers to conceive of maple sugar as a means of curbing the trans-Atlantic traffic in enslaved peoples, A.Z. urges them to see this agricultural practice as a more generative means of achieving political change. Or, to put it another way, the proposal argues Quakers should abandon advocating for deprivation and taxation and instead invest in a fledgling domestic industry marked by a better ethical praxis. The letter advances this argument by implying that attempts to deprive "women and children" from their "habituated" use of sugar was a fool's errand. Building on this, the letter critiques the idea that cane sugar should be taxed to such an extent that it would restrain usage since such a policy would actually lead to an even more brutal treatment of enslaved people as planters sought to maximize profit margins. A better way to cripple this insidious system would be to render cane sugar products more expensive than maple ones without pushing those costs onto consumers. Quakers could achieve this goal, the letter argues, if they would pledge to only consume maple sugar and thus "set an example that will be followed by every patriotic character." They could, in other words, enact a transformation in habit and taste, which would more realistically produce the social justice they were struggling for.[41]

By the winter of 1793, New York's Agricultural Society had grown an offshoot. With the original Society's blessing, the New York Maple Sugar Society made a presentation to the state legislature to lobby for "premiums" for farmers who pro-duced maple sugar.[42] After a celebratory presentation of samples, the Society "immediately appointed" a subcommittee "of seventeen" members and tasked them with creating "a bill in favor of granting liberal premiums for the manufac-ture of sugar."[43] These maple sugar legislative efforts in New York aimed at preserving the productive potential of the trees themselves, while also rebranding New York's place in external trade networks. Nurturing a new domestic industry would secure the larger mid-Atlantic region with a precious commodity that would not flourish in other domestic climes.[44] Considered in this light, the advocacy for maple tapping was a time-sensitive argument against thoughtless deforestation. Additionally, these promoters for maple products sought to increase the importance of New York agriculture by removing the time-consuming necessity of clearing to enable the planting of grains. Fostering the maple industry, if successful, would generate incredible wealth for elite New York landowners, and presumably insure their future profits by preventing further deforestation and predetermining the agricultural future of the state.[45]

Sugary Accumulations

In *Specters of the Atlantic* (2005), Ian Baucom challenges the normative figuration of the past as a temporal modality distinct from the time of the now. Following Walter Benjamin's articulation of how the past and the present are complicated constellations, Baucom argues, "time does not pass, it accumulates."[46] Instead of thinking of time as linear and potentially progressive, Baucom deploys an economic metaphor to capture how the present consists of stockpiled deposits of previous actions. His description does not erase the possibility for change, but rather figures the present as constituted by accumulated pasts. Fundamentally, Baucom's invocation of aggregation to describe the Black Atlantic overtly links questions of temporality to the emergence of a credit-based system of global capital. Within the logic of this emergent eighteenth-century system, the time of the "now" is never simply the present because of how the past dwells within speculative attempts to predict futurity. Baucom's figuration of time allows us to probe the conditions of possibility created by thinking about the simultaneity of the non-simultaneous. In other words, his reclassification of the past as always present *in* the present allows us to consider how the older "seed funds" of the past are constitutive of the larger aggregation of the present.[47] By foregrounding the temporalities of accumulation, we can better understand how the contingencies of the past are constitutive of the time of the now even if they are not overtly accounted for or acknowledged.[48] This might be an especially apt way to think about a market in flux, something Baucom keenly makes visible in his work. By emphasizing how Europe embraced the heretofore unseen riches of New World cultivation, Baucom stresses that they also understood the risk involved in the much more unstable oceanic trade in humans, sugar, molasses, and rum.[49] To mitigate these new risks, European capitalists formed the insurance industry as a means of acknowledging how past transactions might undermine present profits because of the unforeseen difficulties of expanded commercial routes.

Without question, this investment only deepens in the early nineteenth century. The outbreak of revolution in Haiti not only disrupted Caribbean trade but (via the Louisianan Purchase) afforded the United States a more central presence in the circum-Atlantic basin. Indeed, in many ways the U.S. sense of itself as a theoretically unfolding economic and potentially imperial power was as much grounded in its interest in the Caribbean as it was in any territories west of the Mississippi in the first two decades of the nineteenth century.[50] This intensification manifests itself in how early-nineteenth-century U.S. novels register an apparent obsession with the impact of the Haitian Revolution—sometimes encoded in passing allusions to the events themselves and others in muted discussions of a fractured market economy, or via the promotion of maple sugar production, or by a turn toward East Indies trade routes. Yet, more than just cataloging the impact of a foreign event on the formation of the geopolitical development of the United States, these texts predominantly figure the Haitian Revolution as part of an accumulated temporality of revolutions. As I will explore in more detail below, Isaac Mitchell's *The Asylum; or, Alonzo and Melissa* (1804/11) is a paradigmatic example of how these early-nineteenth-century American novels represented economic instabilities and the accumulated temporality of revolutions. In essence, novels like *The Asylum* reverberate with Baucom's figuration of temporality, which is itself rooted in an examination of the interdependence of enslavement, commodity circulation, and the insurance of capital accumulation. Similar to Baucom's conception of what we might call a Black Atlantic temporality, these novels encode the ways in which the Haitian Revolution is and was and would always be intimately connected to "past" revolutions still unfolding across the circum-Atlantic world.

Entrenched within maple sugar narratives was an investment in promoting the work of self-sufficient laborers who did not need to handle maple to the degree that enslaved laborers were constantly in contact with cane. This most clearly surfaces in the recurrent anecdotal turn to the singular farmer who produced a surplus of sugar with little effort involved in cultivation and production. As such, aggregated in any figuration of cane sugar was both the violence of Black Atlantic enslavement and, after 1791, the possibility of Black resistance. In comparison, since maple harvesting required such a distinctly different labor scale it symbolically became associated with free and independent (and thus peaceful) laborers. Maple sugar promotional materials routinely mark how cane sugar bears a level of contamination because of where and how it was produced. Aside from its utility as a promotional tool for the supposed purity of maple sugar, this rhetorical pattern simultaneously stresses that the sap of maple trees can be foraged for without the stains associated with the barbaric traffic in humans that structured other sugar economies. These arguments recognize that the traces of laboring hands (and the residues of sites of production) are always present within commodities. Planted within cane sugar were all the accumulated problems of racial

capitalism and its exploitation of enslaved peoples. What the maple sugar enthu-
siasts sought to promote was a vision of a mid-Atlantic economy unburdened by
the need for labor-intensive plantations. In this regard, these maple sugar georgics
hearken back to the genre of the seventeenth-century country house poem, which
often promoted the idea of a self-yielding earth. As Raymond Williams has deftly
detailed, the country house poem celebrated elite figures while erasing the laboring bodies that actually cultivated and catered to these aristocratic spaces.[51] The
celebration of infinite sap freely flowing from ancient trees resonates with a similar politics in that it suggests generative bounty without the need for actual workers to produce it.

Mark Sturgess argues that the 1790s promotion of maple sugaring as a counter
to foreign cane might best be understood as a kind of "maple sugar bubble."[52] He
suggests that if we attend to how its boosters "employed multiple forms of print
media and literary aesthetics," we can better understand "the relationship among
political discourse, agricultural reform, and artistic production in the early
Republic."[53] For Sturgess, these "maple sugar georgics" labored to "imagine a progressive form of agriculture and economic resistance to the injustices of slavery"
as he reads these texts as largely abolitionist or proto-abolitionist in bent.[54]
Tracing the ways in which the proponents of maple sugar "failed to acknowledge
other forms of resistance, both cultural and environmental" that eventually disrupted "their sweet dreams," Sturgess moves to read the hopes of the 1790s against
the reflections of the 1820s.[55] More specifically, Sturgess registers an insightful
consideration of James Fenimore Cooper's 1823 novel *The Pioneers,* which
unfolds during the early years of his father's settlement of Cooperstown (fictionalized in the novel as Templeton). By repeating the longstanding trope of leaping
over the first two decades of the nineteenth century, and replicating the problematic linkage of the 1790s with the 1820s as if nothing had occurred in the interstitial period, Sturgess mutes the influence of the Haitian Revolution on debates
about maple sugar. He circumnavigates the question of why French sugar importation had been disrupted and why the U.S. turned to the purchase of an inferior
and more expensive product from the British West Indies. In short, he favors following a somewhat familiar Anglo-American (routed through the northeastern
seaboard) narrative about capitalism, environmentalism, and abolitionism by
sailing away from the turbulent currents of the French and Haitian Revolutions.[56]

The arguments for maple sugaring as a laborless bounty were as invested in
reifying large-scale landowners in North America as country house poems were
in celebrating aristocratic wealth and power.[57] Heedless of their own oversized
calculations, maple promoters blindly counted the profits of innumerable casks of
maple sugar on the horizons of the future. Yet, changes in weather patterns,
unseasonal temperature fluctuations, and tree exhaustion could all cause variations in the yield of sap runs, alterations that were seldom accounted for in their
fantasies about a liberating cottage industry. The push to establish maple sugaring

as a sustainable replacement industry did by the early nineteenth century prove a gossamer fantasy. But, it was one that also formed a central subplot in one of the nineteenth century's most popular novels, Isaac Mitchell's *The Asylum*, a text that interrogates the fluctuations of the circum-Atlantic economy as a result of the Haitian Revolution. By embellishing the possibilities of maple sugaring to forge independent fortunes for mid-Atlantic homesteaders, Mitchell's novel hearkens back to maple tapping as a pathway to self-sufficiency. The novel charts a complex geography, and its plot roams across the unsettled interior districts of the mid-Atlantic colonies, to Europe, to the southern districts of the United States, only to find its resolution on a bluff in Connecticut overlooking the Long Island sound where a newly married post-revolutionary couple happily plant roots and forgo oceanic ventures. Mitchell's novel considers the compounding of revolutions into one another as he locates Haitian revolutionary era economic issues in a narrative staged against the American Revolution itself. In short, *The Asylum* resonates with Baucom's accounting of past accumulations within present circumstances to question how to disassociate the United States from a dependence on the fluctuations of unstable oceanic commerce.

The Sugar Maple of America

Isaac Mitchell's *The Asylum* turns to the maple sugar bubble to record a poignant interest in the relationship between circulation and national security. In so doing, Mitchell deploys maple sugaring as a measure of the temporal amalgamations of revolutions, inequalities, and dependencies. While the plot of the novel ostensibly revolves around the damaging social and economic fluctuations engendered by the Revolutionary War, its actual concerns are firmly rooted in the unsettled state of the Republic in the early nineteenth century.[58] By thinking about how early-nineteenth-century trade was increasingly destabilized by European conflicts in the circum-Atlantic basin, Mitchell's novel invests in the georgic possibilities of maple sugaring to reify a vision of economic nationalism defined by white settler freedom as the key to the future of the United States. The centering of white freedom as defined by an isolation from the instabilities of Caribbean trade becomes more central to Mitchell's argument as he revised and expanded the novel which has a complicated textual history. The text first appeared in semi-regular installments (from early June to late October in 1804) in the *Political Barometer* (Poughkeepsie), a paper which Mitchell edited for four years in the early nineteenth century. In 1811, Mitchell published an expanded two-volume edition of the novel that added a lengthy prehistory to the tale which more directly locates the economic concerns of the text in the fluctuations of the first decade of the nineteenth century. The fact that there are two versions of Mitchell's text only further compounds the muddled nature of a critical engagement with the narrative.[59]

The serialized account appeared at the height of Democratic-Republican political power in both New York and in the country more broadly, and as a partisan newspaper editor, Mitchell was deeply invested in his party's cause. By 1811, Democratic-Republican authority (both locally and nationally) had begun to wane, and alongside this loss of influence was the emergence of a much more fractured economic system that further embroiled the United States in circum-Atlantic trade networks. As Joseph Fichtelberg contends, one of the strengths of "Mitchell's text" emerged from how it "was able to articulate a new set of ideological problems in comforting and familiar terms"; it did so by using "the language of sentiment in an attempt to understand an emerging liberal world."[60] While the tropes of sentimentalism registered a kind of universalism for writers and readers in the Anglophone world across the eighteenth century, the capacity for this aesthetic strategy to represent the geographic excesses of the emerging Western world forged by racial capitalism was utterly strained by the first decade of the nineteenth century. The second version of Mitchell's text reflects his attempts to navigate the wider territorial concerns of the early nineteenth century as a means of lamenting the loss of cultural coherence amid the ongoing political fluctuations of the later stages of the Age of Revolutions.

Mitchell routinely reprinted news concerning Haiti and the Louisiana Purchase in the pages of the *Political Barometer* (Poughkeepsie). So while critics often consider the text in its standalone form, it was initially consumed in segments nestled in-between overlapping reports of foreign unrest, national expansion, and commodity pricing. Early readers of Mitchell's text would have encountered his fictionalized allusions to domestic production, frontier settlement, and revolution as literally adjacent to reports about seemingly distant foreign spaces. In this regard, his first readers were invited to engage his literary argument as part of a constellation formed by larger non-national, circum-Atlantic experiences. The sentimental concerns of the marriage plot between Alonzo and Melissa within the original print context were juxtaposed with other generic forms which undoubtedly shaped the perceptions of readers. This invitation to think of the narrative as part of a discursive collage was absent in the standalone publication. However, the addition of the para-textual material duplicated some of the contextualizing work of the earlier discursive abutments present in the serialized form. The additional material in the standalone volume, particularly Mitchell's inclusion of lengthy narrative about the Berghers, which foreshadows the problems that will plague Alonzo and Melissa, creates a similar complication of sentimentalism by implanting the text amid contemporary concerns. By drawing attention to the cultural contexts that readers themselves currently inhabited (the time of the now), these materials framed the past of the American Revolution against contemporary socio-political events. As such, the notes and preface ask readers to consider present circumstances amid the revolutionary era plot in such a way as to present the past and the present as simultaneous modalities. Thus, the para-textual apparatus evinces a sense of how the history of the Revolution remains accumulated within larger, still-emerging social and economic concerns.

While the novel presents itself as primarily concerned with the Revolutionary War, both versions invited readers to think of that history alongside their own contemporary moment. So while the narrative surface appears chiefly invested in a past history, it is more accurate to understand the novel as folding seemingly discrete historical periods into one another. The complexities of history are presented as a process of accumulation rather than as one of progression. In this regard, Mitchell shares a vision of temporality with Baucom as both insist that readers attend to how the compounded pasts aggregate in contemporary cultural formations. In embracing such an accumulative vision of history, Mitchell resurrects seemingly dormant histories and displays their interconnectivity with the present. In effect, Mitchell turns back to the (by 1811) now failed project of maple sugaring to access how it prophesized a pathway to economic independence and stability.[61] He does so to exhibit the instabilities inherent in a continued attachment to the fluctuating uncertainties of foreign trade. As such, Mitchell disinters the post-revolutionary faith in the ability of the Republic to cultivate a domestic agricultural industry that could potentially immunize it against foreign contagions. Perhaps, more importantly, he did so in the context of cane sugar production, which was already rooting itself in American soil.

In the spring of 1803, Robert Livingston completed the Louisiana Purchase, which doubled the size of the United States, ostensibly removed France from the U.S.'s western border, and brought the port of New Orleans under the Republic's control. This last item was perhaps the most crucial, for as Jefferson noted in a defense of the purchase, "the produce of three-eighths of our territory must pass [thru New Orleans] to market."[62] By gaining control of the southern terminus of the Mississippi, Jefferson hoped that the United States could more advantageously direct the flow of imports and exports into and out of the Republic. On New Year's Day 1804, Dessalines gathered a congregation of officers to sign the Haitian Declaration of Independence and form the second independent Republic in the Americas.[63] The seemingly disparate events are interrelated in several ways, but for the purposes of this chapter, I want to highlight two ways in which these events conjoined to spur a North American cane sugar industry. If Napoleon had not needed to fund his last ditch efforts to recolonize St. Domingo, he never would have considered the sale of the Louisiana Territories. As the U.S. negotiators understood perfectly, Napoleon intended to use the profits from the sale of Louisiana to finance an expedition to retake St. Domingo, which had always been the more valuable colonial territory. Second, many of the Creole planters who had fled Cape François for New Orleans also attempted to transplant their lucrative cane sugar production to their new environs. These planters had made a fortune by providing sugar to the world, and they intended to reclaim their lost revenues by using the knowledge they had gained in Haiti to rebuild the now collapsed cane sugar market. Essentially, just as the Haitian Revolution had made the acqui-sition of Louisiana possible, national expansion rooted the brutal realities of cane sugar harvesting more systemically into the domestic sphere.

While Jean Étienne Boré formed the first sugar plantation in North America in Louisiana in 1795 (then still French territory), the industry only really began to flourish as more refugees from the Haitian Revolution arrived in the Louisiana territory.[64] Boré managed to transplant the techniques utilized by French enslav-ers in Haiti to Louisiana, and he soon proved that cane sugar production could thrive in this new locale. This news provided hope to exiled French planters to consider Louisiana as a site where they could establish new plantations. So prior to the acquisition of the Louisianan territories by Jefferson's administration, the agricultural future of the southernmost region had already been seeded. The American appetite for sugar was hardly curtailed despite the sharp increases in prices that flowed from how the Haitian Revolution had brought cane production to a grinding halt. Boré, and the planters who followed him, sought to capture the sugar market by turning the regions surrounding New Orleans into the new export hub for the global sugar trade. This production of cane sugar emerged alongside the multiple attempts by landowners in the mid-Atlantic region to pro-mote maple sugar as a replacement staple. Yet, as Mitchell knew full well by 1811, these maple sugaring efforts had failed to successfully change the tastes of American consumers.

The alterations enacted by the para-textual materials, of Mitchell's 1811 version takes stock of the how the decline of Democratic-Republican power impacted the Republic in terms of its place with the larger contextual framing of the circum-Atlantic world. If there had still been some hope for the possibility in 1804, by 1811 maple sugaring was a failed deposit in the accumulation of the Republic's attempts to cultivate a northern-based economic nationalism. By thickening his maple sugar interests within his revised text, Mitchell resurfaces the belief in self-sufficient yeoman farmers providing the spinal column of American growth. Yet, he did so even as he fully understood that this was a residual concern and a failed economic venture. Still, about a third of the way into the 1811 edition of *The Asylum* appears a curiously detailed and sizable footnote that presides over the majority of four pages of the text. The para-textual rupture of this lengthy foot-note unveils Mitchell's layered approach to detailing the uncertainties of quotid-ian life in the circum-Atlantic world. It does so by drawing the reader's attention out of the temporality of the novel into a consideration of contemporary eco-nomic concerns. Echoing, the same kinds of outsized predictions for that William Cooper and others had promoted decades earlier, Mitchell's text resurrects these possibilities of a maple sugar-driven independence to sound out the contours of an agrarian philosophy predicated on economic self-sufficiency.

On the surface, the note authenticates a story about two penniless European immigrants who achieve financial independence in the wilds of Connecticut by harvesting maple sugar. The narrative figures this couple, the Berghers, as wishful evidence of the hopes that William Cooper and others had for how farmers might turn an otherwise fallow time in their yearly agricultural labors into a fountain of excess. The Berghers had eloped, since their families objected to their union, and had fled Europe to escape persecution. They eventually settled into a backcountry farm in Connecticut (first as tenant farmers and eventually as property managers themselves) where groves of sugar maples provided them financial security and independence. This couple effectively serves as posterchildren for the now dormant promotion of post-revolutionary maple sugaring as a key to domestic self-reliance. The embedded episode about the Berghers (and their story of self-emancipation from cantankerous parents) prefigures the plot machinations that plague the titular star-crossed lovers of Mitchell's narrative, providing a model of companionate marriage for his readers and characters alike. Moreover, the culmination of that marriage plot in a crescendo of independence through maple sugaring resonates across the length of the novel.

By unpacking some of these sugaring reverberations, the ways in which the footnote embeds the novel's political ambitions become more readily interpretable. Various nodes of connection between sugar production, settlement practices, commodity circulation, and revolutions that resonate across the plot surface most visibly through the para-textual interruption of the lengthy footnote. Before further speculating about this footnote, let me briefly recount Mitchell's plot—for although it was the most popular gothic novel in the United States across the nineteenth century, it remains relatively underexamined.[65] The novel begins in pre-revolutionary Connecticut, initially focusing on Melissa Bloomfield, the daughter of a wealthy landowner. Early on, Melissa encounters the Bergher family, the very same family that has been able to secure their independence through maple sugaring. For the first time in their lifelong relationship, in part because Melissa is beginning to contemplate her own marriage, they decide to tell her their story. The Berghers decided to marry against the objections of the bride's father and as a result of this defiance they fled Europe for North America. Pursued across the Atlantic, they finally settle in a sparsely populated district in Connecticut where they have lived in peace and relative comfort ever since. This narrative about the difficulties of securing a companionate marriage effectively anticipates Melissa's own soon-to-unfold future troubles.

After the lengthy exposition of the Berghers, the remainder of the first volume of the 1811 edition details Melissa courtship by two friends who are both vying for her affection. After the usual indecision, Alonzo's sincerity and good character shine through and Melissa confesses her attraction to him. At first, Melissa's family favors the match, and all seems to be moving toward a harmonious union. The only ominous note amid Alonzo and Melissa's impending union surfaces as an aside about an outbreak of "open hostilities" between England and her rebellious North American colonies (70). Effectively, the fathers offer halfhearted expressions of attachment to one side or another, but both appear more concerned with how any hostilities will disrupt the economic activities of North American merchants.

The second half of the novel opens with disastrous news. Alonzo's father, a commercial speculator with global interests, discovers that British authorities have seized his cargo in both the Atlantic and the Caribbean, effectively bank-rupting him. With Alonzo's family now destitute, Mr. Bloomfield forbids the pro-posed marriage. Despite Melissa's best efforts at persuasion, Bloomfield remains intractable and forbids his daughter from having any further contact with her former fiancée. To separate the pair and prevent a possible elopement, Melissa's family imprisons her in a "castle-like building" that was "built of rude stone" in the seventeenth century to defend Anglo-American settlers from indigenous Americans (87). Melissa is locked in this ruinous heap and soon believes it to be haunted when she sees a variety of unusual ghost-like apparitions moving through the building at night. As Kerry Dean Carso argues, "the castle scenes in *Alonzo and Melissa*," while "wildly anachronistic," serve as a means of presenting "the classic Gothic locked door mystery" within an American context.[66] Yet, more than that, this setting reminds the audience that such residual architectural designs, and the order they represent, could never really endure when trans-planted to American soil. By the conclusion of the novel, Mitchell reveals these apparitions as Loyalist smugglers who had been using the castle as a base of oper-ations from which they maintained "a secret and illegal commerce with the British Army on Long Island," part of which entailed them spreading "counterfeit money" in order to weaken the American economy (238). These smugglers have altered the castle so that it now includes subterranean passages and secret doors, turning the previously impenetrable seventeenth-century fortification into a veri-table eighteenth-century sieve for villainous anti-American activities.

Heartbroken by the forced separation, Alonzo searches for Melissa and only abandons hope when he reads an obituary that was falsely planted in a newspa-per. This leads the distraught Alonzo to enlist in the Continental Army, and he subsequently serves at Bunker Hill. Eventually captured by the British during a naval battle, Alonzo is transported across the Atlantic in the hold of a prison ship and finally locked away in an English jail. Alonzo eventually escapes and encoun-ters a British citizen, Mr. Simpson, whose humanity leads to their overcoming their political differences. Simpson ultimately helps Alonzo cross the channel into France, where he encounters agents representing the U.S. cause. At the conclusion of the text, Alonzo rewards Simpson for his timely assistance, and in a fit of grati-tude, this British solider opens a pub that he names "The Grateful American" in the text's most blatant attempt to signal a new amity between England and the United States (276).

After she finally breaks free from the castle, Melissa absconds southward to Charleston to live with her uncle. In order to teach her father a lesson, she fakes her own death and then disguises herself as her cousin who had indeed passed away. Meanwhile, in France, Alonzo encounters Benjamin Franklin, who delivers a rousing and patriotic speech which reawakens Alonzo's dormant patriotic sentiments. With a renewed sense of national duty, Alonzo agrees to carry some crucial papers for Franklin back to North America.[67] Intent on rejoining the war effort, Alonzo sets sails for Baltimore, but a storm disrupts his voyage and capsizes his ship. He washes ashore, in Charleston, as the sole survivor of the shipwreck, and here (after a final bit of misdirection) he reunites reunited with Melissa. They decide, despite any possible lingering familial objections, to finally marry and return to Connecticut, looking to build their future. The last pages of the novel include a variety of revelations, including the capture of the smugglers and noting that the castle has been destroyed during the war. Moreover, because of information in his possession, Franklin effectively restores the fortune that Alonzo's family thought they had lost, and Melissa's father has a change of heart and blesses their union. The Revolutionary War comes to a relatively quiet end, as the novel optimistically frames the reestablishment of Anglo-American social, if not political, relations. Importantly, it does so not by suggesting the stability of trans-Atlantic mobility, but rather through propagating the importance of staid settlement within telluric spaces.

Across the novel the sea functions as a destabilizing force, as Mitchell meticulously details the instability of marine travel. The site of ruinous naval battles, of imperiled cargoes, of shipwrecks, and of widespread smuggling operations, Mitchell positions the Atlantic to create a sharp divide between domestic landscapes and the lawless antagonisms of international waterways. Every waterborne endeavor ends in disaster; a theme highlighted by the multiplicity of fractured oceanic ventures. While Laura Doyle has framed the trope of an "Atlantic crossing" as a staple representation of freedom in long-eighteenth-century Anglo-American literature, it does not function as such within Mitchell's text.[68] As Christian Knirsch has observed, "the Atlantic crossings [in *The Asylum*] are less of a sign of homecoming or manifest destiny…but one of oscillation between Britain and the U.S."[69] The turbulence of oceanic crossings is something to be suffered and hopefully overcome, not because it brings freedom but rather because it affords the possibility of avoiding future waterborne endeavors.

As the conclusion makes clear, after their long-deferred nuptials, Alonzo and Melissa want nothing more than to build a home to shelter from the uncertainties of speculative mobility. As Knirsch notes, "they want to live on their land, enacting an early American ideal of self-sustaining existence known as Jeffersonian agrarianism."[70] And to extend the insights of Knirsch's observation, this Jeffersonian vision of settlement depends upon the presumption that indigenous peoples had already been displaced by English colonialization and that small-scale farmers would not need excessive amounts of enslaved labor to secure their own wealth. The vision in other words is a fantasy about white supremacist independence in which violence against (or even interaction with) people of color is always off-stage or framed as unnecessary. As such, this concluding image, the christening of their farmstead as an "Asylum" from the tribulations that have plagued them up until this point, circles back to the central narrative concern of the first volume, which details how the Berghers faced similar predicaments. This overlapping of narrative trajectories conjoins both married couples to stylized visions of Jeffersonian agrarianism in an effort to claim this ideology as foundational for the American Republic.

While there are other footnotes in the novel, none of them run anywhere near the length of Mitchell's para-textual appendage on maple sugar. Configured as a kind of intricate primer for maple sugaring, the footnote begins by noting that "the sugar-maple of America is an article eminently entitled to the attention of every new settler," and quickly follows this by noting that, "indeed, it may be asked whether its cultivation be not an object for legislative consideration and patronage"(180). Echoing the sentiments of maple sugar proponents of almost two decades earlier, Mitchell contends that if "liberal premiums" were "offered, in proportion to the quantity and quality of sugar annually produced," it would be possible "to reduce the price and diminish the importation of that commodity" (180). The protection of maple groves and the harvesting of the tree's sweet sap could reverse national economic practices. In essence, it would mean that the United States could "perhaps finally to exclude the use of foreign sugars," an economic transformation which would save "millions" every year for "the states" (180–1).

Instead of paying foreign powers for a quotidian commodity, relocating the sugar trade would transfer the profits from sugar sales to American producers. The nurturing of a nascent domestic industry would also yield another substantial benefit; Mitchell stresses that if maple production could replace that of cane, the United States would protect itself from the uncertainties of circum-Atlantic trade. "In case of war, or other event, by which our commerce might be expelled" from international oceanic trade, Mitchell argues, domestic production "would secure to us the use of this delicacy, which habit has possibly rendered indispensable" (181). Stressing that "the tree is easily cultivated," Mitchell projects a way for individual farmers to "readily supply themselves with sufficient quantities of sugar for family use" if they just shifted away from using maples as "timber and firewood" (181–2).

The second lengthy paragraph of the footnote provides a primer for the harvesting of maple sap and the transformation of this liquid into crystalline sugar:

The method of preparing or manufacturing sugar from the maple, is as follows: in the months of February and March, when the weather is such as to freeze in the night and thaw in the day, when the vital juice of plants begins to circulate, and before the buds swell, the trees are tapped, by boring several holes diagonally into their trunks, about one fourth of an inch diameter, three or four inches deep, from eighteen to twenty inches apart, and from two to five feet from the root; tubes, composed of wood or hollow weeds are inserted in these holes, which serve to conduct the sap into troughs prepared to receive it; nothing more is necessary, but to strain and boil the sap to the consistence of sugar, taking off the scum as the liquor heats, before it boils, and carefully stirring it as it grows thick to prevent it from burning. Brass boilers or kettles make the best coloured sugar. The trees will bear tapping every other year, and frequently every year, if large and thrifty; they will yield from thirty to one hundred gallons of sap, each, in a season; every gallon of sap will make about four ounces of sugar.   (181–2)

The footnote provides a high level of detail, systematically plotting out, from start to finish, how famers might produce ample quantities of sugar with relative ease. With a minimal investment in new equipment—just a few taps, buckets, and kettles—Mitchell projects that farmers might follow the fictive example of the Berghers. In short, Mitchell argues that American farmers could easily produce enough of this quotidian staple to meet their own needs, with the implication being that, with negligible further effort, they could then produce an excess to provide themselves with a new source of revenue.

With details from "the spring of 1808," the lengthy third paragraph of the note attempts to give flesh to Mitchell's argument by way of concrete example detailing the efforts of "a farmer in the back settlements of Massachusetts" to harvest maple sap (183). The note outlines how this farmer, just three years prior to the publication of this novel, had "inserted twenty taps into one tree on his own farm," from which (according to Mitchell) he extracted "twenty-three gallons and three quarts of sap in one day, which produced seven pounds and four ounces of sugar" (183–4). Continuing his outsized accounting, Mitchell asserts that this solitary farmer reportedly produced "thirty three pounds" of sugar with relatively ease (184). In case this promotional pitch should not prove persuasive enough to encourage interest in domestic sugaring, Mitchell continues by listing a variety of other domestic staples whose ingredients could be extracted from maple sap. The initial draw of sap "is an agreeable and cooling *beverage*," one that "by a fermentative process" can be transformed into "very pleasant *beer*, which" itself becomes "vinegar" when it goes stale (185). When "boiled to a certain consistence," the sap can be cooked into an "excellent *molasses*," and if this is "submitted to distillation" the yield would be "ardent spirits of a rich taste and fine flavor" (185). In sum, "when manufactured with care, the *sugar* is inferior to none that we import," and Mitchell notes that he has himself "seen Maple-Sugar which in texture, colour, and taste, was equal to any he had ever met with manufactured from the Cane" (185).

Moving to add a patriotic dimension to his public relations campaign, Mitchell states in the fourth paragraph of the footnote that:

During the American revolution, molasses, spirits, and sugar, were made from the stalks of Indian corn, by a process similar to that adopted with the Cane.— Sugar has also been extracted from carrots, beets, and some other roots and vegetables, but much inferior in quality to that manufactured from the maple.   (185)

Harking back to an earlier moment of disrupted trade (which, because of embargoes and naval blockades, mirrored early-nineteenth-century disruptions in circum-Atlantic trade), Mitchell recalls the actions of revolutionary era patriots to forge an object lesson for his contemporary readers. Demonstrating how earlier generations had made do, out of necessity, with inferior sweeteners during the war, Mitchell celebrates these forefathers for their adaptability and inventiveness. In so doing, the footnote complicates the temporality of the novel by effectively blurring the periodicity of North American settlement by linking early-nineteenth-century westward expansion to colonial homesteading. By displaying how maple sugaring offered North American settlers (past, present, and future) the opportunity to profit by virtue of their environmental bounty, the footnote transforms a moment of curious exception about the Berghers into an unending possibility for domestic solidarity. The footnote blends colonial era husbandry into the narrative time of the novel (ostensibly the revolutionary era). Moreover, this para-textual insertion urges the reader to think of their own time alongside that of the revolutionary era by suggesting how domestic accumulation could liberate (in deep time, in nearer time, and in the time of the now) the U.S. from damaging dependencies which had, were, and might once again force the Republic into contaminating economic networks. Like his revolutionary predecessors, the industrious 1808 Massachusetts farmer demonstrates his independence by providing for himself by extracting all he needed from his own environment rather than risking the fluctuations of waterborne commerce.

On the page, the boundaries between the modalities of the past, present, and future blur as Mitchell resurrects the superseded possibilities of the failed maple sugar bubble in an effort to project them into the future. The rich tradition of maple sugaring serves as a withdrawal from an accumulative tradition that connects seemingly disparate social formations into a solitary American tradition. Contemporary readers of Mitchell's text understood disruptions to cane sugar production as symptomatic of all-too-familiar Caribbean unrest. The conflation of cane sugar and Caribbean enslavement was perhaps *so familiar* that it was unnecessary to actually name them as referents given the implied geographies of "foreign sugars." While Mitchell deploys the word "American" to fix his referent to a singular event, the connections he intimates between foreign revolutionary movements and imported agricultural commodities unmoor that fixity. The production of sugar and variously related commodities like molasses and whiskey were as much about the domestic trade networks as they were about foreign entanglements.

By promoting the substitution of maple for cane, Mitchell both imbricates the U.S. in non-national networks of association and reframes the nation's past, present, and future agricultural practices away from a plantation-based economic model. At their core, fantasies about the harvesting of maple sugar share an overblown sense that the production of this domestic commodity—from tapping trees to collecting sap to boiling it down into caked sugar—could be completed without the need for a surplus labor force. In this regard, these maple sugar georgics share the same erasure of enslaved laborers (or even wage laborers) that reverberated through the Jeffersonian vision of agrarianism and the country house poem tradition that in part inflected that vision.[71] The promotion of maple sugaring as a legacy of the American Revolution attempts to delink the horrors of enslaved labor from the history of the emerging Republic. It stakes a claim, in other words, about how the self-sufficient labor of white European immigrants who cultivated a living from the North American "wilderness" provided the bedrock of the social order of the Republic. The allusion to the solitary Massachusetts farmer who just recently produced over 7 pounds of sugar in one day serves as an advertisement for this mythic autonomy. The tangible example works in harmony with the references to the Revolution to make a case about Republican self-sufficiency in the face of external disorders.

The Berghers' narrative stresses how the tapping of maple trees afforded them not only "the delicacies of the Indies," but also quickly generated much needed capital that allowed them to become independent (180). As an appendix to this anecdotal description of self-generating commodity and self-sufficiency, the footnote lobbies for the cultivation of maple sugar to be nurtured by federal intervention. Such proactive legislation would situate the U.S. within an alternative pattern of accumulation not shaped by the traumas and instabilities of cane sugar production. It would seemingly also disassociate the United States from the enslavement that was central to the production of cane sugar. The delusory promise of saved "millions," and the projected comfort of insuring access to some form of saccharine seasoning even during moments of crisis, offers a protectionist logic that moves to divest the U.S. of foreign entanglements (181). Mitchell hypothesizes that by turning to the forests of North America instead of the agitated waters of the Atlantic, Americans could immure themselves against chaotic fluctuations. The para-textual addition of the footnote makes self-sufficiency a serialized practice: for just as maple sugaring secured the Berghers' freedoms in mid-eighteenth-century North America, so too can the backcountry Massachusetts farmer in 1808 follow the same path. Maple sugaring, magically, is never tethered to a particular time or place. Instead, as a willful hope for laborless harvesting, Mitchell's maple sugar object lesson functions as a detemporalized self-generating process for self-determination. In so doing, it promises abundant surety rather than chaotic dependence, so much so that the Berghers' past becomes a serial element constitutive of the present and of futurity.

Mitchell's footnote makes visible how the entire novel crumples time to rearticulate how Caribbean unrest and its interruption of cane sugar production should engender a reconfiguration of operant economic practices. A change in consumptive habits—and alteration in the Republic's taste—from a praxis rooted in past legacies would administer a different set of future possibilities.[72] By having both a colonial era and a contemporary example of the benefits of maple sugaring, Mitchell promotes an non-linear flow of time to champion a reformatted vision of Jeffersonianism, a political ideology that had increasingly lost its national sway. In many ways, Mitchell's conflation of discrete historical moments embraces the idea that time, as Michel Serres has argued in a different context, flows "according to an extraordinary complex mixture, as though it reflected stopping points, ruptures, deep wells, chimneys of thunderous acceleration, rendings, gaps, all sown at random, at least in a visible disorder."[73] In any given moment, this complex mixture of temporal forces was shaping the possibility for American futurity and peaceful Western expansion. To counter the gravity of the ruptures and gaps enacted on the contemporary nation by the disruptions of oceanic commerce, Mitchell proposes a turn toward domestic resource extraction, a tapping into local climatological advantages as a means of preserving prosperity. His disaggregated narrative temporality emphasizes that the time of self-sufficient possibility has not past; rather it remains an as yet inactivated legacy of the accumulative mass of revolutionary era history.

Our Sweet Tastes

Aside from the extended lines snaking along Kent Avenue in Williamsburg in the spring of 2014, the first aspect of Kara Walker's installation at the Domino Sugar Refinery that confronted visitors was an artist's statement painted on the factory's crumbling façade. Declaring that Walker has "confected, a Subtlety; or, the Marvelous Sugar Baby" as "an homage to the unpaid and overworked artisans who refined our sweet tastes from the cane fields to the kitchens of the new world," this overture served as an *amuse-bouche* for the encounter yet to come.[74] A pungent aroma of blackstrap molasses saturated the air, almost demanding that visitors absorb the candied history of the location prior to witnessing Walker's forceful confections.

Erected on the banks of the East River by the Havemeyer family in 1856, the Domino compound was the largest cane sugar refinery in the United States in the nineteenth century. By the 1870s, workers at this site were processing over 1,500 tons of sugar per day, a staggering productivity that accounted for about 50 per cent of the sugar refined in the U.S. per year well into the twentieth century.[75] The viscous remains of all that toil—a mixture of caramel, sweat, molasses, coal smoke, ambrosia, and countless other industrial byproducts—was still seeping from the walls and skeletal rafters during Walker's exhibition. Gazing at the interior of the building, still caked at every turn in old sugary remains, it was possible to imagine the structure as continuously weeping half-congealed saccharine tears.[76]

Within the walls of the decommissioned factory-turned-temporary-gallery, Kara Walker's enormous sphinx-like sculpture with an epidermis comprised of gleaming cane sugar crystals proffered an array of complex meanings. Fronted by an enlarged kerchief-wearing Black female face, the voluptuous naked figure coterminously embodied the racist stereotypes of the mythic caregiver and the overly sexualized Black female body. A Subtlety vividly evoked the racist histories of these all-too-familiar tropes, even as it more delicately called forth a third by signaling their connection to sugar production. Through her inventive use of 30 tons of bleached white sugar crystals to form the surface of the sphinx sculpture, Walker reminded her audience that these racist caricatures of Black woman as simultaneously sexually available and quintessential "mammies" have their roots in new world sugar plantations.[77] Bleached sugar provides the material through which Walker concretizes the *longue durée* of racist ideologies which have delimited figurations of Black womanhood under a white supremacist gaze. The sculpture emphasizes, as Hilton Als argued in a review of the exhibit, that "Americans live, still, in an atmosphere of phantasmagorical genocide."[78] For Als, the ways in which the sculpture manifests fantasies about Blackness through the medium of a dazzlingly white substance demands a reckoning of what these colors mean and what they have meant in the construction of contemporary American society. By bringing attention to the underlying power structures which have confected American culture, Walker's exhibit, in the words of Als, calls into question "those who have the language to make the world and map it, and those who work that claimed land for them with no remuneration, no hope, and then degradation and death."[79]

The sphinx began to crumble almost immediately upon the opening of the exhibit, as Walker intended the sculpture to melt in the uncompromising heat of New York's late spring, as well as to have its sparkling surface stained by the detritus raining down upon it. A coterie of smaller statues of largely unclothed African boys, in almost no mappable relationship to the gigantic sphinx itself, were scattered around the exhibition hall. Redolent of enslaved child laborers, these figures were manufactured out of molasses and a resin-like candy. These bodies, also intentionally ephemeral, hemorrhaged dark syrupy trails that gathered in pools at their feet as these figures decomposed in the warm environment of the temporary gallery. By the middle of the period of the exhibition, a few of these statues had already lost limbs as they could no longer sustain the weight of the burdens they had mutely toted since Walker had opened the space in early May of 2014.

Routinely labeled by critics a blockbuster in countless reviews, Walker's *A Subtlety* called forth a phalanx of implications about race, labor, industry, corruption, violence, corrosion, sexual objectification, inequality, and historiography. Capitalizing on the shock of laboring and subjugated bodies housed within a superannuated factory, the exhibit conjured multivalent ways of thinking about the complexities of New World accumulation and production. Moreover, since the installation was designed as site-specific, it is important to consider how the exhibit intended to call for specific histories of its own location. In other words, central to Walker's theorizations of the connections between sugar production and the exploitations of racial capitalism stands the role New York played in the continued production of each of these violent histories. It was without question a discomforting space, one made even more disconcerting by the throngs of viewers who posed for mocking and exploitative pictures with the protruding breasts and vulva of the sphinx.[80] Alarmingly, many viewers flooded social media with these sexist and racist souvenirs; these images both decontextualized the intervention of the project and demonstrated the perpetuation of the very troubling ideologies the colossal sculpture was intended to critique.[81]

While a myriad provocative threads emerge from Walker's visceral exhibition, perhaps the most intriguing surfaces through how Walker presents cane sugar as a means of crafting the conditions of possibility for viewing multiple geographies and multiple temporalities simultaneously. Neither the procession of semi-clothed African, or perhaps African American or diasporic African, children, hauling baskets of sugar and cane stalks, nor the naked-aside-from-a-kerchief figure of a Black woman would likely never have roamed the floors of this Brooklyn factory; yet, their labor, their presence, and their histories would have ghosted every granule of refined superfluity produced within its walls. Their hands would have harvested the cane that produced the bleached luxuries, and their labor would have seasoned countless dishes (for innumerable American tables) with the commodities produced here.[82] Hauntingly, these statues testified to the *compounded* before-and-after labor histories that freely roamed this factory before it was decommissioned and before it was destined to become luxury housing. For the brief few weeks that the exhibition occupied the derelict hulk of a ruined Brooklyn factory, Walker managed to conjure a way to envision manifold temporalities coterminously occupying a singular space. The crumbling structure also testified to the dislocation of industrial work from a neighborhood and a waterfront that had once blossomed because of it; yet, even as statues supplanted (or stood in for) displaced workers, they added creative capital to the gentrifying neighborhood, enacting another cycle of luxury and precarity far too difficult to ignore.

Collectively, the abandoned factory and the evocative sculptures instantiate how enslavement and other forms of labor exploitation were never just local issues, with crops from one space transformed into quotidian staples in another.

While Walker's exhibit more vividly represented the horrific violences of Black Atlantic history, within her confection resided traces of the arguments that William Cooper and Isaac Mitchell made about the economic future of New York and the production and consumption of sugar. In the very detritus, which rained down from the decades of production and darkened the sugary epidermis of the sphinx, Walker echoed (albeit with a very different politics) the concerns that Cooper had about the surface-level contaminations of cane sugar production. Both deployed these telling stains to expose their audiences to the realities of cane sugar production. Cooper's racist implications about the unsanitary contaminants forever blended into cane sugar were intended to drive Americans away from continued connections to enslaved laborers. Two centuries later, Walker sought to position her audience alongside these exploited peoples to persuade them to unearth a submerged and seldom acknowledged history of abuse. Considered in a certain slant of light, they share a rhetorical purpose in that they move to convince their audiences of the relationship between the exploitation of diasporic Africans and the delicacies adorning their daily tables. While Cooper hoped Americans would divorce themselves from a dependence on Black Atlantic production, Walker insisted that such a separation through refinement could never actually occur. Moreover, by resurrecting the presence of cane sugar production on the shores of the East River, Walker reminded her audience that northern factories were a facet of an industry so often imagined only as a southern or Caribbean industry.

Walker's exhibit accentuated how the national serves as an illusory rubric by which to think through the histories she so creatively assembled. The installation did so by insisting that viewers attend to how the forcible capture and enslavement of diasporic Africans who harvested New World crops meant that all consumption and production was always already a global exchange. Sugar, in its different forms, from cultivated stem to refined crystal, grew in many areas and was touched by many hands before it ever sweetened anyone's tea. All of these geographical spaces and all of these seemingly divergent temporalities accumulated in the exhibit; all of them were in residence alongside and merged into one another.[83] Across the *longue durée* of Western history, sugar has represented a delicacy that flavors our cultural praxis. The racial capitalism that cultivated those tastes, as Walker made manifest, are inseparable from its cultivation and production. The charge of Walker's installation, as I see it, was for viewers to unpack all of the dimensions of this sugary accumulation. Her *Subtlety* then, stubbornly implored viewers to consider the past as compounded in the present, to reflect on how cane sugar and the people forced to produce it destabilize our residual attraction to nationally bound progressive histories. In essence, Walker theorizes how isolationist fantasies about nation formation provide a stark reminder that the kinds of generative white settler self-sufficiency that Cooper and Mitchell sought to ferment never happened. In this sense, her confectionary installation in 2014 essentially provided a different kind of monument to the still unrealized potentiality of maple sugaring by recrystallizing the lengthy racialized history of elite New Yorkers profiting from sugar production in the region. Moreover, given the presence of so many African Americans and Caribbean immigrants on the factory floor of the Domino Sugar Factory before it closed, Walker's saccharine Black laborers also memorialize the role that diasporic Africans played in New York's capital accumulation.

A *Subtlety* dramatically unsettled scores of its many visitors by fostering recognition of the intimate relation between sugar and enslavement, between northern factories and the middle passage, in consumption and production, and within the very violent margins of global capitalism. The revolutionary potential of Walker's illumination emerged out of how the objects, the subjects, and the industrial compound interfuse to form a constellation of accumulations. In this vein, her installation mobilized a similar kind of layered temporality to Mitchell's maple sugar footnote, to provide a stark reminder of the horrendous and almost incalculable violence of cane sugar production and its imbrication in the development of the American economic and cultural order. Her argument took the massive shape of a 75-foot-long and 35-foot-high sugar sphinx so that its brute force could compel viewers to understand these multiplicities as inseparably conjoined. Her transitory installation within a deteriorating factory pushed the audience to bear witness to how their molasses covered contemporary footsteps were intimately connected to the traumas of Black Atlantic history. Mitchell had sought to make a similar argument about the relationship between American development and enslavement through the production of his para-textual material, although his fantasy about divestment was built on a more permeable foundation than even Walker's temporary statues were.

Walker's confection testified to the centrality of sugar production in New York beginning in nineteenth-century America, albeit not in the ways in which Cooper or Mitchell had prognosticated. When the Havemeyer family erected their first factory in Williamsburg in 1856, and even more so with their expanded 1882 second version after a fire consumed the initial structure, New York became intimately linked to cane sugar refinement. By the close of the first decade of the nineteenth century, interest in maple sugaring as a large-scale countereconomy to that of cane sugar had become a distant memory, as Louisianan planters had successfully cultivated cane fields with great financial success. So for over a century and half, before Kara Walker reignited these dormant Black Atlantic histories, the Domino Sugar Factory had long mocked early post-revolutionary hopes for the Republic to find an easy way to disaggregate itself from the centrality of enslavement as the driving force of its development. By the last quarter of the nineteenth century, the Williamsburg refinery produced the bulk of the cane sugar consumed in the United States, a living embodiment of the intimate connections between northern labor and both southern U.S. and Caribbean circuits of racial capitalism. William Cooper and Isaac Mitchell's dreams of New York sugar sweetening the kitchens of America had occurred, even as Walker's *A Subtlety* reminds us that these confectionary dreams never took shape without the exploitation of diasporic Africans at its delectable core.

4

Transmitted to America

Zelica's Incipient Fever and the Legacies of the Haitian Revolution

The London publisher William Fearman announced the publication of *Zelica, the Creole* in 1820, identifying the author of the three-volume novel as "An American."[1] Such geographically derived aliases were ubiquitous in the early-nineteenth-century literary marketplace where actual authorial nomination remained a rarity. Still, the initial advertisement implies that this "American" had a great deal to contribute to London's print public sphere since it promotes two other novels, *The Scarlet Handkerchief* and *The Stranger in Mexico*, "by the same author" as already "In the Press" (I:2). In the space of a few lines, Fearman attempts to rouse prospective readers' curiosity about these novels by triangulating the United States (through the identity of the author), the West Indies (through the signifier "Creole"), and Mexico (through the location of the stranger) while routing these spaces through a singular "American" perspective. This assemblage of titles, in sum, markets these novels as offering portals into a variety of Anglophone fantasy objects in terms of space, place, populations, and cultural mores. Even without offering any details about their plots, Fearman's advert draws attention to these objects as sensationalist pathways into alien structures of feeling. When *Zelica, the Creole* appeared in Philadelphia the following year, the author was similarly identified as "An American."[2] While the U.S. edition was not linked in any of the domestic marketing materials to the two novels supposedly written by the same author, the vague coordinates marked in the title no doubt functioned similarly as a promise of access to exotic themes, characters, and spaces.[3]

Both the English and the American editions of *Zelica, the Creole* share a key commonality: each essentially juxtaposes the presumptive U.S. nationality of the author against the racial ambiguity raised by the signifier "Creole" and the non-Western name preceding it.[4] Detached from any tangible surname, Zelica's solitary given name divorces her from any genealogical connections. As such, from the outset her identity is mediated by a term that both blurred and defined boundaries between natal origins and racialized genealogies. While intimating that Zelica is possibly of European descent, the term Creole also implies her birthplace is in a colony or formerly colonized space even as it intimates a mixed-racial heritage. The dislocated positioning embedded in the title's nominative work precedes, or perhaps counters, whatever fixity (in terms of nationality as

The Haitian Revolution in the Early Republic of Letters: Incipient Fevers. Duncan Faherty, Oxford University Press.

well as race) "An American" posits. At the very least, the juxtaposition encodes a distance between author and titular subject, highlighting that while linked on the title page, there remains something essential to each which alienates them from one another. While the author's identifier does not locate her (or him) within a personalized family tree, it does mark her as a citizen of a nation-state. In contrast, Zelica lacks any such clear connection, but rather stands positioned as part of a deterritorialized ethno-group. Or, to put it another way, the juxtaposition of American and Creole effectively draws a distinction between the specificities of the Anglo-North America and the vagueness of a Francophone Caribbean.

Aside from a handful of nineteenth-century newspaper reviews, *Zelica* received scant attention until quite recently. In the wake of the rapid canonization of Lenora Sansay's *Secret History; or, the Horrors of St. Domingo* (1808), ignited by Michael Drexler's recovery of the text with his Broadview edition in 2007, critics familiarized themselves with *Zelica* because of their supposition that Sansay also wrote this later text.[5] This line of thinking regrettably pigeonholes *Zelica* as primarily of interest as an extension of *Secret History*, and few critics examine the later text without deploying the earlier one as an interpretive keystone. While the evidence to support the assertion of Sansay's authorship of *Zelica* remains, at best, inconclusive, the conflation of the 1820 and 1808 texts has effectively sublimated the later novel into figurations of the earlier one.[6] Without question, similarities between the two texts exist in terms of plot, character names, and setting, but to proffer these correspondences as conclusive evidence overlooks the vastly different tenor and terroir of their narrative concerns.[7] But the subordination of *Zelica* to the status of a second attempt by Sansay to profit from her experiences in Cape François elides these significant differences as unworthy of attention.[8] While Sansay may well have needed money in 1820, especially after her separation from her husband and her continued dislocation from Aaron Burr, such suppositions hardly explain why she would produce such a lengthy second (and third and fourth if Fearman's advertisement is accurate) text in an effort to find financial security. Moreover, the plot of *Zelica* lacks the very insider perspective and scandalous access to power that was so central to the framing (and marketing) of Sansay's 1808 narrative. The shifts in tone, content, plot, and structure between these two texts are considerable; yet, all too often critics have skimmed over these differences to shoehorn *Zelica* into the much smaller footprint of *Secret History*.

Taxonomizing these two texts as sequential surreptitiously renders the importance of the Haitian Revolution for and on early American cultural production as static. Such renderings overwrite the differences between an 1808 meditation on the late stages of the Revolution and those of 1820 as presumptively inconsequential, a critical blind spot hampering contemporary criticism of both novels. By failing to see how the 1820 publication date of *Zelica* creates a distinctive contextual environment, critics undervalue the full import of the later novel. The original publication of the *Secret History* overtly trades on the currency of the still nascent republic of Haiti and the cotemporaneous scandal surrounding Aaron Burr's exile.[9] Sansay understood these factors as important selling points to the extent that they feature prominently on the title page of her 1808 text which promises an eyewitness account of important contemporary events.

By 1820, Haiti had been an independent Republic for over fifteen years. While many readers took comfort in the fact that the struggle for self-emancipation in Haiti had not sparked successful revolutions elsewhere, its continued endurance in the print public sphere—despite embargos, blockades, and non-recognition from both the United States and various European powers—testified to the fact that Haiti continued to haunt the American imagination in enumerable ways. Rather than elide the differences rendered by over a decade of events separating their publication, this chapter circumnavigates a consideration of *Zelica* as simply a revision of *Secret History* to explore the tangible differences between them. I do not undertake this separation simply because the connections grounded in authorship remain tenuous. The differences in form, genre, style, and publication history reveal *Zelica* as a historical novel with pronounced concerns about how the past impacts present cultural formations. In the twelve years separating the publication of these two texts, U.S. concerns (and perhaps even those of Sansay herself) about Haiti—now an established Republic rather than an incendiary flashpoint—had evolved beyond the conventions of the sensationalized memoir.

Finally, this critical tendency of artificially coupling these two texts willfully ignores how a range of early American texts quite consciously framed themselves as responses to earlier productions.[10] Plots and character names were routed in contending directions by new authors, and the lack of coherent copyright laws and the inability to adjudicate claims of intellectual property meant that the print public sphere was extremely fluid. Indeed, early American textual production, in novel form but also in the period's periodical culture (as Jared Gardner and Meredith McGill have demonstrated), was suffused with widespread patterns of adaptation and piracy.[11] Within this climate of recursive intertextuality, the idea that *Zelica*'s and *Secret History*'s similarities reveal anything concrete seems simultaneously ungrounded and anachronistic. The evidentiary chain that presumes linkage proves faulty; yet its protracted impact has hampered a detailed consideration of *Zelica* as a textual object in and of itself. We have fixated on originality and mappable authorship in constructing our canon, a praxis that has obscured how texts were habitually reflections of other texts and reanimations of previous productions. Given the variety of textual mimicking occurring during the period, it remains just as likely that the restaging of *Secret History* embedded within *Zelica* may have involved a second author as much as it proves Sansay's retooling.

Clara's Mobility / Clara's Stasis

From the ambit of plot summaries, similarities between these two texts abound. At the core of each resides the unhappy plight of Clara St. Louis, an American citizen married to a refugee Creole planter. While the initial presentation of the marriage in *Secret History* frames it as strained, from the outset of *Zelica* St. Louis appears as a scoundrel unworthy of the virtuous Clara.[12] On a surface level, what constitutes a companionate marriage (and charting under what conditions such a union might thrive) drives each narrative's plot.[13] The action of these novels unfolds with Clara accompanying her husband on his return to Cape François in 1802 as part of Napoleon's efforts to recolonize the island, and both describe the conditions facing the planters who returned to restore the colonial relation. The futile efforts of the French to reenslave (or forcibly remove) the self-emancipated diasporic Africans who controlled St. Domingo contextualizes each of these novels.

Each text scrutinizes the meaning of whiteness by creating the conditions of possibility for interrogating how U.S. Americaness, Frenchness, and Creoleness were distinct, and perhaps incompatible, identity formations. They do so by featuring characters intended to embody the supposedly varying moral and ethical positions reductively associated with these ethnicities and nationalities. Both plots characterize the Creole St. Louis as an abusive husband incapable of a companionate marriage with his unambiguously superior American wife to lament the fate of women forced to marry inferior men. Similarly, these texts emphasize the bonds between women under the debilitating conditions of a patriarchal culture rife with licentious men. They likewise juxtapose American sexual mores over and against those of the French and Creoles to suggest the more conservative expectations Americans have for heteronormative relationships. Finally, each text concludes with a reverse migration: they culminate by charting the flight of all the surviving white protagonists from the island. Beyond all of these correspondences between plots, *Zelica* also co-opts the language of the earlier text in several instances with little or no variation. The later novel, in sum, cherry picks certain characters and experiences from the earlier text and rearranges the circumstances in which they find themselves.

Yet, fundamental differences abound, some just as visible from the same aerial remove. Primarily, *Zelica* comprises three volumes and almost 900 pages, whereas the single-volume *Secret History* consists of 225 pages, or essentially one-quarter of *Zelica*'s length. While size alone hardly measures anything, this tabulation demonstrates the vast differences in volume. This issue of scale also reveals differences in the publishing industry between 1808 and 1820; few three-volume novels appeared in 1808, but innovations in manufacturing had made larger volumes more viable by 1820. Even more important than these developments in print technologies, generic evolutions unfolded in the twelve years separating these two texts that changed the reading habits of Anglophone readers, including the prominent rise of the English-language version of the historical novel. There has been much fruitful debate about how to best classify *Secret History* generically. Even at its moment of modern recovery, Michael Drexler insightfully described the text as a proto-feminist autobiography rather than simply labeling it a novel.[14] More recently, Gretchen Woertendyke generatively reads it within the genre of the secret history itself as a means of recuperating the importance of that form in the circum-Atlantic world.[15] Still, even those critics who consider it a novel (the default genre of early American literary studies) would have to admit that the parameters of that genre shifted dramatically in the period separating the composition and publishing of these two texts. Like other early historical novels, *Zelica* envisions a broad view of a past social order by suggesting how the private lives of a group of fictional characters and stylized portraits of real people reflect important shifts in historical conjunctures.[16]

The title page of *Secret History* hints at an intimate exposé by inscribing it as "a series of letters, written by a Lady at Cape François." Indeed, critical reactions to *Secret History* have largely embraced the text for its ability to provide access to an English-language participant observer of events in St. Domingo in 1802. Arguably, the experiential eyewitness elements of the text fueled its meteoric rediscovery, effectively propelling it into becoming one of the most rapidly canonized texts in American literary history.[17] In effect, Drexler's recovery of the text opened up a shipping lane for U.S. Americanists to consider traffic between the early Republic and the Caribbean in a way that no other text had previously enabled. Sansay's own emblazoning of her connection to the infamous Aaron Burr has only further fueled the field's investments in it as a socio-political map.[18] This dedication further amplifies speculations about the veracity of the text because of how it hints at historically informed threads of biographical information. The linkage to a founding father (albeit the one founder who serves as an outlying fantasy object then and now, as Michael Drexler and Ed White have persuasively argued) provides a hefty gravitational pull on contemporary critics.[19] This tendency to decode the historical accuracy of the letters hardly surprises us given how the invocation of Burr's name intentionally fueled conjectures about "a Lady" being a politically connected eyewitness.

Secret History, essentially, fits almost like a missing puzzle piece in the field's desire to form a canon around biographically interpretable texts with overt connections to political flashpoints. Sansay's dedication also dredges up many of the rumors swirling around Burr in the aftermath of his scandalous downfall, especially when one considers that his trial had only concluded a few months before the first printings (presumably timed to capitalize on the trial) of the text appeared.[20] Thus, even before one reads the text—then or now—intrigue bleeds through the title page. In effect, the front matter encodes these letters as private correspondence from a witness of the final turns of the Haiti Revolution to the then vice president of the United States (since the setting is 1802). By the time of publication, this late vice president had just willingly accepted his exile from the United States on suspicion of plotting some form of mysterious expedition in the Spanish territories west of New Orleans and was thus at the peak of his notoriety. As such, the inscriptions on the title page promise insight into important contemporary events and the roles that scandalous public figures played in them. While fictive portraits of founders had appeared in historical dramas prior to *Secret History*—for example, George Washington's brief appearance in Royal Tyler's *The Contrast* (1790) or Isaac Mitchell's depiction of Benjamin Franklin in *The Asylum* (1804)—no previous text had attempted the level of intimate access that Sansay's so brazenly promised.[21]

Whatever attraction period readers may have had to this tantalizing promise of insider access pales in comparison to how these facets of *Secret History* have animated contemporary Americanist critics hungry for ways to consider the importance of Haiti for the early American Republic. Almost all of the critical attention focused on *Secret History*, a veritable explosion since 2007, has privileged the first third of the novel (set in St. Domingo) despite the fact that the text has a much more promiscuous geographical imagination. In terms of pagination, more of the text unfolds in Cuba and Jamaica than in St. Domingo. Of the thirty-two epistles comprising the novel, the first fourteen are addressed from Cape François and the final eighteen are written either in Cuba (thirteen of which are drafted from three different locations on the island) or from Kingston, Jamaica (five). Given this wider territorial scope, we might better understand the ambition of the earlier text as mapping how events in Haiti reverberated across the Caribbean and potentially washed into colonial holdings of other European empires (like those of the Spanish and the English). Although often framed as providing access to U.S. American concerns about Haiti, *Secret History* actually presents the Caribbean as an archipelagic network of varying economic and political models. Moreover, the text routinely emphasizes how each island within this interconnected string has its own localized concerns and relationships with continental North America. As Clara and Mary roam across the Caribbean, they remain attuned to detailing the stability of the current state of various colony's political, economic, and socials orders. To some extent, *Secret History* drafts a preliminary map of the ways in which Americanness circulates in these alternate colonial spaces even as it measures how receptive other spaces might be to reorganization and an increased American influence. Arguably, the specter of Burr and rampant speculations about his involvement in territorial expansion might well resonate more forcefully across the parts of the text not set in Haiti than critics have typically noted.

While none of these other spaces seems poised for revolution, they do appear ripe for intervention. Such a figuration underscores that another facet of what it means to be an American observer in the revolutionary Caribbean might well have been an attempt to *discover* possible new sites of connection. Perhaps the best example of this occurs during Clara's flight from St. Louis when she finds herself hiding out on a poorly functioning Spanish ranch that has thousands of heads of cattle yet, as she openly laments, no capacity to provide her with a glass of milk.[22] This scene culminates in Clara's brief musings about how better supervision might turn this primitive space into a profitable enterprise. The episode evinces the relationship between leadership and the monetization of natural resources, and the indolence of the Spanish society contrasts with the more pragmatic concerns of the American heroines.[23] If the French love of pleasure fueled the ruinous mismanagement of colonial St. Domingo, then the Spanish failures to maximize their profits also provides a fundamental lesson in resource extraction. All of those heads of cattle—under the guidance of a different system of husbandry—could easily transform Cuba into revenue generating space. This moment allows the reader to imagine the economic possibilities of ranching against the failed economy of sugar harvesting. The scene, effectively, hints at the generative possibilities of a different economic order taking control, one that required less physically taxing work and fewer workers (and thus was less susceptible to revolution) but could still yield immense profits.

Even as the novel concludes with Clara and Mary's return voyage to Burr and Philadelphia, it places a variety of geographical mediators between Haiti and the United States as if to uncouple them from a simple casual relation. In so doing, the text contrasts a variety of systems of colonial power. Given this wide-ranging ethnographic element, the invocation of Burr and his mysterious ambitions haunts the text in manifold ways. By recording the economic inefficacies of other islands, particularly those controlled by the Spanish, Burr's fictive correspondent theoretically provides him insider information about which U.S. adjacent spaces might be ripe for exploitation. In this sense, the text markets its associations with potential expansion by providing a primer for annexation possibilities. As such, the narrative enacts a vision of what Andy Doolen marks as territorialization, a notion of geographical affiliation informed by first-hand reportage about the primitive agricultural and cultural systems already in place.[24]

In contrast, the entirety of Zelica occurs on the island of St. Domingo (aside from the final pages of the novel that are staged on board ships anchored just off the island's coast). This reduction in geographical scope dramatically differentiates the two novels; furthermore, it also embodies one of the largest shifts in the cultural imagination about St. Domingo that had occurred in the twelve years separating their publication. While Secret History consistently framed Haiti as one node in a larger constellation of colonial islands, Zelica does not chart the potential spread of revolutionary fervor with a distinctly archipelagic territoriality. From the outset, Zelica demonstrates very little concern with Haiti's proximity to or potential interconnectedness with other islands; indeed, few mentions of other Caribbean spaces occur within the novel. One way to read this shrinking scope would be as a manifestation of a monocular territorial imagination in the 1820 text. Another way to consider this shift is as a magnification of the importance of this singularity as a political entity that demanded recognition in and of itself. Both texts locate their action around 1802, but the meaning of that historical conjecture would have significantly varied for readers in 1820 as opposed to in

1808. Many readers in 1808 would likely have feared that the revolutionary fires in Haiti would enkindle disruptions elsewhere. Others still might have hoped that the restoration of European control to counter the self-emancipation of the island was still possible. Few, if any, readers would have entertained such thoughts by 1820 since Haiti had not sparked a global revolution even as it had remained free from external domination.

As Christopher Taylor has recently argued, in the wake of Haitian Independence, the British adopted a set of policies that forged an "empire of neglect" in their Caribbean holdings.[25] Taylor defines this new mandate as shaped by a loosening of cultural and political ties between metropole and colonial periphery in favor of a more nakedly defined set of economic relations. Such a shift emphasizes how in the decade after Haiti declared itself free, European powers sought to quarantine it from other colonial holdings. Moreover, as Taylor advances, these same European powers (especially the British) began to remove themselves from binding connections with any Caribbean colony to insure themselves against possible sympathetic liberation movements. Still, as Lisa Lowe argues, these attempts at reconfiguration worked hand in glove with articulating new forms of labor exploitation to avoid the kinds of racialized revolution that had occurred in Haiti.[26] It is within this shifting climate of a desire for starker distinctions between colony and colonizer that *Zelica* emerged. Moreover, the novel's setting matches this evolution in operant circum-Atlantic conceptions of the Caribbean by treating the island of Haiti as sequestered from other Caribbean spaces.

While traces of Haiti's revolutionary potential being uncontainable linger in *Zelica*, this later text lacks the overall sense (as *Secret History* does) that an intimate connection between islands was inevitable. If the *Secret History* presented revolution as a potential pandemic (already spilling beyond the shores of Haiti by the middle of the text), *Zelica* attempts to diagnose the circumstances of a site-specific outbreak. In so doing, the narrative maintains vital concerns about the potential spread of revolutionary contagions, but it does not present them as imminent gothic horrors pouring out of an erupting Haiti. This shift in the notions of territoriality permeating these two plots exhibits why reducing them to a sequential relationship fails to capture their divergent investments in charting cotemporaneous political and cultural geographies.

Genres of Revolutionary History

Alongside the alterations in territoriality, the texts dramatically diverge in their narrative perspectives. Most significantly, *Zelica* is not an epistolary narrative and the shift to an omniscient narrator significantly alters the novel's stylistic possibilities. In one sense the fluidity of Clara's and Mary's movements in *Secret History* lends itself to the epistolary format, as the missives account for their myriad separations both from Burr (the chief recipient of the letters) and then later from one another.[27] The fractured lines of communication mirror the disruptions in the social fabric that plague Mary and Clara, and their chaotic mobility informs the text's epistles. The sisters produce longer letters during moments of relative calm and more fractured missives during the fugitive migrations of the text's second half. Sansay artfully manipulates the parameters of the epistolary mode as she uses the form to afford a clearer sense of her characters evolving interiority: both in their own self-authored confessions and through the structure of the letters themselves. As the text progresses, these shifts in epistolary form belie the unstable circumstances the two sisters inhabit. The overreliance on biographical information, which fuels a tendency to overread the text as reportage, often subsumes any examination of the aesthetic dimensions of *Secret History*. Thus, Sansay's deft orchestration of the epistolary form to tether sensationalism to the shape of the letters themselves largely remains undervalued.

Less concerned with formally embodying a sense of rapidly increasing crisis, *Zelica* deploys a narrative structure that features the interior monologues of a wide range of characters (everyone from the diasporic African General Christophe to the mixed-race Zelica herself). By comparison, in *Secret History*, Mary pens the first twenty-six (out of thirty-two) letters. The final six letters of *Secret History* are comprised of two letters from Clara to Mary, three letters from Mary to Clara, and the final letter returns to the original orbit of correspondence (Mary to Burr). Mary and Burr do not exist, either on or off stage, as referents in *Zelica*; and while the novel does retain a sororal kinship as a central element, the position of Mary becomes replaced by Clara's non-biological connection to the titular protagonist Zelica. The child of an octoroon enslaved woman and a plantation owner in St. Domingo who both enslaves and marries her mother, Zelica's complex heritage emplots this later novel with narrative concerns alien to *Secret History*.[28] After her mother's death, Zelica's father ships his infant daughter to a boarding school in France for an education she could not receive in Cape François, and she has only just returned to St. Domingo as the novel opens. Her kinship to Clara (a white U.S. American) who has arrived in St. Domingo at almost the same time symbolically reflects the text's concerns about the prospects for hemispheric social reproduction. In many ways, what Elizabeth Maddock Dillon has called the "intimate distance" of the colonial relation defines the relationship of the characters and the readers of *Zelica* to Blackness.[29] For Dillon, intimate distance functions both as a spatial designation and as a marker of interpersonal reliance, as a phrase that manifests fluency between bodies concurrently coded as dissimilar.

Thinking alongside Dillon, *Zelica* registers how the Haitian Revolution exposed the contractedness of the idea of intimate distance. The consequence of an eroded colonial relation blatantly suffuses *Zelica*, even as this question only covertly arises in *Secret History*. *Zelica* features two diasporic African military officers who manifest an ardent desire to marry women that the text largely codes as white, and details why these men fantasize about how such a union will legitimize their authority. Far from uniform in its perspective, the intimate distance featured in *Zelica* emerges from multiple perspectives including most shockingly in the form of the unprecedented behavior of Zelica's father (De la Riviere) a former planto-crat who undergoes a procedure to turn his epidermis Black. Across the length of the *Secret History*, Blackness largely remains an abstraction, one held in abeyance on the margins of the text; but (as I will argue in more detail in this chapter's closing section) De la Riviere's self-imposed Blackwashing as an indication of his commitment to the revolutionary cause centers questions of Blackness on the very outer layers of *Zelica*'s plot. Many of the diasporic Africans portrayed in *Zelica* possess agency, a narrative perspective that offers readers direct access to their personal and political motivations. In *Secret History*, readers only encounter diasporic Africans through mediated transcriptions or secondhand rumors. Arguably, Sansay's 1808 text remains more invested in finding a new space in which to reboot a hierarchical colonial relation now that St. Domingo has become undone. To put it another way, from its dedication to Burr and throughout its treatment of other Caribbean islands, *Secret History* remains invested in an under-articulated hope for a potential new colonial order formed elsewhere, a space in which the reality of self-emancipated diasporic Africans can be glossed over. By contrast, *Zelica* refutes the possibility of preserving the colonial relation as it existed before Haitian liberation.

Kimberly Snyder Manganelli classifies *Secret History* as an "epistolary trave-logue with moments of gothic terror," a definition which, in short, registers how Sansay mines the conventions of voyeuristic natural history writing to inscribe racial taxonomies and perpetuate socio-climatic cultural distinctions.[30] Manganelli's figuration foregrounds Sansay's creation of an authorial voice with both a physical and temporal proximity to the rupture of the Haitian Revolution. Moreover, by framing her protagonists as circumstantial foreign correspondents Sansay underscores that what they witness exists within a wider circuit of com-munication far exceeding localized confines. As the political theorist Massimialno Toomba has recently argued, the Haitian Revolution created "new political and social configurations" as potentialities across the circum-Atlantic world.[31] In *Secret History*, Sansay conjoins questions about gender and struggles for self-emancipation in ways that speak to Toomba's conception of how the Revolution opened up new conceptions of emancipation across a variety of trajectories. Indeed, as Aimee Cesaire has argued, "to study Saint-Dominque is to study one of the origins, one of the sources, of contemporary Western civilization."[32] Building upon Cesaire's observations, Toomba asserts that Saint-Dominque "shaped a con-stellation whose spatial-temporal boundaries exceeded nationality, built bridges with other excluded subject, and introduced a new radical concept of universality, whose legacy branches into many trajectories of human-emancipation."[33] Even as

Toomba's concerns reside with the relationship of visions of freedom articulated by the Haitian Revolution in comparison with that of the French Revolution, the way he scales the legacy of Haiti to think about new forms of freedom offers a way to register *Secret History*'s complex alignment of a critique of patriarchal power with the terrors of white supremacy. Indeed, Toomba's conception of the seismic force of these event reverberate with Manganelli's reading of the novel as an observational travelogue that records how freedom and unfreedom define a variety of territorial spaces in a moment when wide-scale mobility has fractured the solidity of national borders.

In contradistinction to her reading of *Secret History*, Manganelli defines *Zelica* as a novel "in which all efforts at categorization and differentiation are futile: French colonists are mistaken for British sailors, women disguised themselves as men, and whites paint their faces Black to escape the revolution."[34] Manganelli remains one of the few critics to significantly distinguish between the two texts, and her attention to how each text very differently considers questions about the stability of identity in the wake of revolution opens up fruitful interpretive pathways. We might also think of this difference as encapsulated in how the authorial identity of each text echoes with what Toomba defines as the opening of "spatial-temporal boundaries."[35] What, in other words, arises from the differences between being "a Lady at Cape Francois" versus "An American" amid an event that unsettles the possibilities of the borders of the nation-state and traditional forms of social configuration? Each authorial marker establishes claims about the perspective of the narrative voice; yet, the later reasserts the role of the nation-state as a marker of distinction and, as such, perhaps provides the only fixed form of categorization contained within the novel.

Building upon Manganelli's observations about these inconsistencies, I want to stress that this destabilization of racial, ethnic, and national taxonomies in *Zelica* stems from more than just a generic alteration. These variations simultaneously reveal the changes in the function of Haiti in the early American imagination which occurred in the twelve years separating their publications. By 1820, when *Zelica* first appeared, Haiti had established itself as the second Republic, born from a revolution against colonial power in the Western Hemisphere.[36] While still not afforded official U.S. recognition, it had become rooted in the cultural imagination in ways that would have been impossible to predict in 1808. Still, even as Haiti remained a haunting presence, there was also some reassurance that it had not totally upended white supremacist power. The potential bridges this insurgency had made imaginable, to return to Toomba's figuration, had been contained by the fact that the Revolution had not spread across the Caribbean. Haiti, by 1820, was fast becoming an isolated and indebted nation and not a continual conduit to new forms of social belonging that were liberated from the nation-state.[37] Broadly speaking, the Caribbean still remained under European authority in 1808, and while Haiti's self-assertion of independence troubled that totality, it did not upend it. By 1820, in the wake of over a decade of self-rule, the fact that no other successful large-scale revolution against enslavement had occurred tempered perceptions about how an enduring Haiti might inspire resistance elsewhere. By 1820, in other words, Haiti remained a political singularity; thus attempts to delink it from a Caribbean archipelago inscribe a fretful hope in its continued isolation. To think of Haiti as an exceptional space was less likely in 1808 than it was in 1820; to think of it as a discrete political entity perhaps even more so. Despite its considerable length, *Zelica* possesses a much less capacious geographical imagination than *Secret History*; this reflects, arguably, the temporal difference in their composition histories and the shifting dynamics in U.S. American conceptions of what the impact of Haitian liberation would mean for circum-Atlantic futurity.

When Clara and Mary depart Cape François to escape the advancing revolutionary army, they first find their way to Barracoa and then to St. Jago in Cuba (where they are separated), eventually arriving in Kingston, Jamaica (Mary) and Bayam, Cuba (Clara), before reuniting in Jamaica and finally repatriating to Philadelphia. The Revolution in St. Domingo spills across the Caribbean basin in *Secret History*: refugees flee in almost every direction, transported on a motley flotilla of British, American, and French vessels to whatever port of call will receive them. This directionless retreat exhibits how events in Haiti carried into nearby spaces and brought with them waves of uncertainties. No such sense of proximity or affiliation shapes the depiction of Haiti in *Zelica*. In the 1820 text, the British blockade ringing the island appears impenetrable; instead of enduring a scattershot flight to whatever harbor would shield them, the survivors find themselves all ensconced aboard the same British naval vessel. Finally, no mention of any other Caribbean island, nation, colony, or space appears in this end turn—the journey undertaken by refugees in *Zelica* follows a northern trajectory toward the United States.

The temptation to collapse these two texts into an undeviating sequence stems from three intertwined factors: an overreliance on authorial biography as a critical lens, a longstanding neglect of U.S. cultural production about the Haitian Revolution, and a sustained inattention to U.S. literature published in the first two decades of the nineteenth century. Critical reactions to Sansay's *Secret History* remain driven by the first of these factors, even as the text itself becomes the singular exception to the rule of the other two. Our neglect of the larger textual horizons makes the two narratives—despite their pronounced differences—appear consanguineous even as differences abound. Critics draw a straight line between them because *Secret History* serves as *the* North Star in a blatantly unexamined firmament. To put it more bluntly, the figuration of Sansay as the author of *Zelica* serves as the simplest solution to a series of complex problems many scholars customarily circumnavigate. By liberating *Zelica* from its habitual confinement as intimately codependent with *Secret History*, the remainder of this chapter explores the later text's more complex figuration of Blackness and the intimate distance of a post-liberation colonial relation.

Caribbean Romanticisms

The epigraph at the threshold of *Zelica* foreshadows the complicated intertextual history of the novel beyond its connections to *Secret History*. Directly underneath the title, the text reproduces eight of the first nineteen lines of Lord Byron's "The Bride of Abydos" (1813).[38] Byron's poem revolves around the heartrending story of Zuleika and Selim, a pair of star-crossed lovers kept apart by an unfeeling patriarch. Zuleika's father deceives them by suggesting that they are his children by different mothers, when in fact they have no biological relationship. After Selim discovers the truth about his genealogy, he attempts to marry Zuleika but instead finds himself executed for disobedience. Overcome by sorrow, Zuleika (in a commonplace sentimental trope) quickly withers away. The poem proved so popular that William Diamond converted it into tragedy for the London stage in 1818.[39] The Philadelphia Theatre promoted a version of Diamond's play as their featured presentation on November 13, 1819. The broadside advertising the production emphasized (in enlarged print) "A Characteristic Eastern Dance" by no less than six of the company's female actors as a noteworthy attraction.[40] Understanding how the poem deployed titillating access to supposedly aberrant sexual practices, Diamond sought to capitalize on Byron's orientalism by leaning into the exotic temptations of a mythic East. The alluring dance of a coterie of women was meant to offset the pathos of watching young lovers denied the bliss of a companionate union.

The coded reference adorning *Zelica*'s opening page excises all the phrases from Byron's poem that locates it in Turkey. These careful edits transport all of Byron's site-specific allusions into a new locale in a clear effort to de-territorialize their resonances. By muting certain descriptive anchors, the sensuous tragedies of the Middle East poetically migrate to a new climate, even as the carefully sculpted lines register the interchangeability of the two spaces for an Anglo-American imagination.[41] In these spaces of cypress groves and citrus bowers, one can find both sorrow and stimulation. For some readers, the citation may have presaged the concerns of the novel, or at least the portion of it centered on Zelica's own doomed love plot. Still, even if readers did not immediately make this connection, the epigraph introduces the reader into erotic spaces where non-normative moral codes reflect the fecundity of the lush environment. Furthermore, the last reproduced couplet signals that the spirit of man alone prevents this otherwise Edenic space from being paradisiac, declaring that this is a space "Where the maidens are sweet as the roses they twine / And all, save the spirit of man, is divine" (I:1). If nothing else, the inclusion of Byron's prescient lines indicates the literariness of the text itself, accentuating how the author considers her novel as part of a larger textual conversation about the issues of free will, patriarchal authority, and struggles for self-definition. Moreover, given how the extraction from the poem concludes with an emphasis on female beauty and man's corruption, the lines also gesture toward some of the central concerns of the narrative it introduces.

The opening pages of the novel further imprint the connection between the Caribbean and the larger world by detailing that the French forces sent to reclaim St. Domingo arrive straight from Napoleon's conquests in Europe. Setting the temporality of the plot as just after "the peace of Amiens had given a momentary respite to France," the text commences by recording how by the late spring of 1802 Napoleon's armies found themselves "without employment" for the first time since the outbreak of the French Revolution (I:1–2). The narrator characterizes these soldiers as restless and perhaps posing an internal threat to Napoleon's "own recently-established empire" unless they could be otherwise occupied (I:2). The novel's second paragraph offers St. Domingo—"celebrated for its wealth, the luxurious softness of its climate, the beauty of its women, and the voluptuous manners of its inhabitants"—as the perfect solution to this potential danger (I:20). In the Caribbean, these soldiers "who had conquered Italy" could find a new "theatre" of action or "lose in its bowers of soul-dissolving delight the energy that was thought inimical to the repose of their native land" (I:20). While a turn to the "New World" might not offer any "additional glory" to what the "soldiers had already attained," the narrator maintains that "it held forth the promise of a rich harvest of gold to reward their toils in less propitious climes" (I:4). The opening sentences thus represent this campaign not as one of financial necessity for France (reeling economically after having lost St. Domingo), but rather as one that would guarantee Europe's hard-won peace by employing Napoleon's restive veterans.

The text returns to the amatory sentiments of its Byronic allusions by casting St. Domingo as "the country where the fabled delights of the Cyprian isle" can be found (I:3). The text continues its geographical obfuscation by declaring Haiti bursting with "the exhaustless treasures of the Indian mines" (3). Despite the relative scarcity of precious metals on an island, the comparison marks St. Domingo as the repository of all kinds of Euro-American fantasies about the "New World" as rife with innumerable, interchangeable, and seemingly inexhaustible resources. All these imagined pleasures and illusory riches conjoin "in the imagination of the French" to foolishly convince them that there was "no obstacle to their success" (3). In a pique of ironic hyperbole, the narrator suggests that even "the most ardent enthusiast in the cause of liberty would not have indulged the visionary thought" that the formerly enslaved inhabitants of St. Domingo, who had "broke by their own efforts the fetters of bondage," could successfully pit "their undisciplined courage" against "the bravery of well-appointed troops, accustomed to conquest" (3). Given that readers of this 1820 novel were well aware that these

French troops were destined to be repelled, the tenor of this representation recalls just how unthinkable their defeat has been to white supremacists in 1802.

These early paragraphs effectively remind readers that these troops, embarking on what will be an unsuccessful recolonization campaign, had just conquered much of continental Europe. And, as if to utterly hammer this point home, the narrator continues by reminding readers that they had "arrested the flight of the Austrian Eagle,—subdued the descendants of the Caesars,—and inscribed their claims to immortality on the imperishable Pyramids of Egypt" (I:4). Their eventual failure to reconquer their former colony, the narrator argues, results from General LeClerc and his "temporizing measures," including the opening up of an attempted "correspondence with Christophe" (1:5-6). This protracted correspondence between LeClerc and Christophe allows "the negroes...time to reflect and to form an estimate of their own force," and to recognize that their sheer numbers ("upwards of five hundred thousand men") could ward off the French incursion (I:9). While seeming to lament the lack of a quick French strike, the narrator also evinces an appreciation for those who struggled for self-emancipated. For even as the narrator notes "the wildest excesses" that had accompanied the Revolution, she still nonetheless conveys a sense of appreciation for the devotion to liberty held by the formerly enslaved people, along with the intelligence of the leaders of the anti-colonial resistance (framed in the text by fictionalized portraits of Toussaint and Christophe; I:9).

Glossing over the violence of the Revolution and the attendant "excesses shocking to humanity," the narrator notes that this initial "season of anarchy and confusion," marked by "unheard of cruelties," had passed by 1802 (I:9). Echoing the tone of *Secret History*, *Zelica* professes sympathy for how enslaved people who "had been rendered ferocious by their sufferings" could easily become "intoxicated with a desire for revenge" (I:9). Amidst all this understandable horror the narrative cautions against thinking that formerly enslaved people subscribed to unhinged violence by noting that a few had protected some planters by helping them "escape from a country where they could no longer find safety" (I:12). This carefully balanced portrait of the early revolutionary history of St. Domingo stresses what white readers likely would have expected of any account of the island's recent history. While far from taking an anti-racist position, the author does assert that the inhumane conditions in Haiti engendered the extreme resistance which determined the fate of the colony. This figuration of the brutality of French planters in pre-revolutionary Haiti serves as another instantiation of the novel's investment in thinking of this space as distinctive from the rest of the plantocracy.

The text introduces a third party who troubles the binary opposition of valiant French troops and self-emancipated, formerly enslaved people, and does so as a means of distinguishing between the various white people currently on the island. While the text does not use the term "Creole" to define either the white people who remained on the island or those who recently returned to reclaim their property, it nonetheless marks these people as distinct from "the Europeans" (I:13). It presents these "native" white people as "inhabitants" that labored to forge some new relationship with "the blacks," who at first treat them as equals until the return of the French causes them to treat these remaining white people "with suspicion" (I:14). Further complicating this otherwise totalizing sense of whiteness, the text details what it offers as the differences in Christophe and Toussaint's attitudes toward racial identities. While Toussaint orders Christophe to withdraw from Cape François, Christophe resists because he imagines holding onto the city and forcing the white settlers "to make with their bodies a rampart to oppose" the French (14). Deferring to his commander's dictates, Christophe sets fire to the city and during his retreat an abandoned powder magazine ignites causing a ravaging explosion. But the exchange between the two offers readers a glimpse into Christophe's aggressive inclinations and Toussaint's more ameliorating vision. At the same time, Christophe reveals his fixation on the symbolic potential of whiteness. Whereas the narrative presents Toussaint as invested in creating a lasting peace through *détente*, its characterization of Christophe remains charged. Indeed, immediately after his retreat Christophe muses on how Zelica's whiteness might afford him the means to further his own personal ambitions and consolidate his political power.

As he watches the city burn from a nearby mountaintop, Christophe drifts into a reverie about his ardor for the still unnamed Zelica. Christophe, the narrator informs the readers, "loved a maid—the fairest of the race that he had devoted to destruction" (I:22). The text emphasizes the intensity of Christophe's desire by noting that "whilst his imagination rioted among heaps of slain and scenes of devastation, it pointed as the reward for all his toils to some distant tranquil bower of that delicious country, where embalmed in fragrance, soothed by melody and surrounded by delight, he could devote his life to love" (I:22–3). As admixture of orientalist fantasies and representations of planter excess, Christophe's blood-soaked imagination overdoses on fantasies about whiteness and power. Yet, somehow, even in his frantic imaginings, Zelica manages to escape him as the opening chapter concludes by noting that while "he panted to obtain her, even in his dreams" she "eluded the grasp with which he sought to hold her fair and frowning image" (I:25).

The name Zelica first appears in the epigraph opening the second chapter, another edited selection from a Romantic era orientalist poem. This citation reproduces six lines from the fourth tale of Thomas Moore's 1817 *Lalla Rookh*, a volume which widely circulated in both England and the United States.[42] Indeed, Moore's work was so popular that *The North-American Review and Miscellaneous Journal* devoted the first twenty-five pages of its November 1817 issue to a charged consideration of the text.[43] The overarching plot of *Lalla Rookh* concerns a beautiful "princess of Hindostan" whose parents arrange for her to marry a prince of

Cashmere. Since she has never met him, this princess remains wary of their impending union; but her protests are ignored since her father intends for her marriage to secure certain political alliances. The poem (which the writer in *The North-American Review* continually lambasts for its "conceit and debauchery") explores how a humble poet offers to entertain the princess during her journey to her future husband.[44] Along the way, this poet dazzles her with tales of oriental romances that feature women who find themselves on the cusp of unwelcome marriages. By the end of the text, Moore reveals the poet as none other than bridegroom prince of Cashmere, and, of course, by this time the princess has fallen for him ensuring that their marriage will not be loveless.

The source for several operatic and theatrical adaptations, the plot of *Lalla Rookh* may well have been familiar to many of *Zelica*'s readers. At the very least, this second epigraph further advances the author's strategy of embedding this Caribbean tale within an Anglo-American orientalist imaginary. Or again, this second epigraph roots orientalist fantasies about exotic, imperiled women in the French colonial world, a transplantation which underscores the function of St. Domingo in the American imagination. The citation of Moore's work, in other words, locates the novel within a slipstream of Romanticist tropes about sensuous racial others. Moreover, it positions revolutionary Haiti as akin to the destabilized and morally ambiguous fantasy space half a world away (though with a more complex figuration of whiteness and people of color than British Romantic poetry typically registered). Such a redirecting of desire serves as an introduction to *Zelica*, a remapping that revises the slightly more factual figuration on offer in the *Secret History*.

The description of Zelica that appears soon after the second epigraph further situates her within Romantic frameworks by describing her "large black eyes" (defined by their "melting languor") and her "gracefully indolent movements" (I:46). Carefully walking the (color) line between framing her as an exotic other and detailing her European education and manners, the narrative casts Zelica as "a perfect enchantress" (I:47). Almost instantaneously, her physical beauty bewitches all the white men around, who are further aroused by her seeming "wholly insensible" to their "flattery or gallantry" (I:47). Later in this same chapter, St. Louis (a white "native of St. Domingo") and Belmont (a Frenchman) impenitently discuss Zelica's beauty and confess their mutual desire to seduce her (I:55). During the conversation, Belmont describes her as combining "the beauty of the houris with all the graces only to be acquired in Paris, and the irresistible languor created by this voluptuous climate" (I:55). Belmont casts Zelica as an amalgamation of long-eighteenth-century misogynistic and racialized stereotypes, freely associating her with paradisiacal virgins, Parisian coquettes, and a luxurious ennui racistly projected onto mixed-race women in the Caribbean. For Belmont, Zelica is "an enchantress whose slightest motion enslaves," raising the specter of unfreedom and linking it to her via the typical exploitative tropes of the seduction genre (1:55).[45] In short, Belmont fixates on Zelica as representing the culmination of a variety of geographically distinct acquisitive desires.

This delicate shadowing of Zelica's biography contrasts with the text's presentation of her ally and foil (in terms of competing problematic registers of femininity), Clara, the American wife of the Creole St. Louis. In apposition with the vivid depiction of Zelica's physical appearance, the narrative describes Clara as "an elegantly-formed female, closely wrapped in a large veil," presumably to shield her from the sun and heat, but which also affords her a certain modesty (I:28). Aside from this brief introductory notation, and a description of her husband and the circumstances by which the pair find themselves prisoners of the diasporic African General Glaude, the narrative fixates on Clara's national origins in defining her. The text advances the idea that her Americanness was "for her a fortunate circumstance," since "though all white people of French origin were treated with insolent severity by the blacks, they felt great respect for the Anglo-Americans, from whose country they had caught the glorious flame of liberty, and from which they probably expected assistance" (I:30–1). Clara's Americanness, then, offers her a buffer against prejudicial treatment and registers how nationality might matter more for the formerly enslaved people of St. Domingo than color in terms of defining their attitudes toward foreign white people.

Optimistically casting the United States as "at once their model and their hope," the text fabricates alliances between emergent Republics when there were in fact (certainly by 1820) few mutually held reciprocities (1:30). This narrative thread further complicates whiteness along national lines by suggesting that the self-emancipated diasporic Africans of St. Domingo held some kinship with Americans (despite the continued participation of the United States in systems of enslavement) because of their mutual commitments to liberty. More importantly, Clara's natal origins afford her license within the text, not only in terms of how the revolutionaries themselves treat her, but also by how the narrative itself refrains from focusing simply on her physical appearance in positioning her for readers. Her citizenship, in this regard, serves as another covering to protect her pale skin from the harsh tropical climate, the rapacious sexual appetites of the local population, and the voyeurism of expectant readers.

The narrative figures self-emancipated diasporic Africans as cathecting to the United States and rejecting further association with France. These revolutionaries look to America for a potential alliance, while envisioning France as having abandoned the most capacious definitions of *liberté*, *égalité*, and *fraternité* circulating in the earliest days of the French Revolution.[46] For Christophe, the French have descended into a kind of "madness," marked by a profound "inconsistency," in the wake of "having raised the banners of liberty in France on the altar and the throne they had overturned" (1:25). Despite having achieved this freedom, the French have subsequently "become in their own land the slaves of a stranger, and crouched beneath the throne of a despot" (I:25). Declaring his countrymen as capable of resisting the despotic Napoleon's unquenchable thirst for "power," Christophe holds out "hope" that the Haitians will retain their revolutionary principals and avoid a resurgence of despotism (I:25). Within the novel, France no longer represents a conjoined sister rebellion, but a counterformation to Haitian liberation. In essence, Christophe maintains that the shared political ideologies of New World Republics should prove more powerful than the shared white supremacy of the French and the Americans. Such a distinction offers an overly optimistic prospect for what was a largely non-existent political solidarity. Yet, it also has the effect within the text of placing Clara in a unique position since her American citizenship affords her the respect of all those around her. Clara's Americaness allows her to intercede on Zelica's behalf and offer her some protection at the beginning of the text, an act that forms their quasi-sororal alliance.[47]

The novel devotes significant attention to twinning Zelica and Clara. Even as most of the white French and Creole men in the text fantasize about them (although in different registers of familiarity), both Zelica and Clara become symbolic love objects for diasporic African military officers who presume that a potential union with whiteness will secure them unrivaled power. Unlike the third most prominent woman in the early portions of the text, French Creole Madame Senat, Clara and Zelica both maintain orthodox conceptions of marriage. The widow of a planter murdered "at the commencement of the revolution," Madame Senat has remained in Clara's social circle because of her brazen affair with Clara's husband (1:34). As such, even if Clara and Zelica maintain a more progressive hope for companionate marriages, their shared moral conceptions of sexuality (as defined by religiously sanctioned heteronormative coupling) link them. This sense of kinship unites them, but it also places them in the same besieged situation vis-à-vis a range of predatory men. Different facets of their identities do offer some protection: Clara's American identity affords her special recognition and Zelica's mixed-race status and her father's brokered promise of engagement to Christophe allows her to transgress the unsettled political boundaries of the novel.

Deprived of any capacity to impact the social and political struggles unfolding around them except in minor ways, the two women bond over their shared superior moral and intellectual characters. As Clara discovers her husband's infidelities, the two women also share a similar predicament in that they are in (or about to be forced into) ill-suited marriages. Sensing that they occupy similar positions, they each move to protect and assist the other, even as they strive to improve the conditions of yet others (especially women) around them. Since everyone aside from Clara in the text understands (with the readers) that Zelica is mixed race, Clara is at times at variance with them, having a different sense than everyone else around them of the potential kinship ties between herself and Zelica. Clara reads racial categories as being starkly defined and thus fails to imagine Zelica, who largely passes as white, as anything other than what her pigmentation suggests.[48]

Clara's blindness to the realities around her marks one of the key dividing lines between the two women. This tension surfaces most clearly in the novel's Blackface episode, in which Clara's inability to read the complexities of racial taxonomies is readily apparent. When Zelica proposes to Clara that they adopt Blackface to evade detection as they attempt to escape the revolutionaries, Clara initially cannot fathom how they can successfully pretend to be Black. Indeed, it is during this episode that Clara discovers Zelica's mixed-racial heritage. This unexpected revelation forces Clara to rethink her assumptions about whiteness, Blackness, and the imagined stability of the color line. The narrative casts Clara's naïveté as a reflection of her upbringing in Philadelphia, intimating that those more habituated to the horrors of enslavement have a more nuanced understanding of racial taxonomies.

For many of those around her, Clara's U.S. Americanness equates her with an overarching commitment to liberty and personal freedom. By contrast, Zelica understands the complexities of both Caribbean and European racial taxonomies while possessing a keener awareness of what the Revolution in St. Domingo means for circum-Atlantic social relations. Zelica's desire not to further connect herself to Christophe arises not simply from her affection for her French fiancée, but also from a strong inclination to distance herself from Blackness. Indeed, part of her attachment to Clara may well spring from Clara's inability to read Zelica's hybridity. Most of the other characters, including Christophe (who yearns for Zelica in order to instantiate his own power) or St. Louis and Belmont (enflamed by white supremacist fantasies about the hypersexuality of women of color), seek to capitalize on Zelica's biracial vulnerability. In contrast, since Clara remains ignorant of Zelica's heritage she assumes that they are equally beset white women. Given how Clara serves as proxy for a U.S. perspective, she reflects an American adherence to an imagined stabilizing color line and blind to any uncertainties within this bifurcation.

Across the novel, the narrator carefully defines the relationship between Clara and Zelica as informed by their reciprocal recognition of their susceptibilities to patriarchal abuses. In this regard, the text explores the possibilities for sororal kinship (or sororal friendship) to afford women a means of navigating (and to a degree resisting) the dangers of misogyny. For Clara, their individual and collective attempts at subverting the operant power structures around them stems from their mutual position as "white" women. Yet, as Marlene Daut persuasively argues, this sense of whiteness as a counterformation to political instability serves as another form of Clara's blindness, since (as Daut argues) "Zelica's powers of protection and Clara's attempts at resistance are only bolstered at every turn by the color black itself."[49] In showing how Clara's ignorance of racial taxonomies reveals another dimension of her inability to fully comprehend sororal solidarity, Daut convincingly notes that the novel's presentation of Blackface, which includes Zelica very performatively darkening herself, as a means of transgression also works to make "more apparent the 'delicacy' and 'fragility' of 'white' female status in Saint-Domingue."[50] To this argument, I would add that Clara's Americanness remains inseparable from her white womanhood. Building on the logic of Daut's insights, Clara's subject position (even though she fails to see it) remains buttressed by Blackness itself in that her (white) nationality affords her a position of largely unchecked privilege. As such, the various interplays of citizenship, rights, and possibility charted to this point reveal the fragility and delicacy of Clara's American identity.

Zelica's hybridity, and its centrality within the novel, marks the greatest thematic difference between *Zelica* and Sansay's *Secret History*. Zelica's Blackness, or her access to Blackness, reorients Clara from the biological sororal relationship that defines the narrative concerns of her relationship with Mary in *Secret History*. By featuring non-biological kinship, *Zelica* presents a nuanced rethinking of the relationship between whiteness, Americanness, and womanhood. The color line, as presented in 1808, remains hard and fast, perhaps unbreachable, and while the earlier text does invest in thinking about the differences (in moral character and behavior) of various forms of European whiteness, it never broaches (aside from some tragic asides about mixed-race women) the idea of passing as a tangible possibility. In the 1808 text Clara's, or anyone else's for that matter, whiteness never becomes destabilized. However, by aligning Clara's whiteness with her Americanness in *Zelica*, the later narrative ponders how hybridity—embodied in a figure like Zelica who routinely passes across a suddenly very porous divide—potentially undermines the solidity of any identifying markers. The attachment that all the Black revolutionaries have for Americanness (as a symbol of Republican brotherhood) further extends this narrative element. All of the featured revolutionaries defer to Clara's citizenship because of the causal relationship they imagine between the two nations and their supposedly inherent commitments to liberty. Still, while Zelica never attempts to pass as an American, her proximity to Clara raises the question of just what constitutes an American.

On the surface, Clara's national identity provides her certain protections. At the same time, the text reveals how these benefits depend on Blackness to recognize and permit these distinctions over and against other forms of whiteness. Without that recognition, Clara's citizenship stands as fragile and abstract. If not for her American whiteness, Clara would simply be yet another dispossessed planter's wife adrift on an island that has no use for her. Therefore, while Clara can cling to her white American womanhood as if it were an anchor, the entirety of the text records this as a gossamer fantasy. This reversal in the seeming stability of the American citizenship opens up the possibility that national identity itself has become unmoored. Since Zelica proves capable of traversing the supposed solidity of the color line, her nuanced mutability opens up the possibility that she might cross over the supposedly fast boundaries of nationalities. Given how she both claims and disclaims herself to be French and a native of St. Domingo, she has already embraced fluidity in ways that few other figures in the narrative appear capable of replicating. This shift in figuring the porosity of U.S. borders, their susceptibility to possible invisible incursion, reflects how *Zelica* moves from thinking about the Haitian Revolution as a Caribbean flashpoint (as Sansay did in 1808) to stressing that it was an event with potentially hemispheric implications but operating on a different, more personalized scale. The ways in which the Revolution could, to return to Toomba's terms, shape "a constellation whose spatial-temporal boundaries" might "exceed nationality" becomes reflected in how Clara and Zelica are figured as conjoined victims of patriarchal abuse despite their differences in heritage and citizenship.[51] These divergent issues all come to a head in the final scenes of the novel, wherein the novel's exploration of citizenship and identity transforms into a deeper interrogation of the relationship between race and nation.

Ambiguous Migrations

Staged during the final French retreat, the climax of *Zelica* unfolds on a craggy ridge on the outskirts of Cape François. The drama arises from the desperate attempt by Zelica and her father De la Riviere to guide Clara to a British vessel waiting to transport her to the United States; Clara's husband, already onboard the same British ship, anxiously paces its deck anticipating her arrival. Amid this fraught indecipherability, the narrative moves to rescript its exploration of the distinctions between race and citizenship. The end turn makes it clear that the self-emancipated, diasporic Africans have successfully resisted reenslavement. As a result of this realization of impending defeat, the differences between Frenchness, Britishness, white Creoleness, and Americanness dissipate as all of the various white figures join forces to escape the island. No longer motivated by their various contrasting agendas, these various white ethnicities now work together in spite of their former differences. Clara and Zelica remain, pursued by the diasporic African officers who have sought to force them into marriage, and this fervent pursuit fills the final section with an ominous foreboding.

As Clara, Zelica, and De la Riviere arrive near the rendezvous point, General Glaude suddenly leaps from the shadows in a final attempt to kidnap Clara. In his pursuit, Glaude has become monomaniacal in his obsession with how Clara's white Americaness could consolidate his future standing in the new Haitian society due to emerge after the defeat of the French. On the cusp of her safe egress from the island, Glaude finally catches up with Clara and triggers a jumble of confused, rapid action. Without warning, a disembodied "voice of thunder" cries out, "Traitor!" and the scene dissolves into chaos as indistinguishable combatants' frantically lunge at one another (III:290). Leaping from out the darkness, Glaude "plunged a sword into the heart of De la Riviere." In turn, the confused De la

Riviere "buried his dagger in the breast" of an obscured figure off to his side (III:291). The sudden arrival of "a thousand torches" seen to be "descending among the rocks" grinds the action to a halt (III:292).

What proves to be a mysterious procession of diasporic Africans is conducted by an "enchantress" bearing a "magical image in one hand" and "an enormous torch of resinous wood in the other" (III:292). The intimidating column quickly forms a ring around the lifeless combatants, and Madeleine, a formerly enslaved woman who has remained loyal to St. Louis and his family, steps out, having fashioned this obeah fetish in a religious ceremony in the woods. Her followers bring "a blaze of light over the wild scene," and in a prevision of poetic justice, the lambent glow of the assemblage of torches illuminates "the lovely corpse of Clara— lovely even in death" (III:292). Instead of wounding Glaude, De la Riviere has mistakenly stabbed "the heart of Clara" with such violence that she "expired without a groan" (III:293). As the throngs of torchbearers reverently guard Clara's body, Glaude retreats into the darkness from which he had emerged. Momentarily stunned by the rapid action, Zelica mutely gazes at the motionless bodies of her father and her quasi-sister before melodramatically uttering "one wild heartbroken shriek," extending "her arms to heaven" and plunging off the cliff "into the waves" in a suicide attempt (III:293). As "the short but splendid dawn of a tropical sky" begins to irradiate "the horizon," Madeleine directs her followers to "fantastically" adorn Clara's corpse with "flowers like a bride bound by her companions in sportiveness with fragrant fetters—not like a victim destined to the grave" (III:294). Silently laboring to create a "rustic bier," strewn "with flowers," out of "a net-work of strong flexible twigs," Madeleine orders Clara's body elevated from the ground and shielded from "insects" by the continuous fanning of "flowery branches" (III:294). Confident her directions will be followed, Madeleine leaves the torchbearers as a solemn cortege while she returns to Cape François to find a priest "to read the service of the dead" for her "murdered mistress" (III:295). No one moves to afford De la Riviere the same ceremonious care nor do they attempt to discover what has happened to Zelica; rather, the 1,000 assembled bodies all appear galvanized by Clara's flower-strewn corpse.

Instead of preparing for three funerals, Madeleine appears absorbed in preparing an ecumenical wedding. While Madeleine's motives emanate from her deep affection for "her mistress," her reactions to the presumptive deaths of the two other figures is telling (III:295). This solitary focus reifies Clara's purity and legibility against the more troubling legacies of De la Riviere and Zelica. If Zelica personifies tragedy within the text, then her father embodies mystery. About midway through the three volumes, readers learn that De la Riviere had been a wealthy French plantocrat who had abandoned his property because of his commitment to the revolutionary cause. His pronounced sympathetic identification with the rights of diasporic Africans convinces him to undergo a "chemical preparation" to become (seemingly permanently) phenotypically Black (III:201).

Whether his desire to overwrite his white skin is an attempt to atone for his sins as an enslaver, or whether he imagines that Blackness is essential to freedom remains ambiguous. Yet De la Riviere's sense that whiteness needs to be removed from the island if it is to become truly free may well serve as a precondition for his commitment to altering his own appearance. In a final effort to concretize his devotion to Christophe (the diasporic African general in charge of the revolutionary army), De la Riviere—despite his daughter's pronounced objections—promises him Zelica's hand in marriage. For De la Riviere, this engagement serves as the best means of demonstrating to Christophe "the good faith of white men" (III:288).

Zelica remains defined against an array of Black and Blackfaced masculinities. Even after he meets Lastour, the French solider that Zelica had fallen in love with prior to her return to St. Domingo, De la Riviere persists in demanding that she acquiesce to his wishes because he has "pledged to support" the "cause of freedom" with "all the powers of his soul" (III:288). His daughter's devotion to Clara and Lastour drive De la Riviere to try and secret them from the island; yet he does so in the hopes that once they are removed he will be able to fully commit his entire family (and his posterity) to the revolutionary cause. In the face of her father's unbending radicalism, Zelica suppresses her own desires and submits to his patriarchal precepts. In a sense, Zelica functions as a mediator between competing conceptions of freedom, striving to insure that Clara remains unsullied by the revolutionary upheaval, even as she simultaneously resigns herself to becoming a pawn in her father's machinations. Zelica's failure to protect Clara leads to her suicidal leap, and this reaction implies that Zelica has embraced the sacrifice her father demanded only in so far as it can insure Clara's futurity.

Readers soon discover that Zelica has not perished, as a British longboat fishes her "apparently lifeless" body out of the crashing surf (III:302). Her rescuers reunite her with Lastour who is already aboard their British naval vessel (III:302). While she has survived her suicidal leap, Zelica remains senseless in the wake of Clara's murder as the shock has robbed her of her sanity. Unlike all of the other figures close to her, Zelica outlives the upheaval of the revolutionary struggle on the island. Despite the text's titular focus on Zelica, the novel's primary victims of revolutionary violence in St. Domingo are Clara and De la Riviere. Crucially, these two deaths rupture the primary tenets of the novel. Despite the polytonal faith previously attached to the immutability of the color line or the protective benefits of U.S. citizenship, the identities of the departed evacuate them of any coherence. Across the novel a vast array of characters maintain that U.S. citizenship—the envy of the French, the Creole, and the diasporic Africans alike—guarantees its bearer immunity from the dangers of colonial and revolutionary violence.[52] Yet the most prominent American in the novel, Clara, never departs the island. Her final resting place becomes a flowery bower constructed and guarded by a Catholic priest and a Vondou priestess, who orchestrate its construction as a shrine to freedom. Far from providing Clara with a passport out of revolutionary turmoil, her American citizenship only insures her recognition as a martyr. In sum, Clara's tomb effectively becomes a reliquary in the wilds outside Cape François.

Another maxim suffusing the text asserts the impassability of the color line. Just as the climactic struggle cancels Clara's supposed invulnerability, De la Riviere's Blackened corpse similarly unsettles any presumptive faith in the stability of systems of phenotypical classification. In a sense, his altered epidermis mimics the inconstancy of the French pervading the opening paragraphs of the novel by literally blurring the boundaries between French citizens and diasporic Africans. De la Riviere's corporeal modification evinces the novel's early fixation on the inconstancy of the French, of their willingness to compromise their own freedoms and become enslaved to another master (Napoleon) after they have broken the yoke of aristocratic control. Given how De la Riviere willingly upends his own subject position—by forsaking his ill-gotten wealth and joining Christophe's inner circle of advisors—he transforms himself into an incarnation of radicalism. Moreover, he manifests this attachment to revolutionary ideology through his co-option of literal Blackness. He undergoes the chemical preparation to embody (on a visual level) his commitment to Christophe's aim of erasing whiteness from the island. His attempts to control who his daughter marries implicitly manifests his desire to wed her to Blackness, to fix the futurity of his lineage to Blackness in the same way he has permanently transformed his own skin.

While repulsed by her father's proposed arrangement, Zelica trades on Christophe's desires when she identifies herself as his intended to claim the authority to advocate for Clara. Despite her heritage, or perhaps because of it, Zelica cannot fully comprehend interracial solidarity or full equality for people of color. While she feels the pressure of filial duty, she resists this obligation as long as she can. At the beginning of the text, in part because of De la Riviere Blackwashing, she believes her father has died and quietly embraces how his passing has extracted her from an unwanted engagement. After she discovers her father's chemical masquerade, she reluctantly adheres to his dictates to save Clara. In some ways, Zelica's narrative trajectory mirrors the conventional concerns normally associated with the tragic mulatto figure (someone both part and not part of two socially distinct worlds).[53] Yet, because she represents a certain transnational mobility, Zelica firmly believes that she can disassociate herself from her natal home to pursue a life elsewhere. Apparently capable of passing (depending on geographical location), Zelica embraces this fluidity as an avenue to freedom even if the novel seems uncomfortable with that potential trajectory.

The fact that Zelica becomes speechless after her suicidal shriek accelerates this disquietude, as if her undecipherable fever has affected her capacity to define herself. To put it another way, if Clara and De la Riviere remain entombed by certain posthumous interpretations of them, then Zelica's survival means she persists as the solitary figure of illegibility. The passing of the two figures that plotted Zelica through a relational positioning turns her into an abandoned star in search of a new constellation. Previously, she had been caught up in her father's attempts to trade on her Blackness to authenticate his own passing and in Clara's utter failure to recognize her mixed-racial heritage. During this period, Zelica navigated this fluidity through the power of speech. Robbed of her voice, Zelica now mutely resides at the mercy of external examiners and whatever calculus of contingency they deploy to fix her identity.[54]

This transformation of Zelica into a voiceless cipher begins shortly after sailors' pull her from the ocean. Unbelievably, Lastour does not recognize her even though he was on board the longboat that rescued her. He explains his oversight as caused by the fact that "her face was quite concealed by her hair, and [his] agitation" over present dangers which had "deprived" him "of all presence of mind" (III:303). Lastour's confusion matches that of St. Louis, who believes the recovered woman might be Clara. These misapprehensions read as deeply contrived, a metafictional disruption that totally blurs the identities of the two women to emphasize the complexity of Zelica's own position (especially given that readers are already aware of Clara's fate). As if to further stress Zelica's newfound ambiguity, the ship's doctor informs the two apprehensive men that "there were strong symptoms of incipient fever in the patient;" and again Zelica's life appears to hang by a narrative thread (III:304).

Lastour languishes outside her sick room, "alternatively elevated by hope and depressed by fear," while the narrative focuses on St. Louis's despair over Clara's fate (III:304). Still believing his wife alive, St. Louis attempts to convince the ship's captain to return to Cape François. His pleas are countered with the reminder that as "an American lady," Clara "can be in no danger; they will not dare to offer her any harm" (III:304). Finally, "on the morning of the third day," St. Louis learns that his wife has died and that her American citizenship has not offered her any security.[55] The allusion to a temporality of resurrection calls forth the Christian miraculous, but perhaps only to underscore that no divine intervention would be forthcoming. Despite all the ministrations of the "priest" and the "enchantress," Clara and the sanctity of her American citizenship have transitioned into a new symbolic realm. Whatever Clara's unimpeachable Americanness signified remains entombed in Haiti, while whatever Zelica's indecipherable hybridity embodies now migrates northward in its stead.

Instead of defining Americanness as a buffer against revolutionary uncertainties, the novel stresses the susceptibility of American bodies—and its body politic—to these foreign contagions. Plagued by her histories and her circumstances, and pushed forward by contending circum-Atlantic tides, Zelica functions as a floating signifier: an infected mystery in motion, a contagious personification of circum-Atlantic relations. The text concludes in this liminal oceanic space, pregnant with anticipation and on the brink of arrival. We leave Zelica—an amalgamation of revolutionary Black Atlantic signifiers—in a chrysalis stage without any indication of what will emerge from her febrile cocoon. The text mentions her "soft voice" comforting St. Louis when he falls into a melancholy coma after learning of Clara's passing, but readers can no longer hear her voice. Zelica's soft tones have effectively become untranscribable background noise, capable of propping up damaged white masculinity but seemingly capable of little else. This apparent loss of translatability foreshadows the uncertainty of how to classify Zelica upon her arrival in the United States. While St. Domingo might have been a space wherein identity could fluctuate, no such mutability would exist for the taxonomizing eyes of U.S. customs authorities. These border agents would hermeneutically fix Zelica's legal identity at her point of entry. The issue would be a matter of local jurisprudence, meaning that Zelica's freedom might entirely depend on whatever port the British vessel drifts into. Would she be fixed as French? Would she be accepted as a free woman of color? Would she be classified as the property of Lastour? Of St. Louis? Of the ship's captain? Would she ever speak again?

Toward the conclusion of the first volume, in a fit of pique at the instability of the situation she found herself in, Clara had decried, "everything in this country is false—everything delusive" (I:200). This outburst revealed Clara's inability to properly distinguish between truth and masquerade. Yet, given the ways in which St. Domingo's ethnoscape figures as being composed of peoples from elsewhere, a reader would be hard-pressed to find evidence that any other national space was less complex. Indeed, Clara's own personal history suggests that she was deluded into thinking St. Louis capable of a companionate relationship, and his incessant philandering utterly destroys their marriage. This plot point reveals that false-hoods are equally at home in the United States or might be brought there by the arrival of foreigners. So while it might be tempting to read Clara's declarations about falsity as geographically rooted, it would be foolish to embrace her territorial exceptionalism as meaningful in a world predicated on seemingly endless mobility.

A desensitized voyeuristic quality suffuses *Zelica*, percolating as a tendency to eroticize mixed-race women and to blur revolutionary political desires with sexual ones. Yet, such embodiments of socio-political forces beat at the heart of the emerging early-nineteenth-century genre of the historical novel in English. While the Caribbean setting, and the gestures toward mythic Orientalized pleasures, allow for a charged eroticism absent in the work of Sir Walter Scott or James Fennimore Cooper, at the core of the text nonetheless reside questions about nation formation and futurity. Central to this uncertainty remains a recursive questioning of the relationship between Haiti and the United States. From the novel's opening pages through Clara's enshrinement as a martyr, the function of the United States as a potential sibling Republic stands clear. Yet the function of Haiti for the United States remains notably obscure: perhaps rendered even more cryptic because it depends on the now-muted Zelica for definition. Will other Americans be as unable as Clara to read Zelica's hybridity? How will her father's death affect her sense obligation moving forward? Has she finally been struck by revolutionary fever after having been immune to it for so long? Has she decisively escaped the instability that has plagued her since the opening of the novel? Or, does she still carry these unsettling incipient fevers with her to the United States?

5

"UNIVERSAL EMANCIPATION!"

New York's Print Public Sphere and the Haunting Legacies of the Black Atlantic

On July 4, 1799, New York State enacted a Gradual Emancipation Act that freed enslaved children born after that date; yet this liberation only came into effect after a lengthy period of continued exploitation.[1] The legislation called for the daughters of enslaved mothers to be freed after the age of 25, while sons of enslaved mothers continued in bondage till their 28th birthday. In essence, the Emancipation Act encoded the idea of compensation for enslavers as a necessary precondition for abolition. Despite these remunerative measures, state-wide debates about emancipation engendered an increased animosity toward African Americans in the region. As Leslie Harris argues, coterminous with the passage of the legislation was an increase in attempts by "various groups of whites" to "limit free blacks' access to political, social, and economic equality."[2] Just as elite New Yorkers feared the consequences of lost revenues from curtailed exploitation, working-class white people were anxious about increased competition for low wage jobs. Both groups were nervous about the ability of formerly enslaved people to, as Harris suggests, "live as equals in a republican society."[3] In many ways, the law was a temporary solution to a structural problem. Providing no future provisions for enslaved people born prior to July of 1799, the legislation also failed to help newly emancipated people transition into their slowly gained new legal status. In particular, the legislation did not provide emancipated people any recompense for their decades of forced servitude.

Realizing that the 1799 legislation had failed to solve anything, New York State acted again in 1817 when it granted deferred freedom to all enslaved people in the state regardless of their birthdate. Like its predecessor this second Act also carried delaying provisions, since it did not take effect until July of 1827.[4] Moreover, it similarly failed to address what Harris terms the prevalent "ambivalent feelings about the free black urban presence."[5] Apprehensions about integrating formerly enslaved people into the political, social, and economic fabric of the city festered in the wake of this second legislation, leading to increased discrimination and the adoption of additional methods of racialized policing. Adding to these apprehensions was Manhattan's centrality in the wider national and international trading system that remained predicated on the exploitation of enslaved workers. The docks of New York remained crowded with evidence of the structuring power of

The Haitian Revolution in the Early Republic of Letters: Incipient Fevers. Duncan Faherty, Oxford University Press.
© Duncan Faherty 2023. DOI: 10.1093/oso/9780192889157.003.0006

enslavement, as countless shipping manifests registered the city's entanglement in trade networks built on the continuing horrors of Black Atlantic capitalism. Many of the commodities daily unloaded along the city's waterfront were the byprod-ucts of the global plantation system, and some of these vessels undoubtedly counted enslaved peoples among their crews.

Given the evidence all around them, it was likely difficult for New Yorkers to imagine that their localized solution could successfully quarantine the region from the instabilities that enslavement produced elsewhere. Indeed, New York's newspapers teemed with rumors about insurrections of enslaved people across the globe almost as soon as that information reached the city's pressman. As fret-ful as white New Yorkers may have been about the assimilation of formerly enslaved people into a republican order—defined as it was by whiteness—the knowledge that diasporic Africans elsewhere were actively seeking liberation only exacerbated local unease. Gradual emancipation, in other words, hardly amelio-rated concerns that racial insurrection could return to Manhattan; indeed this dread of domestic uprisings remained a prevalent fear across the second decade of the nineteenth century.[6] Like every other major city in the United States, when news of a domestic insurrection broke, New Yorkers were quick to seize on reports of possible connections to the legacies of the Haitian Revolution. Endlessly swimming alongside any report of Black resistance was always some insinuation about the presence of a Black Jacobin influence. One such instance of these unsubstantiated rumors occurred in the aftermath of the second Emancipation Act, a moment when the horizons of localized manumission were just beginning to be legible even as they remained a deferred actuality.

Reports of a suppressed rebellion in Georgia first reached Manhattan on May 19, 1819, when the *New-York Daily Advertiser* printed a brief notice in the middle of the third column on its second page:

Insurrection in the South.—A friend has favored us with an extract of a letter from Augusta, Georgia; from which it appears that a plot against the white inhabitants, which was to have been extensive in its operation, has been happily defeated. We are informed that the writer of the letter is a gentleman of the first respectability: — "AUGUSTA," May 6th, 1819.

"A plot of insurrection of the blacks of this place and surrounding country, as well digested as that of St. Domingo, and which was to have been executed on Saturday week last, but for providential interference, was yesterday fortunately discovered, and many of the ringleaders are now committed for trial, who will probably soon meet the sentence which awaits them."

While the article contains just a single vivid sentence from the unnamed observer's open letter, the editors of the *Daily Advertiser* nevertheless framed it as a prelude to a sensational drama. Even as the citation concludes with mention of a sham trial—given the predetermined death sentence—the notice plots an expansive geography in the juxtaposition of the "fortunate discovery" with the notation of an uprising "as well digested as that of St. Domingo." This reference to a successful struggle for emancipation complicates the surety of resolution the piece attempts to communicate. The conciliatory work of "providential interference," in short, resides uncomfortably alongside the terrifying potentially massive scale of this aborted rebellion.[7]

These scant eighteen lines of type include an alarming array of unsettling details. In marking the suppressed event as "extensive in its operation," and suggesting that "many" (and therefore not all) of "the ringleaders" had been apprehended, the article does not entirely foreclose this unnerving "plot against the white inhabitants" of Georgia. Central to this disquietude was the idea that Augusta had only narrowly avoided becoming an American Cape François. Even fifteen years after the end of the Haitian Revolution, the specter of a formerly opulent trading center that had been burned to the ground still haunted the American print public sphere. Coupled with this ghostly image of a smoldering city was the knowledge of how a free Black population had been central in planning the Haitian Revolution. Fears about diasporic African solidarity, above any connections brought about by citizenship or geographical location, were part and parcel of the apprehensions about integration. Indeed, even the briefest mention of St. Domingo in this report likely triggered New Yorkers' never actually dormant concerns about Haiti liberation.

The *New-York Gazette & General Advertiser* carried an even shorter notice on the same Wednesday as the *Daily Advertiser*'s initial account, and by Friday of the same week expanded reports surfaced in several other papers including the *New-York Spectator*, the *Mercantile Advertiser*, *The New-York Evening Post*, the *Commercial Advertiser*, and *The New-York Columbian*.[8] According to the *Commercial Advertiser* and *The New-York Columbian* (likely both using the same issue (May 10, 1819) of the *Augusta Chronicle* as their source), one of the suspected leaders of the failed insurrection (an enslaved man "named Coco") had been "an active brigand in the insurrection and massacre at St. Domingo in the year '93."[9] More details emerged in various other newspapers concerning Coco's ambitious plans to distract the white inhabitants of Augusta by setting fire to various buildings and preventing their escape by cutting down the town's bridge and unmooring all the boats in the harbor.[10]

Additional particulars soon arrived in Manhattan, like those printed in *The New-York Evening Post*, which hyperbolically suggested that Coco had reached an alliance with "a body of negroes in Edgefield, South Carolina" (roughly 26 miles north of Augusta) and with "some in the swamp, who were provided with arms."[11] Submerged in this reference to a maroon community in the outskirts of Augusta was another dimension of the fear about a "free" Black population that occupied para-social communities within otherwise white controlled districts. The article further speculates that Coco planned to take "possession of the shipping at Savannah" and to retreat to the "Spanish dominions," "Florida," or "St. Domingo" if the uprising proved incapable of taking the town.[12] Given that only five enslaved men had apparently been arrested, all of the additional details about the scale of the supposed conspiracy must have been alarming. These concerns could only have been exacerbated by the idea that Coco—a supposed veteran of the earliest days of the Haitian Revolution—had been living in Georgia for some time, presumably awaiting an opportunity to spark a domestic rebellion. While some readers may well have taken comfort in an averted crisis, for others, the coverage of the suppressed rebellion assuredly raised concerns about how many more Cocos (and how many more potential maroon allies) were already within the United States. How had this band of insurgents managed to collectivize and form such elaborate plans? Permeating the framing of the narrative resides a conjunction between Blackness and internationalism, a linkage that counters the unarticulated notion of whiteness and U.S. citizenship that remained an ongoing concern for New Yorkers amid the glacial unfolding of gradual emancipation. Or, to put it another way, white American concerns about the impossibility of free Black people fully integrating into American society were always animated by the unspoken notion that Americanness equaled whiteness.

As historians such as Alfred Hunt, David Patrick Geggus, and Douglas Egerton have argued, few accounts of uprisings of enslaved people in the United States in the nineteenth century failed to surface rumors of a connection to the Haitian Revolution.[13] The ways in which rampant paranoia about the Haitian Revolution percolated through all these accounts of domestic rebellions not only demonstrates how the legacies of Haiti self-emancipation shaped the American imagination, but it also reveals how fervently Americans tried to suppress the idea that resistance to enslavement was never a home grown problem. The need to attribute insurrection to foreign influences registers how many Americans believed that the conditions of enslavement within the United States were not deplorable enough to warrant resistance. If the cause of this unsettlement could be diagnosed as an external threat, than the possibility of finding some way to ban its importation could conceivably prevent future uprisings. Such a familiar pattern of distancing expressed a recursive desire to transform insurrection into a problems of geography and foreign brutality rather than admitting that it was a response to the structuring violences inherent in Black Atlantic racial capitalism itself.

Fantasies about Haiti as rebellious revenant were reanimated whenever a domestic upheaval required explanation. As a result, no explanation for how Coco arrived in the United States after his supposed participation in the 1793 uprising (over a quarter of a century before he supposedly planned a wide-scale rebellion in Georgia) was ever produced.[14] Indeed, specific details were not necessary to cast him into the preordained role of needing-to-be-executed Haitian villain. Somehow, his decades old involvement in an external rebellion fully explained his radicalism. As Hunt and Geggus both assert, this operant fantasy about Haiti as "the foremost model of black autonomy" was always already on hand in the American cultural imagination to inflect troubling events.[15] Central to this model was a belief in how the Haitian Revolution had sparked a revolutionary internationalism among diasporic Africans, a borderless political sensibility at odds with American domestic stability.

This chapter explores how a strange and largely neglected early American text, *The Black Vampyre; A Legend of St. Domingo* (1819), sought to exploit and reconfigure these widespread fears about diasporic African revolutionary internationalism. While the novella ostensibly sought to capitalize on a contemporary interest in vampire tales, it does so by rooting its sensationalism in contemporary concerns about Haitian inspired resistance, uncertainties about the western spread of enslavement within the United States, and deep-seated fears about emancipated African Americans attempting to live as equals within the New York area. The novella, in other words, seizes upon the fears registered in New York periodical cultural about the potential threats to white American stability by sensationalizing the possibilities of Black solidarities and Black resistance. While I am not proposing that Coco serves in any way as a model for the titular figure of *The Black Vampyre*, the fact that New York's print culture produced two exaggerated figures of Black radical resistance with Haitian connections in such a short span of time underscores how conjoined St. Domingo and domestic revolutionaries were in the American imagination well into the late 1810s. The novella, in sum and as I will argue below, plays with a variety of operant narratives about foreign insurrection and domestic stability in order to create a uniquely American fantasy about undying Black solidarities.

Coco in New York

For readers of New York newspapers during the third week of May of 1819, the suppressed rebellion in Augusta was a proto-star in a constellation of information around the legacies of freedom and unfreedom. Numerous additional references to Augusta appeared in a variety of New York papers that same week. As the *New-York Gazette & General Advertiser* registered, President James Monroe (on a tour of the southern states and eventually bound for New Orleans) was expected to arrive in Augusta on May 13th (or just five days after Coco's supposed plot was discovered).[16] Both *The New-York Evening Post* and the *Commercial Advertiser* printed the same letter (alongside news about Coco's rebellion) written by the Reverend William Mead, an agent of the American Colonization Society, detailing his efforts to expose violations of the ban against the importation of foreign born enslaved people.[17] Mead's missive solicited contributions from northern abolitionists to purchase the freedom of illegally trafficked diasporic Africans, and his letter concludes by announcing that he too was headed to Augusta in the company of a group of unlawfully enslaved people he had tracked down in rural Georgia.[18]

The disjointed temporalities of early-nineteenth-century reprinting networks, as Trish Loughran has powerfully demonstrated, render it difficult to trust the timelines of early American newspapers as factually synchronous.[19] Still, a suggestive imagined community might be formed around the idea that Monroe and/or Mead could have reached Augusta during Coco's trial or his execution. Such an act of critical speculation would allow us to think (even fleetingly) that it was possible that either Monroe or Mead could have arrived in Augusta amid an ongoing rebellion. In one sense, Monroe and Mead represent opposing trajectories for the future of enslavement in the United States; yet if either of them (or both) had appeared in the midst of an active rebellion, their presence would have exacerbated an already volatile situation. In the midst of managing heated congressional debates about the future of the Missouri territory, Monroe had ventured south and west toward New Orleans (and its rapidly growing sugar plantations) on a tour of newly incorporated western territories.[20] Mead, heading east and north, was traveling in the company of newly liberated Africans who he hoped to repatriate back across the Atlantic, but he did so as an orchestrated performance intended to draw attention to the continued illegal international traffic in enslaved people. Complicating these oppositional white itineraries were the extra-national territorial connections linked to Coco through his supposed associations not just with St. Domingo, but also with maroons inhabiting swamps surrounding Augusta. These nearly avoided intersections reveal the multivalent ways in which the haunting legacies of the Haitian Revolution suffused the American imagination. Indeed anxieties about Haiti permeated almost every debate about westward expansion (and a further spread of enslavement) even as they fueled abolitionist attempts to remove the stain of America's "peculiar institution" from the Republic. Readers of New York periodicals would have encountered news of each of these events in rapid succession, revealing how the gutters of newspaper columns could barely separate the excessive interconnections of the stories they published.[21]

Several other adjacent articles about the Augusta rebellion may have prompted readers to think hemispherically about the relationship between the American Republic and circum-Atlantic racial capitalism. Several area papers, including the *Columbian Gazette*, the *Commercial Advertiser*, *The New-York Evening Post*, the *Westchester Herald*, the *New-York Advertiser*, the *Trenton True American*, the *Columbian Gazette*, and *The New-York Columbian*, all reported on rumors that the Spanish were on the verge of surrendering Cuba to Great Britain.[22] While these reports proved unfounded, the idea that Cuba might fall under British rule was another piece of unsettling news. A range of Americans, including the presidential administrations of Thomas Jefferson and John Adams, had debated the feasibility of annexing Cuba as a means offshoring large-scale plantations.

These fantasies about Cuba ranged from conceiving of it as a way to expand U.S. influence southwards to figuring it as a repository for relocating existing North American plantations away from the North American continent. In each case, this Cuba fixation aimed at constraining the risks of domestic insurrections by trying to imagine ways to reduce the possibilities for free African Americans to interact with still enslaved people.[23]

These speculations about Cuba's future drifted into a floodtide of ongoing debate about the future of domestic enslavement reignited by Missouri's petition for statehood. A number of New York politicians featured prominently in these deliberations, especially Congressman James Tallmadge Jr. who represented New York's 4th congressional district. Tallmadge sponsored an amendment that proposed limiting the numbers of enslaved people allowed into Missouri and contained a codicil which called for a gradual emancipation policy for the territory as a precondition for recognizing Missouri as a state.[24] Modeling his proposal on New York's own attempts at gradual emancipation, Tallmadge hoped his compromise would create mediating strategies for westward expansion. New York newspapers were bursting with attention to Tallmadge, with some reporting that he was the presumptive Democratic-Republican nominee for the upcoming senatorial election.[25] Tallmadge was a partisan star on the rise, and some party hopefuls believed that his attempts to curtail enslavement (both territorially and temporally) could propel their New York model onto the national stage. Yet Tallmadge struggled to find support for his amendment, even as he moved to placate widespread concerns over how free African Americans intermingling with enslaved people supposedly posed a danger to white populations. Given just how enflamed tensions were by New York's own gradual emancipation project, it is hard to think that Tallmadge's concerns about integration and the anxieties over free people of color dwelling amid both free white people and enslaved people did not also shape his thinking about the formation of new states. To counter what seemed like the inevitability of racialized unrest, Tallmadge advocated lengthy stretches of indenture followed by continual exploitation through increased competition for low-wage work in the hopes of averting the disasters that had consumed Haiti.[26]

Again, these adjacent narratives may have moved newspaper readers to think about the connections between histories of hemispheric coloniality, hopes for U.S. expansion, the resistance of enslaved people, and the continuing Black Atlantic's traffic in human beings. At the very least, the proximity of these narratives registers how the American print public sphere was littered with various satellites orbiting (some closely, some loosely) with the gravitational pull of the Republic's investments in Black Atlantic capitalism. Still, while a range of New York papers could print extracts (or full versions) of Tallmadge's condemnations of the spread of enslavement, they could not imagine any self-authored attempts at liberation on the part of diasporic Africans as anything other than criminal. The print public sphere in New York seemed incapable of disassociating Black liberation from potentially constituting a vital threat to white Republican stability. Even those, like Tallmadge, who professed a moral opposition to enslavement were still consumed by fears about an intermingling of free and enslaved Black people within an otherwise white Republican citizenry. Indeed, even for many abolitionists, it was easier to conceive of a territorial sequestering of enslavement rather than integration. Underlying all these circulating reports about racialized unrest, threats to futurity, endangered white citizens, and national expansion was the shared sense that any question regarding enslavement was never simply a domestic issue. From Mead's proof that southerners were openly violating the supposed ban on the importation of enslaved people to speculations about Coco's foreign origins, evidence abounded that the United States remained engrossed in a global network of Black Atlantic exchange.

Even within the rising isolationism and nationalism of the Era of Good Feelings a shared sense of internationalism permeated public thinking. These anxieties about wider circuits of exchange may well have further kindled the charged feelings in both regional and congressional political debates about the future of enslavement, since they routinely questioned if any sort of domestic legislation could settle historically global problems. Or, perhaps, they invigorated a coterminous understanding that no matter what laws were enacted to prohibit the mobility of free African Americans and enslaved people across national, regional, or even local borders, these prohibitions were inevitably going to be subject to quotidian violations.[27] Either way, these anxieties about scale, mobility, rebellion, and integration gave rise to the sensationalized gothic undertones that typified how American readers consumed accounts concerning the legacies of enslavement and the ghostly matter of Haitian liberation. In sum, in the spring of 1819 New Yorkers occupied a textual ecosystem saturated with opinions about how St. Domingo functioned as the apocalyptic specter underwriting debates about the future of domestic enslavement and national economic prosperity.

Speedily Published

While the identity of the author of *The Black Vampyre; A Legend of St. Domingo* (1819) remains uncertain—possible candidates include Uriah Derick D'Arcy, Robert Sands, and Richard Varick Dey—Katie Bray has persuasively argued it was Dey by registering just how immersed he was in New York's print public sphere.[28] Allusions to articles, reviews, and advertisements which had recently circulated in Manhattan just prior to the text's appearance saturate the novella. From its juvenile bickering with James Kirke Paulding, to its dedication to the author of a recent play lampooning the Panic of 1819, the text exhibits a blood-curdling knowledge of the local literary scene.[29] Indeed, one cotemporary reviewer lamented the text's thinly veiled portraits of notable local personalities.[30] Finally, the text unquestionably rerouted fears about racialized unrest (which had been percolating in the city for several months) by nakedly attempting to capitalize on the recently arrived vampire craze.

While measuring the readership of the text remains nearly impossible, this satiric remodeling of a popular British import clearly captured the attention of booksellers and newspaper reviewers. No fewer than three New York newspapers carried advanced notice that the book was "in press" and would "be speedily published."[31] All of these papers subsequently advertised the book for sale, a missive which appeared in several other local papers as well.[32] Advertisements were not limited to the New York area, as notices quickly appeared in New Haven, Pennsylvania, and South Carolina.[33] Typically, all of these advertisements list *The Black Vampyre* alongside two other recently published works, "The Sketch Book, by Geoffrey Crayon, gent" and "The Vampyre, by Lord Byron."[34] That *The Black Vampyre* even briefly occupied the same pride of place as these two successful texts registers the publisher's hopes for the volume.[35] The recent importation of the British novella *The Vampyre* (1819) had sparked something of a vampire craze in the United States, perhaps especially so since for much of the spring and summer of 1819 it was assumed to have been written by the infamous Lord Byron. While this text was actually written by John Polidori, its mistaken ascription to the celebrated Byron no doubt contributed to the text's notoriety.[36] Readers familiar with *The Vampyre* would have recognized *The Black Vampyre* as a parody, while also understanding it as a significant revision. Central to these modifications was *The Black Vampyre*'s indebtedness to the local print public ecosystem out of which it had emerged, given its deep investments in racial assimilation, racialized revolution, and the economies of speculation and enslavement. At first glance, *The Black Vampyre* appears as an absurd reworking of the British original, yet on a deeper consideration, it aggressively domesticates the European source by reanimating the sensationalism about vampires into concerns about Black radicalism. Dey's novella, in other words, transformed a legendary Old World monster into an entirely New World production.

One of the novella's first reviews, published in the *Commercial Advertiser*, artfully avoids mentioning the topic of race despite the declarative nature of the title. At the same time, the reviewer seems deeply unnerved by the reorientation of the vampire myth from the Near East to the Caribbean.[37] In faulting the text for failing to conform "in every respect" to "the superstition," the review condemns *The Black Vampyre* without actually stating what distinguishes it from Polidori's production.[38] This avowal by avoidance comes to a head in the reviewers' assertion that *The Black Vampyre* contains "the absurdity of supposing that any sane woman could fall desperately in love with the character of a Vampyre" without mentioning that the vampire, in this case, was African.[39] Well aware of Polidori's text, which it appraises alongside Dey's, the reviewer fails to fault the British import for revolving around its titular vampire's seduction of not one, but two, innocent white women. In many ways, Polidori's text recast vampires for Anglo-American readers by transforming the figure from a zombie-like figure into a Byronic aristocrat.[40] By mocking his former employer's infamous reputation in his monstrous protagonist, Polidori sexualizes the vampire and transforms it into a romanticized persona that has endured to this day. Despite Polidori's presentation of vampires as bewitching, the reviewer in the *Commercial Advertiser* fails to critique him for his depictions of a white vampire seducing white women. Instead, the reviewer harps on how presenting a *Black* vampire as alluring violates Polidori's gothic construction.

Dey describes the Black Vampyre as the epitome of aesthetic beauty, noting that he "was a coloured gentleman, of remarkable height, and deep jetty blackness; a perfect model of the CONGO Apollo" (20).[41] Moreover, Dey soft peddles the attraction of the lone female character in the narrative by hinting it stems as much from nefarious black magic as it does from actual physical attraction. That this women becomes impregnated by the Black Vampire during the consummation of their wedding, suggests that it is miscegenation that really irks the reviewer. Arguing that such behavior was not possible for a sane woman serves as a coded way of declaring interracial sex as irrational. While the review notes the centrality of the seduction plot to both vampire narratives and *The Black Vampyre* in particular, it doubles down on what it marks as the otherworldliness of procreative sex between a white woman and a black man. In many ways, the review intimates a great deal about the plot of *The Black Vampyre* in its strategic refusal to name the text's most pronounced concerns. Since it creates the conditions of possibility for interracial sex, Dey's largest violation of canonical standards may be the relocating of vampirism from eastern Europe to the African continent. By circumventing any direct mention of Blackness in the review, the critic dances around how the text details the extractive violence of Black Atlantic capitalism. This evasion proves tricky, since the novella foregrounds links between the inhumane traffic in Africans and the instabilities of capitalism. Indeed, the text asserts that both systems inherently drain the life force of workers to satisfy the inhumane cravings of elite profiteers. Rather than deal head-on with the complexities of *The Black Vampyre*'s plot, the reviewer questions its author's sanity to sidestep the overt implications of interracial sex and the text's decidedly anti-capitalist message.

Fit for No Work

The Black Vampyre opens with a vignette about lost profits. The second sentence of the narrative details how a "French ship" forcibly transporting enslaved people "from the eastern coast of GUNIEA" sold them "remarkably cheap" upon its arrival in "ST. DOMINGO" (16). These enslaved people had been "reduced to mere skeletons by the yaws on the passage" and all but one "died shortly after" disembarking (16). This young boy, "of a very slender constitution" and clearly "fit for no work whatever," was purchased by a French planter who, according to the text, "charitably knocked out his brains" and threw him in the "ocean" (16). Disguising murder as mercy, the planter represents the cruelty of those who seek to profit from the extractive violence of human trafficking. This opening scene tabulates the devastating costs of the Middle Passage to implicitly calculate the impossibility of profiting from such horrors. The twisted gesture of the "Planter," in other words, frames his sense of this doomed ship's Atlantic crossing as a total write off, one he assumes should be washed away by the harbor's tides rather than spark a reappraisal of the debilitating losses of Black Atlantic trade.

From the start, this critique of the barbaric traffic resides alongside a counter-narrative, one that marks that a "MR. ANTHONY GIBBONS, a "gentleman of African extraction," would survive as "a descendent of these dead slaves" (16). This seeming impossibility becomes a reality as "the little corpse" the planter attempted to kill swims ashore and "begged for some bread and butter" to remedy the "pain in his bowels" (16). "Supposing that his business to have been half done," the Planter kicks the boy "back into the water" (16). Across the next few paragraphs, the planter repeatedly reenacts his charitable violence: first by tying a weight to the boy and attempting to drown him again, ordering him beaten to death, and finally by directing the building of a large pyre on which he plans to burn the child. Despite the boy's persistent survival, the planter never considers extending him any actual benevolence; instead, he understands "his business," despite numerous failures, to be murder (16). Animated by pathological devotion to his perverted sense of charity, the planter relentlessly tries to eradicate the child. Yet, to the planter's dismay, the child remains undead. Figuring the undying boy as "Satan, Obi, or some other worthy, with whom he had to deal," the planter defines his actions as a quasi-religious mission (16).

In the ensuing struggle to immolate the boy, the planter ironically becomes the victim of his own designs as he winds up atop the burning pyre himself. He survives long enough to have a brief conversation with his wife, Euphemia, in which the planter discovers that their still unbaptized infant has been mysteriously "sucked, like an unripe orange," and that "nothing" was now left of him but his "beautiful and tender skin" (19). At first, the text pithily suggests that the planter's passing was "much regretted by all who had the honor of his acquaintance" (19). But as the text shifts its gaze from his mourning wife to his enslaved laborers this is reversed, as the narrator sardonically notes that his passing was mourned "particularly by his negroes; who could not soon forget him; as he had left too many sincere marks of his regard on their backs, to be ever obliterated from their recollections" (19). This figuration of mocking remorse on the part of the enslaved people forced to labor for the deceased planter emphasizes his brutality, and underscores how his self-imagined charity was in fact just another facet of his violent anti-Blackness. As such, this opening vignette lays out the stakes of the tale's investments in exploring the ways in which white supremacist "charity" aims at foreclosing sociality for diasporic Africans by attempting to reduce them into being legible only as laboring figures who can produce capital for white enslavers.

In what follows, this chapter explores how *The Black Vampyre* interrogates white anxieties about diasporic African sociality by considering what it frames as the joint threats to white stability of miscegenation and radical Black collectivity. In many ways, the plot of *The Black Vampyre* echoes many of the tenets that Elizabeth Young has defined as central to figurations of Black Frankensteins in that it serves as "a story about a monster whose body incarnates the political ideas of collectivity and reawakening and whose behavior signals political revolt."[42] While there are significant differences between cultural representations of vampires and Frankensteins, Young's sense of the ways in which fears about fictionalized monsters were racialized across the nineteenth century provides a useful means of thinking about some of the aims of *The Black Vampyre*. In particular, and perhaps even more so than the largely mute and simply brutish Frankenstein figure, the titular monster in *The Black Vampyre* is particularly threatening for the ways in which he "menaced the supreme icons if domesticity, white women," while simultaneously threatening to penetrate "the most volatile whiter interior of all: the psyche."[43] In the case of *The Black Vampyre*, that penetration is literal as well as figurative in that the threat to a white woman actually takes the form of a seduction which results in both marriage and pregnancy. Dey's creation, in this sense, is less the muted brute that Shelly's imitators had in mind when they envisioned the hypermusicalized threat of a Black Frankenstein, and a more harrowing reconfiguration of the more alluring figure of the early-nineteenth-century vampire.

Dey most vividly alters the traditional vampire tale, or Polidori's version of the vampire tale, by reterritorializing the origins of vampirism. By defining vampirism as having African roots, Dey links real world brutalities to superstitious gothic sensations.[44] This rerouting of orthodox tropes reveals how the predatory nature of vampirism serves as the perfect metaphor for circum-Atlantic capitalism (built on draining the life force of its enslaved victims to maximize profitability). The monstrosity of the planter suffuses this configuration, especially when he congratulates himself on his charitable attempts at murder. Since the boy appears "fit for no work whatever," the planter understands him as disposable: too far gone to even be considered a refuse slave who could be nursed back into health and resold into further exploitation (16).[45] Since returning the child to forced labor seems impossible, the planter envisions no possible social role for the boy outside of death, effectively reducing any living but unable to work diasporic African into a corpse. In this regard, the planter refracts what Sylvia Wynter has called the ideology of "homoeconmics," in that Western man defines himself by his capacity to practice "accumulation in the name of (economic) freedom," and he does so in part by defining others as beyond the borders of such a figuration.[46] A body unable to accumulate, or to be pressed into the service of accumulating for others, fails to have any value within this horrific system of human relations. But the boy's African heritage (or the portion of his African heritage which is connected to vampirism) provides him the means to resist being foreclosed on by this white supremacist ideological thinking. Or, to put it another way, the boy's undying gothic inheritance liberates him from being confined by the planter's desire to fix him as a laboring body or as a corpse.

While previous figurations of vampires largely presented solitary monsters, Dey frames vampirism as a structural and, perhaps, inescapable pandemic. Central to this reconceptualization remains Dey's multivalent attempts to transfuse vampirism with operant early-nineteenth-century preconceptions about a variety of non-Christian religions, including several forms of paganism, but also distorted renditions of Islam and Obeah. By amalgamating myriad religious practices, some of which had African roots, with vampirism, the text extends its consideration of Christian charity into a structural engagement with the ethics of plantation economies more broadly. Dey's initial association of enslavement and vampirism sets the stage for this consideration. In depicting the slender African boy who survived the Middle Passage as unfit for life (because he was deemed unfit for labor) as the titular revenant of the narrative, Dey opens his text by imploring readers to think about the afterlives of enslavement and the economic system that drives it. Elizabeth Maddock Dillion has deftly coined the term "bare labor" to describe the lives of enslaved people, a term that she explains signals "a life stripped of official access to forms of social life, identity, and belonging."[47] The planter's actions demonstrate his attachment to a colonial ideology of bare labor in that he can envision no social role for an enslaved person beyond that of forced servitude. In the planter's eyes, diasporic Africans incapable of labor are irrelevant; as such, he perversely figures his own actions as mercifully inevitable.

The revenant's endless returns demonstrate the depths of his resistance. A byproduct of his mysterious condition, the boy's refusal to be defined by the planter's corrupt ideology stands as both a singular and a collective project carried with him across the Atlantic. As a result of his assumption that the boy cannot work, the planter presumes him useless upon arrival at the site of production (St. Domingo). Dey's text upends that configuration by fashioning the boy as a kind of embodiment of what Elizabeth Maddock Dillon calls the "impossible commons," a space outside the imagination of "imperial and capitalist structures and sensibilities."[48] The un-laboring body that refuses to die concretizes a living symbol of resistance to a racist ideology that equates Blackness with either exploitation or annihilation.

Obviously, the young vampire's imperviousness to harm evinces his otherworldliness. On the surface, he occupies a commons closed off from everyone else around him. Yet, on a deeper level, the satiric thrust of the opening few para-graphs belies the extractive nature of a calculus which judges certain people as disposable.[49] The boy's political possibilities reside in his refusal to be pigeon-holed as either a productive cog or an unwanted part. Wynter's figuration of *homoeconmicus* usefully indexes how the boy occupies a space outside of the Planter's operant definition of humanity, one predicated on the idea of an acquir-ing body as the paragon of Western human virtue. As such, one thread of the text explores the limitations of such an economically driven conception of life. Since the planter taxonomizes him as worthless, he understands him as already dead even as he remains living. Or again, the planter judges the boy incapable of life despite his undying persistence. The horrifying performance of the planter's myr-iad attempts to fix him as valueless, as opposed to the agential undead position he occupies as a result of his vampirism, highlights how the boy resists the enclosing machinations of racial capitalism. The Planter may believe that his initial actions signal his virtuousness, yet his self-imagined sympathy for the plight of others actually registers his depravity.

The text frames the planter as an archetype of a white elite male, a fact perhaps best encoded in how he initially has no signifier beyond that of his occupation. On the threshold of the text, the Planter does not need to be personalized beyond having this marker of economic relation since he stands in for any number of predatory actors. Even after Dey personalizes him, by revealing his surname as Personne, he still remains a blank slate since the French word translates as either "person" or, more commonly, "nobody."[50] As such, the opening of the text reverses the normative order of presenting diasporic Africans and Euro-Americans in the New World. In other words, the text overturns the traditional operation of nomi-native power. On the one hand, the text does everything in its power to disentan-gle the planter from any meaningful set of genealogical connections (he remains an occupation at best or nobody at worst). On the other, the sickly diasporic African child (whose birthplace on the eastern coast of Guinea is recorded as part of his biography) is identified as the ancestor of "Mr. Anthony Gibbons, a gentle-man of African extraction" (16). This reversal of racist genealogical hierarchies flows as a subtle undercurrent in the opening frame of *The Black Vampyre*, but one that emphasizes the text's interest in exposing the brutal racialized hierar-chies of the plantocracy. By investing in the futurity of the enslaved and glossing any specifics about Mr. Nobody, Dey registers his larger investments in thinking about the exploitative nature of Black Atlantic trade. Coterminously, he raises a variety of questions about freedom and unfreedom by linking them to the very definitions of life and undying death.

From the opening frame, and through the naïve lamentations of Personne, the text intertwines vampirism with a variety of non-Western religious practices. In effect, Dey declares the "OBEAH mysterious" as the source of the power held by "the immortal bloodsuckers" (35). The narrative's vision of Obeah blurs it with stock renditions of Islam, as if to suggest that these two distinct systems of belief are interchangeable since they are both alien to Personne's orthodoxy. Given the ways in which Personne serves as a representative type, the implications of this figuration are more than personal and extend to an ideological break between Euro-Americans and Africans. Religious systems, in other words, take on geographical affiliations, creating maps of belief systems and racial cartographies of belonging. Thus, in some ways, the text conjoins Christianity and capitalism and posits that they are at odds with other forms of belief and economic possibility.

At the heart of his tale, Dey conjures a phantasmagoric scene set in a cavern underneath St. Domingo in which enslaved people and vampires gather to swear a blood oath to fight for "UNIVERSAL EMANCIPATION!!!" (36). Here, Dey mobilizes a critique of Black Atlantic capitalism through his staging of vampirism as entering the Euro-American world via the transportation of enslaved people from Africa. But the text also surreptitiously links Christianity and capitalism as systems fueled by subjugation and exploitation. By linking the discord of the undead to New World colonization, Dey turns his satire into a pointed critique of the actual bloodletting of racial capitalism. This conjunction informs not just the blending of all non-European forms of belonging into a singularity, but also the Black Vampyre's attempts to forge solidarity between enslaved people and his fellow vampires:

> But to come to the object of our present meeting. Sublime and soul-elevating theme!—The emancipation of the Negroes!—The consecration of the soil of ST. DOMINGO to the manes of murdered patriots in all ages!—No matter whether the bill of sale was scrawled in French or in English;—No matter whether we were taken prisoners, in a battle between the LEOPHARES and the JAKOFFS, or in a skirmish between the SAMBOES and the SAWPITS;—No matter whether we were bought for calico and cotton, or for gunpowder or for shot;—No matter whether we were transported in chains or in ropes—in a brig, or a schooner, or a seventy-four—the first moment we come ashore on ST. DOMINGO, our souls shall swell like a sponge in the liquid element;—our bodies shall burst from their fetters, glorious as a curculio from its shell;—our minds shall soar like the car of the æronaut, when its ligaments are cut; in a word, O my brethren, we shall be free!— (36)

In this rousing call to collectivity, the titular Black Vampyre calls upon the assembled potential revolutionaries to ignore whatever divides them. He argues that their various origins and experiences no longer matter because their presence in St. Domingo—"from the first moment"—unifies them in a crucial way (36). The Middle Passage, and the economic system which drives it, attempts to remove all distinctions between these people in order to render them interchangeable commodities. The Black Vampyre's call to arms asks each of these groups to transform this enforced commonality into the means by which to combat their unfreedom. Only when they are free and therefore individualized subjects can these particularities matter again; until then, he argues, such socially constructed divisions should be understood as white supremacist attempts to dissipate their capacity for resistance.

The speech unfolds by pondering the various circumstances by which the crowd had been forcibly transported to St. Domingo, cataloging these differences to redefine their import. Casting St. Domingo's soil as sanctified by the spirits of the martyrs who proceeded them ("manes" in the Latin sense), the speech depicts these ancestors as "murdered patriots"—presumably as either advocates for a national space or in the secondary sense of being committed to freedom (36). Rather than viewing St. Domingo as the crucible of unfreedom, as the space of social death or bare labor, the Black Vampyre theorizes the space as the site of production for an earthshattering counternarrative.[51] The speech marks the Middle Passage as enacting a transition; however not in the white supremacist sense of person to commodity, but from person to potential revolutionary. In refusing to allow abduction (or even the languages governing this theft, or the form of currency used to transact this insidious business) to become reductively defining, the speech implores the assemble crowd to hold their personal histories and disconnections in abeyance so as to form a powerful collective.

The speech redefines the erasure of kinship so often associated with the Middle Passage by asserting a nascent pan-Africanism predicated on a direct lineage between the martyrs who had heralded them and the current diasporic Africans in St. Domingo. As an invective against the oppressive regimes of the plantocracy, the oration details how the policing powers of white supremacy rely on the cultivation of difference. In effect, the Black Vampyre suggests that while enslavers flatten individuality in order to dehumanize, they simultaneously do so to undermine the potentialities of solidarity.[52] Instead of allowing racist taxonomies to divide them, the speech insists upon the potential power of aggregation. The capacity to enslave and police diasporic Africans was always provisionally dependent on the ability to divide them. As such, the constant central fear of white supremacists was of Black collectivity. Indeed, any resistance to systems of partition, to those dividing means of suppression, would have activated the most gothic of terrors for Euro-American readers. Lingering on the Middle Passage, the speech surreptitiously gestures to the concept of shipmates as a crucial point of connection. As Ramesh Mallipeddi argues, the concept of shipmates, seen in popular abolitionist texts such as Maria Edgeworth's "The Grateful Negro" (1804), was imagined as providing a point of connection between enslaved people.[53] Mallipeddi contends that the concept of shipmates represented the collective experience of the Middle Passage as a coalescing force on one scale (i.e. that of the actual ship). Dey's Black Vampyre extrapolates this concept in an effort to think structurally about a refusal of weakened division on a much grander scale. Since plantation management was predicated on a debasing subdivision, the speech disavows all forms of disassociation to call for collective resistance. Thus, the meeting in the cavern mimics actual moments of assemblage associated with the Haitian Revolution to frame collective resistance as possible, as necessary, and as world altering. In so doing, the text activates perhaps the most central fears of white supremacists about diasporic African solidarity and the ways in which such collectivities could successfully challenge racialized hierarchies and continued exploitation. But prior to this vignette about solidarity and resistance, the text grapples with another white supremacist anxiety about interracial sex and diasporic African male beauty, a cultural unease which the text uses to set the stage for the Black Vampyre's gravitas and overall ability to persuade others to join his cause.

Undead Unions

Dey flaunts existing cultural taboos around miscegenation, and *The Black Vampyre* may be one of the earliest publicly printed U.S. accounts that represents a sexual relationship between a Black man and a white woman.[54] The gothic sensationalism of the text provides some cover for the depiction, but the relationship between the Black Vampyre and Euphemia remains striking for its boldness and more shockingly so because it results in pregnancy. Predating Lydia Maria Child's more famous depiction of Charles Hobomok Conant—the child of the indigenous Hobomok and the Puritan settler-colonist Mary Conant—by several years (as *Hobomok* was published in 1824), the mixed-race son of the Black Vampyre haunts the text in manifold ways. The conclusion of *Hobomok*, so often criticized by contemporary critics for its depiction of miscegenation (most famously by James Fenimore Cooper, whose sterile *Last of the Mohicans* sought to rebut Child's narrative), moves to erase Charles Hobomok Contant's indigeneity by concluding with the pronouncement that any trace of his patrilineal heritage conveniently vanishes as he matures.[55] No such expedient evaporation occurs in Dey's text. This difference may result from the generic possibilities of the gothic over that of the historical romance, or Dey may well have felt that his pseudonymity would provide a shield unavailable to Child who would certainly have faced public censure as a woman writer. While the supernatural elements obscure some of the implications of Dey's depiction of a mixed-race union, the birth of a son (whose monstrosity resurfaces in the concluding paragraph of the text) remains noteworthy. This child, "a mulatto" with "Vampyrish propensities; of which his mother and Mr. Personne were never able to entirely cure him" serves as a living reminder of the violent legacies of the revolutionary Black Atlantic (39).

Dey prepares the way for the Black Vampyre's seduction of Euphemia with an extensive attention to his physical beauty, perhaps in some way justifying their shocking union. Some of this descriptive language replicates a variety of racist stereotypes, and much of this scurrilous language draws from influential accounts written by the Abbé Reynal and the planter Brian Edwards concerning the lives of enslaved people in the Caribbean. However, these figurations are complicated by how the text figures the Black Vampyre as possessing an "irresistible charm" and a "regal port" (21). Moreover, Dey turns to other canonical sources, with allusions to Shakespeare's *Two Gentleman of Verona* and *Julius Caesar*, to praise African beauty.[56] These contending representations peak in Dey's use of the term "Congo Apollo" to define the beauty of the Black Vampyre (20). This allusion compares the African Prince to the Apollo Belvedere, a much-touted marble statue from antiquity that, in the long eighteenth century, was often praised as representing the epitome of the ideal white masculine form.[57] John G. Bogert, then serving on the board of Manhattan's American Academy of the Fine Arts had just recently brought a copy of this statue to New York. As part of his work for the museum, Bogert procured cast copies of major European sculptures, including a large number of well-known busts such as that of the famous Apollo Belvedere.[58] By riffing on the currency of the Apollo Belvedere as the ideal white male form, Dey presents the Vampyre as the pinnacle of diasporic African beauty. In a kind of inverted figuration of aesthetic sensibilities, Dey marks the Black Vampyre as separately but equally beautiful to the most revered Western masculine form in the long eighteenth century.

Utterly overwhelmed by the Black Vampyre's charm, Euphemia marries him on the evening of their first meeting. Almost within minutes of their first encounter, "the beauty then, the royalty, gentility, and various accomplishments of" the Black Vampyre had "made captive of the too sensible heart of the French widow" (22). The Black Vampyre's poetic pleas of affection further enkindle the initial spark of attraction, especially after he loquaciously celebrates her unparalleled beauty.[59] Like a monstrous version of Othello, the Black Vampyre's melodious charms and physical magnificence quickly overwhelm Euphemia. Despite the objections of the family chaplain, who warns Euphemia against "the impropriety of marrying a negro," their union commences without delay (23).

After the nuptials and just before the vividly implied consummation, the narrative draws a revealing curtain over the couple. This gossamer veil lifts in the following paragraph with the Prince awakening his slumbering page, who confusingly finds himself staring at Euphemia dressed in an "enchanting dishabille" (23). The married pair spends their post-coital evening not in a solitary remove, but in a moonlight stroll with their page to the nearby graveyard where the supernatural bent of the narrative vigorously reemerges. This gothic turn takes the form of the Vampyre's resurrection of Euphemia's previous husbands, a scene punctuated by several references to the glossed over intercourse of the newly married couple. As Euphemia wanders in the graveyard and "vague terrors" begin to seize her mind, the bride's thoughts turn to "the comfortable bed" she has just departed and to her overall state of "undress" (24). While the erotic and the gothic often overlap in their suggestive figurations, Dey's text overtly conjoins these narrative elements in startling ways. The conversion of the white Byronic creature into a character with African origins amplifies all of the still-emerging anxieties about the vampire as a figure of gothic penetration. Moreover, it accelerates these fears by moving them quite clearly into a racialized arena in which the desires of white women mirror that of a supposedly overly sexual diasporic African man. Euphemia's Francophone heritage (so often associated in Anglophone literature with sexual promiscuity) slightly tempers the sensationalism of this episode, even as the tale's Caribbean setting (repeatedly imagined in Anglophone writing as the site of charged sexual appetites and questionable mores) also safely displaces her actions to a foreign locale.[60] Still, even with these qualifications in place, Dey nevertheless presents this sexual activity as happening within the sanctity of marriage as if to curb some of the shocking excesses his narrative registers.

Euphemia denies the Black Vampyre one request when she refuses to consume the noxious potion he commands her to drink as a pledge of fidelity. Leaning heavily (and simultaneously indiscriminatingly) on Bryan Edwards accounts of Obeah practices (likely from volume II of *History of the British Colonies in the West Indies* (1794/1805)), Dey amalgamates a variety of non-Western religious practices in his vampire-esque resurrection scene.[61] He gestures toward Islamic burial practices by noting the presence of two male figures that, while facing east, perform a variety of "antic prostrations" and throw "handfuls of earth three times over their heads" (25). These inaccurate, but telling, feints toward Islamic rituals disjointedly merge with another borrowing from Edwards's descriptions of diasporic African religious ceremonies. Following Edwards conception of Obeah rituals, Dey has the Vampyre concoct an admixture of blood, earth, and water into a potion he orders Euphemia to drink. Since Euphemia refuses this potion, the Vampyre turns her by biting her breast and sucking her blood; soon after this, Euphemia finds herself having "certain carnivorous cravings in her maw" (27).

The text takes a comic turn after the Black Vampyre reanimates Euphemia's three deceased husbands as they immediately begin fighting for recognition as her legitimate spouse. The second and third husbands first grapple with one another, but are soon vanquished by her first husband Mr. Personne, who immediately expresses consternation over her marriage to a Black man. While the Prince moves to befriend Personne by acknowledging the planter's preexisting claim on Euphemia; Personne responds with the admonishment that Black Vampyre should not "be too familiar, Blackey" signaling the planter's undying racism (29). However, the Black Vampyre, that "generous monarch," simply "pocketed the affront," and reveals himself as none other than the young enslaved boy who Personne had attempted to "mercifully" murder at the tale's opening (30). Declaring that Personne has been "sufficiently rewarded, for the cruelties you practiced upon my person, several years ago," the Black Vampyre declares

"I forgive you, my dear sir," and indicates that he will not stand in the way of the Personnes reunion (30). He further informs the Personnes that his page, Zembo, is in fact their son, who has "grown considerably," adding further, "I assure you that his education has not been neglected" (30).

The Black Vampyre then urges the reunited couple and their long missing child to leave the island, offering them passage on "a vessel" docked in the harbor and "ready to sail to Europe in an hour" (30). He concludes this address to them by noting, "The Island is no longer a place for you" (30). Given this invitation for a safe passage off the island, Dey represents the Black Vampyre as possessing a magnanimity that the planter neither shares nor can fully comprehend. While at first willing to follow the Black Vampyre's directions, their long-thought-dead son (the Black Vampyre's erstwhile page) directs them to follow him. However, instead of taking his parents to safety, Zembo takes them to witness a secret revolutionary meeting.

Dey again leans on Edwards in depicting a meeting at which enslaved people congregate to plan an insurrection by setting the meeting within the subterranean cavern previously discussed above. Dey's footnote cites Edwards as registering how Vincent Ogé, a free person of color executed for leading a revolt in St. Domingo in 1790, and other "ring-leaders held their meetings in certain subterranean passages or caves, in the parish of the La Grande Rivierec" (31) to provide a historical basis for his revolutionary meeting hall.[62] Dey depicts the subterranean cavern of his text as utterly resplendent, likening the space to "a vast hall of Arabian romance" (34). This exotic characterization emphasizes the cavern as a manufactured space (presumably by the diasporic Africans); as the text notes, its roof was "supported by immense shafts" which were "studded with precious stones" (34). Dey further notes that these "different spars assumed" a variety of "beautiful hues" since they were illuminated by "light of an hundred torches, blazing in every quarter" (34).

The depiction of the cavern as an ornately decorated underground hall rather than a natural cavity shifts the backdrop for this clandestine meeting from that of a chance unpoliced space to a secret location purposely built in defiance of colonial authorities. While in keeping with the sensationalized tenor of the overall narrative, this site also hints at a much wider network of anti-colonial struggle on the part of diasporic Africans. Capable of securing precious stones and adorning their meeting space with them, the description of the cave asserts that this meeting space has a long history. The description further indicates that this congregation has secretly amassed a dazzling amount of wealth. In essence, this episode depicts a sub-rosa society that has flourished while passing under the radar of the white colonial gaze, managing to construct a highly developed space of intricate design and with an organized membership.

The "the beaks of parrots," "the teeth of dogs, and alligators," the "bones of cats," and "broken glass and eggshells," and a variety of "other appendages" adorn the walls of the subterranean hall (32). According to the text, the space contains all "the implements of NEGRO witchcraft!" (32). Again borrowing heavily from Edwards's descriptions of Obeah practices, Dey conjures a vivid scene replete with a "vast amphitheater," occupied by "rudely attired" enslaved people and a band of musicians playing African instruments (the "MERRIWANG," the "DUNDO," the "GOOMBAY") (33). At the head of this congregation, standing around a "natural throne," gather several vampires. (32). The narrative reveals the space as a kind of Obeah temple; or, more accurately, it conjures an Anglo-American fantasy of what the composition of such a space might appear to be. The "discordant harmony" of the orchestra creates a soundscape that would "frighten all of the hosts of Pandemonium," further associating the meeting hall with a satanic majesty (33).

Spectacularly adorned with jewels and fragments of skeletons, and painted helter-skelter with blood, the meeting hall combines under one roof a myriad possible associations with non-Christian behaviors. The description reads like a set design for a mid-twentieth-century B movie serial, constructed to simultaneously suggest spectacular wealth and uncultivated primitivism. Moreover, as was usually the case in those B movies, this site appears primed for colonial reassertion. While the description stresses an accumulation of wealth on the one hand, on the other, it implies a failure to generate anything other than adornment with this affluence. Despite their having created a space festooned with all these multi-hued jewels, the gathered crowd have remained unequivocally unfree, and thus unable to use this wealth in any way that the wider capitalist system that surrounds them would recognize as demonstrating success. The temple, in other words, represents a kind of non-capitalist accumulation since its occupants appear uninterested in monetizing its riches. This reflection on fantastical wealth brings to the surface themes of accumulation and white supremacy that Dey weaves into his meditation on the politics of racial capitalism. The cavern recalls Wynter's argument that those who refuse to conform to the operant notion of accretion as the defining principle of humanity are ostracized from the Western definition of the human.[63] While this scene functions as a moment of dark humor within the text, it also reveals how capitalist logics displace certain groups (uninterested in extractive capitalism) from its delimited sense of just who should be classified as human.

Dey moves from describing the gothic splendors of the assembly hall and the various groups gathered within the space to recenter the text on the Black Vampyre's attempt to foment a revolution. At one point comparing the Black Vampyre to Edmund Burke (for their individual abilities to "thunder out" their intentions despite murmured disapproval from the crowd), Dey casts him as a compelling orator intent on uniting various factions into a coherent anti-colonial whole. The sermon begins with two contending opening lines, each of which upsets one subgroup within the general assembly. Obviously, this chatter is comical, but it also pushes the reader to think more broadly about the relationship between vampires and humans. At first, the "African Prince" (the new name for the titular Black Vampyre) opens with "Gentlemen and Vampyres!" but the "resentment" expressed by the Vampyres for being placed second stirs the Prince to switch his order of address (33). Quickly, he tries "Vampyres and Gentlemen" as an opening retort a "loud growl accompanied by a hiss" emerges from the assembled "NEGROES" who are also reluctant "to come last" (33). The Black Prince decides to press on and justifies his second figuration by stressing to the audience "the immortal should precede the mortal" and following this with a brief history of the vampires and the various names by which they have been known (33).

This call and response draws attention to this assembly as a carnivalesque scene, replete with references to a reversal of normative political authority since a diasporic African prince presides over the anti-colonial assembly. At the same time, the unequal (in the sense of serial address) equalization of these two categories produces a relationship between enslavement and gothic immortality. Or, to put it another way, the conjunction of the terms begs the question of just who is socially dead (or socially undead) in this world? The history of vampirism offered by the Prince reveals that there are only two ways out of this inflicted condition: through death or the use of a potion produced by the "OBEAH mysteries" (33). Given the tenor of the text, these methods of transcendence would also appear to be the only two possible pathways out of enslavement. Effectively, the narrative suggests that enslaved people have to choose an Obeah fueled struggle for liberty or accept the death sentence that racial capitalism has ascribed to them.

This linkage is further consolidated through Dey's use of the word "fee-tail" to describe "the estate of Vampyrism" (33). A legal term indicating a particular type of inheritance, a fee-tail is an inheritance "limited to some particular class of heirs of the person to whom it is granted."[64] In using a term about the restriction of a group of heirs to inherit (or not) property, the term fee-tail signals a patriarchal right of privilege to decide who will or will not be recognized as a legitimate heir. To borrow from the foundational work of Hortense Spillers, a fee-tail inheritance represents a version of "poppa's maybe" in the sense that it requires a public declaration of who would or would not be recognized by, and thus linked to, the patrimony privilege of the fee-tail.[65] Under a fee-tail inheritance, the father embraces his authority to decide who he wants to recognize as an heir. The concept of a fee-tail has its roots in Roman law but also corresponds to versions of feudal inheritance that allowed specific lands to be entailed upon certain lineal descendants. Put another way, it demarcates a system of inheritance that allows a patriarch to determine a line of inheritance beyond a single generation. This, in essence, allows that singular figure to determine in perpetuity who shall be considered a legitimate heir and who would be marked as outside an inheriting line of descent.

As Spillers' so generatively proves in her seminal work on this subject, diasporic Africans in the United States (because of the violence of non-recognition on the part of white supremacists) have no "Father to speak of—his Name, his Law, his Symbolic function mark the impressive missing agencies in the essential life of the black community." Given that Black children in America had their identity "determined through the line of the mother," they are effectively governed by a fee-tail inheritance based on an enduring non-recognition by white fathers. Effectively, and effectively universally, Black American children were deemed outside the bounds of inheritance by a racist fee-tail act. Spillers' argues for the importance of "a distinction in this case between 'body' and 'flesh'," in articulating the complexities of the savage violence of Black Atlantic human trafficking. This crucial distinction between a subject position, a body, which can be recognized by juridical and social codes in ways that flesh, as a kind of "concentration" seldom "acknowledge[d] nor discourse[d] away," to again borrow from Spillers, becomes in many ways the part of no part. Or, again, those marked as flesh and not as bodies remain forever unrecognized by the tenets of inheritance, dwelling outside the bounds of the fee-tail as designated by the undead white male patriarchs of the past.[66] But in a rhetorical thrust, the Black Vampyre attempts to forge a solidarity between the members as he moves to suggest that the fee-tail inheritances of vampirism should serve as a legacy beyond the scope of white supremacist control, representing a bequest that cannot be denied or disregarded by the violences of colonizers attempting to overwrite the strength of African legacies. In this regard, he represents the heirloom of vampiric power as an oppositional force to counter the horrors of Black Atlantic violence and erasure.

After sketching a brief history of vampirism, the Prince attempts to conjoin the various groups assembled in the hall by arguing that the condition of enslavement overrides any other possible differences among them. When the enslaved people and the vampires can understand themselves as a collective, then, he enjoins, "O my brethren, we shall be free!" (35). Reaching the crescendo of his speech, the Prince concludes by declaring, "Our fetters discandied, and our chains dissolved, we shall stand liberated,—and redeemed—emancipated,—and disenthralled by the irresistible genius of UNIVERSAL EMANCIPATION!!!" (35). The Prince's "fiery oratory" so inspired "the auditors, that the whole mass of their thick blood leaped with the quickening pulse of anticipated freedom" and they reacted with "*unparalleled bursts of unprecedented applause!!!*" (35). With all hearts now beating as one, the speech transforms the crowd into that of an almost unimaginable solidarity. Sensing they are on the verge of a transubstantiation from unfree flesh into free bodies, the crowd becomes a singular congregation, with Dey comparing them to "perfect Corybantes" ready to perform their "Phyrricks" (36). Further associating their behavior with that of pagan religious practices, the text marks the fevered pitch of their various wild dances and preparations for martial action in an expression of a divine connection with the idea of freedom (36).

For a flickering moment, the tale sensationally hovers on the cusp of a confrontation with the white supremacist regime through retaliatory violence. The Prince's speech has inspired the crowd to imagine the possibility of a new set of social relations, and they energetically prepare to deploy their unified strength. Yet as soon as this solidarity (and its entire radical potentiality) is enkindled, it is snuffed out by the sudden arrival of French colonial troops. The return of the policing force of imperial troops forecloses all of the erstwhile revolutionary force of the gathering. As the "glittering bayonets" poured "in from every quarter" and "hemmed them in," the enslaved people "seeing how the business was likely to terminate, prudently sneaked off," while the French combatted the vampires (37). Zembo betrays the vampires by informing the soldiers how to kill the undead, and in short order the French carry out a massacre. Using against him the knowledge Zembo has acquired by his association with the Prince, Zembo effectively turns another form of diasporic African knowledge into yet another tool of colonial oppression. During the "desperate conflict," the Personnes steal the Obeah potion which can cure vampires so that they can rid themselves of the Black Vampyre's unnatural influence (37).

Even as everything appears lost to the French onslaught, the Prince continues to resist in a somewhat mock-heroic struggle for freedom. Here Dey compares him to both the Gaetulian lion (a North African lion famous for its ferocity) and Enceladus, a giant of Greek mythology who Athena buries under Mt. Etnea after a legendary struggle. These allusions further ostracize the Prince by linking him to fabled opponents of classical Western authority; moreover, each of these associations reproduces familiar white supremacist registers for depicting rebellious enslaved people. First, Dey frames the Prince as a legendary wild animal whose bloodthirsty behavior poses a threat to human society; and then subsequently he connects him to the destructive force of volcanic eruptions. This second allusion surfaces an infamous metaphor long associated with the Haitian Revolution. "The masters of the Caribbean," the comte de Mirabeau declared in response to the outbreak of revolution in St. Domingo, "were 'sleeping at the foot of Vesuvius.'"[67] This sense, as Dubois argues, of living on the edge of an inevitable disaster, of borrowing time against an inevitable eruption, defines "the political theater" of a space in which "all sides constantly referred to the potential for revolution among" enslaved people.[68] Dubois's point, as well as Mirabeau's, records how the plantocracy always felt a sense of impending doom, even if an actual eruption was met with a great deal of performative surprise.

The gothic terror of *The Black Vampyre* resides in its capacity to allow its readers to enter into this performance of recognition and horror, and then to have the cathartic release produced by the restoration of established (white) power. It presents an unworldly scene, pervaded with the outlandish, only to largely evacuate it of all of its revolutionary possibility. Except, of course, for the point, registered at the opening of the text (almost as an aside), that the Prince's descendants were currently living in New Jersey. As such, the text raises the possibility that the Black Vampyre's offspring may nonetheless have brought a monstrous inheritance into the United States. This child with a revolutionary heritage lingers as the final implication of the horrific in the novella. In this sense, the death of the immortal Black Vampyre bears with it the seed of a potential resurrection. In almost every figuration of them, vampires seldom suffer an eternal death, and this sense of their undying power is perhaps even more acute in a text that features the inherited "vampirish tendencies" of his offspring in its final lines (39). In essence, the Prince will always be a revenant; a presence demanding recognition if not also restitution from the readers who cannot so easily close the book on his potential revolutionary sensibilities.

Revolutionary Offspring

In returning in his final lines to the opening of his novella, Dey closes the circle on the mysterious Anthony Gibbons, the gentleman of "African extraction" named in the first paragraph as the Black Vampyre's descendent. In essence, the conclusion triangulates Gibbons, Personne, and the Black Vampyre by reminding readers that the same white planter who charitably attempted to murder a young African child was now raising that child's son in the United States. Even after his second death, the young enslaved boy / Black Vampyre / Prince refuses definition or reduction into mere flesh since his spirit continues to animate his offspring. Although their union proved to be an extremely brief one, the Vampyre had impregnated Euphemia and she has born this child in the United States after the Personnes have relocated there following the failed rebellion. Despite their best attempts to cure him, this child never loses his monstrous propensities and the lingering vampiric legacy haunts the ending by creating a forceful circularity. In essence, the text is bookended with reminders that a free diasporic African with a deep connection to revolutionary movements in Haiti was living as a free man in the New York region. By declaring that this child of a vampiric revolutionary leader was dwelling within the American domestic scene, the narrative in effect culminates by activating many of the anxieties which had been circulating in New York's print public sphere during the text's gestation; in the sense that the text awakens concerns about potential trans-national diasporic African solidarities, fears about free people of color attempting to integrate into an otherwise white Republican social order, and the potential presence of Haitian revolutionary connections enkindling domestic rebellions. Indeed, these concerns were so prevalent across the New York area that Dey only really needs to hint at them in order to presumably bring home to his readers the terror he gestures toward.

The Black Vampyre's enduring legacy may well be the son that takes after him, no matter what his mother and stepfather try to do to alter his nature.

This conclusion transforms the novella from an exotic gothic tale set in an extra-national space into a foreboding sensationalist domestic tale of terror. Just as Dey had borrowed the impetus for his satiric critique of rapacious capitalism, he also seemingly pilfered his conclusion from the headlines of local papers that had been absorbed by the terror inducing prospects of domestically located Black radicals with connections to revolutionary St. Domingo; and outsized concerns about how free people of color were disrupting the traditional stability of the city as they sought to establish themselves after their gradual emancipation. The horrifying legacy of the Black Vampyre evolves out of his own undying body and routes itself through that of his descendent who has taken up residence in New Jersey. Would this child possess his father's enduring desire to upend racist hierarchies? Did he innately have the charismatic capacity to persuade others to his cause as his father had? What form of radical behavior would his vampiric tendencies take?

The idea of an undying diasporic African—someone constitutionally committed to resisting enslavement and with political inclinations inseminated in St. Domingo—now passing as free in the United States defines the real terror within *The Black Vampyre*. For readers of New York periodicals, who consumed the same waves of anxious information that Dey did, this narrative twist at the end of *The Black Vampyre* may well have been understood as a fantastical extension of pieces they encountered on a quotidian basis. In many ways, the serial effusion of concerns about Haiti's influence on American culture animates Dey's attempt to transplant vampirism to St. Domingo. The novella's solidarity, in other words, resides more with domestic fears of racialized resistance to continued enslavement than it does with Polidori's lampoon of Byron. Despite a paucity of evidence to support their fears, white Americans (almost as an unquestioned reflex) constantly fantasized about restaging the Haitian Revolution as a domestic event (even as they always hoped for an alternative outcome). This tendency suffuses the circulation of information concerning Coco's attempts to liberate Augusta and the surrounding districts, as well as countless other representations of attempts at self-liberation. It is this profound anxiety about events in St. Domingo inspiring further resistance to white supremacy and racial capitalism in the United States that haunts Dey's text. The Black Vampyre's child lingers in the United States as a reminder that the problem of racialized revolution was not a geographically distant phenomenon but, rather, one that might erupt domestically at any moment.

By virtue of his connections to Africa and St. Domingo, this child brings with him to the United States similar latent anxieties about an international Black radical solidarity that the supposed origins of Coco incited when news of his connection to Haiti circulated just a few weeks prior to the publication of *The Black Vampyre*. In both cases, the legacies of Haiti lingered like an undead revenant haunting the supposedly paternalistic practices of enslavement in the United States. Both cases prove how all the benign rhetoric about merciful behavior (insidiously used to prop up the violent regime of white supremacist power) barely disguised how so many white people in the United States also believed they too sleep at the foot of Vesuvius. This fear about racial retribution surfaced in the racist assumptions circulating in New York's print public sphere about how free African Americans could not successfully assimilate into dominate white culture, that they would no doubt move to violently upend social stability because they were presumed incapable of becoming equal citizens. Moreover, the specter of Haitian connections (and the knowledge of the role free Black people played in the Haitian Revolution) accelerated the terror of these aborted rebellions by dredging up barely submerged fears about the possibility of international Black solidarity.

Whatever differences—geographical, social, or topographical—that separated a pre-revolutionary Cape François or Augusta from New York, they were over-written by the shared fear of how an uprising of diasporic Africans intent on liberation could potentially compromise the fragile white social fabric. This commonly held sense of an imperiled whiteness may well explain why bookdealers imagined that readers in South Carolina would be interested in Dey's text. Just as readers in New York maintained an interest in unsuccessful southern rebellions of enslaved people, so too did southerners continued to think about how the undying legacies of the Haitian rebellion haunted the American imagination on a national level. An interest in the revolutionary countertopography of the circum-Atlantic world animates both the plot and the marketing of *The Black Vampyre*. Dey's satiric New-Worlding of old world terrors brings home how the Haitian Revolution had already rooted itself in the American psyche.

No evidence of Coco's origins circulated outside of the initial rumors about his Haitian connection.[69] While the possibility exists that Coco was forced to migrate to North America with a refugee French or Creole planter fleeing the Revolution in St. Domingo, it is just as likely, given the speed of suppositions about connections to Haiti, that his supposed revolutionary genealogy was simply annexed to his attempt at rebellion as a shopworn explanatory cause.[70] The American imagination was always quick to link any domestic uprising, either rumored or suppressed, to Haiti. Accompanying this readily accessible explanation, then, was the assumption that all diasporic Africans with a connection to St. Domingo, even the fictionalized Anthony Gibbons, would likely have revolutionary intent. The force of these assumptions combined to suppress any possible examination of the horrible conditions of enslavement within the United States by providing white Americans with a foreign locus in which to invest their attention. The idea of Haitian rebels secreted within the United States, clandestinely working to foment unrest, was perhaps the most circulated gothic tale of the American nineteenth century. From endless whispers to countless periodicals accounts, these haunting fears about imagined Haitian connections were always readily reanimated, no matter what specific situation had actually occurred. This was the real serial revenant, the un-killable legacy that nobody, no Personne, could vanquish despite their repeated attempts to murder the source of their anxieties.

Coda

"What's Past Is Epilogue"

On June 2nd, 2020, @Noushiex3 posted two photos on Instagram of herself at a Black Lives Matter protest in Boston. In both images, she holds a hand-lettered sign above her head declaring that "Haiti did it in 1804; this is just Round 2 We Got You!"[1] @Noushiex3's original post registered almost 9,000 "likes," and has to date garnered over 340 comments. A brief caption accompanies the post, which @Noushiex3 begins with the lines, "It's not impossible. Don't tell me it can't be done." The post ends with five hashtags, the last of which are "#NoJusticeNoPeace" and "#MyBlackLifeMatters." Out of the dozens of figures in the first photo, only @Noushiex3 gazes back at the viewer. With half her face covered by a light blue surgical mask, @Noushiex3's presence testifies to her participation—in the middle of a global pandemic—in a public struggle against anti-Black violence a week after the murder of George Floyd by Minneapolis police officers. Lingering with this social media post allows us to almost feel @Noushiex3's embodied urgency in representing Haitian self-emancipation as a vital precursor to contemporary American social justice reforms.

The first of the two images posted by @Noushiex3 became a viral text.[2] Perhaps more accurately, the first image became two viral texts: one, which circulated as an affirmation of the connections between Haitian liberation and histories of oppression in the United States; and another, which evoked the history of white supremacist counteractions to Haiti's independence that the early chapters of this book have explored. For example, a Facebook group called "The Haitian American" shared the photo two days later; this post received 2,162 "likes" and was shared an additional 1,242 times by other Facebook users.[3] While there were some dissenting comments posted in response to the reposted photo, by and large users reacted positively to @Noushiex3 theorizing a long hemispheric history of resistance to anti-Blackness. Many of these comments, like one posted by Caly King Momi, register Haiti as an inspiration for liberation of other diasporic Africans, or as Momi argues, "Haiti's courage extended to other Caribbean countries who rebelled and were freed."[4] In essence, Momi endorses @Noushiex3's vocalization of the ways in which the Haitian Revolution engendered both the formation of an independent Black Republic as well as a trans-national sense of new forms of Black political possibilities.

The Haitian Revolution in the Early Republic of Letters: Incipient Fevers. Duncan Faherty, Oxford University Press.
© Duncan Faherty 2023. DOI: 10.1093/oso/9780192889157.003.0007

Essentially, these circulations of @Noushiex3's image affirm her declaration that the Haitian Revolution had changed world history. This reposting of the image simultaneously signal-boost her theorization of how the horrifying legacies of U.S. enslavement did not end with the 1865 passage of the 13th Amendment, but instead have endured as tangible infrastructures of anti-Blackness in contemporary American society. By affirming @Noushiex3's message, these supporters (effectively and affectively) co-sign her assertions that these horrors morphed into racist policing practices in the United States; in effect, @Noushiex3 emphasizes the connection between enslavement and the carceral state, as Michelle Alexander (among others) has so persuasively demonstrated.[5] Indeed, the clearest argument inscribed in the sign stems from its contention that the past resonates in the present. Following the generative work of Tina M. Campt, we can also understand how "the muscular tension" captured in @Noushiex3's portrait "constitutes a state of black powerfulness in the midst of debility, a form of resistance expressed through a refusal to accept or acquiesce to defeat."[6] The image posits an alternative vision for American futurity, one in which Black solidarities find inspiration and power from the implied struggle to win round one. The geographical and temporal distances between the time of the now and Haiti in 1804 collapse because of @Noushiex3's resolve to register these seemingly disconnected moments as intermingled, serialized iterations of a contiguous struggle for fundamental change.[7]

In utterly predictable ways, a significant number of observers of the image actively reinterpreted @Noushiex3's sign as somehow revealing that #BLM activists were intent on fomenting violent retribution.[8] The hate speech of this counterformation denounced the sign's insistence on a emancipatory vision of history to reactivate a conservative early American understanding of the Haitian Revolution as representing a threat to the foundational privileges of whiteness that animate American democracy.[9] Refusing to comprehend "we got you" as an expression of Black solidarity, disavowing it as a repudiation of resurging anti-Black violence, these alt-right social media users attempted to convince others that the sign presents proof of an international conspiracy to eradicate the Republic.[10] Moreover, by imagining the "we" indicates proof of international conspiracies, these conservative trolls also attempted to label African Americans as unpatriotic by linking them not with any American protest tradition but with (and only with) a supposedly radical and foreign ideology.[11]

The idea that Haiti might provide a generative model for African American equality remains an anathema in white American culture. Undeniably, for any reader of the early American print public sphere, the racist reactions to @Noushiex3's theorization of reverberating hopefulness are hauntingly familiar. Without question, these contemporary alt-right social media users move to obliterate any possible solidarities between the U.S. and Haiti with as much vitriol as many of the conservative figures examined in this book's previous chapters.

These contemporary anxieties about the influence that Haiti might have on the United States reverberate with the same palpable force as any of those crafted by early American partisan periodical writers two centuries before them. This linkage in discursive strategy reveals how the internet has provided a forum for partisan writing perhaps unmatched at any moment between the early American print public sphere and our own siloes of circulating media streams.[12] Considered as part of a lengthy tradition of conservative vilifications of Haiti, these alt-right reactions to @Noushiex3 posts are a contemporary manifestation of a long American aversion to the idea of Haiti as a space of freedom.

At the same time, @Noushiex3 reminds us that these attempts at dismissal willfully ignore a multitude of other historical connections between Haiti and the early American Republic. Yet, @Noushiex3's declaration has its own exigent intellectual genealogy, one whose roots can be traced back to the efforts of early-nineteenth-century African American writers who worked to cast Haiti otherwise.[13] While the texts examined in this book have largely focused on the first two decades of the nineteenth century, a different interpretative trajectory concerning the meaning of Haiti began to emerge at the tail end of this period with the rise of African American owned and operated print networks. This African American-centered print public sphere forms the cornerstone of the tradition invoked by the hand-lettered protest sign that so vividly unsettled thousands of contemporary white supremacists. This tradition, which would be the subject of another book altogether, begins to unfold in the very first issue of *Freedom's Journal*, and suggests how a parallel genealogy over how to best interpret the legacies of Haiti began to enter into the American print public sphere.

By way of concluding this project, the Coda briefly examines how this alternative imagination of Haiti complicated the racialized panic that circulated (often unchallenged) for so long in the early American Republic of letters. As representations of Haiti as a beacon of freedom began to compete for attention with the figurations of Haiti as a space of infectious danger, the larger white dominated print public sphere actively sought to disarticulate the influence of the Haitian Revolution on the United States as a means of silencing this dissent. The burgeoning circulation of these counter figurations, which often actively rewrote the tropes of these white supremacist figurations of Haiti, effectively draws to a close the canonical interregnum examined in this book.

"To Our Patrons"

Plans to commemorate Emancipation Day were underway all across New York State in the spring of 1827, since—after a lengthy process that had begun twenty-seven years earlier—the state's legislative efforts to outlaw slavery within its borders were finally being realized. To commemorate this unprecedented legal change, a variety of prominent free Africans Americans in Manhattan sought to amplify the influence of Black owned and operated civic, religious, and social organizations and institutions that, they believed, might provide proper infrastructures of support for the soon to be emancipated. As Leslie M. Harris has demonstrated, these efforts brought to the surface "some of the conflicts among blacks as to what the community's public presence should be, as well as the beginnings of class tensions among New York City's antebellum blacks." As Harris argues, the city's "black middle class" was concerned about the potential unruliness of public celebrations and attempted to preempt spontaneous demonstrations by promoting "new" traditions "of moral reform activism" as the optimal commemorations. They hoped, in essence, to turn the vast majority of soon to be emancipated Black New Yorkers into "observers and spectators," who could be guided by "the more educated and religious" sections of New York's elite African American community.[14]

While a profound class bias suffuses these sentiments, they also reveal well-founded anxieties about how the white community was going to react to localized emancipation. As Robert Levine has observed, these fears about predictable white backlash against Black freedom exhibit how these middle-class freemen were keenly aware of "the limitations of New York's emancipation act in a nation in which slavery remained the laws of the land."[15] New York's Emancipation Act was fragile not simply in geographical terms, but also because its effectiveness entirely depended on a white police apparatus and a white juridical system to insure its effectiveness. It would take little effort, these middle-class freemen understood, for white spectators, property owners, and police officers to erroneously reclassify spontaneous public celebrations as riots. Especially given how "blackness" in American society, as Kevin Quashie insightfully argues, is "commonly understood" as "expressive, dramatic, or loud," and how the "dominant expectation we have of black culture" is perceived to be "resistance."[16] This restrictive figuration, as Quashie details, lends itself to figuring "black subjectivity" as existing "for its social and political meaningfulness rather than as a marker of the human individuality of the person who is black."[17] This interpolation of Blackness as resistance also lends itself to white supremacist policing strategies that retain the power to determine when public expression becomes public nuisance or when loudness becomes the soundtrack to criminal behavior. Attempting to limit animated, flamboyant celebrations of Emancipation Day were, simultaneously, also efforts to forestall white counterreactions in the form of harassment, arrests, and lynching.

To make their case for civil and stoic commemorations, these middle-class freemen sought to educate the wider African American community about how best to plan both for Emancipation Day itself and for life afterwards. One such effort, organized by John Wilk, Peter Williams, Jr., and William Hamilton among others, was the formation of the *Freedom's Journal*, designed to be the first newspaper owned, operated, published, and edited by African Americans in the United States. The founders of the paper hired John B. Russwurm and Samuel Cornish to be the inaugural editors early in 1827, and under their joint steward-ship, the first issue of *Freedom's Journal* appeared in Manhattan on March 16, 1827. From the outset of their plans, the publishers felt it was imperative to culti-vate a Black print public sphere in advance of juridical emancipation. This sense of urgency reflected the organizers hopes that the paper itself might become a forum through which its readers might think through the complex dimensions of localized liberation within a nation still defined by its investments in enslave-ment, and in a Western world still largely defined by anti-Blackness. They hoped, in short, that *Freedom's Journal* would serve as both a conduit of information and a pedagogic device to educate the vast majority of New York's African American population as they began the difficult and uncertain work of transitioning out of enslavement.

While Russwurm and Cornish were unlikely collaborators (indeed their part-nership was short lived), their efforts at establishing a nascent African American print network to promote and circulate the *Freedom's Journal* were nothing short of remarkable.[18] When the inaugural issue appeared, there were over 300,000 free African Americans within the United States and an estimated 16,000 living in New York itself.[19] Over one hundred weekly editions of the four-page, four-column paper appeared before it eventually folded in 1829. At its peak, the paper boasted a national readership that stretched across eleven states as well as the District of Columbia, with additional international subscribers in Canada, the United Kingdom, and Haiti. Few other American periodicals had anything approaching such a dispersed readership, and the fact that the *Freedom's Journal* did so underscores the immense efforts necessary to move beyond a print culture overseen by white editors and white publishers who catered to white readers. In many ways, to be a participant in the Black print public sphere in the spring of 1827 meant reading a copy of *Freedom's Journal*, since it was unlikely that any of its materials would recirculate within white centered print networks.

The infrastructure needed to reach readers interested in *Freedom's Journal* was groundbreaking, especially given the legal prohibitions against non-white people transporting letters and printed matter enacted by the U.S. postal system.[20] Given all the highly developed ways in which white supremacists in the United States sought to deter and undermine the formation of Black solidarities across space and time, the cultivation of a geographically disparate readership for *Freedom's Journal* was in almost every sense of the term revolutionary. As Gordon Fraser has noted, Cornish and Russwurm created "a network that included forty-seven authorized agents and extended from Waterloo, Ontario, to rural North Carolina, from Port-au-Prince to Liverpool to Richmond, Baltimore, and New Orleans" in an effort to distribute the "the more than eight hundred [weekly] issues" of the paper.[21] At a local level, as Jaqueline Bacon has argued, the paper labored to counter the racist figurations of free African Americans frequently circulated in early-nineteenth-century New York (and penned by such anti-Black writers as the infamous Mordecai Noah, whose vile caricatures appeared on an almost quotidian basis in a variety of New York periodicals).[22]

The first issue of *Freedom's Journal* included a "To Our Patrons" column comprising nearly three-quarters of the first page. In this declaration of purpose, Cornish and Russwurm detailed their intention to cover a broad range of issues and to connect with Black readers in ways never before achieved. Embracing the opportunity to "plead our own case," since for "too long have others spoken for us," Cornish and Russwurm endeavored to shift the boundaries of the American print public sphere by creating a periodical unfettered by the demands and desires of the white publishing industry.[23] Redressing how materials within American periodicals had been overdetermined (on every subject) by white writers and white editors focused on the concerns of white readers, Cornish and Russwurm aimed at exposing how the American print public sphere, to borrow a devastatingly acute phrase from Benjamin Fagan, was in reality devoted to "chronicling white America."[24]

The "misrepresentations" that have "deceived" the "public" about the capacities and moral character of diasporic Africans, Cornish and Russwurm maintained, effectively policed African American lives whether now free or still enslaved.[25] To put it another way, the decidedly anti-Black representations routinely permeating the U.S. print public sphere justified a multipronged campaign to prevent Africans Americans from achieving political, economic, or social equality. By endlessly publishing negative examples to buttress white domination, the mainstream white periodical press continued to subjugate African Americans by associating them with "vice" and "poverty."[26] These delusory associations implied that African Americans were incapable of actual equality and thus effectively underwrote efforts to curtail their social mobility. Yet, as Russwurm and Cornish knew full well, since New York's Emancipation Acts did not provide any compensation for decades spent in enslavement, the freedoms that it was producing were, at best, incomplete. The legislation's failure to create secure pathways to equality meant that it effectively underwrote the formation of new forms of exploitation and continued discrimination.

The mission statement of *Freedom's Journal* diagnosed the enduring material and psychic effects of enslavement "because no sufficient efforts" arose—even on the part of the "many in society who exercise toward us benevolent feelings"—to consider the needs of individuals whose "minds [were] contracted by slavery." Public efforts around emancipation, in sum, oversimplified the physical, emotional, and mental traumas of enslavement by endlessly disavowing the existence of structural racism. In sum, Cornish and Russwurm maintained that since little actual support materialized to help formerly enslaved people to transition toward freedom, they were likely destined to remain second-class citizens. Since "no publication, as yet, has been devoted to" the concerns of African Americans readers, they announce their plan to create "a public channel" to address this void. In order to fulfill this ambition, the editors realized that they needed to extend their reach beyond regional concerns and to bear in mind that simply advocating for expanded abolition would not adequately address either the short- or long-term needs of African Americans. To counter the machinations of a culture intent on enacting post-emancipatory avenues for continued segregation and exploita-tion, Cornish and Russwurm implored their readers to think about the deeper meanings of freedom and equality beyond the horizon of emancipation. As such, the editors' open letter invited readers to actively participate in the production of the paper rather than simply passively consume its information.[27]

While "mindful" of the urgent needs of "our brethren who are still in the iron fetters of bondage," the editors pledged to campaign against enslavement in part by disseminating information about Africa and diasporic Africans outside the United States.[28] They did so because they understood how anti-Blackness was not (and could never be) simply a domestic phenomenon. By drawing attention to global Black histories and cultures, they hoped to provide anti-racist examples to combat the centrality of white supremacist thought within American culture. They aimed not simply to end the plantocracy and enslavement, but to address how the larger white supremacist American society had continued to disenfran-chise free people of color after emancipation. Keenly aware of how white society carefully nourished incipient strategies for unremitting subjection, Cornish and Russwurm declared that *Freedom's Journal* intended to oppose anti-Blackness writ large.

As I argued in Chapter 5, the ever-increasing backlash against free people of color was particularly true in New York, as the process of gradual emancipation had generated insidious new forms of anti-Blackness.[29] As emancipated African Americans entered the wage-earning work force, they routinely encountered attempts to delimit their social and economic mobility. New York was, in short, a hotbed of nascent proto-Jim Crowism that curtailed the conditions of possibility for African American New Yorkers.[30] While countering these tendencies was part of the aim of *Freedom's Journal*, the editors made clear that simply speaking back would not effectively counter widespread racist demagoguery. "To Our Patrons" attempts to shift what social theorist James P. Overton defines as "the window of discourse," or what political theorists more commonly refer to now as "the Overton window."[31] By broadcasting their ambitions as greater than cataloging the myriad injustices of enslavement, Cornish and Russwurm defined their mis-sion as theorizing new conditions of possibility of and for freedom itself. In essence, they sought to shift the terrain of the print public sphere by widening the range of acceptable discourses around citizenship and equality by creating a space for Black writing that could reach the public unfiltered by the concerns of white editors and white publishers.

While they did not explicitly make this claim, they intimated that racist thinking (perhaps benign but racist nonetheless) animated white writing about African Americans, since that writing remained predicated on the question of enslavement rather than on the question of freedom. For Cornish and Russwurm, this distinction exists as both fundamental and indispensable as they move to liberate African Americans from the position of simply providing testimony or explanatory evidence for white abolitionists. Cornish and Russwurm, like everyone else involved in the founding of *Freedom's Journal*, knew full well that emancipation laws did little in 1827 (or indeed 1863 or 1865 or 1868) to address the structural violence of forcing people to endure decades in bondage.[32] These juridical Acts provided a present tense change without addressing the *longue durée* of anti-Blackness. Cornish and Russwurm frame this sentiment in their articulation of how "our vices and degradations are ever arrayed against us, but our virtues are passed by unnoticed."[33] Worst still were the ways in which even "our friends" have "from these causes" effectively "fallen into the current of popular feeling."[34] As such, these otherwise steadfast white allies are "actually living in the practice of prejudice, while they abjure it in theory, and feel it not in their hearts."[35]

In many ways, Cornish and Russwurm anticipated Saidiya Hartman's argument in *Scenes of Subjection* concerning how quickly emancipation discourses morphed into new liberal forms of domination. While focused on the failures of Reconstruction, Hartman argues, "emancipation appears less the grand event of liberation than a point of transition between modes of servitude and racial subjection." Yet her claim also aptly describes how New York's transition from legitimatizing enslavement to legally prohibiting it did not actually produce freedom or equality in the state. Indeed, one might say that New York became a breeding ground for the development and instantiation of nascent forms of discrimination that begrudgingly admitted an end to legalized enslavement but continued to refuse to include African Americans within "the appellation 'human.'" Witnessing the advent of these new constraints on Black freedom first-hand in New York, Cornish and Russwurm emphasized coverage of spaces independent of white authority as a means of disassociating Black equality from white benevolence. The habituated anti-Blackness that routinely circulated in the U.S. print public sphere long served as a means of retrenching African American freedom by perpetuating racist stereotypes about these spaces as incapable of actual democratic self-government. Cornish and Russwurm knew that since enslavement was never just a domestic concern, advancing the cause of Black freedom could not simply adhere to national boundaries. In other words, they understood how the specters of anti-Blackness, which shaped American perceptions about the rest of the world, had a direct impact on African American futurity. To counter how falsified knowledge about Africa and Haiti were used to restrict African American participation in the American polity, Cornish and Russwurm sought to use *Freedom's Journal* to realign the operant Overton window. They aimed to do so by underscoring how essential the depictions of extra-national spaces of Black life were for the cultivation of a new form of a U.S. print public sphere.[36]

As I have argued in this book, a wide range of white American writers seized on Haiti to diminish the capabilities of diasporic Africans and to sound out the nightmarish possibilities of what Black freedom and solidarity might mean for the white citizens of the United States.[37] Some of this attention to Haiti was a result of geographic proximity but, more importantly, it also stemmed from how the French colony of Saint-Domingue represented both the nadir and the apex of the plantocracy. More so than any other space on the globe, the majority of Americans figured Haiti as a lodestone for thinking about the conditions of possibility for maintaining or ending enslavement in the United States. Highly aware of this fixation on Haiti as a nexus in the American imagination, Russwurm and Cornish sought to alter this recurring denigration by reeducating the public about the import of Haiti. In so doing, they sought to enact new structures of thought and feeling about domestic forms of social justice, freedom, and equality. Since Haiti served as a locus for white American anxieties about emancipation and larger questions of racialized freedom, altering perceptions about Haiti was a central tenet of the mission of *Freedom's Journal*.[38] Mary Grace Albanese registers that Cornish and Russwurm "regularly printed laudatory articles about Haiti's past and present, including a biography of Toussaint Louverture."[39] As Albanese proposes, the attention to Haiti in *Freedom's Journal* exhibits how "the Haitian Revolution emerges within this climate"—one which imagined Haiti "as an appealing model of universal rights" and "as a crucial actor in early African American cultural formations."[40] Similarly, Ben Fagan observes, the paper continually deployed the rhetoric of Protestant revivalism and "black chosenness," a term he deploys to underscore how the early Black periodical press labored to depict Black freedom as divinely inspired.[41] Haiti had a special role in the formation of chosenness in that it provided a real world example of Black liberation. In this regard, Cornish and Russwurm understood how it might function as a city on a hill for African Americans. So too did white supremacist Americans, who were so deeply motivated by their fears about Haiti's example that they actively struggled to disavow it as an inspiration for new forms of Black freedom and belonging.

In promulgating Haiti as a model of possibility, as a space which might help further the cause of African American freedom, Cornish and Russwurm sought to interrupt white supremacist efforts to make diasporic Africans pay for the *privilege* of their freedom. Just two years prior to the foundation of *Freedom's Journal*, an 1825 French naval blockade of Haiti had demanded a payment of 150 million francs to compensate French enslavers for what they declared were the lost revenues resulting from Haitian independence. The nefarious imposition of this debt (which the United States helped to enforce), calculated to be a contemporary payment equivalent to over twenty-one billion dollars, was somewhat resolved—over a full century later—in 1947.[42] The gradual approach to emancipation enacted in New York had likewise effectively forced African Americans to prepay for an end to their own enslavement through protracted decades of continued servitude. Conscious as well of their position as part of a minority free Black population in the United States, Cornish and Russwurm felt the urgent need to oppose the imposition of new forms of dominion aimed at making African Americans continual debtors for the "gift" of their freedom.

As I have tried to exhibit in this book, since the outbreak of organized resistance in St. Domingo began in 1791, the former French colony had functioned as a wellspring of anxiety, fear, and revolutionary possibility for white Americans. Repeatedly, American readers had encountered a variety of meditations on these foreign events that enjoined them to consider Haiti as predictive of terrifyingly dreadful futures for the United States. By exporting concerns about the futurity of the Republic offshore to St. Domingo, white American writers sought to stage Haiti as a means of interrogating the state of domestic stability. By transferring anxieties about racial injustice elsewhere, these early Americans could still fervently cling to the hope that isolation and immunization could forestall the need to reimagine racialized hierarchies in the United States. Following the legacies of this logic into our own contemporary moment, we can see how the contemporary alt-right resurrects longstanding reactionary tropes about the Haiti Revolution when it moves to deploy them as buffers against demands for social justice.

Despite the ways in which Americanists have long maintained that early-nineteenth-century African Americans were hesitant to invoke Haiti as a potential model of freedom, as Sara Fanning argues, "neither Haiti's instability nor internal discord could erase the undeniable significance of the revolution to contemporary thought on the slave system."[43] As Fanning impressively demonstrates, beginning in the mid-1820s, "American supporters of Haitian recognition" presented a "major challenge" to the "emerging ideology of white supremacy," which actively labored to efface Haiti's potential emergence as an object lesson for the United States.[44] Those who advocated for these overt connections, including free African Americans who immigrated to Haiti, sought to articulate freedom and emancipation as extra-national issues and to bring the lessons of 1804 to bear on domestic American cultural. One such prominent example of this emergent thinking appeared in *Freedom's Journal* in early 1828.

"A Haytien Tale"

When Frances Smith Foster recovered "Theresa—a Haytien Tale" in 2006, she introduces her discovery by questioning the critical fascination with precedents. Given that the first installment of "Theresa" appeared in the January 18, 1828, issue of *Freedom's Journal* (with the final section published a month later), Foster notes (with caveats about texts not yet identified) that it may well be the earliest published African American fictional text. For Foster, the possibility that "Theresa" offers a canonical origin point affords Americanists an opportunity to rethink the traditional genealogies of American literary history. On the one hand, the text's appearance in the first African American newspaper prompts us to think harder about the various genres published in *Freedom's Journal*. At the same time, the publication date of "Theresa" challenges longstanding assumptions about the development of an African American literary culture so often imagined as rooted in the middle of the nineteenth century. The recovery of "Theresa," Foster argues, evidences the necessity of approaching early African American cultural production "with the knowledge that slavery was not the only—nor always the most pressing—interest in pre-Civil War America." Moreover, she argues, critics must "realize that freedom was understood to have many forms, some more individual and some more communal than others," and that African American cultural production "was not an unmediated mirror of dominant Euro-American" ideologies.[45] The narrative concerns of "Theresa," read in light of Foster's injunctions, constitute as many challenges to our traditional conceptual frameworks as its publication history does for our timelines of American literary production.

As Eric Gardner has observed, critics all too often perpetuate the erroneous "slippage" between "African American literary works" and "slave narratives," as if the latter always encompasses the former in categorizing African American cultural production before Reconstruction, an inaccuracy which reduces all nineteenth-century "black literature into a single genre—albeit a rich one."[46] Such imprecision dangerously blinds readers to how "Theresa" prompts readers to think beyond emancipation, and inhibits the ability to see its speculations about the struggles of free people of color to maintain freedom in the face of renewed white supremacist violence. Furthermore, such slippage makes it harder to see how "Theresa" actively reacts to the white archive of American Haitian texts that this book has examined, and especially the reinscription of Haiti's meaning in the American print public sphere. In centering its plot on free Black women working to maintain their freedom, "Theresa" rejects the multivalent commitments of white authors to extend their shared anti-Blackness by habitually linking the emancipated with the enslaved (effectively always linking them to the past rather than to the future). In this regard, "Theresa" helps us consider what remains embedded within and occluded by residual forms of reading African American literature as always already a reaction to white conceptions of Black life and Black freedom. Of course works by Black authors from or about Haiti were concerned with literal bondage. But, as I have shown throughout this study, white authors in the U.S. were so preoccupied by the specter of Haiti precisely because they already intuited what Frances Foster would remind us of so many decades later: that the incipient freedoms captured by the Haitian imaginary in Black literature generated a conception of liberation so far in excess from emancipation alone.

Foremost among the questions raised by "Theresa" is how do we interpret the ramifications of the geography plotted by the text's subtitle? How, in other words, do we comprehend the possibility that the first published fictional text by an African American was "A Haytian Tale?" These questions beg other questions: what do we make of the fact that this text is also very clearly a fantasy about Haitian history? How do we taxonomize a text less invested in the actualities of the actual Revolution and more concerned with reimagining Haiti as a site of Black belonging whose roots seemingly date back to before French colonialization? Our canonical figurations of the late 1820s have long depicted this period as defined by an increased attention to nationally grounded plots and themes, routinely representing this era as marked by the rise of writers such as Washington Irving and James Fenimore Cooper (renowned for their domestically situated narratives). Even after the explosion of work unpacking the circum-Atlantic coordinates of post-revolutionary writers across the last several decades, the late 1820s have for much of American literary history been understood (if they have received any attention at all) as an era marked by a pivoting inward. Typically, these residual critical genealogies suggest that the increased nationalism post the War of 1812 period helped cultivate a domestic marketplace of new forms of decidedly American fictions.

"Theresa" unsettles the saliency of these critical paradigms, as even the nominative coordinates of its subtitle underscore a more complex geography than typically afforded American cultural production from this period. Moreover, the subtitle disrupts the pigeonholing of "antebellum" African American writing as defined by a south to north trajectory intended to shorthand an imagined movement from enslavement to freedom. "Theresa" refutes these presumptions by locating Black freedom not within northern U.S. confines (or migrating freedom further northwards into Canada), but actually in a foreign Caribbean island south of U.S. borders.[47] Foster's generative insights about how we should not compartmentalize African American writing as an "unmediated mirror" of dominant white ideologies offers us one way to understand the more complex geography of "Theresa." Foster, in effect, entreats us to read early African American texts for evidence of how they sought to think beyond questions of enslavement in an effort to speculate about new forms of freedom. In essence, "Theresa" presents a fundamental provocation to the residual contours of nineteenth-century American literary studies by virtue of how its aesthetic strategies resist confinement by our received critical frameworks.

In imploring scholars to read differently—in cautioning against simply seeking in African American cultural production a reiteration of the heteronormative, religious, and universalist impulses animating canonical white cultural production— Foster calls for a recognition of how early African American writing valued "expediency, imagination, and improvisation."[48] Following these injunctions, I want to consider positioning "Theresa" as an example of how African American writers sought to rescript the function of Haiti as a proxy for domestic *American* nightmares beginning in the late 1820s, or to think of how "Theresa" positions Haiti as a site of Black belonging and Black possibility. Moreover, I want to underscore how the text positions itself as a corrective to the endless attempts circulating in the white print public sphere to exhibit Haiti as the antithesis of American democracy. Finally, I suggest that in so doing "Theresa" moves to highlight how these white fantasies about Haiti routinely gloss over the centrality of whiteness in promulgating the tenets of that political formation.

Just as Cornish and Russwurm had understood the need to combat racist figurations of Haiti as a space of violence and anti-democratic corruption—a tradition that to this day has been kept burning by American white supremacists—"S" (the pseudonymous author of "Theresa") sought to remap Haiti as a space of Black national belonging. By depicting Haiti not through the lens of anti-Blackness but as a beacon of possibility for African Americans, "S" produces a radical reconfiguration of Haiti for American readers. "S" does so by reversing the partisan doctrines which for so long had circulated in the United States about the Haitian Revolution. Instead of figuring Haiti as a space of radical freedom after a lengthy struggle against colonial exploitation, "S" conjures an ancestral homeland disrupted by a recent incursion of "French barbarity." Indeed, from the outset, despite the fact that the Revolution has not yet ended in the narrative temporality of the text, the titular hero and her family fear for their safety because of "the inhumanity of her country's enemy." This white violence against the "the oppressed natives of Saint Nicholas," leads the mother of the tale's titular protagonist to conclude, "she must depart from the endeared village of her innocent childhood" in order to safeguard her daughters from harm.[49]

The text opens by emphasizing how a family of free Black women possesses a generational nationalism despite the fact that the plot unfolds before the founding of Haitian Republic as an independent state. The text, essentially, conjures a patriotism that might seem more believable after 1804 than at the moment of the tale's narrative setting. Thinking of how "S" manufactures an anachronistic pre-revolutionary diasporic African patriotic attachment to a post-revolutionary Haiti allows the ways in which "Theresa" presents an improvised version of history to surface. While this conjured future past remains less invested in the actualities of the Haitian Republic, it does intriguingly register "S"'s investments in the inherent possibilities of creating a useable Haitian national past for African American readers.[50] In this sense, Foster's figuration of the plot as "relatively simple" obscures how it is only deceptively so. "Theresa" intimates that diasporic Africans might share an attachment to Haitian liberation and nationhood, and locates these affective bonds in a historical moment when such a commitment was more an unrealized potentiality than an assured possibility.[51] Reading the tale in this way accentuates how "Theresa" concretizes questions of Black life and Black freedom after emancipation into the foreground of its narrative concerns. Moreover, it affords the opportunity to see these thematic concerns—grounded in a theorization of how to hold on to an endangered freedom—resonate with the editorial vision of Russwurm and Cornish as embodied in their mission statement for *Freedom's Journal* itself. In looking toward the example of how free people of color in Haiti had to struggle to maintain their freedom and safeguard both historical attachments and kinship relations, "S" forges a tale about Haiti that is not centered in the fight for emancipation, but rather in the enduring struggle to maintain freedoms already obtained.

Set prior to Toussaint L'Overture's arrest and deportation to France in 1802 (where he would die in prison a year later), the text revolves around the actions of Madame Paulina and her two daughters Amanda and Theresa. At the start of the narrative, fearing for the safety of her family, Madame Pauline decides to flee their ancestral village and venture to a remote "hut" she had once spotted during a previous "summer's excursion" to escape the advancing French army. Disguising herself as a French officer, Madame Pauline travels with forged documents identifying her daughters as prisoners of war so that they can fool any passing French troops. During their travels through verdant groves and resplendent vistas, Theresa overhears some information about a planned surprise attack against Toussaint. Fearing for her country's future, Theresa leaves her mother and her sister to find the general and warn him of this imminent danger. Theresa's intervention allows Toussaint to launch a preemptive counterattack and save the Haitian army from ruin. Although Theresa is left fearing that the French have massacred her family, the text ends by implying that all three women have survived their harrowing flight from French cruelty.

From the outset, the histories of the three female protagonists seems tangled, in large part due to how the text subtly reverses what we think of as the defining tropes of this period. Based on the consistent form of address afforded Madame Paulina and the lack of any indication that any of these women were enslaved, the text clearly refutes any of the conventional ways in which white authored texts habitually featured women of African descent within a plantation setting. In effect, "S" subverts the tropes of mainstream Euro-American Haiti fictions by centering her plot on a Black mother (with discernable genealogical and kinship connections) anxious about white predators menacing her daughters. Habitually in white authored texts set in the Caribbean, the terms would be the inverse, obsessively plotting to guard the imperiled chastity of white women preyed upon by overly sexualized Black men. Within its opening gambit, "Theresa" casts the mass of undifferentiated and animalistic French as the terrorizing perpetrators. Through this counterformation of canonical tropes, "S" moves to dislodge the totality of the anti-Blackness suffusing depictions, of Haiti as an existential threat to American domesticity (in both senses of the word), so familiar in the white American print public sphere. Deeply aware of how popular gothic and sentimental tropes, customarily deployed by white writers, frame rebellious Black figures as dangerous brutes, "S" reverses the subjects of these familiar generic characterizations even as she reanimates the moods they create for her own decidedly different narrative ends. This dynamic recrafting reveals the depths of "S"'s familiarity with the racist conventions of the white print public sphere even as it exhibits her ambition to address a reading audience not accounted for by white writers.[52]

A few paragraphs later, "S" expands the scale of the French devastations as Madame Pauline ponders the recent destruction of agricultural production in Haiti. In reflecting on what has happened to her native country, she laments that "the once flourishing plantations" of Haiti stood "ruined" because of the current conflict, and that the nation, which had "once" been "the granary of the West Indies," was now an "abode of wretchedness."[53] Given the overinvestment of French colonial authorities in producing cane sugar, the colony was never a net exporter of foodstuffs. Without question, the vast majority of the agricultural products exported from colonial Haiti—whether they took the form of cane sugar, molasses, or rum—were destined for markets in Europe or North America, satisfying the cravings of white Euro-Americans who relied on access to cheap sugar no matter the human cost paid in its production.[54] So not only does "S" replant the verdant fields of Haiti with nourishing grains instead of superfluous commodities, but she also remaps the flow of trade to and from the nation. As such, the text insists that what disrupted this imaginary free circulation of grain were not the revolutionary actions of enslaved peoples, but a French incursion into what the text frames as previously peaceful territories. In essence, "S" frames "Theresa" as a refutation of the relentless ways in which white authored texts about Haiti fixated on how the Revolution had economically ruined white families. As previous chapters have argued, by examining the fractured white families at the center of *Monima* and *The Asylum*, white writers consistently sought to harvest sympathy for lost white profits by relentlessly intimating that the struggle for self-emancipation in Haiti had rendered formerly "good" white patriarchs destitute. By reorienting readers via a speculative mapping of Haiti's place in the circum-Atlantic trade system, "S" registers Haiti as a wellspring of nourishing foodstuffs for Black consumers, as opposed to a sugar factory whose enslaved workers were often nearly starved in order to suppress possible dissent. In so doing, "S" counters Haiti's function as a white fantasy space of depravity, sexual licentiousness, and endlessly extractable wealth in favor of framing it as a long-standing site of Black possibility.

As Marlene Daut persuasively argues, "Theresa" falls short of accurately depicting Haiti; the text's accounting of geography, of flora and fauna, of Toussaint's life, or even the trajectory of the Revolution itself clearly emerges as fiction and not fact.[55] Daut correctly assesses the lack of veracity in "S"'s reconstruction of Haiti, and as she notes in her compelling reading of "Theresa," these inconsistences perhaps reveal that the author had little first-hand knowledge of the Haitian

Republic.[56] Still, rather than fault "S" for propagating misinformation, my own inclination is to read the text as a conscious rebuttal of the slanderous depictions of white American writers, who for so long had controlled how Haiti was depicted in the American print public sphere. Reading in this way opens up the possibility for understanding "S" as unsettling the constrained representation of Haiti implanted in the American imagination. In essence, I want to assert that "S," following the injunctions of Russwurm and Cornish's mission statement, and their arguments about the need to think about free Black life outside of North America, moves to write back against popular white supremacist renderings in an effort to remap the import of Haiti. In reconceptualizing the dominant image of Haiti for the American print public sphere—the habitual use of Haiti as a proxy to stage anxieties about white security and white democracy—"S" rearticulates Haiti as a symbol of Black freedom and Black citizenship for the readers of the *Freedom's Journal.*[57]

Instead of attempting to correct misapprehensions about Haiti, "S" constructs a portrait of Haiti that takes seriously the projection of a new kind of fantasy about the relationship between diasporic Africans and "New World" settlements. One way to consider the narrative ambitions of "Theresa" is to recognize it as an attempt to deploy fabulation as a means to articulate liberation. As Saidiya Hartman has argued in defining critical fabulation, the archival materials that we have inherited function so as to marginalize the history of the oppressed (and especially the enslaved) and thus remain overdetermined by white supremacy.[58] Improvising through fabulation offers a pathway toward disavowing the supremacy of white erasures that predetermined Haiti's treatment in white American periodicals. Given the suppression of first-hand accounts that reflected the thoughts, experiences, and hopes of diasporic Africans in St. Domingo during the Revolution—an almost non-existent archive in the American print public sphere—"S" embraces the aesthetics of critical fabulation to forge potential connections between African Americans and Black Haitians. Considered in this vein, the text posits that belonging and ancestral connections as facets of diasporic African identities in the Americas, instead of just defining them through stifling forms of alienation and dislocation. Moreover, given how Haiti was a locus for almost every imaginable anxiety for mainstream American ideologies, to think otherwise (regardless of geographical and botanical misnomers) stands as a revolutionary act of fabulation in and of itself. The rhetorical thrust of "Theresa," in short, positions marginalized voices not simply as refuters of white supremacist distortions, but as agents capable of defending Black families and Black citizens against its hegemonic force.

While the plot of "Theresa" may be deceptively simple, the text nevertheless holds a pivotal place in American literary history, existing as one of the earliest attempts to redraw, fictively, the boundaries of the American experience to marginalize white subjectivities. In effect, we might consider "Theresa" as a harbinger of the sign forged by @Noushiex3: both texts insist that Haiti provides an example that African Americans might follow. "Theresa" may not record a realistic account of the Haitian Revolution, but it also resists representing that history as a threat to the United States. It may not render the environmental history of the island properly, but the reconfiguration of the agricultural production of the island it posits transforms Haiti into a granary for Black futurity. The text does not promote unhinged violence against white people; instead, it culminates in detailing a defensive set of maneuvers that preserve Black life. The celebratory tone in the text resonates in its descriptions of an army (guided by the selfless Theresa) that fights to preserve freedom and safeguard Black kinship. "Theresa" is not a war song or a revenge fantasy but rather a ballad that lovingly positions an idea of Haiti as creating the conditions of possibility for Black solidarities. In short, "S" was well aware of how the white print public sphere had delimited the meaning of the version of Haiti that circulated within in the United States, and "Theresa" represents her attempts to counter these enclosing tropes. "S" undertakes this work by narratively reversing the by now all too familiar moves which these white authors had relied on to denigrate Haitian independence. In essence, she flips the white supremacist script that disavowed the insurgent theorizations of freedom embodied in the Haitian Republic.

At its core, "Theresa" works to highlight the life affirming promises of Black kinship, Black patriotism, and Black belonging. The text achieves this by transposing many of the white American distortions of Haitian liberation in order to elevate Black possibility and Black survival. In so doing, "Theresa" revises the fantasies of such white American fictions as "The Story of Makandal" and *The Black Vampyre* to empower readers to see the Haitian Revolution as engendering incipient hope instead of only fear, and to see its legacies as fomenting incipient forms of freedom rather than recirculating forms of terror. Written for the pages of the first African American periodical, "Theresa" authors an improvised version of Haitian possibility for the readers of the *Freedom's Journal* in total sympathy with mission statement of that paper's editors. "S," to put it another way, mirrors the efforts of Russwurm and Cornish to instantiate new meanings of Haiti for African American readers. Extending and amplifying the paper's editorial orientations, "S" rebukes the *fictions* crafted by white authors which habitually arrayed Haitian "vices and degradations" to disavow global Black freedoms and circum-Atlantic Black solidarities.[59] In short, "Theresa" conjures a new vision of what a "Haytian tale" could offer the American print public sphere: one that erects a new foundation of possibility above the ruinous groundwork fabricated in countless white supremacist disavowals.

A Tale of Two Archives

The foundational fiction inaugurated by "S" in "Theresa" was, of course, far from the last African American reconfiguration of the meaning of Haiti as offering a beacon of possibility for national futurity. Indeed, similar reconceptualizations of the import of Haiti suffuse a range of later-nineteenth-century texts. Just a year after the publication of "Theresa," David Walker's *Appeal to the Colored Citizens of the World* (1829) began to circulate up and down the eastern seaboard of the United States. Walker celebrates Haiti as a sanctified space of solidarity and protection for African Americans.[60] A wide range of prominent mid-nineteenth-century African American reformers and activists, including James McCune Smith, William Wells Brown, and Frederick Douglass, made frequent references to Toussaint and to the Haitian Revolution in public orations and lectures.[61] Toward the close of the nineteenth century, Pauline Hopkins's *Of One Blood* (first serialized in 1902–3) explores the Haitian valences of radical possibility by mining her earlier theorizations about Haiti's anti-imperialist example that previously appeared in *The Colored American*.[62] Even this somewhat scattershot and gestural accounting registers the ways in which countless African American writers, intellectuals, artists, orators, politicians, religious leaders, activists, and theorists turned and returned to the possibilities of Haitian freedom as a means of thinking about American anti-Blackness and the potential for domestic social justice reforms.

If "Theresa" serves as the first of these iterations of African American concepts of Haitian possibility it was far from the last. All across the nineteenth century—in everything from whispered conversations to public printed declarations—African Americans actively refuted the delimiting white supremacist insistence on figuring Haiti as the antithesis of American democracy. This counterformation was, in many ways, compelled to tackle the oppressive ways white writers across the era of ungood feelings had labored to immunize the American political ecosystem from the incipient fever of Haitian forms of Black belonging. Indeed, from the earliest days of the Republic to our own contemporary moment, the idea that African Americans might look elsewhere—beyond the enclosing powers of white American authority—for models of belonging undeniably works against the centrality of white cultural hegemony. Yet it is also important to recall that these alternative models were not always necessarily proposing violence as the means of resistance. The radical potential of treating Haiti as a site of political and social inspiration, rather than as a locus for fearmongering, lays bare how Haiti has for so long served as a black mirror for the white American imagination.[63] Then and now, homegrown fantasies about Haiti have haunted the formation of the American Republic of letters in ways that we are only yet beginning to account for.

Without question, there would have been readers in 1828 who reacted to the publication of "Theresa" in much the same way as the cotemporary alt-right responded to @Noushiex3's Instagram posts. Then and now American white supremacists react with vitriolic horror to any affirmation of the idea that Haiti's liberation created conditions of possibility for a reconstitution of American conceptions of belonging and democracy. Then and now in their disavowals of any connections between Haiti and the United States, these conservative actors seek to broadcast their limited notions of American nationalism even as they seek to whitewash their delimited configuration of the American polity. Then and now these active forgings of connections between the two Republics, these insistences of the possibility of a circum-Atlantic Black solidarity that might circumnavigate the repressive forces of an equally global white supremacy, unsettle normative forms of domination and spark outrageous fantasies of violence. In this sense, Haiti has always functioned as a tale of two archives in the American cultural imagination. Anthony Bogues asserts that the "idea" of Haiti has always "generated multiple archives that regularly collided," serving as locus for "an idea of freedom about the capacity of the black body for sovereignty," as a "colonial fantasy," and as a reminder for white Euro-Americans of "the 'horrors' of St Dominque."[64] For Bogues, these collisions and inflections range across the entirety of Western modernity and Western historiography, and his sense of the seismic force of the idea of Haiti within Western culture remains undeniable. The particular American disarticulations and enunciations of these recursive collisions are, as such, only a fragment of the larger story. Still, attending to this neglected splinter of American literary history allows us to short-circuit the presumptive logics of imagining that a whiggish progressivism was the hallmark of nineteenth century American cultural production.

The aim of this book has been to recover the ways in which one idea of Haiti infused the early American Republic of letters as a consistent and divisive means of thinking about the futurity of the United States. This long neglected but still significant archive of American literary production was widely circulated across the first two decades of the nineteenth century; moreover, these tropes about the horrors of St Dominque routinely shaped the ways in which white American writers and readers interpolated questions of Black freedom both domestically and internationally. The neglect of this archive has allowed the sedimentary patterns of periodization that formed alongside the birth of the field to retain their primacy within American literary history. Perhaps even more problematically, the neglect of this archive has also helped bolster disavowals of the importance of the other idea of Haiti, the one that opens an archive of political possibility. The muting of the foundational function of texts from the first two decades of the nineteenth century in our accounting of American literary history has allowed the import of that celebratory idea of Haiti to remain marginalized. Just as "S" repudiated these attempts at effacement in designing a vision of Haiti as a nexus for thinking about African American liberation, @Noushiex3's defiant stasis sounds out how the past resonates in contemporary social justice movements as well as within our operant notions of cultural history. Engaging with texts published during the canonical interregnum teaches us the hollowness in thinking of the United States as an isolationist imaginary. Such xenophobic mappings may well be the most fictional elements of our narratives about national development.

By returning to these neglected archives, I hope that the field can move beyond the stiflingly reductive focus on the chronotopes of "antebellum" and "postbellum" as figurations of freedom and unfreedom in the American nineteenth century.[65] Such a fixation endlessly distorts how sectionalism, partisanship, and white anxieties about Black equality and freedom were and are always colliding within the archives of American literary history.

Notes

Introduction

1. The three volumes of *Zelica, the Creole; a Novel* (London: W. Fearman, 1820), were first printed in London under the byline "An American." The text was advertised alongside two other novels (*The Stranger in Mexico* and *The Scarlet Handkerchief*) purportedly written by the same author which had recently been "transmitted to the Publisher from America." All citations from the novel are from this edition. See *Zelica*, 3: 290–1.

2. One notable exception to this tendency is the important intervention made by the essays collected in a project edited by Elizabeth Maddock Dillion and Michael Drexler. This collection provides one of the most comprehensive attempts to map out the complex ways in which the early U.S. struggled with how to interpret the meaning of the Haitian Revolution. Indeed, Dillion and Drexler's introduction to the volume serves as a crucial survey of critical figurations of this evolving phenomenon of U.S. interpretations of the meaning of Haiti for the early American Republic. See Elizabeth Maddock Dillion and Michael Drexler, "Haiti and the Early United States, Entwined," in *The Haitian Revolution and the Early United States: Histories, Textualities, Geographies*, ed. Elizabeth Maddock Dillon and Michael J. Drexler (Philadelphia: University of Pennsylvania Press, 2016), 1–15.

3. Lisa Lowe deftly charts how liberal versions of freedom, narrativized as an overcoming of enslavement and oppression, were deeply connected to the expansion of Anglo-American empires. Central to her work is the argument that the abstracting promises of freedom often obscure their own embeddedness within racist colonial conditions. In many ways, what Lowe describes helps us unpack the embedded logics of canon formation. See especially the fifth chapter, "Freedoms Yet to Come," of Lowe's *The Intimacies of Four Continents* (Durham: Duke University Press, 2015).

4. One example of the serial attention afforded news of the Haitian Revolution is the way in which an 1802 rumor of invasion by French "negroes" sparked the declaration of martial law in South Carolina. For more information on this event and its aftermath, see my recent essay, Duncan Faherty, "'The Mischief that Awaits Us': Revolution, Rumor, and Serial Unrest in the Early Republic," in *The Haitian Revolution and the Early United States: Histories, Textualities, Geographies*, ed. Elizabeth Maddock Dillon and Michael Drexler (Philadelphia: University of Pennsylvania Press, 2016), 58–80.

5. Avery Gordon's concept of haunting as a mode of social analysis invites us to think about how a lingering presence, simultaneously present and absent, shapes how knowledge production occurs by "forcing a confrontation, forking the future and the past" (xvii). Ghostly matters, in this sense, blur distinctions between temporal modalities, and provide a useful way to consider how Haiti shaped knowledge production in the early United States. See Avery, Gordon, *Ghostly Matters: Haunting and The*

Sociological Imagination (Minneapolis: University of Minnesota Press, 1997), 8. My own thinking about hauntology more closely aligns with the work of Gordon because of her explicit focus of the importance of race in thinking about the cultural ramifications of haunting. Still, without question, Gordon's work and most of the work around the concept of haunting within the Western imagination builds upon Jacques Derrida's formative work in *Specters of Marx: The State of the Debt, the Work of Mourning and the New International* (New York: Routledge 1994). Derrida crucially articulates a variety of processes by which liberal framings of progressivism overwrite and neglect the lingering impact of historical violences that continue to produce suffering in the contemporary world.

6. This assertion echoes the formative work of a range of scholars who have labored to make the import of the Haitian Revolution more visible in our collective view of the late-eighteenth-century circum-Atlantic world. Such important critics including the groundbreaking work of C.L.R. James in *The Black Jacobins: Toussaint L'Ouverture and the San Domingo Revolution* (New York: Random House, 1938), as well as Michel-Rolph Trouillot's *Silencing the Past: Power and the Production of History* (New York: Beacon Press, 1995), Colin Dayan's *Haiti, History, and the Gods* (Berkeley: University of California Press, 1995), and more recently Julius S. Scott's *The Common Wind: Afro-American Currents in the Age of the Haitian Revolution* (London: Verso, 2018). As this project argues much more so than the French Revolution (even as many citizens of the early American Republic saw these two events as inseparable and intimately connected), the Haitian Revolution had a profound impact on how Americans constructed both their own conceptions of democracy as well as their own national futurity. Following the work of James, Trouillot, Dayan, and Scott in asserting the climacteric effects of the Haitian Revolution on the entire Atlantic world, my project moves to further explicate one portion of that impact by attending to the United States across the first two decades of the nineteenth century.

7. Elizabeth Maddock Dillon, *New World Drama: The Performative Commons in the Atlantic World, 1649–1849* (Durham: Duke University Press, 2014), 59.

8. Some important examples of this work include: Sean X. Goudie, *Creole America: The West Indies and the Formation of Literature and Culture in the New Republic* (Philadelphia: University of Pennsylvania Press, 2006); Chris Iannini, *Fatal Revolutions: Natural History, West Indian Slavery, and the Routes of American Literature* (Chapel Hill: The University of North Carolina Press, 2012); Andy Doolen, *Territories of Empire: U.S. Writing from the Louisiana Purchase to Mexican Independence* (New York: Oxford University Press, 2014); Monique Allewaert, *Ariel's Ecology: Personhood and Colonialism in the American Tropics, 1760–1820* (Minneapolis: University of Minnesota Press, 2013); Elizabeth Maddock Dillion, *New World Drama: The Performative Commons in the Atlantic World, 1649–1849* (Durham: Duke University Press, 2014); Michael Drexler and Ed White, *The Traumatic Colonel: The Founding Fathers, Slavery, and the Phantasmatic Aaron Burr* New York: NYU Press, 2014); and Marlene Daut, *Tropics of Haiti: Race and the Literary History of the Haitian Revolution in the Atlantic World, 1789–1865* (Liverpool: Liverpool University Press, 2015).

9. The tendency may well be exemplified by an essay published by Nancy Armstrong and Leonard Tennenhouse in which they use Sansay's text as a pivot to connect Barbary and North American captivity narratives to the cruelty of the gothic elements

of Harriet Beecher Stowe's *Uncle Tom's Cabin*. For Armstrong and Tennenhouse, what *Secret History* "reveals" is less about "the bloody business of slavery," and more about "the amatory cruelty of the colonial elites" (674). As such, even as they note the violences of colonial elites they read the text as a kind of precursor to mid-nineteenth-century American concerns rather than understanding it as invested in early-nineteenth-century questions of enslavement, colonization, and liberation. In other words, the text provides them another means of shoring up preexisting notions of canonicity and periodization. See Nancy Armstrong and Leonard Tennenhouse, "The Problem of Population and the Form of the American Novel," *American Literary History* 20, no. 3 (2008): 667–85.

10. Upon disembarking in the United States, Zelica's legal status would be determined by how customs officials decided to fix her identity. Unlike many Caribbean and South American countries and colonies, the United States did not legally recognize a multi-plicity of racial categories and so Zelica's identity upon entry into an American port would have either been fixed as Black or white. Moreover, while it remains somewhat unclear, the novel seems to suggest that the British ship carrying Zelica to the United States is bound for New Orleans (likely the closet major American port). As such, readers may have made a connection between this migration of people associated with the Haitian Revolution and the 1811 German Coast uprising. While ultimately unsuccessful, the German Coast uprising was the largest insurgency of enslaved peo-ple in the United States. Countless periodical accounts of the event drew a direct con-nection between this domestic insurgency and the migration of enslaved and formerly enslaved people to Louisiana from Haiti.

11. This issue about how American perceptions of the import of Haiti shifted over time between the publication dates of these two novels is taken up in more detail in Chapter 4 of this book.

12. In this regard, this project shares a sympathetic methodology with that of the work critics such as Jesse Alemán, Kirsten Silva Gruesz, and Anna Brickhouse who have individually and collectively urged the field to grapple with how early American cul-tural production was less rooted in Anglophilia than we have typically imagined. In short, each of these critics has argued that (in the words of Alemán) the long nine-teenth century was the "age of US Latinidad" and urged a reorientation of Americanist work around a deeper engagement with Spanish language production. While this book remains focused on English language texts (or texts in translation which circu-lated in the Anglophone print public sphere of the early Republic), it still remains committed to urging the field to rethink its habitual lines of influence. See Jesse Alemán, "The Age of U.S. Latinidad," in *Timelines of American Literature* (Baltimore: Johns Hopkins University Press, 2019), 162.

13. In terms of the development of this project, Marlene L. Daut's *Tropics of Haiti: Race and the Literary History of the Haitian Revolution in the Atlantic World, 1789–1865* (Liverpool: Liverpool University Press, 2015) has been an indispensable interlocutor. Daut's impressive volume recovers a wide range of what she calls "literary fictions of the Haitian Revolution" from a variety of linguistic traditions including English, French, Portuguese, German, and Haitian Creole. Where these projects differ is that my book is primarily invested in the function of and the circulation of fantasies about Haiti in the formation of American literary culture and less so in the veracity of

information about Haiti. This project aims not to catalog the volume of material that Daut examines but to think deeply about why the first two decades of the nineteenth century (during which time early American writers were deeply cathected to information about Haiti as a means of thinking about U.S. nation formation) have largely been ignored by American literary history.

14. In thinking in this way, this project seeks to build on the work of Jennifer Rae Greeson and Christopher P. Iannini who have both persuasively argued for the field to expand and complicate its received sense of the geographical coordinates of American literary history. Greeson's *Our South: Geographic Fantasy and the Rise of National Literature* (Cambridge: Harvard University Press, 2010) challenged the field to take seriously the ways in which fantasies about a primitive south were deployed to frame the ascendency of a supposedly more progressive north as the means by which the United States transformed into a world power. Equally important for the challenges it posed to the field of early American studies, Iannini's *Fatal Revolutions: Natural History, West Indian Slavery, and the Routes of American Literature* (Chapel Hill: The University of North Carolina Press, 2012) unearths the ways in which the development of the genre of natural history writing was dramatically tethered to colonial understandings of the Caribbean plantation system and how this genre wormed its way into shaping cultural production on a much broader scale. In essence, both Greeson and Iannini have urged the field to take more seriously the ways in which canonical northern cultural production has deep roots and still unexplored routes of connection with how the United States interpolated the Caribbean plantation system.

15. Sara E. Johnson's work is indispensable for thinking about the force of this Haitian fear thesis on critical engagements with the impact of the Haitian Revolution. See the "Preface" to Sara E. Johnson's *The Fear of French Negroes* (Berkeley: University of California Press, 2012) for more information on this phenomenon. The rise of the term "French negro" to describe revolutionary diasporic Africans became a commonplace trope in the late eighteenth century, and as Johnson details, these widespread fears often resulted in legal restrictions on the mobility of people previously enslaved by the French.

16. One root cause of this disregard concerning the first two decades of the nineteenth century can be traced back to Lillie Deming Loshe's formative bibliographic work *The Early American Novel* (1907). Within that text, Loshe advances the erroneous idea that there was a rapid decline in both the number of novels and the initiate authors published in the United States after 1800. According to Loshe, the last decade of the eighteenth century was the zenith of novel production in the United States and it was followed by a prolonged period of inactivity. Yet, as the work of Lyle Wright demonstrates, Loshe's accounting was incomplete. As Wright establishes in his informative *American Fiction 1774–1850: A Contribution toward a Bibliography*, a text whose very subtitle underscores its incompleteness, more domestically authored American novels were in fact published between 1801 and 1811 than in the previous decade. Despite Wright's intervention, Loshe's calculus still operates as a truism. To think of it another way, Loshe's miscalculations have loitered for so long in timelines of American literary history that they have been grandfathered into possessing a kind of squatter's rights.

17. In this regard, the project moves to take up the injunction of the political theorist Ariella Aïsha Azoulay who implores us "to engage with the histories and modalities of

the archive from outside the position it shapes for us as citizens or as scholars" by "unlearning its latent progressive temporality." See Azoulay, *Potential History: Unlearning Imperialism* (New York: Verso, 2019), 167.

18. One version of this magnification of cultural influence, for example, surfaces in the ways in which what is termed "American Romanticism" (roughly imagined as beginning in 1820) is often understood as an outgrowth of British Romanticism; instead of considering how writers like Washington Irving and Walter Scott mutually influenced one another (given their individual connections to such figures as Sydney Smith, and their professed admiration for each other's work). American writers are almost always labeled as inheritors of influence rather than enactors of it. A similar tendency has dominated figurations of sentimentalism as a generic form, where lines of influence are routinely only plotted as only moving from Europe to North America.

19. A useful summation of this controversy can be found in Adam Serwer, "The Fight Over the 1619 Project Is Not about the Facts," *The Atlantic*, December 23, 2019, see https://www.theatlantic.com/ideas/archive/2019/12/historians-clash-1619-project/604093/

20. In many ways this is problematic history of the field is the subject of Amy Kalplan's introduction to *Cultures of United States Imperialism*, which she famously begins with perhaps the most ironic line to open a reappraisal of a the birth of a field: "The field of American studies was conceived on the banks of the Congo" (3). As Kaplan demonstrates, she derives this genealogy through a close reading of Perry Miller's *Errand into the Wilderness* (1956), which was both a foundational text for the field and one that insisted on the primacy of New England. The omnipresence of New England in early formations of American literary studies had been the subject of a variety of scholarly investigations, all of which are in many ways indebted to Nina Baym's articulation of this problem in an important essay in the first volume of *American Literary History*. Part of the strength of Baym's insights resides in her attention to the presentation of cultural objects and the production of nationalism, something she attends to by thinking about the production of textbooks and their function in introducing cultural history. Baym also further underscores how the periodization of American literature grows out of an attachment to the success of New England writers. See Kaplan " 'Left Alone in America': The Absence of Empire in the Study of American Culture," in *Cultures of United States Imperialism*, ed. Amy Kaplan and Donald Pease (Durham: Duke University Press 1993), 3–22; and Baym, "Early Histories of American Literature: A Chapter in the Institution of New England," *American Literary History* 1, no. 3 (1989): 459–88.

21. While almost completely forgotten, Pattee's critique carried a great deal of symbolic authority when it first appeared. Pattee was a renowned public intellectual whose prominence could be traced back as far as his groundbreaking 1896 article, aptly titled "Is There an American Literature?" Dedicating his career to establishing American literature as distinct from British traditions, Pattee helped found both the Modern Language Association's *American Literature Group* and the field's first flagship journal *American Literature*. His lengthy career was devoted to recovery, foundational editorial projects, and to expanding the discipline. The sheer volume of this work makes his dire reappraisal of the field's critical genealogies all the more surprising. His 1924 elegy was, of course, far from the last critical monody about the field imaginary, as

this kind of recursive methodological questioning remains a fundamental element of U.S. literary studies. Still, his discomfort with operant classificatory systems (which had already—by 1924—seemingly circumscribed scholarship into solidified patterns) suggests the intimate relations between periodization, specialization, and the possibilities for scholarly innovation. See Pattee, "Call for a Literary Historian," *American Mercury* 2, no. 6 (June 1924): 134.

22. Pattee's description of what would later be repackaged by F.O. Matthiessen as the American Renaissance rightfully marks this group of writers as by and large reflective of New England literary culture. This unacknowledged regional frame still lingers in later attempts to examine the "other" American Renaissance by Joyce Warren or to look beneath Matthiessen's canon by David Reynolds. While there have been recursive attempts to rethink the periodization of American literary history across the development of the discipline, it has remained largely as stagnant as Pattee feared.

23. One recent notable exception to this inertia is the generative collection of essays edited by Cody Marrs and Christopher Hage entitled *Timelines of American Literature* (Baltimore: Johns Hopkins University Press, 2019).

24. For the detailed contents of each edition of the *Norton Anthology of American Literature* (both long and short versions) since its first publication in 1979, see the indispensable digital humanities project "Early American Literature Anthologies" (https://talus.artsci.wustl.edu/anthology_graph_sites/index.html). The site also catalogs the authors included in every iteration of the Heath anthology.

25. One of the most interesting filters of this site's search function is the ability to collate the birthplace of all the included authors, and by using this tool what emerges is that almost 50 per cent of all writers in every edition of the *Norton* have had New England origins. In many ways the information that this digital humanities project registers confirms the regional predisposition of anthologies and points to how periods and literary movements in which New England writers were at best peripheral figures often remain un-anthologized. See https://talus.artsci.wustl.edu/anthology_graph_sites/index.html

26. Matthew Wilkens has very generatively employed digital humanities tools and methods to track the references to place that appear in canonical mid-nineteenth-century texts in order to "define and assess the geographical imagination of American fiction around the Civil War" (804). In so doing, Wilkens reveals the overemphasis on New England's overall importance within American literary history even for thinking about the Civil War era, a geographical constriction that skews which writers and which works habitually surface in our work regardless of the period in question. See Wilkens, "The Geographic Imagination of Civil War-Era American Fiction," *American Literary History* 25, no. 3 (2013): 803–40.

27. While cataloging the various attempts at canonical interventions undertaken by a range of editors and anthology projects resides outside the scope of this Introduction, as should be clear here, no major volume of American literature intended for classroom use since the publication of *Norton*'s initial effort has afforded the period of 1800–20 much attention. Part of the rationale for this arises from how publishers believe that instructors are reluctant to violate canonical standards.

28. Attempts to produce multicultural versions of American literary history are not without controversy in their own right, and as Jodi Melamad has argued, "concepts of

literature's function and value remain as central to neoliberal multiculturalism's ideological consolidation and its racializing procedures as they were (and are) for racial liberalism and liberal multiculturalism." See Jodi Melamad, *Represent and Destroy: Rationalizing Violence in the New Racial Capitalism* (Minneapolis: University cf Minnesota Press, 2011), 140.

29. While Haiti is not overtly present in her thinking about this issue, Sandra Gustafson has taken up the issue of the methodological schism dividing the study of American literature before Reconstruction into disconnected fields. In Gustafson's accounting, this partitioning effectively decouples the fractious debates about national expansion and growth which circulated in the aftermath of the American Revolution from nineteenth-century cultural production in ways that delimit our understanding of the complexities of the evolution of national culture. While her intervention usefully updates the diagnosis which Pattee had previously offered by underscoring the space between, her method stops short of actually attending to any textual objects produced in the interstitial period. In effect, she imagines a bridge without any sustaining structural support undergirding its midsection. See Gustafson, "Histories of Democracy and Empire," *American Quarterly* 59, no. 1 (2007): 107–33.

30. The Oxford series intended to capitalize on the important intervention that its general editor, Cathy Davidson, had made with the publication of her groundbreaking book *Revolution and the Word: The Rise of the Novel in America* (New York: Oxford University Press, 1986), which itself had sought to recover the important work of a number of early American writers. All told, the Oxford series produced five volumes of recovered texts including the first modern classroom editions of Susanna Rowson's *Charlotte Temple* (1791), Hannah Webster Foster's *The Coquette* (1797), Tabitha Gilman Tenney's *Female Quixotism* (1801), Rebecca Rush's *Kelroy* (1812), and Catharine Maria Sedgwick's *A New-England Tale* (1822). A project which evolved a bit later, organized by Rutgers University Press, the "American Women Writers" series, published at least eighteen recovery volumes which were primarily invested in mid- to late-nineteenth century cultural production, with only a few volumes from as early as the 1830s.

31. This has largely remained true of scholarship which has focused on the texts recovered by the Oxford series, with the notable exception of the chapter in Michael Drexler and Ed White's *The Traumatic Colonel: The Founding Fathers, Slavery, and the Phantasmatic Aaron Burr* (New York: NYU Press, 2014), which focuses on the important role of an enslaved character in Tabitha Tenney's *Female Quixotism*.

32. Gaul primarily focuses on the state of scholarship on early American women writers and the role that journals like *Legacy* can play in fostering work focused on neglected authors, texts, and periods, but her argument also speaks more generally to issues around recovery and the canonical privileging. See Theresa Strouth Gaul, "Recovering Recovery: Early American Women and *Legacy*'s Future," *Legacy* 26, no. 2 (2009): 262, 276.

33. Ed White, "Divided We Stand: Emergent Conservatism in Royall Tyler's *The Algerine Captive*," *Studies in American Fiction* 37, no. 1 (2010): 5.

34. Stovall's insightful work around the limitations of Enlightenment conceptions of freedom, the ways in which questions of race have bifurcated operant conceptions of freedom despite attempts at redefinition during the age of revolutions, challenges the

idea that racism is somehow a paradox or contradiction within the democratic tradition. Indeed, as his work evinces, the very idea of freedom across the Western liberal democratic tradition has always been understood to mean white freedom. See Stovall, *White Freedom: The Racial History of an* Idea (Princeton: Princeton University Press, 2021), 131.

35. This attempted differentiation suffuses the plot of Sansay's *Secret History*. For example, from its opening pages Sansay continuingly ruminates on the distinctions between American, French, and Creole mores when it comes to both political and interpersonal interactions. I am also indebted to Elizabeth Maddock Dillion's thinking on this issue in a variety of lectures, perhaps most notably a talk at the annual meeting of the MLA in 2017 entitled "Creole Erasure: Anglo-Whiteness and Coloniality."

36. These efforts at fabricating the idea that enslavement was almost entirely a southern problem have had a long afterlife in the American cultural imagination. While these early-nineteenth-century efforts generally attempted to draw a distinction between the corruptions of large-scale plantations and smaller forms of racialized exploitation, they have morphed into the distorted commonly held belief that plantation enslavement was the only form of enslavement in U.S. history. In many ways, these resonances demonstrate just how successful these early-nineteenth-century attempts at shifting public perceptions around enslavement have proven.

37. In other words, these discourse streams suggested that even those people who had been emancipated were incapable of equality or integration in the dominant social order because of their experiences under enslavement.

38. Eric J. Sundquist, *To Wake the Nations: Race in the Making of American Literature* (Cambridge: Harvard University Press, 1993), 143.

39. As Sundquist himself observes, Melville transforms the date of Delano's encounter from 1804 to 1799. This alteration locates the reversal of fortune on the *San Dominick* not at the beginning of the Haitian Republic but in the midst of the late stages of the Revolution. If anything, this change further registers Melville's investments in thinking about a long eighteenth-century rupture, rather than a mid-nineteenth century one yet to come.

40. Perhaps the most informative historical account of the emergence of the structures of feeling associated with the harmony of Monroe's rise to power remains George Dangerfield's *The Era of Good Feelings* (New York: Harcourt, Brace and Co., 1952).

41. Theodore Dwight, who served as the secretary of the Hartford Convention, opened his "history" of the gathering by arguing that, "No political subject that has ever occupied the attention, or excited the feelings of the great body of the people of these United States, has ever been the theme of more gross misrepresentation, or constant reproach, than the assembly of delegates from several of the New-England states, which met at Hartford, in the State of Connecticut, in December 1814, commonly called the 'Hartford Convention'" (1). That Dwight so empathically attempted to correct these still prevalent misapprehensions over sixteen years later speaks to the enduring impact of this threatened succession. See Dwight, *History of the Hartford Convention: With A Review of the Policy of the United States Government which led to the War of 1812* (New York: N. & J. White, 1833).

42. My use here of ungood as measure of value is in part driven by Sianne Ngai's generative attention to how minor and politically ambiguous affects, or what she terms

non-cathartic states of feeling, provide a suitable way to diagnose the conditions of modernity. See especially the introduction to Ngai, *Ugly Feelings* (Cambridge: Harvard University Press, 2007).

43. The term "U.S. Americanists" has been coined to define scholars working primarily on the last two-thirds of the nineteenth century.

44. In a provocative challenge to the ways in which "circulation" has long served as a key "critical category" for early American studies because of "the term's capaciousness," Christy L. Pottroff urges scholars to take more seriously the "many different entry points for thinking about information exchange" (621). After tracing the critical gene-alogies of key methods for examining circulation in early America, Pottroff considers the racialized dimensions of early American print circulation by inspecting materials from the archive of the United States Postal Service. In so doing, Pottroff uncovers not simply "how the circulation of information in early America worked, but also [explores how scholars might] be better attuned to the ways in which circulatory sys-tems shaped and constrained information itself" (624). In particular, Pottroff explores the ramifications of an 1802 policy which "dictated," that no one other than "a free white person shall be employed in carrying the mail," a policy which Pottroff notes was adopted in response to the Haitian Revolution. For Pottroff, the policy demon-strates how the very idea of "a networked African American community bound together by mobile black postal workers" was an "inherently dangerous" idea to white politicians and civil servants (624). At the heart of Pottroff's essay resides the keen observation that "racial inequality and exclusion structured access to circulation" within the early American Republic, and underscores the ways in which the state sought to sanction only information about Haiti that aligned with own desires to pre-serve white supremacist authority (625); see Pottroff, "Circulation," *Early American Studies* 16, no. 3 (2018): 621–7.

Chapter 1: "Not an End"

1. See Edward W.R. Pitcher, *Fiction in American Magazines before 1800: An Annotated Catalogue* (Schenectady: Union College Press, 1993), 1.

2. See Meredith L. McGill, *American Literature and the Culture of Reprinting, 1834–1853* (Philadelphia: University of Pennsylvania Press, 2007).

3. One of the real strengths of Pitcher's introduction is the frankness with which he underscores how any recovery project (especially one as ambitious and unprece-dented as this one) will always be incomplete. Indeed, Pitcher highlights the innumer-able challenges he faced, including: his struggle to locate and access extant copies of know magazines; coming up with a working definition of what he meant by "major" in deciding which periodicals to focus on; attempting to decipher if texts were origi-nal "American" productions or recirculations of foreign objects; and, finally, strug-gling to attach retroactive generic classifications to texts produced during a period in which there was a much more fluid understanding of the relationship between fact and fiction. Given just how little attention critics had paid to early American periodi-cal writing (especially compared to critical attention to the novel) up till the point that Pitcher started work on his project, in many ways his volume is really one of the

earliest serious attempts to think about the scope and scale of early American fiction outside of the canonical form of the novel.

4. Jared Gardner, *The Rise and Fall of Early American Magazine Culture* (Urbana: University of Illinois Press, 2012), 3.

5. This stands in stark contrast to the reading practices of critics of early American literature, who almost from the inception of the field have spurned periodical texts and still habitually obsess over the national origins of literary texts in thinking about the field imaginary. See Gardner, *The Rise and Fall*, 4.

6. Gardner, *The Rise and Fall*, 4.

7. In his important new book *American Fragments* (2022), Daniel Dietz Couch challenges the field to take seriously the import of short periodical pieces in order to better comprehend how these popular fragmentary forms "generated a spectrum of possible completions, and thereby unveiled new, forward-thinking terrain in the construction of identity" (5). Couch refutes the centrality of the novel within early American studies by attending to how a wide range of writers crafted "fictionalized version[s]" of "marginalized individuals" in order to interrogate "the sociopolitical circumstances" of the very "conceptual frameworks" which defined belonging in the early Republic (6). See Couch, *American Fragments: The Political Aesthetics of Unfinished Forms in the Early Republic* (Philadelphia: University of Pennsylvania Press, 2022).

8. While many periodical editors in the United States used regional or national signifiers in crafting the titles of their productions, the realities of textual production were such that the publication of unaccredited materials from foreign sources was routine. Moreover, the lack of copyright laws or attribution practices meant that many of these pirated texts were not even necessarily identified as foreign productions.

9. Given the incredible volume of titles cataloged by Pitcher, quantifying his findings remains difficult, but following the operant long-eighteenth-century patterns for narrative nomination, many of the titles he registers feature non-Anglo names, classical allusions, foreign places, or exotic circumstances as a means of attracting the reader's attentions.

10. Jim Egan's landmark work on how "the specter of the East" haunts American literary history (from its British colonial origins through the middle of the nineteenth century) serves as an indispensable guide to thinking about the function of references to the East in a range of canonical American writers; see Egan, *Oriental Shadows: The Presence of the East in Early American Literature* (Columbus: Ohio State University Press, 2011).

11. Leonard Tennenhouse, "Libertine America," *Differences: A Journal of Feminist Cultural Studies* 11, no. 3 (1999): 1–28. Painting with a broad brush, Tennenhouse is admittedly less interested in thinking about the particularities of any specific narrative in an effort to trace the larger structural ways in which libertines functioned as a representational figure in the literary archive. His investments, in other words, reside with thinking about the social value of the libertine figure absent some of its more specific political and economic coordinates.

12. Jacob Crane convincingly demonstrates how a range of early American writers repeatedly deployed "North African Muslim figures in print to intervene in public debates

and situate local issues within the punctuated temporality of national and transatlantic crises" (334). While Crane is focused on domestically authored American texts, his observations about how readers in the early Republic would have been accustomed to reading about North African Muslims as proxies to index concerns about domestic enslavement and foreign threats to domestic security provides one way to consider the popularity of this text (with its own investment in Makandal's knowledge of Arabic suggesting his possible Muslim identity) as a means of thinking about American national stability. See Crane, "Barbary(an) Invasions: The North African Figure in Republican Print Culture," *Early American Literature* 50, no. 2 (2015): 331–58.

13. Pitcher, *Fiction in American Magazines*, 149.
14. Pitcher, *Fiction in American Magazines*, 149.
15. Pitcher, *Fiction in American Magazines*, 1.
16. Laurent Dubois, *The Banjo: America's First African Instrument* (Cambridge: Harvard University Press, 2016), 182.
17. As I will argue below, part of the work of "The Story of Makandal" resides within how it frames a fictionalized biographical portrait to critique the bad management practices which the text frames as sparking rebellion, and Couch's sense of the relationship between portraits of marginalized figures and social reform deftly articulates how in this sense the text participates in a wider spectrum of discursive practices which were routinely featured in early American periodicals.
18. Carolyn E. Fick, *The Making of Haiti: The Saint Domingue Revolution from Below* (Knoxville: University of Tennessee Press, 1990), 62.
19. Fick, *The Making of Haiti*, 62.
20. Fick, *The Making of Haiti*, 62.
21. In *Sentient Flesh: Thinking in Disorder, Poiesis in Black*, R.A. Judy includes Makandal among a range of important figures in "the Americas" who represent the ways in which diasporic African struggles for liberation cannot be reduced to the "pursuit of individual vainglory"; instead "what is celebrated about these Black heroes, by and large, is their sacrifice in pursuit of collective freedom" (297–8). See R.A. Judy, *Sentient Flesh: Thinking in Disorder, Poiesis in Black* (Durham: Duke University Press, 2020).
22. In his classic account of the Haitian Revolution, C.L.R James (in *The Black Jacobins*) describes these accounts and the details are repeated by almost every treatment of the event by later historians. For a recent accounting of this, see Monique Allewaert, "Super Fly: François Makandal's Colonial Semiotics," *American Literature* 91, no. 3 (2019): 459–90.
23. References to Makandal as a revolutionary agent still saturate popular culture, including a distorted version that provides the basis for a character that appears in several installments of the popular *Assassin's Creed* video game series. Makandal is also the likely inspiration for an African god (Agasu) presented in Neil Gaiman's novel *American Gods* (2001) and is perhaps most directly portrayed in Alejo Carpentier's magical-realist novel *The Kingdom of this World* (1949). I am indebted to the work of Kate Simpkins for thinking about these contemporary resonances and would highly recommend "The Makandal Text Network" exhibit (which Simpkins is a part of) for more information about this (https://ecda.northeastern.edu/makandal-exhibit-introduction/). This exhibit is part of the invaluable Early Caribbean Digital Archive (https://ecda.northeastern.

edu/) co-directed by Nicole Aljoe and Elizabeth Maddock Dillon at Northeastern University.

24. See Jeremy D. Popkin, *Revolutionary News: The Press in France, 1789–1799* (Durham: Duke University Press, 1990), 19.

25. I am deeply indebted to Ed White, my partner in the "Just Teach One" digital recovery project, for all of his literary forensic work in tracking down these various editions of the text while we were working on our edition of "The Account of a Remarkable Conspiracy."

26. The best source of information on the *King Caesar* pantomime drama is Kate Simpkins' unpublished dissertation, *The Absent Agronomist and the Lord of Poison: Cultivating Modernity in Transatlantic Literature, 1758–1854*, especially chapter two "The Strange Empire" which offers an extended reading of the script, its songs, and considers the early performance history of this text. See https://repository.library.northeastern.edu/files/neu:cj82nc446/fulltext.pdf

27. For a more detailed accounting of these textual variations, see the textual introduction and the notes for the "Just Teach One" edition of "The Account of a Remarkable Conspiracy" for more information.

28. Every U.S. version, with the exception of the *Washington Patrol* printing, seems to have used the version that appeared in the *LMBR* in 1789. My catalog is based on searches in the "Redex Newspaper" and the "Proquest Periodicals" databases, but this accounting remains far from exhaustive, particularly given how so many newspapers and periodicals have not survived while others have not been properly cataloged, archived, preserved, or digitized, rendering the entirety of their contents difficult to account for.

29. See Avery F. Gordon, *Ghostly Matters: Haunting and the Sociological Imagination* (Minneapolis: University of Minnesota Press, 2008).

30. In this regard, the text serves to remind readers of both a specific instance and any number of attempted rebellions, which as Eve Tuck and C. Ree argue reflects how hauntings make it impossible to separate "the particular from the general, the hosted from the host, personal from the public, the foot(note) from the head(line), the place from the larger narrative of nation, the people from specific places" (640). By thinking with Tuck and Ree we can see how the tensions in this text, between a settler colonial desire to fix a particular meaning to the story of Makandal and the ways in which the very recursivity of its reanimation underscores how it functions as a revenant memory haunting the white supremacist imagination. See Tuck and Ree, "A Glossary of Haunting," *Handbook of Autoethnography*, ed. Stacey Holman Jones, Tony E. Adams, and Carolyn Ellis (New York: Routledge, 2013), 639–58.

31. See the preface to Sara E. Johnson's *The Fear of French Negroes* (Berkeley: University of California Press, 2012) for more information on this phenomenon. The rise of the term to describe revolutionary diasporic Africans became a commonplace trope in the late eighteenth century, and, as Johnson details, these widespread fears often resulted in legal restrictions on the mobility of people who had been enslaved by the French.

32. Elizabeth Maddock Dillon, *New World Drama* (Durham: Duke University Press, 2014), 43.

33. As Dillion traces in her analysis of attempts to regulate public mobility in Charleston, concerns over the intermixing of races in spaces like the theater resulted in local officials regulating audience accessibility and enacting an increased control over what she calls the "performative commons" in the early Republic. In particular, Charleston city officials became increasingly anxious about the enslaved people that French refugees had brought with them to the city in flight from the Revolution, and prohibited these enslaved people from intermingling with the local population. See Dillon, *New World Drama*, 42.

34. In a previous essay about how events in Haiti sparked rumor-driven unrest in the United States, I trace the ebbs and flows of one example of this kind of serial haunting. See Duncan Faherty, " 'The Mischief That Awaits Us': Revolution, Rumor, and Serial Unrest in the Early Republic," in *The Haitian Revolution and the Early United States: Histories, Textualities, Geographies*, ed. Elizabeth Maddock Dillon and Michael Drexler (Philadelphia: University of Pennsylvania Press, 2016), 58–79.

35. See March 27, 1802, *Philadelphia Repository and Weekly Register* (Philadelphia).

36. To perhaps provide a more familiar context, the headnote which accompanied the first installment of "The Story of Makandal" in the *Philadelphia Repository* appeared about seven weeks after Lenora Sansay sailed for St. Domingo to reclaim her husband's lost planation, the unfolding of which forms the basis for her semi-autobiographical novel *Secret History* (1808). The popularity of Sansay's *Secret History* as the key touchstone for early Americanists who want to explore connections between Haiti and the early Republic is further explored in Chapter 4.

37. One of the most important recent biographical portraits of Toussaint is Marlene Daut's "The Wrongful Death of Toussaint Louverture," *History Today* 70, no.6(2020),https://www.historytoday.com/archive/feature/wrongful-death-toussaint-louverture. Daut's work on Toussaint is invaluable both for its details about his own actions as well as for providing a deeper understanding of the later events of the Haitian revolution itself. See https://www.historytoday.com/archive/feature/wrongful-death-toussaint-louverture

38. Neil Roberts, *Freedom as Marronage* (Chicago: The University of Chicago Press, 2015), 29.

39. Trouillot's work on the importance of the Haitian Revolution was a groundbreaking intervention into our understanding of the seismic importance of the rupture enacted by this struggle for self-emancipation. At the same time, reductive distillations of his argument have distorted his notion of silence to suggest that reactions to these events were muted or scattershot, rather than widespread and frequent.

40. Roberts, *Freedom as Marronage*, 29.

41. Lisa Lowe, "History Hesitant," *Social Text* 33, no. 4 (125) (2015): 85.

42. Lowe, "History Hesitant," 85 and 86.

43. Lowe, "History Hesitant," 98.

44. Lowe, "History Hesitant," 98.

45. Lowe, "History Hesitant," 89.

46. Lowe, "History Hesitant," 89 and 92.

47. C.L.R. James, *The Black Jacobins: Toussaint L'Ouverture and the San Domingo Revolution* (New York: Random House, 1936), 20–1.

48. Fick, *The Making of Haiti*, 68.
49. David Geggus, *Haitian Revolutionary Studies* (Bloomington: Indiana University Press, 2002), 75.
50. Laurent Dubois, *Avengers of the New World: The Story of the Haitian Revolution* (Cambridge: Harvard University Press, 2004), 52.
51. Sylviane A. Diouf, *Servants of Allah: African Muslims Enslaved in the Americas* (New York: NYU Press, 1998), 216–17.
52. See the very useful timeline created by Colin Dayan in *Haiti, History, and the Gods* (Berkeley: University of California Press, 1998). This timeline is also reprinted in Michael Drexler's edition of *Secret History* (Peterborough, Ontario: Broadview Press, 2007).
53. Diouf, *Servants of Allah*, 217.
54. Diouf, *Servants of Allah*, 217.
55. The attention to fiction founded on fact has been a central theme of early American literary studies since the field's inception and has long guided critical treatments of these novels. Jane Tompkins' *Sensational Designs: The Cultural Work of American Fiction, 1790–1860* (New York: Oxford University Press, 1986) was not the first critical text to make the case for thinking about the factual origins of early American literature but it may well have been the most influential.
56. The unchecked assertions that pepper the social media feeds of contemporary America, with partisans seemingly occupying wildly different media-driven understandings of current conditions, may well appear at an unheralded pace, but they reflect in some ways the divergent media streams of a pre-objective notion of journalism that dominated the early Republic's periodical culture.
57. As Tom Koenigs has recently argued the early American print public sphere produced a vast array of what we might think of as extra-novelistic imaginative writing which frequently made divergent claims about textual authority and verisimilitude. According to Koenigs, many of these texts offered "widely divergent conceptions of fictional 'truth,' a term that might refer to a narrative's moral vision, its mimetic accuracy, or its aesthetic impact" (3)." See Koenigs, *Founded in Fiction: The Uses of Fiction in the Early United States* (Princeton: Princeton University Press, 2021).
58. See Henry R. Warfel, *Charles Brockden Brown: American Gothic Novelist* (Gainesville: University of Florida Press, 1949), 100.
59. See Frank Mott, *A History of American Magazines 1741–1850* (Cambridge: Harvard University Press, 1957); and Peter Hutchinson, "A Publisher's History of American Magazines Eighteenth-Century American Magazines" (2008), http://www.themagazinist.com/uploads/Part_One_Birth_of_American_Magazines.pdf
60. See Cathy Davidson, *Revolution and the Word* (New York: Oxford University Press: 1986), 12–19.
61. See Nazera Sadiq Wright, *Blackgirlhood in the Nineteenth Century* (Urbana: University of Illinois Press, 2016), 8–10.
62. Scruggs, "Photographs to Answer Our Purposes: Representations of the Liberian Landscape in Colonization Print Culture," in *Early African American Print* Culture, ed. Laura Langer Cohen and Jordan Stein (Philadelphia: University of Pennsylvania Press, 2012), 230.

63. Kyla Schuller, *The Biopolitics of Feeling: Race, Sex, and Science in the Nineteenth Century* (Durham: Duke University Press, 2018), 157.

64. All citations for "The Story of Makandal" are from the "Just Teach One" edition of the text and will be citied parenthetically within the chapter. See http://jto.common-place.org/just-teach-one-homepage/account-of-a-remarkable-conspiracy-makandal/

65. This strand of the narrative, which highlights Makandal's ability to heal common maladies through his knowledge of botanicals, echoes a popular periodical piece which was widely reprinted as early as 1750 and then reappeared for several decades usually under some version of the title "The Negro Cesar's Cure for Poison." As Keri Holt argues, texts like Cesar's cure exemplify how publications like "the South Carolina and Georgia almanacs" regularly contained "domestic advice [that] was acquired from slaves" which was subsequently reprinted in other venues; see Holt, *Reading These United States: Federal Literacy in the Early republic, 1176–1830* (Athens: University of Georgia Press, 2019), 65. For more information on the circulation of "Cesar's Cure," see Duncan Faherty and Ed White, "Late 18C Anti-Slavery Texts," https://jto.americanantiquarian.org/wp-content/uploads/2021/03/Early-Abolitionist-Texts-for-JTO-final.pdf

66. In their insightful essay on the cultural legacies of Makandal's knowledge, Elizabeth Maddock Dillion and Kate Simpkins argue that "in the literary and historical figure of François Makandal, a vital alternative mode of thinking appears, albeit one that has been largely exiled from the realm of historical and scientific knowledge"; in tracing the racist dimensions of this erasure, Dillon and Simpkins, "turn to Makandal as a source of anticolonial, Black speculative knowledge that has direct bearing" on present circumstances (724). See Dillon and Simpkins, "Makandal and Pandemic Knowledge: Literature, Fetish, and Health in the Plantationocene," *American Literature* 92, no. 3 (2020): 723–35.

67. Dillon, *New World Drama*, 27.

68. Agamben's framing of bare life arises from his attempt to rethink our understanding of the Holocaust through a consideration of Roman Law, and while his insights are useful for considering the horrors of Nazi ideologies, attempts by subsequent critics to retrospectively use this term to consider New World enslavement fail to account for how exploitation was the central guiding principal of the Black Atlantic and that the violence of eradication was directed at indigenous populations and not enslaved ones. As scholars such as Alexander G. Weheliye, Zakiyyah Iman Jackson, and Gwen Bergner (among many others) have argued, all too often theorists of biopolitics have neglected race, New World enslavement, and the violences of colonialism and the forced transit of the Black Atlantic in their configurations of state violence and inequality. See Bergner, "Introduction: The Plantation, the Postplantation, and the Afterlives of Slavery," *American Literature* 91, no. 3 (2019): 447–57; Zakiyyah Iman Jackson, "Animal: New Directions on the Theorization of Race and Posthumanism," *Feminist Studies* 39, no. 3 (2013): 669–85; and Alexander G. Weheliye, *Habeus Viscus: Racializing Assemblages, Biopolitics, and Black Feminist Theories of the Human* (Durham: Duke University Press, 2014), 32–6.

69. As Great LaFleur has persuasively demonstrated a widespread pattern of "binding contemporary understandings of racial difference and sexual aberrance" informed the

genre of "criminal execution narratives," which repeatedly presented "racial blackness, in particular" as "articulated through criminalized sexual behaviors, and criminalized sexual behaviors are in turn characterized through an esthetics of spiritual and moral darkness" (105–6). In many ways the same rhetorical patterns that LaFleur measures in execution narratives frames how Makandal is presented here; see especially chapter three of LaFleur, *The Natural History of Sexuality in Early America* (Baltimore: Johns Hopkins University Press, 2018).

70. For a detailed account of the strict legal limitations placed on enslaved women granting consent, see Jennifer Morgan's *Laboring Women: Gender and Reproduction in the Making of New World Slavery* (Philadelphia: University of Pennsylvania Press, 2004). In addition, as Ned and Constance Sublette trace in their impactful history of the sexual violence against enslaved women, the forced impregnation of enslaved women generated "human capital" for enslavers. See *The American Slave Coast: A History of the Slave-Breeding Industry* (New York: Lawrence Hill Books, 2015).

71. As bell hooks has argued, sexual violence against enslaved women needs to be understood as "an institutionalized method of terrorism" so that the violences of this endemic attempt at domination can be understood as a technology of systemic oppression. That "The Story of Makandal" glosses over the threat of sexual violence and rape is another important form of the text's attempts to whitewash the violences and terrors of enslavement. See hooks, *Ain't I a Woman: Black Women and Feminism* (Abington: Routledge, 2013), 27.

72. The narrative's failure to provide a name for this enslaved woman, despite her prominence in the plot's pivotal turning point, is indicative of the ways in which the colonial archive habitually erased the individuality of enslaved women. Marisa J. Fuentes argues in the epilogue to *Dispossessed Lives* colonial records routinely presented enslaved women "as stripped bare of all that was meaningful in their lives" (145). As Fuentes outlines, historians concerned with the lives of enslaved women have to confront "the paucity of materials about enslaved women, the complete absence of material by enslaved women, and the intensity of archival and physical violence on enslaved women" (144). This tendency toward erasure was so prevalent that even within a highly stylized fictive biographical portrait the enslaved women whose imagined choice effectively sparks Makandal's rebellion against colonial exploitation and enslavement is rendered nameless. See Fuentes, *Dispossessed Lives: Enslaved Women, Violence, and the Archive* (Philadelphia: University of Pennsylvania Press, 2016).

73. Another way to read this rhetorical call for sympathetic identification, following the important work of Elizabeth Polcha on John Steadman's coded depictions of sexual domination, is as a stylistic framing which "tantalizes" readers "with a suggestion of sexual indecency" which enables readers to participate in "a fantasy" through which they can imagine "what is behind" what Steadman terms the "Sable Curtain" (689); in other words they can participate in a Euro-American fantasy about interracial sex without having to consider the violence which so often defined it. As Polcha persuasively argues "the literary history of the colonial Americas has a deep-seated investment in sexual exploitation," and "The Story of Makandal"'s attempt to mute these investments is revealing (704). See Polcha, "Voyeur in the Torrid Zone," *Early American Literature* 54, no. 3 (2019): 673–710.

74. While it is difficult to find direct evidence of work slowdowns on the part of enslaved laborers as evidence of attempts to control one's own time, the monomaniacal attempts to quantify labor on the part of enslavers evinces the ways in which they understood this as a possible means of resistance. One example of such anxiety about slowdowns can be found in Kelly Houston Jones, "'A Rough, Saucy Set of Hands to Manage': Slave Resistance in Arkansas," *The Arkansas Historical Quarterly* 71, no. 1 (2012), 1–21.

75. The work of Sylviane A. Diouf is indispensable for thinking about maroon societies and what the references of them in other texts encode. See Diouf, *Slavery's Exiles* (New York: New York University Press, 2015). I have also learned a great deal about maroon culture and representations of maroon life from Sean Gerrity, whose book *A Canada in the South: Maroons in American Literature* (in progress) deftly maps out a new understanding of African American thinking about the para-social possibilities of maroon societies in the *antebellum* period.

76. According to Stewart R. King, the "maréchaussées" of Saint-Domingue were all of African origin by 1733, and their primary responsibility was policing the enslaved population. See "The Maréchaussée of Saint-Domingue: Balancing the Ancien Régime and Modernity," *Journal of Colonialism and Colonial History* 5, no. 2 (2004), doi:10.1353/cch.2004.0052.

77. See especially chapter 1 of Kyla Wazana Tompkins, *Racial Indigestion: Eating Bodies in the 19th Century* (New York: New York University Press, 2012).

78. Tompkins, *Racial Indigestion*, 52.

79. See for example, the arguments about spatial understanding and racial hierarchies that Rebecca Ginsburg has made in "Escaping through a Black Landscape," in *Cabin, Quarter, Plantation: Architecture and Landscapes of North America*, ed. Clifton Ellis and Rebecca Ginsburg (New Haven: Yale University Press, 2010), 51–67.

80. David Luis-Brown has reconfigured the relationship between the formation of racialized identities and the sentimental mode by arguing that, "sentimentalism, then, is a highly protean form that aspires to persuade readers in various ways to adopt attitudes of sympathy toward those who suffer" (47). Crucially, Luis-Brown registers our need to move beyond the work of Adam Smith in order to fully comprehend "the precise political significance of sentimentalism" since it so deeply depends on a "combination" of "discourses" and "political ideals" to fully impact readers (47). While he is largely concerned with later contexts, Luis-Brown's work enables us to see how the protean use of sympathy within "The Story of Makandal" aims at highlighting how bad plantation management compounded the suffering of enslaved people even as it disavows their revolutionary potential. See Luis-Brown, *Waves of Decolonization: Discourses of Race and Hemispheric Citizenship in Cuba, Mexico, and the United States* (Durham: Duke University Press, 2008).

81. This attempt to silence the ways in which the actual Makandal remained a figure of inspiration for later generations of revolutionaries in St. Domingo and elsewhere had clear counterrevolutionary intentions, but failed to overwrite his actual significance. As a wide range of scholars have argued Mankandal's memory was invoked at the Bois Caïman ceremony in August of 1791 (which took place on the same plantation on which Makandal had been enslaved) that was presided over by Dutty Boukman and

has long been understood as a pivotal moment of assemblage which resulted in the Haitian Revolution. Recently Kieran M. Murphy has written about a range of late-eighteenth- and early-nineteenth-century materials which reference Makandal in relation to the Bois Caïman ceremony, see Murphy, "What Was Tragedy during the Haitian Revolution?," *Modern Language Quarterly* 82, no. 3 (2021): 417–40.

82. This figuration echoes the ways Makandal's knowledge of medicinal herbs was denigrated as climatological homeopathy in contrast to the supposedly superior scientific knowledge of European trained physicians. These various denigrating threads unravel his abilities as a socio-political agent capable of either persuasion or enacting lasting change.

83. The lone exception to this routinized dismissal of the centrality of serialized fiction in the early Republic has long remained the field's attention to the figure of the libertine. The serialized libertine has served as a chestnut for scholarly considerations of both "orientalist" tales and critical readings of sentimental motifs and seduction narratives, yet much of this attention still endeavors to isolate the libertine figure from the intimate networks of association that define slave economies, or economies of indenture for that matter. Seldom, in other words, do critics consider the pervasiveness of sexual violence and exploitation that libertines are perhaps intended to represent beyond threats to imperiled white womanhood, which has both legal and cultural recourses to resistance. This illusion that choice was always a viable option (unless the threat of sexual violence occurs in some exotic local) serves as a kind of distorted proxy for the commonplace realities of racialized sexual violence in the eighteenth-century circum-Atlantic world.

84. In his recent dissertation, "Creating the Cold War Canon: A History of the Center for Editions of American Authors," Matthew Ryan Blackwell argues that the state-sponsored initiative to create classroom editions of major nineteenth-century American writers was in large part guided by "a context in which the opposition between the U.S. and the U.S.S.R. was often reduced to an opposition between the abstract concepts of 'individual freedom' versus 'totalitarianism,' the notion that the products of individual authors' inherent freedom of expression could be recovered from the historical record was ideologically aligned with propaganda efforts that began in the 1950s" (28). Blackwell's institutional history of publishing initiatives lays bare the ways in which what became the dominant teaching canon of nineteenth-century American literary studies was carefully scripted to produce a particular vision of American cultural history as progressive and centered around the freedom of white protagonists and authors. See Matthew Ryan Blackwell, "Creating the Cold War Canon: A History of the Center for Editions of American Authors" (PhD diss. University of Iowa, 2019).

Chapter 2: Sympathy in the Era of Ungood Feelings

1. "For the Gazette of the United States. to Thomas M'Kean, Esquire," *Gazette of the United States* XXI, no. 2888 (January 1, 1802): [2].

2. Almost immediately after taking office McKean began a systematic campaign to replace Federalist or Federalist leaning state officials with his own campaign cronies.

Chapter 21, entitled "Governor McKean," of David McKean's biography of his ancestor, *Suspected of Independence: The Life of Thomas McKean, America's First Power
Broker* (New York: Public Affairs, 2016) provides a detailed account of Governor
McKean's purging of "dozens of Federalist state employees" after he assumed
office (191).

3. "For the Gazette of the United States. to Thomas M'Kean, Esquire," January 1, 1802, [2].
4. This election cycle was so contentious that historians have long referred to it as the
   Revolution of 1800. Perhaps the most formative work on the partisanship of this election can be found in the impressive collection James J. Horn, Jan Ellen Lewis, and
   Peter S. Onuf, eds., *The Revolution of 1800: Democracy, Race, and the New Republic*
   (Charlottesville: University of Virginia Press, 2002). In particular Michael A. Bellesiles's
   contribution, " 'The Soil Will Be Soaked with Blood': Taking the Revolution of 1800
   Seriously," provides a deft introduction to the charged rhetoric suffusing periodical
   electioneering efforts for both parties. See Thomas Jefferson, "First Inaugural
   Address," *The Papers of Thomas Jefferson*, Vol. 33: *17 February to 30 April 1801*
   (Princeton: Princeton University Press, 2006), 151.
5. "For the Gazette of the United States. to Thomas M'Kean, Esquire," January 1, 1802, [2].
6. "For the Gazette of the United States. to Thomas M'Kean, Esquire," January 1, 1802, [2].
7. "For the Gazette of the United States. to Thomas M'Kean, Esquire," January 1, 1802, [2].
8. "For the Gazette of the United States. to Thomas M'Kean, Esquire," January 1, 1802, [2].
9. "For the Gazette of the United States. to Thomas M'Kean, Esquire," January 1, 1802, [2].
10. While many founders and other heroes of "seventy-six" were still occupying promi-
    nent national and regional positions, after the passing of George Washington in
    December of 1799, a renewed reverence of the revolutionary generation began to take
    hold of the popular imagination. Michael D. Hattem's recent work on the cultural
    memory of the revolutionary era generation provides a useful complication of Michael
    Kammen's longstanding centrality in such discussions. Kammen's argument tends to
    gloss over the very early nineteenth century and its more reverential figurations in
    favor of focusing increased attention on the mid- to late-nineteenth-century attempts
    to underscore cultural progress since the revolutionary period. See Hattem,
    "Citizenship and the Memory of the American Revolution in Nineteenth-Century
    Political Culture," *New York History* 101, no. 1 (2020): 30–53; and also, Michael
    Kammen, *A Season of Youth: The American Revolution and the Historical Imagination*
    (New York: Alfred A Knopf, 1978). Across the last two decades there has been a
    noticeable increase in public attention to the meaning of the Founders, a cultural phe-
    nomenon which can be seen, for example, in the widespread popularity of Lin-Manuel
    Miranda's smash 2015 hit musical *Hamilton* (as well as the attendant critique of how
    this production whitewashes history). To this might be added the even more recent
    widespread public debates about the presence of statues of the founders as public
    monuments across the United States.
11. Courtney Chatellier, " 'Not of the Modern French School': Literary Conservatism and
    the Ancien Régime in Early American Periodicals," *Early American Studies: An
    Interdisciplinary Journal* 16, no. 3 (2018): 493.
12. Chatellier, " 'Not of the Modern French School'," 493.
13. "For the Gazette of the United States. to Thomas M'Kean, Esquire," January 1, 1802, [2].

14. "For the Gazette of the United States. to Thomas M'Kean, Esquire," January 1, 1802, [2].

15. Obviously McKean's understanding of his own actions differed from that of this Federalist critique, but in a letter he wrote to an associate, he compared his actions in cleaning out the statehouse of Federalist workers to that of "Hercules" washing out the decades of accumulated filth from "the Augean stables"; see McKean, *Suspected of Independence*, 191. The metaphor may well be self-serving, but it does provide an indication of just how many Federalist appointees and career bureaucrats McKean intended to force out of civil service.

16. "For the Gazette of the United States. to Thomas M'Kean, Esquire," January 1, 1802, [2].

17. "For the Gazette of the United States. to Thomas M'Kean, Esquire," January 1, 1802, [2].

18. William C. Dowling, *Literary Federalism in the Age of Jefferson: Joseph Dennie and* The Port Folio, *1801–1811* (Columbia: University of South Carolina Press, 1999), xi. Ed White's work on the conservative turns of early American fiction crucially complicates Dowling's formative work, especially in terms of how White argues that the field has habitually adhered to "the default characterization of the early U.S. novel as generically and socially radical." In White's accounting this critical doxa has for too long imagined that "the *word* is part of the *revolution*," in a stylized underscoring of just how much of an impact Cathy Davidson's seminal work *Revolution and the Word: The Rise of the Novel in America* (New York: Oxford University Press, 1994) has had on the field imaginary; see White, "Divided We Stand: Emergent Conservatism in Royall Tyler's *The Algerine Captive*," *Studies in American Fiction* 37, no. 1 (2010): 5.

19. While Dowling's work generatively began to map a more complex notion of Federalist literary culture in the early Republic, his sense of this influence almost exclusively addresses connections between European and North American cultural and political actors, resulting in an erasure of any sense that events in the Caribbean contributed to these cross-cultural exchanges.

20. Rachel Hope Cleves, *The Reign of Terror in America: Visions of Violence from Anti-Jacobinism to Antislavery* (New York: Cambridge University Press, 2009), 4.

21. Cleves, *The Reign of Terror in America*, 4.

22. James Callender began openly referring to "Sally" in a series of columns attacking Jefferson shortly after the election of 1800, and his vitriol was echoed by any number of Federalist columnists. For a more detailed account of this, see Annette Gordon-Reed, *Thomas Jefferson and Sally Hemings: An American Controversy* (Charlottesville: University of Virginia Press, 1997).

23. There were at least thirteen columns published under the pseudonym "Burleigh" that originally appeared in *The Connecticut Courant* in the late summer and early fall of 1800. The tenor of these articles is demagogic Federalism as Burleigh seems intent on terrifying voters into supporting his party's cause. The columns were widely reprinted in Federalist newspapers across the country, and were likewise consistently cited by Democratic-Republican papers as a prime example of the partisanship of their opposition. Burleigh's weekly screeds, for example, were reprinted by Federalist venues across September and October of 1800—in such papers as *The South Carolina State Gazette* (Charleston), *The Massachusetts Mercury* (Boston), *The Philadelphia Gazette*, *The New York Gazette*, *The Washington Federalist*, and *Jenk's Portland Gazette* (Maine). Democratic-Republican newspapers, like *The Impartial Observer* (Providence, RI),

openly rebutted Burleigh's accusations before the printer's ink was barely dry, decrying him as "a hot-headed, violent, and strenuous party-man" intent on slander and malice (*The Imperial Observer*, September 1, 1800). This piece, signed by the "Friends to Truth," is but one instance of these direct replies to Burleigh, and indeed a majority of the issues of *The Impartial Observer* contain a response to Burleigh in September and October of 1800. For examples of historians who have cited Burleigh, see Michael A. Bellesiles, "The Soil Will be Soaked with Blood," in *The Revolution of 1800*, ed. James Horn, Jan Ellen Lewis, and Peter Onuf (Charlottesville: University of Virginia Press, 2002), 59–87; John Ferling, *Adams vs. Jefferson: The Tumultuous Election of 1800* (New York: Oxford University Press, 2004); and David Hackett Fischer, *The Revolution of American Conservatism: The Federalist Party in the Era of Jeffersonian Democracy* (New York: Harper & Row, 1965). Burleigh's predictions about murder and incest can be found in *The Connecticut Courant*, September 20, 1800.

24. Chatellier, "'Not of the Modern French School'," 509.

25. Chatellier, "'Not of the Modern French School'," 509.

26. The connection between these two seemingly discrete registers is even more apparent if we begin to account for the importance of serialized publication for fiction and political polemics alike. For more on the importance of seriality, see Jared Gardner, *The Rise and Fall of Early American Magazine Culture* (Chicago: The University of Illinois Press, 2012).

27. As Linda Frost has argued, Adams included this famous quip in an 1804 letter which was in many ways a meditation on Jefferson's presidency. See Frost, "The Body Politic in Tabitha Tenney's *Female Quixotism*," *Early American Literature* 32, no. 2 (1997): 113–34.

28. For Daniel Couch, Adams's letter reveals "attacks" both on "the failing Federalist party as well as what he perceives to be the machinations of Jefferson's administration"; in that it "more broadly" expresses "his apprehension for the future of the country" (97). Thinking with Couch allows us to better understand how not all Federalists embraced the idea that what had been a heated political struggle was becoming a kind of early American culture war. Moreover, Couch's work proves how Federalists both disagree on how to regain their lost authority and still continue to hope for renewed victories at the ballot box. See Couch, *American Fragments: The Political Aesthetic of Unfinished Forms in the Early Republic* (Philadelphia: University of Pennsylvania Press, 2022), 97–130.

29. My use of the term ungood here to mark the affective register of the early nineteenth century aims at problematizing the traditional historiographic figuration of the post-war of 1812 period as the era of good feelings. In essence the use of that term works to suggest that the intense partisanship of the first fifteen years of the nineteenth century had been overcome without every really taking this early period seriously as a moment of cultural and political struggle.

30. While "The Story of Makandal" was clearly not written by a Federalist American writer, its exploration of violations of choice as threats to what it imagines as the stabilizing impact of a hierarchically defined social order shares an aesthetic sensibility with the Federalist project and may in some ways account for part of its enduring popularity within the U.S. print public sphere. In a sense it represents the right kind of French influence that the Federalists maintained was still crucial to American futurity.

31. The fear of a French influence was always already racially coded in the U.S. in the early nineteenth century, in large part because Haiti stood as a dramatic reminder of what an attraction to French revolutionary logic entailed. Sara E. Johnson's seminal work, *The Fear of French Negroes: Transcolonial Collaboration in the Revolutionary Americas* (Berkeley: University of California Press, 2012), is a path-breaking register of how what she marks as a "transcolonial black politics" formed out of collective attempts to further the work of the Haitian Revolution. Equally important, Julius S. Scott's *The Common Wind: Afro-American Currents in the Age of the Haitian Revolution* (London: Verso Books, 2020) further underscores just how interconnected diasporic Africans were across the circum-Atlantic world and just how anxious such transcolonial networks made Euro-American white people.

32. In *Specters of the Atlantic*, Ian Baucom challenges our normative figuration of the past as a temporal modality distinct from the time of the now. Following Walter Benjamin's articulation of how the past and the present are complicated constellations, Baucom provocatively argues that "time does not pass, it accumulates." See Ian Baucom, *Specters of the Atlantic: Finance Capital, Slavery, and the Philosophy of History* (Durham: Duke University Press, 2005), 118. As Michel Serres has suggestively argued, "time does not always flow according to a line," but rather "according to an extraordinary complex mixture, as though it reflected stopping points, ruptures, deep wells, chimneys of thunderous acceleration,…all sown at random, at least in a visible disorder." Michel Serres with Bruno Latour, *Conversations on Science, Culture, and Time*, trans. Roxanne Lapidus (Ann Arbor: The University of Michigan Press, 1995), 57.

33. While I am reluctant to project the politics of her male family members onto her, it is true that Read shares this sense of lost authority in both of her novels, and her other extant writing seems to reproduce many of the same tropes as other Federalist writers.

34. Joseph Fichtelberg, "Friendless in Philadelphia: The Feminist Critique of Martha Meredith Read," *Early American Literature* 32, no. 3 (1997): 207. See also, Andrew Cayton, "The Authority of the Imagination in an Age of Wonder," *Journal of the Early Republic* 33, no. 1 (2013): 1–27. for a slightly different take on the question of how Federalist political anxieties found a new generic form in the turn toward fiction.

35. The novel makes a somewhat strange, albeit brief, investment in differentiating between good and bad planters, between those that paternalistically treated enslaved peoples as cared for workers and those who more viscously exploited and abused them. The implication seems to be that the latter enslavers were responsible for causing the Haitian Revolution, which might have been avoided if the leadership style of the former had been more widely embraced. This thread of the novel mirrors its overall attempts to define good wealth (possessed by people with the proper moral sense to use it for the public good) over and against rapacious bad capitalists (whose lack of moral certitude means that they only use their wealth to satisfy their own desires).

36. Ashli White's *Encountering Revolution: Haiti and the Making of the Early Republic* (2010) argues that this notion of a chain reaction has stifled our sense of historical development and reciprocity. While the recent historiography of the colonial era embraces the "fluidity and contingency" of the web of associations that British North America was embedded within, all too often, she laments, "the dominant trope for the revolutionary decades is that of a chain, a sequence in which political principals and activity at one site inform revolution in another." See White, *Encountering Revolution*, 6.

37. In part, Read uses this bastardization of Sonnetton's name to reflect the ways in which Americans have a paltry understanding of either the French language or French culture. But it also functions as a way to separate Sonnetton/Sontine from his American-born wife, Madame Sontine, who neither objects to the mistranslation of her married surname nor later in the novel, when the text refers to Sonnetton by his proper appellation, is afforded the same nominal correction (she remains Madame Sontine across the length of the text as if to underscore how ill-suited this marriage really is). To avoid the shifting nominations used in the novel, in the chapter, I will refer to these figures as Sonnetton and Madame Sontine.

38. Martha Meredith Read, *Monima; or, The Beggar Girl* (New York: T. B. Jansen & Co. Booksellers, 1802). All citations from the novel are from this edition (unless otherwise noted) and will be cited parenthetically in the chapter itself. Read's attempt to display Monima's fragile position by having other characters threaten to treat her as if she was enslaved replicates the racist pattern of early-nineteenth-century American fiction to use allusions to enslavement as a means of underscoring dangers to white womanhood and white citizenship more generally. As I will argue in more detail below, this allusion to Monima's supposed "French negro" origins serves as a means of highlighting the protections of her whiteness and her definable genealogical connections.

39. While this attempt at robbing Monima of the protections of her whiteness serves to narratively reveal the questionable moral character of her antagonist (as I will discuss in more detail below), it simultaneously works to underscore the centrality of whiteness to Read's conception of belonging. In surveying the operant ways in which citizenship and belonging were understood in early America, Cristina Beltrán has argued that "race shaped the boundaries of American membership—creating economic and social conditions for U.S. assertions and enactments of freedom, democracy, and republican values" (42–3). While she is thinking about the very different context of contemporary migrations, Beltrán's assertion that "the noncitizen migrant is the Other that both threatens and consolidates white citizenship" resonates with Read's conception of the problem with Democratic-Republican ideologies which fail to distinguish between good and bad French migrants, the latter of whom for Federalists served as that Other which they felt both imperiled and reified their notions of proper American identities (45). See Beltrán, *Cruelty as Citizenship: How Migrant Suffering Sustains White Democracy* (Minneapolis: University of Minnesota Press, 2020).

40. Three printings of *Monima* appeared in the early nineteenth century, with two editions appearing in New York (both published by T.B. Jansen & Co) and a third Philadelphia edition (printed by Eaken & Mecum in 1803). Both New York editions include a dedication and a preface, while the Philadelphia printing excludes the dedication and offers a revised preface. Both of the prefaces frame the moral intentions of the novel as paramount, albeit in slightly different ways as the Philadelphia edition is more aggressive in its defense of the text as founded on fact.

41. For a detailed and generative discussion of how Federalist concerns animate the early American novel, see Ed White, "Trends and Patterns in the US Novel 1800–1820," in *The Oxford History of the Novel in English: The American Novel to 1870*, ed. J. Gerald Kennedy and Leland S. Person (New York: Oxford University Press, 2014), 73–88.

42. This dedication and the following preface appeared in the two New York editions of 1802 and 1803. The 1803 Philadelphia edition included neither but instead contained

the following preface. See Martha Meredith Read, *Monima; or, The Beggar Girl* (Philadelphia: Eaken & Mecum, 1803), ii.

43. These figurations appear in Read's preface to the Philadelphia edition of *Monima*.

44. Martha Meredith Read, *Margaretta; or The Intricacies of the Heart* (Charleston, SC, 1807), 414.

45. For more information about how Read's *Margaretta* works to draw connections between pre-revolutionary Haiti and the United States in 1800, see Duncan Faherty, "'Murder, Robbery, Rape, Adultery, and Incest': Martha Meredith Read's *Margaretta* and the Function of Federalist Fiction," *Warring for America: Cultural Contests in the Era of 1812* (Chapel Hill: The University of North Carolina Press, 2017), 95–126.

46. Read's social conservativism and her anxieties about the impact of social leveling are in many ways precursors to the same class-based politics that Cooper would become infamous for two decades later. For a more in-depth discussion of how Read's novel anticipates Cooper's own investments in the securing possibilities of properly ordered elite homes, see Duncan Faherty, "'Murder, Robbery, Rape, Adultery, and Incest'," 95–126.

47. "Vagrancy," as Saidya Hartman has argued in terms of understanding its eighteenth-century definitions in English Common Law, "was a status, not a crime" (243). Read's careful presentation of the crimeless Monima registers the ways in which Philadelphians interpolate her status as a vagrant as indicative of vice and moral degeneracy. Hartman continues her interrogation of statutes against vagrancy by noting that, "in short vagrants were the deracinated—migrants, wanderers, fugitives, displaced persons, and strangers," and underscores how "status offenses were critical" to the upholding of "racist order" (243). While Hartman specifically focuses on how "status offenses" became a prevalent way of policing Black mobility in "the aftermath of Emancipation," her crucial insights about how vagrancy is connected to the removal or separation of an individual from their hereditary environments and protections allows us to understand how Read wants Monima's public begging to underscore how she has in fact been deracinated. And, as Hartman vividly articulates and Read intimates, at stake in this dislocation is the secondary meaning of deracination (which I will explore in more detail below) and its implications for Monima's dangerous proximity to losing the protections of her whiteness because of her dispossession. See Hartman, *Wayward Lives, Beautiful Experiments: Intimate Histories of Riotous Black Girls, Troublesome Women, and Queer Radicals* (New York: Norton, 2019).

48. In many ways, Charles Brockden Brown was a committed "Woldwinite," a neologism crafted by Philip Barnard and Stephen Shapiro to describe Brown's investments in the radical reimagining of gender relations put forth in the works of such British intellectuals as William Godwin and Mary Wollstonecraft. The ways in which Read's conservativism differs from Wollstonecraft's, especially around the question of women's rights, is discussed in more detail in the final section of this chapter. For more information on Barnard and Shapiro's conception of "Woldwinite," see their introduction to their edition of Brown's *Ormond; or The Secret Witness* (Indianapolis: Hackett Publishing, 2009).

49. For a useful debate about the radical and conservative responses to the question of mobility and social order, see Nancy Armstrong and Leonard Tennenhouse. "The Problem of Population and the Form of the American Novel," *American Literary History* 20, no. 4 (2008): 667–85; and Bruce Burgett's response to their essay "Every

Document of Civilization Is a Document of Barbary? Nationalism, Cosmopolitanism, and Spaces between: A Response to Nancy Armstrong and Leonard Tennenhouse," *American Literary History* 20, no. 4 (2008): 686–94.

50. Henri Petter, *The Early American Novel* (Columbus: The Ohio State University Press, 1971), 445.

51. Elizabeth Maddock Dillon, *New World Drama* (Durham: Duke University Press, 2014), 27.

52. See Fichtelberg, "Heart-Felt Verities: The Feminism of Martha Meredith Read," *Legacy* 15, no. 2 (1998): 126.

53. Fichtelberg, "Heart-Felt Verities," 126.

54. Martha Meredith Read, "A Second Vindication of the Rights of Women," *Ladies Monitor*, September 5, 1801, 34.

55. Wollstonecraft as cited by Fichtelberg, "Heart-Felt Verities," 126.

56. Wollstonecraft as cited by Fichtelberg, "Heart-Felt Verities," 127.

57. Read, "A Second Vindication of the Rights of Women," 34.

58. Read, "A Second Vindication of the Rights of Women," 34.

59. Read, "A Second Vindication of the Rights of Women," 34.

60. Read, "A Second Vindication of the Rights of Women," 34.

61. Hortense Spillers, "Mama's Baby, Papa's Maybe: An American Grammar Book," *Diacritics* 17, no. 2 (1987): 65–81.

62. Consider the ways in which Federalists, like Burleigh, openly prognosticated that a Democratic-Republican ascendency would in part be defined by an erosion of traditional moral behaviors, with incest often cited as a prime example of planter depravity, to see the connection between Read's promotion of open and "natural" bonds between fathers and daughters as being key to the vindication of their rights, and her implication that secret family connections are the inverse. This theme of incest and the proper strong attraction that fathers have for their daughters is also a feature in Read's *Margaretta*, where the biological father and titular heroine, who do not realize that they are related, feel compulsively drawn to one another in utterly chaste and natural ways.

63. The historian Stephanie E. Jones-Rogers's work on how "white women" are largely ignored in "studies of sexual violence during slavery" has distorted our sense of this violence by registering "sexual and sexualized violence as the province of men" (220). In urging the field to take more seriously the various ways in which white women participated in sexual violence against and the sexual exploitation of Black women, Jones-Rogers reminds us of the various forms that this violence actually took. In this regard, Read's disavowal of Black women from being understood as identifiable as potential victims of sexual exploitation or violence in a treatise on women's rights is (in thinking with Jones-Rogers) another form of how white women often tacitly or in this case literally condoned sexual violence against Black women. See Jones-Rogers, "Rethinking Sexual Violence and the Marketplace of Slavery," in *Sexuality & Slavery: Reclaiming Intimate Histories in the Americas*, ed. Daina Ramey Berry and Leslie M. Harris (Athens: University of Georgia Press, 2018), 109–23. As Marisa J. Fuentes has proven, "white women's bodies were protected from assault" by "men who were not their husbands" (since the concept of "marital rape" did not exist in many parts of United States until the late twentieth century), and as such "they

could essentially be protected from or defended against certain forms of assault" which afforded "them a type of sexual identity, power, and honor unavailable to women of African descent" (87). See Fuentes, *Dispossessed Lives: Enslaved Women, Violence, and the Archive* (Philadelphia: The University of Pennsylvania Press, 2016).

64. Brian Connolly, *Domestic Intimacies: Incest and the Liberal Subject in Nineteenth-Century America* (Philadelphia: University of Pennsylvania Press, 2014), 168.

65. Saidiya Hartman quoted in Judith Butler, "Is Kinship Always Already Heterosexual?," *Differences: A Journal of Feminist Cultural Studies* 13, no. 1 (2002): 15.

66. Butler, "Is Kinship Always Already Heterosexual?," 15.

67. Saidiya Hartman, *Lose Your Mother: A Journey Along the Atlantic Slave Route* (New York, Farrar 2007), 5.

68. Elizabeth Maddock Dillon, "The Original American Novel, or, The American Origin of the Novel," in *A Companion to the Eighteenth-Century English Novel and Culture*, ed. Paula Backscheider and Catherine Ingrassia (London: Blackwell, 2009), 236.

69. These two fragments of the larger texts both appear in the September 5, 1801, issue of the *Ladies' Monitor*.

70. Russ Castronovo, *Fathering the Nation: American Genealogies of Slavery and Freedom* (Berkeley: University of California Press, 1995), 201

Chapter 3: "Free of Every Thing which Can Affect Its Purity"

1. See Society for the Promotion of Agriculture, Arts, and Manufactures, *Transactions of the Society for the Promotion of Agriculture, Arts And Manufactures, Instituted In the State of New York*, [S.l.: s.n.] (1792): iii.

2. Simeon De Witt (December 25, 1756–December 3, 1834) had served the revolutionary cause as the geographer and surveyor of the army for the last three years of the conflict; after the war, De Witt was appointed the first New York State surveyor general, a position he would hold for the next fifty years. Samuel Latham Mitchill (August 20, 1764–September 7, 1831) was a well-respected lawyer and doctor who had successfully negotiated land purchases in western New York from the Iroquois in the late 1780s. A graduate of the University of Edinburgh, Mitchell was a renowned naturalist who taught chemistry, botany, and natural history at Columbia College. Like Livingston and L'Hommedieu, De Witt and Mitchell were elite New Yorkers with a host of longstanding connections and affiliations.

3. In addition to the notable figures elected to serve as officers, the membership rolls of the society included a veritable who's who of post-revolutionary New York. The Society, which changed its name to the Society for the Promotion of Useful Arts in 1804, continued to sporadically publish transactions every few years until at least 1819.

4. George Washington to the mayor, recorder, alderman, etc., of the City of New York, April 10, 1785. While I have not yet located any public reprintings of Washington's letter in New York, it was clearly written for public consumption, and his letter was reprinted in newspapers outside of the New York area, including, for example, *The Essex Journal* (Newburyport, MA), May 25, 1785; and the *Pennsylvania Packet, and Daily Advertiser* (Philadelphia, PA), May 23, 1785.

5. While New York's waterways had long served as important sites of commercial exchange, the fact that the British had occupied Manhattan for the entirety of the war meant that its importance to the emerging United States had long been on pause. The structures of feeling of post-revolutionary New York is something that I discuss in greater detail in "On the Hudson River Line: Postrevolutionary Regionalism, Neo-Tory Sympathy, and 'A Lady of the State of New-York,'" in *Mapping Region in Early American Writing* (Athens: University of Georgia Press, 2015), 138–59.

6. In his insightful study of the settlement of the Hudson Valley, Martin Bruegel asserts by attending to the ways in which rural settlers in the middle and interior of New York State helped shape the emergence of what he calls a market society we can better understand the growth of new forms of cultural, economic, and social life in the aftermath of the Revolutionary War. See Bruegel, *Farm, Shop, Landing: The Rise of a Market Society in the Hudson Valley, 1780–1860* (Durham: Duke University Press, 2002).

7. New York's settlement history is as much defined by the hostility of indigenous dispossession as all of the other former English colonies in North America, but by even the late eighteenth century the region had not undergone the large-scale terraforming activities that marked other English colonial holdings. In this regard, while New Yorkers continued to imagine the displacement of indigenous Americans as central to the growth of the state the ways in which the seized lands would be transformed into profit-making agricultural spaces was still a source of open debate.

8. Much of this history is recounted in great detail in Alan Taylor's *William Cooper's Town: Power and Persuasion on the Frontier of the Early American Republic* (New York: Vintage Books, 1996). The settlement of Cooperstown of course also forms the basis for James Fenimore Cooper's *The Pioneers* (1923), but also suffuses the plots of his Anti-Rent novels, as well as the later dystopian vision of settlement histories recorded in *Wyandotté* (1843).

9. The missive contained inquiries about manure, soil composition, the best depth for tillage given the region's climate, what kinds of grasses were currently in use for pasture, the best variety of apples for cider production, the current habits for bee-keeping, the viability of silk worms being introduced into the state, and a call for suggestions about how to raise "the reputation of our flour in foreign markets." A draft of this open letter is recorded in the first volume of *Transactions of the Society for the Promotion of Agriculture, Arts and Manufactures, instituted in the State of New York* (1792), vii–xiii.

10. *Transactions*, xiii.

11. In her compelling book, *Reading These United States*, Keri Holt argues that the early American print public sphere was invested in promoting regional identities as a means of defining cultural and political order, and as such she revises the problematic fixation on national identity, which has long defined the field of early American studies. See Holt, *Reading These United States: Federal Literacy in the Early Republic, 1776–1830* (Athens: University of Georgia Press, 2019), especially chapter 2, which focuses on regional almanacs.

12. The Society printed William Cooper's missive in the first volume of their *Transactions*. See *Transactions*, 83–7.

13. By far the best treatment of the settlement of Cooper's town is Alan Taylor's *William Cooper's Town* which provides an insightful biography of both the man and his visions for settler colonial development in the upper portion of New York State.

14. *Transactions*, 83.

15. For more information on James Fenimore Cooper's slightly fictionalized portrait of his father, see in addition to Taylor's book, Wayne Franklin's *James Fenimore Cooper: The Early Years* (New Haven: Yale University Press, 2007).

16. *Transactions*, 84.

17. *Transactions*, 85.

18. *Transactions*, 85.

19. *Transactions*, 85.

20. Mirroring the kind of highly structured settlement plan he would later articulate in *A Guide to the Wilderness* (1810), Cooper's vision for New York advanced the careful management of laborers, rather than the unruly prospect of individual yeoman farmers carving out their own homesteads from the "uncultivated wilderness." William Cooper's vision for settlement, as he outlines in *A Guide in the Wilderness; or, The History of the First Settlements in the Western Counties of New York, with Useful Instructions to Future Settlers* (1810), was predicated on large landholders carefully managing the architectural and thus economic development of New York's interior regions, a subject that I examine in the third chapter of *Remodeling the Nation: The Architecture of American Identity, 1776–1858* (Hanover: University Press of New England, 2007). My early work on Cooper does not touch on his promotion of maple sugaring, which also features prominently in his *A Guide* in which he describes the possible wealth extraction from maple sap as part of his overall efforts to recruit new settlers to the region.

21. Cooper's thinking is also inherently predicated on indigenous erasure, which bleeds across much of his writing about land management in New York. Indeed like so many other Anglo-American settler colonial planners in the late eighteenth century, Cooper takes the displacement of indigenous peoples as a given for American expansion, and his concerns here around race are much more overtly centered on his concerns about avoiding the importation of more diasporic Africans into the region.

22. *Transactions*, 86.

23. *Transactions*, 86.

24. *Transactions*, 86.

25. *Transactions*, 86.

26. *Transactions*, 86. For an in-depth examination of the horrible violence of cane sugar harvesting and production, see Sidney W. Mintz, *Sweetness and Power: The Place of Sugar in Modern History* (New York: Penguin Books, 1986).

27. *Transactions*, 86.

28. *Transactions*, 86.

29. In her remarkable work on Benjamin Franklin and Phillis Wheatley, Lauren Klein establishes the ways in which linkages between cane sugar consumption and the horrors of diasporic African enslavement were intimately connected for well over a decade before Cooper's writings on the subject. As Klein argues, "because of its link to 'the pestilential detestable traffic' of the slave trade, sugar came to be viewed by

Franklin, as by many others as the time, as 'thoroughly dyed in scarlet in grain' (*Papers*, 41: 38). It was a clear instance of how the sense of taste could be exercised in order to adhere to the morally correct position" (58). See Klein, *An Archive of Taste: Race and Eating in the Early United States* (Minneapolis: University of Minnesota Press, 2020).

30. The most important work on the ways in which the French Revolution impacted political hopes in Haiti remains C.L.R James's *The Black Jacobins: Toussaint L'Ouverture and the San Domingo Revolution* (1938); for a more recent meditation on how radical French thought migrated to the Caribbean, see Massimiliano Tomba, *Insurgent Universality: An Alternative Legacy of Modernity* (New York: Oxford University Press, 2019).

31. Laurent Dubois, *A Colony of Citizens: Revolution and Slave Emancipation in the French Caribbean, 1787–1804* (Chapel Hill: The University of North Carolina Press, 2004), 47.

32. See "New-York, August 18," *United States Chronicle* [Providence, RI] VII, no. 349, September 2, 1790: [2]; "New York, August 24," *Cumberland Gazette* [Portland, ME] September 6, 1790: [2]. For examples of how versions of this same story spread, see *Spooner's Vermont Journal* [Windsor, VT] VIII, no. 371, September 7, 1790: [3]; "New York August 31," *Hampshire Gazette* [Northampton, MA] V, no. 210, September 8, 1790: [2]; and *Farmer's Journal* [Danbury, CT], September 9, 1790: 2.

33. "Philadelphia, Sept. 9," *The New-York Journal, & Patriotic Register* [New York] XLIV, no. 56, September 14, 1790, [3].

34. "Philadelphia, Sept. 9," September 14, 1790, [3].

35. Kyla Wazana Tompkins, *Racial Indigestion: Eating Bodies in the 19th Century* (New York: New York University Press, 2012), 52.

36. "Philadelphia, Sept. 9," September 14, 1790, [3].

37. "Thoughts on the Importance of the Maple Sugar Tree," *Federal Gazette* [Philadelphia, PA], August 31, 1790, [2].

38. "Thoughts on the Importance of the Maple Sugar Tree," August 31, 1790, [2].

39. Lockean notions of property rights being defined by the appropriation and improvements of "uncultivated" spaces had been central to the insidiousness of North American settler colonialism dating back to the earliest European incursions into the New World, and they remain central to these maple sugaring fantasies. At the same time, the idea that a white landowner (or their agents) could lay claim to vast reservoirs of forests by simply inserting a tap into maple trees downsizes the scale of what is required for improvement to such an extent that this vision of maple tapping would have speeded up the violences of indigenous people's removal from what were their rightful homelands.

40. It is possible that A.Z. is a misprint and that this piece was also written by A.B. as their earlier piece in Philadelphia had been, but I have not been able to confirm this, and the byline is very clearly A.Z. "For the Daily Advertiser," *Daily Advertiser* [New York] VI, no. 1575, March 8, 1790, [2].

41. "For the Daily Advertiser," March 8, 1790, [2].

42. See "Legislative Acts/Legal Proceedings," *Albany Register* [Albany, NY] V, no. 238, January 28, 1793, [3].

43. "Legislative Acts/Legal Proceedings," January 28, 1793, [3].

44. Always prone to agricultural experimentation, Thomas Jefferson flirted with maple sugaring in the 1790s. In addition to regularly purchasing maple sugar and making a bit of a show in terms of using it at his table, Jefferson also sought to promote maple sugaring in New England, and also attempted to grow maple trees in Monticello in an effort to undertake sugaring in Virginia. See the entry for the "Sugar Maple" at the Monitcello website: "Sugar Maple," *Thomas Jefferson Encyclopedia*, https://www.monticello.org/site/house-and-gardens/sugar-maple (accessed June 2020).

45. While many of the maple sugaring proponents had deep ties to New York, they were far from alone in advocating for the support of a new domestic industry as a means of liberating the United States from foreign dependencies. Indeed, a 1791 pamphlet by Benjamin Rush, entitled *An Account of the Sugar Maple-Tree of the United States*, echoes the tenets of many of these other reports. Drafted as an open letter to then Secretary of State Thomas Jefferson and the other members of the American Philosophical Society, the letter presents maple sugar production as an unrivaled and seemingly endlessly renewable source of profit. Casting maple sugar trees as an inexhaustible resource, Rush stresses the compounding value of these tress to small-scale farmers. He does so by adumbrating a variety of ways of promoting maple sugar. But, most importantly, Rush argues, in order "to transmit to future generations, all the advantages which have been enumerated from the maple tree, it will be necessary to protect it by law, or by bounty upon the maple sugar, from being destroyed by the settlers in the maple country." Underscoring that cane sugar was originally imported into the West Indies from the East Indies by the Portuguese, Rush argues for the precedent of transplantation in reshaping the agricultural prospects of vast territories when the question of profit arises. The question of enslavement also enters into Rush's account of the sugar maple. Most dramatically it surfaces in his postscript, in which he notes that his letter was written before "the account of the war, which has lately taken place in Hispaniola, between the white people and their slaves, had reached the city of Philadelphia." Like the other champions of maple sugaring, Rush proclaimed that maple sugar equaled cane in quality, and that harvesting this bounty from the forests of Pennsylvania and New York would produce a surplus commodity that would reroute the sugar trade from Cape Francois to the Susquehanna. While noting that enslavement is "inhuman and unjust," Rush argues that only by weakening the economic system underpinning the sugar plantation could actually end this barbaric traffic. Echoing many other proponents of maple sugaring, Rush figures enslavement as a West Indies phenomenon that the United States is only magically linked to by its participation in the cane sugar trade. Changing the trade, he implies, would not only reroute the profits of the sugar trade from foreign entities to domestic producers, but it would also buffer the United States against the destabilizations of resistance to enslavement already occurring elsewhere. See "*An account of the sugar maple-tree, of the United States, and of the methods of obtaining sugar from it, together with observations upon the advantages both public and private of this sugar.* In a letter to Thomas Jefferson, Esq. secretary of state of the United States, and one of the vice presidents of the American Philosophical Society. Read in the American Philosophical Society, on the 19, of August, 1791, and extracted from the third volume of their Transactions now in the press./By Benjamin Rush, M.D. Professor of the institutes and of clinical medicine in the University of Pennsylvania."

46. Ian Baucom, *Specters of the Atlantic: Finance Capital, Slavery, and the Philosophy of History* (Durham: Duke University Press, 2005), 331.
47. Baucom, *Specters of the Atlantic*, 331.
48. This is a point that Jeannine Marie DeLombard makes in her review of *Specters of the Atlantic* in *Law and History Review* 25, no. 3 (Fall 2007): 656.
49. In this regard Baucom's work dovetails with that of the more literary-focused efforts of Joseph Fichtelberg in his book *Risk Culture: Performance and Danger in Early America* (Ann Arbor: University of Michigan Press, 2010).
50. Christopher P. Iannini's path-breaking *Fatal Revolutions: Natural History, West Indian Slavery, and the Routes of American Literature* (Chapel Hill: University of North Carolina Press, 2012) deftly traces the ways in which the growth of the Caribbean plantation system impacted the formation of late-eighteenth-century American writing in ways that had been previously unaccounted for. Iannini's work in no small part highlights how the routes of American cultural development should actually be plotted on a north-south axis instead of an east-west one.
51. Raymond Williams' first reading of Bern Johnson's 1612 poem "To Penshurst," which he would more fully develop in *The Country and The City* (1973), compellingly makes the case about the erasure of actual laborers in the pastoral mode. See Raymond Williams, "Pastoral and Counter-pastoral," *Critical Quarterly* (1968), 277–9.
52. Mark Sturgess, "Bleed on, Blest Tree!" Maple Sugar Georgics in the Early American Republic," *Early American Studies* 16, no. 2 (2018): 353–80.
53. Sturgess, "'Bleed on, Blest Tree!'," 355.
54. Sturgess, "'Bleed on, Blest Tree!'," 355.
55. Sturgess, "'Bleed on, Blest Tree!'," 354.
56. Almost without exception, these nationalist maple sugar champions do not mention enslavement within the United States. Sturgess deftly untangles how maple sugar promoters in the late eighteenth century flirted with abolitionist rhetoric. Yet, he also comes a bit too close to reproducing the residual configuration of collapsing slavery with large-scale plantations. The anti-slavery rhetoric of maple sugar promoters did not aim to displace the entire regime of enslavement (and its politics are certainly pro-capitalist and in favor of large-scale wealth and landownership); rather, they sought to foster a national industry that could replace importation with an exportable commodity. While Jeffersonian visions of yeoman farmers superficially appear disconnected from the proto-industrial plantations that used the forced labor of enslaved workers to maximize their profitability, it would be a mistake to perpetuate the idea that these smaller farms were somehow configured without either enslaved or exploited wage laborers. While quick to note that 90 per cent of enslaved people worked on harvesting and manufacturing cane sugar, even the more ardently abolitionist maple sugar promotional materials neglect to describe enslavement within the United States especially in terms of the presence of enslaved people in northern states. The systems of enslavement railed against in these pieces are almost exclusively extra-national in their framing since cane production had not yet really taken root in North America. Embedded in these promotional tracts was the sentiment that cane sugar production bore with it the aggregated force of revolutionary potential which might be dissipated with a new form of agricultural production.

57. Again I am leaning on Raymond William's sense of the country house poem here as he advances it in *The Country and The City*.

58. In his chapter on Mitchell's *The Asylum*, Joseph Fichtelberg argues in some detail about how the economic instabilities that percolate through the novel are in fact early-nineteenth-century issues and not really applicable to the temporal setting of the novel. See Fichtelberg, *Critical Fictions: Sentiment and the American Market, 1780–1870* (Athens: University of Georgia Press, 2003).

59. Perhaps it would be better to say that there are three versions since the pirated edition of the text published by Daniel Jackson entitled *Alonzo and Melissa; or, The Unfeeling Father: An American Tale* (1811) continued to be published across the length of the nineteenth century. For more information on the complex publication history of the novel, see Leonard Tennenhouse, *The Importance of Feeling English: American Literature and the British Diaspora, 1750–1850* (Princeton: Princeton University Press, 2007), 101–3.

60. Fichtelberg first considers Mitchell's novel in an 1997 essay, which he later revises as part of his later book on early American novels and speculative economies; see Fichtelberg, "The Sentimental Economy of Isaac Mitchell's 'The Asylum'," *Early American Literature* 32, no. 1 (1997), 2; and, Fichtelberg, *Critical Fictions: Sentiment and the American Market, 1780–870* (Athens: University of Georgia Press, 2003).

61. By the turn of the nineteenth century, cane sugar production had taken root in Louisiana which by the time of the publication of the novel had been incorporated into the United States. Since cane sugar was now a domestic production, the nationalist bent of the maple sugaring argument no longer held as much weight in the larger political and cultural imagination. Moreover, by this time since there had been no intervention to curtail deforestation or land allocation patterns in New York State the idea of a large-scale maple plantation was no longer a viable fantasy.

62. Thomas Jefferson to Robert R. Livingston, April 18, 1802. A digital copy of the letter is available on the Library of Congress website and can be accessed here: https://www.loc.gov/resource/mtj1.026_0131_0134/?st=gallery

63. News of Dessalines's Declaration was the subject of a great deal of newspaper coverage, although not to the same degree that Toussaint's constitution had garnered a few years earlier. As Gordon Fraser has argued, beginning in "August 1801, printers in the United States published and circulated the new constitution of the revolutionized French colony of Saint-Domingue, a political entity that in three years would become the first independent black nation-state in the Western Hemisphere. By 1802, more than twenty newspapers from Virginia to Maine had reprinted the Saint-Domingue constitution." See Fraser, "Review of *The Haitian Revolution and the Early United States: Histories, Textualities, Geographies*, ed. Elizabeth Maddock Dillon and Michael Drexler," *MELUS: Multi-Ethnic Literature of the U.S.* 42, no. 3 (2017): 221. For a detailed discussion of how this text was perhaps "the most widely read piece of literature authored by an African American...until the publication of *Narrative of the Life of Fredrick Douglass*," see Michael Drexler and Ed White, "The Constitution of Toussaint: Another Origin for African American Literature," in *The Haitian Revolution and the Early United States Histories, Textualities, Geographies*, ed. Elizabeth Maddock Dillon and Michael Drexler (Philadelphia: University of Pennsylvania Press, 2016), 213–32.

64. For more information on the early formations of cane planting and harvesting, see J. Carlyle Sitterson, *Sugar Country: The Cane Sugar Industry in the South, 1753–1950* (Lexington: University of Kentucky Press, 1953).

65. Part of this neglect stems from its publication in this glossed-over interstitial period of the first two decades of the nineteenth century. However, our collective inattention to the text perhaps more accurately emerges from the difficultly of aligning Mitchell's sense of a non-national accumulation within our operant master narratives for U.S. literary development. See Cathy Davidson, "Isaac Mitchell's *The Asylum*; or, Gothic Castles in the New Republic," *Prospects* 7 (1982): 281–99, for a detailed review of the publication history of the text. The first modern claim about the popularity of the novel appears in Alexander Cowie, *The Rise of the American Novel* (New York: American Book Company, 1951), 104.

66. Kerry Dean Carso, *American Gothic Art and Architecture in the Age of Romantic Literature* (Cardiff: University of Wales Press, 2015), 98.

67. Mitchell's overly serious depiction of a chance encounter between a naïve young American and Benjamin Franklin is lampooned by Herman Melville in *Israel Potter* (1855). In this episode, Melville turns Mitchell's reverential figuration of Franklin as a self-less statesmen into a rousing portrait of a huckster who uses patriotic glosses to cover the tracks of his own hedonism.

68. See Laura Doyle, *Freedom's Empire: Race and the Rise of the Novel in America* (Durham: Duke University Press, 2008), 4.

69. Christian Knirsch, "Transcultural Gothic: Isaac Mitchhell's *Alonzo and Melissa* as an Early Example of Popular Culture," in *Transnational Gothic: Literary and Social Exchange in the Long Nineteenth Century*, ed. Monika Elbert and Bridget M. Marshall (New York: Routledge, 2016), 45.

70. Knirsch, "Transcultural Gothic," 43.

71. For a more in-depth exploration of this idea, see Elizabeth Hewitt, *Speculative Fictions: Explaining the Economy in the Early United States* (New York: Oxford University Press, 2020), especially chapter two, entitled "Jefferson and the Simple Story of Pastoral Economies."

72. Lauren Klein's groundbreaking work on the relationship between gustatory consumption and an American aesthetics of taste demonstrates the ways in which the relationship between eating, representations of foodstuffs, and the actual laborers who produced that food suffused early American culture. See Klein, *An Archive of Taste*.

73. Michel Serres with Bruno Latour, *Conversations on Science, Culture, and Time*, trans. Roxanne Lapidus (1990; Ann Arbor: University of Michigan Press, 1995), 57.

74. This prefatory statement still resides on the website that was built by the funding organization (CreativeTime) to accompany the project, and can be seen here: https://creativetime.org/projects/karawalker/

75. See: https://creativetime.org/projects/karawalker/domino-sugar-factory/

76. The plant only ceased production in 2004, when it was no longer deemed profitable after its 148-year operating history. Once closed the factory was more or less abandoned and left to rot, with no effort to clean the space. Visitors to the exhibit were required to sign a waiver, which insured that CreativeTime could not be held responsible for the delusory environmental conditions.

77. See Zack Sokol, "How Kara Walker Built a 75-Foot-Long Candy Sphinx in the Abandoned Domino Sugar Factory," *Vice*, May 8, 2014, https://www.vice.com/en_us/article/3d5qaj/how-kara-walker-built-a-75-foot-long-candy-sphinx-in-the-abandoned-domino-sugar-factory

78. See http://www.newyorker.com/online/blogs/culture/2014/05/kara-walker-domino-sugar-factory-sphinx-sculpture.html?utm_source=tny&utm_campaign=generalsocial&utm_medium=facebook&mbid=social_facebook

79. See http://www.newyorker.com/online/blogs/culture/2014/05/kara-walker-domino-sugar-factory-sphinx-sculpture.html?utm_source=tny&utm_campaign=generalsocial&utm_medium=facebook&mbid=social_facebook

80. This is a point that many internet and social media observers made, but a very compelling account can be found in Gloria Malone's piece "What Kara Walker's 'Sugar Baby' Showed Us." See Malone, "What Kara Walker's 'Sugar Baby' Showed Us," *Rewire News*, July 21, 2014, https://rewire.news/article/2014/07/21/kara-walkers-sugar-baby-showed-us/

81. See for example, this piece in artnews: http://news.artnet.com/art-world/kara-walkers-sugar-sphinx-spawns-offensive-instagram-photos-29989 and also Nicolas Powers' column, "Why I Yelled at the Kara Walker Exhibit," which opens with the line " 'You are recreating the very racism this art is supposed to critique,' I yelled." See Powers, "Why I Yelled at the Kara Walker Exhibit," *The Indypendent*, June 30, 2014, https://indypendent.org/2014/06/why-i-yelled-at-the-kara-walker-exhibit/

82. As Walker was almost assuredly aware when she was creating her installation Brooklyn's Domino Sugar Factory was the site of the longest labor strike in New York City's history, a job action which lasted over twenty months. Many of the workers who held out for better working conditions at the factory were African Americans and Caribbean immigrants (as well as eastern European immigrants) from the surrounding working-class neighborhoods of Williamsburg, Red Hook, Bedford-Stuyvesant, and Clinton Hill. In this regard, Walker's confectionary workers resonate with the later labor history of the building that continued to exploit workers of color until its closure in 2004. For more on these connections, see this brief reflection from the July 3, 2014, issue of The *Atlantic* by Leigh Raiford and Robin J. Hayes, "Remembering the Workers of the Domino Sugar Factory."

83. Indeed, many more if we consider the implications of the sphinx itself or Walker's allusion to medieval traditions of patrician sugar sculptures, known as "subtleties," which once adorned aristocratic tables at celebratory feasts.

Chapter 4: Transmitted to America

1. The first edition of *Zelica, the Creole* was published in London in 1820 in three volumes. All references to the novel are from this edition and will be cited parenthetically within the chapter. See An American, *Zelica, the Creole* (London: William Fearman, 1820).

2. Even more so than their British peers, U.S. readers were accustomed to the kind of nationalist pseudonymity engraved by geographical appellations. Indeed, using place names or a regional identity to signify the origins (and therefore, perhaps, the

potential political affiliations) of an author was a commonplace trope for early American novels. See for example, the novels of "A Lady of Philadelphia" later revealed to have been Martha Meredith Read or "The Lady of the State of New-York." As I have argued elsewhere, "A Lady of the State of New York" used this regional signification to align her novels with current political and social post-revolutionary legacies within the New York region. See Duncan Faherty, "On the Hudson River Line: Postrevolutionary Regionalism, Neo-Tory Sympathy, and 'A Lady of the State of New-York'," in *Mapping Region in Early American Writing* (Athens: University of Georgia Press, 2015), 138–59.

3. The American book-trade might have been reticent in committing to printing a barrage of novels without having some tangible prospect of success. It is also possible that, for a variety of reasons (including that these three texts were not in fact written by the same individual), the author (or authors) planned a different publication strategy for the U.S. market. The records concerning the publication backstories for many early-nineteenth-century novels remain fragmentary, and a lack of biographical knowledge about the authors of many of these texts only exacerbates this issue. Given how authorial identification has long shaped patterns of critical praxis in literary history, it is also hardly surprising that none of "An American['s]" novels (if a single author did pen all three) have received much critical attention. Indeed, if not for the geographical location of these texts outside of North America which allows critics to think about the place of U.S. within a circum-Atlantic context, these novels would likely still remain neglected.

4. Certainly, within the U.S. print public sphere the byline "American" would have been understood, by 1820, as a specific type of locator within a national framework. While the phrase did still on occasion define indigenous people in both the United States and England, that sense does not seem to fit here. Given how Fearman wanted to market these texts as exotic, if he could have implied indigenous authorship, he would likely have done so more clearly. Much more likely was the surfacing of the signifier American to link the text to a now decades-old tradition within literary culture, perhaps most famously articulated in Charles Brockden Brown's preface to *Edgar Huntly* (1799), to signify that the concerns of novels located within the New World bore with them different social, political, and historical concerns.

5. Without question Drexler's edited volume not only resurrected the text of *Secret History* (Peterborough, Ontario: Broadview Press, 2007) for the field but it also helped make the latter central to the early American canon. His work in this regard built upon the foundation established by Colin Dayan's formative work in *Haiti, History, and the Gods* (1986). Dayan was the first contemporary critic to really attend to Sansay, and to read the novel not only for its *reportage* around the abortive French attempt to recolonize the island but also for the ways in which Sansay's connection to Burr added a layer of intrigue (especially around U.S. interest in Haiti). Dayan's work sparked the first contemporary interest in Sansay, most directly in the subsection of part three of *Haiti, History, and the Gods* entitled "Lenora Sansay, Aaron Burr, and the Love Letter"; see Dayan *Haiti, History, and the Gods* (Berkeley: University of California Press, 1995), 164–71.

6. As Marlene Daut has persuasively argued, the evidence linking Sansay to the authorship of Zelica relies on two 1821 reviews of the text (one in *The Athenaeum; or Spirit of the English Magazines* (Boston) and *The Edinburgh Review, or Critical Journal*, which

both suggest that "Madame de Sansee" authored the novel. Daut also underscores how "Philip Lapsansky of the Library Company of Philadelphia" has also made this attribution. As Daut notes these debates about attribution are perhaps not the most "important" element in thinking about the function of Zelica as a "quasi-historical novel." See Daut, *Tropics of Haiti: Race and the Literary History of the Haitian Revolution in the Atlantic World* (Liverpool: Liverpool University Press, 2015), 257.

7. I am drawing here on the recent work of Ezra Tawil in my use of "terroir," a term he deploys to think about the ways in which the cultural landscapes of early America impacted the formation of a distinct national aesthetics. What I find most useful in Tawil's use of the term is his attention to how American authors sought to consider the ethnoscape of the emerging Republic as a means of identifying narrative strategies that suited this burgeoning readership. See Tawil, *Literature, American Style: The Originality of Imitation in the Early Republic* (Philadelphia: The University of Pennsylvania Press, 2018).

8. As I will argue below, the aesthetic registers and formal concerns of these two texts could not be more distinct, and the rush to conflate them into a sequential relationship neglects the pointed artistic concerns of each text.

9. The most concise source of information about the relationship between Burr and Sansay remains the introduction to Michael Drexler's edition of the *Secret History*. Another indispensable source on the cultural function of Burr in the early American imagination is Michael J. Drexler and Ed White, *The Traumatic Colonel: The Founding Fathers, Slavery, and the Phantasmatic Aaron Burr* (New York: NYU Press, 2014). But by far the most detailed work on Sansay's biography and her connection to Burr has been undertaken by the independent scholar Jennifer Van Bergen, who has done enormous amounts of archival work to try and piece together a variety of fragmentary records about Sansay's life that are indispensable to our understanding of her. Bergen has published this work in a variety of places, but most prominently in "Reconstructing Leonora Sansay," *Another World Is Possible* 1 (2010).

10. James Fenimore Cooper, quite famously, claimed to have begun his career as a novelist after hubristically betting his wife that he could produce a better novel than Jane Austen's *Persuasion* (1817), which spurred his crafting of *Precaution* in 1820; his later rejection of Lydia Maria Child's representation of early American national identity (which features a somewhat sympathetic, if still highly complex, figuration of miscegenation) in *Hobomok, A Tale of Early Times* (1824) reportedly influenced his intent in framing his empathic dismissal of the possibility of cross-racial unions in *The Last of the Mohicans* (1826). Cooper is far from exceptional in this regard. Think of all the early American texts that deploy some version of the name Constantia (from *The Gleaner* (1798) to *Ormond* (1799), to *Constatius and Pulchera* (1801), naming but a select canonical few) as a wide-scale print public sphere debate about the meaning of constancy in the early Republic. Think of how *Caleb Williams* influenced and shaped the career of Charles Brockden Brown, or the ways in which *Julia and the Illuminated Baron* (1800) responds to *Ormond*, or the countless seduction narratives set against the backdrop of the American Revolution (with *Charlotte Temple* and *Amelia; of the Faithless Briton* being just the most familiar at the tip of a larger iceberg). Or recall Daniel Jackson's famous piracy of Isaac Mitchell's *The Asylum* (1804/11) in

which he defanged the political dimensions of Mitchell's text in order to produce a highly successful edition that was printed no less than twenty-five times in the nineteenth century under a false byline. Think of the European editions of *Wieland*, which attributed Brown's novel to William Godwin and were reviewed and marketed as such for some time. Recall how the authorial function, so crucial to literary historiographies beginning in the twentieth century, had almost no purchase in the largely anonymous or pseudonymous print public sphere of the early Republic. Think of how Royal Tyler's *The Algerine Captive* (1797) rewrites Tobias Smollett's *Roderick Random* (1748); or how *The Female American* (1767) sought to rewrite *Robinson Crusoe* (1719). For more information on these patterns of call and response, see Nina Baym, "How Men and Women Wrote Indian Stories," in *New Essays on Last of the Mohicans*, ed. H. Daniel Peck (New York: Cambridge University Press, 1992); Christian Knirsch, "Transcultural Gothic: Isaac Mitchell's *Alonzo and Melissa* as an Early Example of Popular Culture," in *Transnational Gothic: Literary and Social Exchanges in the Long Nineteenth Century*, ed. Monika M Elbert and Bridget Marshall (London: Routledge, 2016), 35–49; or Eve Tavor Bannet, "The Constantias of the 1790s: Tales of Constancy and Republican Daughters," *Early American Literature* 49, no. 2 (2014): 435–66.

11. See Jared Gardner, *The Rise and Fall of Early American Magazine Culture* (Urbana: The University of Illinois Press, 2012); and Meredith McGill, *American Literature and the Culture of Reprinting, 1834–1853* (Philadelphia: University of Pennsylvania Press, 2007).

12. This significant alteration shifts Clara (in *Secret History*) from being an unhappy woman trying to reconcile her own position in a claustrophobic and sexist environment (in the case of *Zelica*'s Clara) to the much more conventional role of wife of a promiscuous man. Another significant difference in Clara is that in the later novel she is no longer compromised by her flirtatiousness, which suffuses *Secret History*'s figuration of the character.

13. On the question of the racial and social politics of companionate marriages in literary culture in the early Republic, see Melissa M. Adams-Campbell, *New World Courtships: Transatlantic Alternatives to Companionate Marriage* (Hanover: Dartmouth College Press, 2015).

14. Drexler makes this astute point in his introduction to his edition of the text, and this initial classification has in many ways guided the field's response to the text leaning into this sense of it as containing some level of autobiographical confession. See Drexler, *Secret History*, 32.

15. See Wortendyke, "Romance to Novel: A Secret History," *Narrative* 17, no. 3 (2009): 255–73.

16. As far back as 1962, in his path-breaking study *The Historical Novel* (London: Merlin), George Lukács argued for the ways in which the genre grew out of a recognition of social, cultural, and economic changes which resulted from the French Revolution. Given the ways in which mid-twentieth-century critics routinely glossed over the impact of the Haitian Revolution, it is not surprising that events in the Caribbean do not feature in Lukács account. Still his argument that the age of revolutions was the catalyst for the emergence of the genre allows us to see how the Haitian Revolution was a source of inspiration for new generic forms. More recently, Brian Hamnett has argued that the genre emerges in relation to the rise of history as an academic

discipline in the nineteenth century and while his focus is exclusively on European novels one can extend his insights about the desire to forge new forms of historiography to communicate specific ways of understanding past events to wider publics is also a useful way to consider the form of *Zelica*; see Hamnett, *The Historical Novel in Nineteenth-Century Europe: Representations in History and Fiction* (Oxford: Oxford University Press, 2011).

17. Anyone who has attended an early Americanist conference or panel session in the last decade could not help but notice ubiquity of the text in recent presentations; moreover, the volume (because so many teachers have adopted it for use in their classrooms) remains the most successful edition of Broadview's early American series. Indeed, it seems only a matter of time before the narrative becomes co-opted into one of the field's major anthologies.

18. Evidence suggests that the pair were likely lovers before, and perhaps after, Burr convinced Leonora to marry her Creole refugee husband Louis Sansay. Given these salacious associations, the inscription on the text's title page that declares "Colonel Burr, late Vice-President of the United States" as the recipient of "a Lady's" letters effectively promotes intrigue.

19. In their recent exploration of the function of Aaron Burr in the early American imagination, Drexler and White provocatively decode the ways in which the "Founders" functioned as a system of structuring fictions for the nascent Republic. In particular, they underscore how Burr served as a symbolic pivot of intrigue and counterformation. In this regard, the referencing of Burr on the title page of *Secret History* taps into a much larger cultural fascination with Burr as a person of interest. See Drexler and White, *The Traumatic Colonel: The Founding Fathers, Slavery, and the Phantasmatic Aaron Burr* (New York: NYU Press, 2014).

20. Burr's trial occurs in the late summer and early fall of 1807, and while he is not found guilty he is also not fully exonerated, and in early 1808 he leaves for Europe and does not return until 1812.

21. These earlier figurations of "Founders" often presented them as purely public figures without any kind of private motivations beyond that of the public good. Sansay's text, while it does not feature Burr on the stage, does hint at a very different kind of domestic connection than the previous figurations of founders as stock heroic figures. As White and Drexler maintain in their book, Burr was a very different kind of fantasy object for early Americans.

22. This scene is recounted in Letter XXVIII, the first missive from Clara to Mary in which she details what has happened to her since she fled her abusive husband. For a period of time she hides out near Cobre (Cuba) and is amazed to see that while the inhabitants possess "innumerable heads of cattle" they prove incapable of "procuring a little milk," the episode in short reads like a primer for acquisition or better leadership to monetize these resources for more productive ends.

23. Anna Brickhouse's insightful work on the English tradition of disavowing exploitation and brutality against indigenous peoples and diasporic Africans by criticizing Spanish colonial practices, the Anglophone attachment to the legend of Black Spain, offers one way to think about how Sansay's text participates in a long standing tradition of reifying Anglo-American colonial and settler colonial practices through a demonization

of the Spanish as inefficiently brutal. See Anna Brickhouse, "The Indian Slave Trade in Unca Eliza Winkfield's *The Female American*," *The Yearbook of English Studies*, 46 (2016): 115–26.

24. In the introduction to his important book, *Territories of Empire: U.S. Writing from the Louisiana Purchase to Mexican Independence* (New York: Oxford University Press, 2014), Andrew Doolen deploys the term "territorialization" to define the less recognizable forms of expansion and land acquisition which occurred in the early nineteenth century, that is forms of expansion which may or may not have been overly state sanctioned.

25. Christopher Taylor, *Empire of Neglect: The West Indies in the Wake of British Liberalism* (Durham: Duke University Press, 2019).

26. In the first chapter of *The Intimacies of Four Continents* (Durham: Duke University Press, 2015), Lisa Lowe charts how as early as 1803 (as registered in a secret memorandum written by the British colonial official John Sullivan) British capitalists advocated for the importation of indentured male laborers from China who could provide "a free race of cultivators…who from habits and feelings could be kept distinct from Negroes, and who from interest would be inseparably attached to the European proprietors" (21–3). This shift, as Lowe, notes represents the keen awareness of British officials to the instabilities enacted by the resistance to enslavement in Haiti.

27. While there have been considerable efforts to define the form of *Secret History* and to trace the biographical dimensions of the narrative, there has been relatively little attention paid to the aesthetic dimensions of the text. This neglect remains a critical blind spot as Sansay is a gifted writer and deftly manipulates the conventions of the epistolary form to generative ends in the text.

28. In his work on Helen Hunt Jackson's *Ramona* (1884), David Luis-Brown argues that this novel works in part "by soliciting the identification of readers with racially ambiguous subjects" which allows its "shadow plot" to "undermine romantic racialism's tendency to reply on racial difference to construct meaning" (61). While the situations are not entirely analogous (and obviously separated by six decades in terms of their publication histories), the narrative presentation of Zelica does work to elicit a similar kind of sympathetic identification on the part of white readers which troubles (as I will examine in more detail below) the normative ways in which whiteness and Blackness are imagined in a binary hierarchy, for just as *Zelica* seeks to parse out a variety of meanings for whiteness, the presentation of the titular character herself is meant to destabilize readers' understandings of Blackness as well. As Luis-Brown notes, the hemispheric interests of certain forms of romanticism strain our somewhat residual understandings of the genre and its narrative concerns. See Luis-Brown, *Waves of Decolonization: Discourses of Race and Hemispheric Citizenship in Cuba, Mexico, and the United States* (Durham: Duke University Press, 2008), 61.

29. In the introduction to her generative book *New World Drama: The Performative Commons in the Atlantic World, 1649–1849* (Durham: Duke University Press, 2014), Elizabeth Maddock Dillon introduces the concept of "intimate distance," to mark the complexities of distance and dependence that defines the colonial relation. Objects or subjects that are intimately distant enact definition onto one another, even as their disconnectedness belies their distinctiveness. In Dillon's accounting, the phrase

embodies the tension inherent in a system designed to perform two tasks: first, bridging the Atlantic and asserting kinship across oceanic dislocation while, second and conterminously, maintaining an irreconcilable division between white and non-white bodies.

30. Kimberly Snyder Manganelli, *Transatlantic Spectacles of Race: The Tragic Mulatta and the Tragic Muse* (New Brunswick, NJ: Rutgers University Press, 2012), 33.

31. Massimiliano Toomba, *Insurgent Universality: An Alternative Legacy of Modernity* (New York: Oxford University Press, 2019), 20.

32. As cited by Laurent Dubois, *Avengers in the New World: The Story of the Haitian Revolution* (Cambridge: Harvard University Press, 2004), 11.

33. Toomba, *Insurgent Universality*, 44.

34. Manganelli, *Transatlantic Spectacles of Race*, 33.

35. Toomba, *Insurgent Universality*, 44.

36. There was widespread circulation and reprintings of both "Toussaint's Constitution" and the later Haitian Constitution signed by Dessalines across the early nineteenth century in the U.S. print public sphere. Similarly, *reportage* about Haiti did not wane in the aftermath of its declaration of independence, and, as the Coda will argue, the tenor of these figurations began to alter significantly as African American writers more frequently and overtly made reference to Haiti as a beacon of freedom and possibility beginning around the second decade of the nineteenth century. For a deeper understanding of the circulation and impact of Toussaint's Constitution in the United States, see Michael Drexler and Ed White. "The Constitution of Toussaint: Another Origin of African American Literature," *A Companion to African American Literature* (Oxford: Wiley-Blackwell, 2010), 59–74.

37. As Laurent Dubois argues in *Haiti: The Aftershocks of History* (New York: Picador, 2013), almost from the inception of the Haitian Republic it was made destitute by the ways in which Euro-American powers conspired to isolate and bankrupt the emerging nation. The French insistence, backed at various moments across Haiti's history by U.S. military interventions, that Haiti pay for its freedom has had a crippling effect on its capacity to move beyond a racist status as a debtor nation. Given these insidious deprivations, Haiti's ability to enact change either within its own borders or elsewhere has always been curtailed by a continual and pronounced neo-colonial oppression.

38. First published in 1813, Byron's "The Bride of Abydos" was popular in both England and the United States. Indeed, Byron's notoriety in North America during this period has remained an understudied influence on the American print public sphere. Joseph Rezek's work on how London publishers dominated the Anglophone book market and thus impacted the development of national literary traditions in North American, Scotland, and Ireland provides a deep exploration into the circulation of a variety of English authors outside of Britain. However, while he offers intense focus on the popularity of other British Romantic writers, Byron remains somewhat marginalized in Rezek's work; see Rezek, *London and the Making of Provincial Literature: Aesthetics and the Transatlantic Book Trade, 1800–1850* (Philadelphia: University of Pennsylvania Press, 2015). More recently, Daniel Couch has advocated for Americanists to take more seriously how "romanticism" impacted "turn-of-the-century aesthetics" in the early Republic, a critical move which would allow us to move beyond "the theory that American culture develops in a stunted and belated manner," but which would also

demand "that we study concurrent transatlantic practices, even if they were employed uniquely on either side of the ocean" (3). Couch's method which pushes beyond thinking of romanticism as only belatedly (say, with Edgar Allan Poe onward) influencing American cultural production, and to have a more nuanced sense of the fluidity between early American and early-nineteenth-century British texts. See Couch, *American Fragments: The Political Aesthetic of Unfinished Forms in the Early Republic* (Philadelphia: University of Pennsylvania Press, 2022).

39. William Diamond adapted several of Byron's tales for the London stage, including *The Corsair* in 1814 and *The Bride of Abydos* which debuted in Drury Lane in 1818. As Peter J. Manning has noted, the famous actor Edmund Kean starred in the adaption of *The Bride of Abydos* to much acclaim; see Manning "Edmund Kean and Byron's Plays," *Keats-Shelley Journal* 21/2 (1972–3): 188–206.

40. Chestnut Street Theatre (Philadelphia, PA). *Philadelphia Theatre. By desire of many ladies and gentlemen, Monday evening, November 1, 1819, will be presented a favourite play... called The foundling of the forest... [microform] after which, a grand historical and patriotic drama called Sigesmar the Switzer* (Philadelphia, PA: s.n, 1819).

41. This blurring of non-Western spaces, and the association of licentious and sensuous behaviors with non-Christian societies, was a foundational element of white suprem-acist ideologies and in many ways serves as a consistent undercurrent in the myriad depictions of the Middle East which circulated in the early American print public sphere. In surveying the cultural function of seduction narratives in the early Republic, Hugh McIntosh has registered (following the work of Stephen Shapiro and Leonard Tennenhouse) the "transnational issues of bourgeois property at the center of trends in seduction fiction," to which I would add the ways in which distorted figura-tions of harems and wealthy deys provided a means of representing the sexual depri-vations of the plantocracy; see McIntosh, "Constituting the End of Feeling: Interiority in the Seduction Fiction of the Ratification Era," *Early American Literature* 47, no. 2 (2012): 321–48.

42. The author of *Zelica* takes some poetic liberties with this second epigraph as well, since the heroine of tale which she cites is actually "Nourmahal" and not "Zelica." But Moore does employ the name Zelica in the first tale that appears in *Lalla Rookh*, pro-viding another possible literary origin for the titular protagonist of the novel. As Marlene Daut notes, "owing to the popularity of Moore's epic oriental romance, Zelica became a common name in operas in the nineteenth century and led to several other *Lallah-Rookh*-inspired novellas and short stories which also used the name Zelica. Zelica is also the name used in Samuel James Arnold's 1796 *The Creole; or The Haunted Island in Three Volumes*"; see Daut, *Tropics of Haiti*, 260.

43. While the length of the review is somewhat standard for the magazine, the reviewer's consternation at Moore's attempts to be "notorious and popular" in "this age of firm and healthy poetry" demonstrates the high level of disdain for the poem which as the reviewer knew full well was receiving a widespread readership; see *The North-American Review*, November 16, 1817, 1–25.

44. *The North-American Review*, November 16, 1817, 8.

45. While her book project is still in formation, Elizabeth Polcha's dissertation remains one of the best sources on the ways in which long-eighteenth-century white writers moved to rhetorically sexualize women of color in colonial texts about the Caribbean

as a means of elevating their own status and obscuring the important roles these women played in knowledge formation. The male gaze of St. Louis and Belmont as depicted by the narrator in *Zelica* (which moves to turn Zelica into a fantasy object as a way of denying any recognition of her political agency) very much echoes the patterns that Polcha traces in natural history writing. See Polcha, "Redacting Desire: The Sexual Politics of Colonial Science in the Eighteenth-Century Atlantic World" (PhD diss., Northeastern University, 2019).

46. As Michael Drexler deftly argues in the introduction to his edition of *Secret History*, "out of the three great revolutions of the late eighteenth century come three different ideas of freedom. Only in the case of Haiti are all three present" (14). In essence, as Drexler asserts, while the American and French Revolutions advanced ideas about liberty and economic freedoms they did not fully articulate an expansive sense of equality.

47. Clara also proves to be the only character within the text who cannot read the import of the shadows that seem to color everyone else's interactions with Zelica. When Clara finally, toward the final third of the novel, discovers Zelica's mixed-race parentage she is both utterly surprised and dramatically unnerved.

48. While concerned with a different novel, Brigitte Fielder's work on the complexities of female friendships between white, Black, and mixed-raced women in the circum-Atlantic world underscores the ways in which racial fluidity need not always be registered against or read through its connections to whiteness. In this regard, Clara's failures to consider the possibilities of racial solidarities not being anchored in a Black/white binary serves as further evidence of how her way of reading the world is meant to encapsulate the dominate mode of perception operant at the time; see Brigitte Fielder, "*The Woman of Colour* and Black Atlantic Movement," in *Women's Narratives of the Early Americas and the Formation of Empire*, ed. Mary Balkun and Susan Imbarrato (New York: Palgrave, 2016), 171–85.

49. Daut, *Tropics of Haiti*, 270.

50. Daut, *Tropics of Haiti*, 270.

51. Toomba, *Insurgent Universality*, 44.

52. While there is no evidence to suggest that the author of *Zelica* was African American, the text does take up the question of Black citizenship in ways that resonate with Derrick R. Spires' recent work on Absalom Jones and Richard Allen. Indeed, the text particularly foregrounds the ways in which Zelica herself moves to embody a vision of citizenship that, to borrow from Spires' work on late-eighteenth-century Black activists, "is not a thing determined by who one is but rather by what one does" (3). In many ways, the novel presents Zelica as wanting to be defined by what Spires calls "an expansive, practiced based" form " of citizenship" one under which belonging is determined by "political participation, mutual aid, critique and revolution" rather than by the myriad ways in which citizenship was "becoming more racially restrictive" (3). Thinking with Spires allows us to see how the author of *Zelica* may well have been aware of these emerging African American theorizations of new forms of citizenship and sought to frame the figure of Zelica as someone who moved to claim a sense of her own belonging based on these attempts to imagine citizenship more expansively. Given the open ended nature of the novel's conclusion concerning Zelica, we might also think about how the text raises these new possibilities without offering any definitive conclusions about their impact on the American ethnoscape.

53. While there is a long critical history of the tragic mulatto figure largely focused on later mid-nineteenth-century American literature, more recent work focused on earlier Anglophone cultural production has a more complex understanding of the hemispheric dimensions of this figure. Important critical work on this issue includes Fielder, "*The Woman of Colour* and Black Atlantic Movement," 171–85; Jennifer DeVere Brody, *Impossible Purities: Blackness, Femininity, and Victorian Culture* (Durham: Duke University Press, 1998); Patricia Mohammed, "'But Most of All mi Love Me Browning': The Emergence in Eighteenth and Nineteenth-Century Jamaica of the Mulatto Woman as the Desired," *Feminist Review* 65 (2000): 22–48; Manganelli, *Transatlantic Spectacles of Race*; and Sara Salih, *Representing Mixed Race in Jamaica and England from the Abolition Era to the Present* (New York: Routledge, 2011).

54. While focused on late-eighteenth-century early American texts which imagined North African spy-observers entering into North America to detail the sustainability of American democracy for their home nations (such as Peter Markoe's *The Algerine Spy in Pennsylvania* (1787)), Jacob Crane's work on how "the language that constitutes representative government" was potentially destabilized by the speech acts of racialized others resonates with the concerns of *Zelica* as well. Crane notes that these Barbary texts reveal how "the national public were inherently vulnerable to the threat of foreign bodies that speak," which underscores how Zelica has used her voice to resist attempts to fix her identity and instead offer her own self-fashioning; if she regains the power of speech before entering an American port she may well do so again and thus resist the taxonomic power of customs officials to define her status in the United States. In this regard the blurring of Zelica's identity with the North American fantasies about North Africa in the beginning of the novel take on a new resonance around this issue of her capacity to speak. See Crane, "Barbary(an) Invasions: The North African Figure in Republic Print Culture, *Early American Literature* 50, no. 2 (2015): 353.

55. The narrative's depiction of Clara's death as being the byproduct of a struggle between a radical Frenchman and a revolutionary diasporic African echoes the ways in which earlier Federalist text's like Read's *Monima* (as I argued in Chapter 2) sought to frame the United States as endangered by how radical French behaviors had spurred on diasporic African resistance and endangered hemispheric stability.

Chapter 5: "UNIVERSAL EMANCIPATION!"

1. For more information on the political wrangling involved in the passage of this Gradual Emancipation Act, see Arthur Zilversmit, *The First Emancipation: The Abolition of Slavery in the North* (Chicago: University of Chicago Press: 1967).

2. Leslie M. Harris, *In the Shadow of Slavery: African Americans in New York City, 1626–1863* (Chicago: University of Chicago Press: 2003), 96.

3. Harris, *In the Shadow of Slavery*, 96.

4. This second act also had some restrictions, and the 1830 census for the state still registered seventy-five enslaved people living in New York. It was not until the publication of the 1840 census that no enslaved people were registered as living in the state. See https://www.nyhistory.org/community/slavery-end-new-york-state

5. Harris, *In the Shadow of Slavery*, 97.

6. Shane White deftly mines a wide variety of archival materials to reconstruct the ways in which the process of gradual emancipation shaped and curtailed the lives of African Americans in New York in the early nineteenth century. As White makes abundantly clear this process of becoming "somewhat more independent" was often guided by the rise of newsforms of exploitation and domination intended to retain white supremacist hegemony in the area. More focused on white political actors and activists than White, David N. Gellman's book nevertheless usefully maps the various charged public debates about the process of gradual emancipation, and in so doing he provides a vivid index of white anxieties about the process. See Shane White, *Somewhat More Independent: The End of Slavery in New York City, 1770–1810* (Athens: University of Georgia Press, 2012); and David N. Gellman, *Emancipating New York: The Politics of Slavery and Freedom, 1777–1827* (Baton Rouge: LSU Press, 2008).

7. "Insurrection in the South," *New-York Daily Advertiser* [New York] III, no. 653, May 19, 1819: [2].

8. See the *New-York Gazette & General Advertiser* [New York] May 19, 1819; the *New-York Spectator* [New York] May 21, 1819; the *Mercantile Advertiser* (New York, New York) May 21, 1819; *The New-York Evening Post* [New York] May 21, 1819; the *Commercial Advertiser* [New York] May 21, 1819; and *The New-York Columbian* [New York] May 21, 1819.

9. "Conspiracy at Augusta," *Commercial Advertiser* [New York] XXII, no. 60, May 21, 1819: [2].

10. See for example, "Augusta, May 10," *Columbian* [New York] X, no. 2811, May 21, 1819: [2].

11. "Augusta, May 8," *Evening Post* (New York, New York), no. 5282, May 21, 1819: [2].

12. "Augusta, May 8," [2].

13. Alfred Hunt's *Haiti's Influence on Antebellum America* (Baton Rouge: Louisiana State University Press, 1988) remains a groundbreaking account of the recurrent American interest in linking Caribbean struggles for liberation with domestic insurrections; David Geggus's insightful volume *Haitian Revolutionary Studies* (Bloomington: Indiana University Press, 2002) builds on Hunt's formative work by widening the scope of his inquiry; and, finally, Egerton's work on Gabriel's rebellion evinces how particular events in the U.S. were often imagined as having consequential attachments to Haiti even if the connections were mere projections. See Douglas Egerton, *Gabriel's Rebellion: The Virginia Slave Conspiracies of 1800 and 1802* (Chapel Hill: The University of North Carolina Press, 1993).

14. Coverage of Coco and his supposedly terrifying origins quickly faded from accounts of the rebellion in Augusta, replaced by several lengthy stories concerning the one white victim of the event. Several New York newspapers, including the *New-York Daily Advertiser*, the *New-York Gazette & General Advertiser*, the *Commercial Advertiser*, the *Columbian*, and the *Cherry-Valley Gazette*, all reprinted a letter from the May 8th issue of *Augusta Advertiser* which detailed how "a white citizen of Augusta, one Robert Russell," had been fatally wounded by a member "of the volunteer guard" when he "failed to heed" their "warnings." The volunteer who killed Russell, according to these accounts, failed to recognize his old friend because of the

darkened confusion and stress of keeping watch. Many of these reports were published under the pathos inducing headnote "Melancholy," which underscores how readers were meant to understand innocent white people as the victims of potential radical Black uprisings. In sharp contrast to these sentimental accounts of Russell's untimely death, many of these same papers carried graphic stories of how an enslaved man named John who had been "recommend[ed] to mercy" for his role in the attempted insurrection had his sentence "mitigated" to "two hundred and fifty lashes, then to have both his ears cut off, and to be branded with the letter R." See for example "From the Augusta Advertiser, May 8," *New-York Daily Advertiser* [New York] III, no. 656, May 22, 1819: [2]; and "Augusta Conspiracy," *New-York Gazette & General Advertiser* [New York] XXIX, no. 11667, May 25, 1819: [2].

15. Egerton, *Gabriel's Rebellion*, 168.

16. "[Ellen; Savannah; United States]," *New-York Gazette & General Advertiser* [New York] XXIX, no. 11664, May 21, 1819: [2].

17. See "Milledgeville, May 4th, 1819," *Evening Post* [New York] 5282, May 21, 1819: [2].

18. Despite the fact that the United States had "abolished" participation in the international slave trade in 1808, numerous illegally enslaved people were still being traded in southern districts. Mead's venture was one effort among many to draw public attention to this continued illegal traffic.

19. See Trish Loughran, *The Republic In Print: Print Culture in the Age of U.S. Nation Building, 1770–1870* (New York: Columbia University Press, 2007).

20. Tensions about Missouri's petition to be granted statehood, as I will discuss in some detail below, were particularly high, and one of the leading opponents to allowing Missouri to enter the union as a slave state was a New York congressman named James Tallmadge Jr. who had risen to nationwide prominence for his proposal (know commonly known as the Tallmadge Amendment) to delimit Missouri's time as a site of enslavement (by forcing the territory to agree a process of gradual emancipation as a precursor to becoming a state) in order to check the progress of enslavement into western territories.

21. One way to think of the impact of these juxtapositions filling the columns of New York's papers would be to embrace David Scott's formation of "superseded futures past." In *Conscripts of Modernity*, Scott deftly points out that we too often view revolutionary activities as failures if they do not come to fruition, and he urges us to consider the ways in which—even if just for a brief window of time—other potentialities existed in the minds of the contemporary experiencers of these events. He urges us, in other words, to imagine the unrealized potentialities of past actions rather than just think of them as retrospectively foreclosed when we look at the possibilities of emancipatory struggles. Such a way of thinking would allow us to sit with the possibilities that were at play as news of these various possible cross-pollinations unfolded somewhat simultaneously. See David Scott, *Conscripts of Modernity: The Tragedy of Colonial Enlightenment* (Durham: Duke University Press, 2004).

22. See for example "From the Trenton True American," *Columbian Gazette* [Utica, NY] XVII, no. 844, May 18, 1819: [2].

23. A concise introduction to some of these fantasies can be found in Louis A. Perez Jr., "Cuba and the United States: Origins and Antecedents of Relations, 1760s–1860s," *Cuban Studies* 21 (1991): 57–82.

24. See for example this report of a recent meeting of the New York Manumission Society that was published in the *Spectator* (among other places): "New-York, Feb. 24, 1819," *Spectator* [New York] XXII, March 9, 1819: [2].

25. See "Extract from a Correspondent in Poughkeepsie," which details the debates at a meeting of the Duchess County Republicans. *National Advocate for the Country* [New York], March 2, 1819: 1.

26. "Legislative Acts/Legal Proceedings," *Commercial Advertiser* [New York] XXII, no. 60, April 16, 1819, [1].

27. Indeed this theme of the intermingling of free African Americans and enslaved peoples was a consistent touchstone in Tallmadge's congressional speeches about Missouri's petition for statehood many of which were reprinted in full in a variety of New York newspapers. Expressing a sympathetic understanding of "the difficulties and dangers of having free blacks intermingling with slaves," Tallmadge argued in one speech that Missouri's petition needed to be considered alongside Alabama's similar request for statehood. Arguing that the possible transit between people in diametrically different conditions of freedom and unfreedom might undermine the "safety of the white population of the adjoining states," Tallmadge sought to differentiate Alabama from Missouri. He did so by asserting that since Alabama was "surrounded...by slave holding states" it should be admitted into the Republic as site of enslavement to preserve security in the region. But, he maintained, since Missouri was not similarly landlocked by states allowing enslavement, it should be considered in a different light and not become the means by which enslavement would gain a foothold in the west. Portions of this speech were printed in several papers, and published in full in the *Commercial Advertiser*. See Legislative Acts/ Legal Proceedings," April 16, 1819, [1].

28. See Katie Bray, "'A Climate...More Prolific...in Sorcery': *The Black Vampyre* and the Hemispheric Gothic," *American Literature* 87, no. 1 (2015): 1–21. Bray's work on *The Black Vampyre* remains the only extended critical treatment of the text.

29. Dey signals his text's imbrications in New York's literary culture on his very title page, as he dedicates his novella to the author of the play *Wall-Street* by way of declaring that both texts are born from "the Auction Room" (13). By aligning his text with the writer of a contemporary drama that lampoons the instability of financial speculation in New York, Dey locates his text in a discursive exploration of the unhinged speculation that fueled the Panic of 1819. A farce of the perils of the current economic system, *Wall-Street* stages how bankers, merchants, and traders were so consumed by whispers of monumental profits that they habitually outpaced their access to actual specie. The play, in sum, illustrates how inflated returns on unhinged speculations led capitalists to have increasingly fewer concerns about the consequences of their actions. One of the on-the-brink-of-ruin figures depicted in the play is Mr. Merchant whose long overdue shipment of coffee from St. Domingo has left him so cash strapped that he is willing to sell a portion of his expected cargo at a discounted rate in return for a desperately needed cash advance. While the play makes little of this foreign connection, the coffee from St. Domingo nevertheless serves as the only tangible commodity attached to the various promissory notes referenced on stage. That this cargo from St. Domingo serves as the most stable economic signifier in *Wall-Street* may well be the play's most farcical prompt, given how the harvesting of coffee

and sugar on the island had only slowly recovered in the wake of the lengthy revolution. Still linking St. Domingo, even in the most tangential of ways, to the collapse of the U.S. market suggests how referencing the island remained—even in 1819—a byword for economic collapse. Even within the comedic confines of a farce, Merchant's attempts to borrow against Haitian imports clearly signaled a furtive effort, one as unlikely to succeed as all the other figures scrambling for money to pay for their daily needs. St. Domingo haunts the play as a reminder that circum-Atlantic trade remained an unstable business, and this thematic concern of the play resonates throughout the novella which dedicates itself to the author of *Wall-Street*. For the best history of the Panic of 1819, and its implications for the stability of the U.S. economy, see Clyde A. Haulman, *Virginia and the Panic of 1819: The First Great Depression and the Commonwealth* (London: Pickering & Chatto, 2008); and also James Nelson Barker Mead, *Wall-Street, or, Ten Minutes before Three: A Farce in Three Acts* (New York, 1819).

30. *Commercial Advertiser* [New York], June, 28, 1819.

31. See "Advertisement," *Commercial Advertiser* [New York] XXII, no. 60, June 19, 1819: [3]; *New-York Daily Advertiser* [New York] III, no. 679, June 21, 1819: [3]; and "Advertisement," *Evening Post* [New York], no. 5307, June 19, 1819: [3].

32. See, for example, *Spectator* [New York] XXII, September 7, 1819: [3]; and, *National Advocate* [New York] VII, no. 1999, July 5, 1819: [1]. *Readex: America's Historical Newspapers*.

33. See "Advertisement," *Connecticut Journal* [New Haven, CT] LII, no. 2700, July 27, 1819: [4]; "Westchester: Wednesday, September 22, 1819," *Village Record* [West Chester, PA] III, no. 112, September 22, 1819: [4]; and, *Southern Patriot* [Charleston, SC], September 2, 1819: 1.

34. See for example, *Columbian* [New York)] X, no. 2851, July 10, 1819: [3].

35. As Katie Bray insightfully argues, both of the texts which were typically advertised alongside *The Black Vampyre* were by prominent authors (since the fact that Geoffrey Crayon was a pseudonym of Washington Irving was something of an open secret). Moreover, after Byron was revealed not to have written *The Vampyre*, his name still appeared in these ads as booksellers replaced the wrongly ascribed text with a collection of his poems. The printing of a second slightly expanded edition just a few weeks after publication of the first edition perhaps further implies the popularity of *The Black Vampyre*.

36. Polidori's text quickly became a bestseller on both sides of the Atlantic, proving successful enough to require the publication of several editions in its first year. The first several printings of *The Vampyre* attributed the text to Byron, and it was not until the late spring of 1819 that Polidori was publically identified as its actual author. In the U.S. print public sphere, the first edition of *The Black Vampyre* was advertised for sale alongside Byron's *The Vampyre* since news of Polidori's authorship did not reach North America until shortly before the publication of the second edition of *The Black Vampyre* (now being sold alongside various volumes of Byron's poetry). Byron himself had indeed deployed vampire-like figures in several of his poems (most notably "The Giaor," which provides one of the epigraphs for *The Black Vampyre*), which in part fueled the belief that he had authored Polidori's text. Moreover, Byron's verse played an important role in shaping the early Anglophone understanding of vampires,

even as his larger-than-life persona helped popularize representations of vampires as erotic, scandalous, wandering figures. For more information about the connections between Byron and the rise of vampires in Anglo-American literary culture, see D.L. Macdonald and Kathleen Scherf's introduction to their edition of the text in John William Polidori's *The Vampyre and Ernestus Berchtold*, ed. D.L. Macdonald and Kathleen Scherf (New York: City Broadview, 2008), 9–31.

37. "The Vampyre," *Commercial Advertiser* [New York] XXII, no. 60, June 28, 1819: [2].

38. "The Vampyre," [2].

39. "The Vampyre," [2].

40. As Macdonald and Scherf detail, Polidori transforms the figure of the vampire away from its original depictions in eastern European folktales. In these traditional folk-tales, vampires often resembled contemporary representations of zombies in that they were typically depicted as petrifying and largely unintelligent corpses, which had been reanimated by some external force. Polidori was responsible for transforming this folk figure into the more familiar modern version of the vampire as an "articulate, aristocratic, and seductive" rouge (9), and he largely did so by constructing his vampire as a "caricature" of his former employer Lord Byron (11); for more information on this (in addition to the Macdonald and Scherf introduction) see: Conrad Aquilina's "The Deformed Transformed; or, From Bloodsucker to Byronic Hero—Polidori and the Literary Vampire," in *Open Graves, Open Minds: Representations of Vampires and the Undead from Enlightenment to the Present Day* (Manchester: Manchester University Press, 2013), 24–38; Mariam Wassif's "Polidori's The Vampyre and Byron's Portrait," *Wordsworth Circle* 49, no. 1 (2018): 53–61; and, Andrew McConnell Stott's *The Poet and the Vampyre: The Curse of Byron and the Birth of Literature's Greatest Monsters* (New York: City Pegasus Books, 2015). Other scholarship of note on Polidori's text includes J. P. Telotte's "A Parasitic Perspective: Romantic Participation and Polidori's *The Vampyre*," in *The Blood is the Life: Vampires in Literature* (New York: City Bowling Green State University Press, 1999), 9–19; and Carol Senf's "Polidori's *The Vampyre*: Combining the Gothic with Realism," *North Dakota Quarterly* 56, no. 1 (1988): 197–208. For a perceptive exposition of how Polidori's vampire represents the inherent dangers in unregulated self-interest, we recommend Lauren Bailey's "Gothic Economies: Capitalism and Vampirism," in *The Routledge Companion to Literature and Economics* (London: City Routledge, 2018), 89–95.

41. See the "Just Teach One" edition of the first printing of *The Black Vampyre* (1819), edited by Duncan Faherty and Ed White. All citations of the text are from this edition and will be noted parenthetically within the chapter. See http://jto.common-place. org/just-teach-one-homepage/the-black-vampyre/

42. Elizabeth Young, *Black Frankenstein: The Making of An American Metaphor* (New York: New York University Press, 2008), 23.

43. Young deploys this language as a means of underscoring how Nat Turner functioned as a kind of Black Frankenstein in the mind of Virginian politicians in the 1830s, but that sense of the threat, I think, speaks to the import of the plot of *The Black Vampyre* in deeply resonating ways. See Young, *Black Frankenstein*, 21.

44. The text's insistence on the African origins of vampiric power, that it lies outside the boundaries of white control or influence, is perhaps the largest difference between the idea of a Black Vampire and a Black Frankenstein. As Young underscores in her

project, central to Mary Shelley's creation and its subsequent imitators is the idea that the "monster" is out for revenge against a white creator who is framed as totally responsible for the creature's birth; in contrast, Dey continually frames vampiric power as African in origin and fundamentally anti-white supremacist, so it is not a case of destroying the master with the master's tools (as is usually the case with a Frankenstein figure) but rather of deploying something African in origin to counter the violence of Euro-American enslavers. In this regard, the Black Vampyre might be a more terrifying figure than the Black Frankenstein.

45. The historian Marisa J. Fuentes is currently at work on a project about "refuse slaves," a term she identifies as being used to describe "African captives who were refused at purchase or who survived the Middle Passage but died before they could be sold in Atlantic ports." I am indebted to Fuentes for talking with me about her exploration of this term after a talk she gave at The CUNY Graduate Center in the Spring of 2018.

46. Sylvia Wynter and Katherine McKittrick (eds.), *Sylvia Wynter: On Being Human as Praxis* (Durham: Duke University Press, 2015), 10.

47. Elizabeth Maddock Dillon, *New World Drama: The Performative Commons in the Atlantic World, 1649–1849* (Durham: Duke University Press, 2014), 27.

48. Dillon, *New World Drama*, 27.

49. In this regard the narrative reproduces the political logics of anti-Black racism, perhaps best encapsulated in this pointed definition offered by Ruth Wilson Gilmore: "Racism is the state-sanctioned and/or extra-legal production and exploitation of group-differentiated vulnerabilities to premature death, in distinct yet densely interconnected political geographies." See Ruth Wilson Gilmore, "Race and Globalization," in *Geographies of Global Change: Remapping the World*, ed. R. J. Johnston et al. (New York: Wiley-Blackwell, 2002), 261.

50. I am indebted for this information to Ed White who first noticed this important nominative detail in terms of Personne's representation in the text.

51. I am using the term "counternarrative" here in light of how the writer John Keene deploys that term in his 2015 collection of short stories entitled *Counternarratives*. Keene's praxis in the collection is to use archival materials relating to the lives of diasporic Africans in the New World by essentially remixing them and creating narratives where little or no material record actually exists. Keene deploys a kind of fabulation in order to resist erasure and silencing in an attempt to create new ways of thinking about both the past and the present.

52. The text defines this as the processes by which enslavers attempted to make enslaved people see themselves as if they might be "French" or "Spanish" to a limited degree or as if their identities were tethered to particular plantations or regions.

53. See Ramesh Mallipeddi, *Spectacular Suffering: Witnessing Slavery in the Eighteenth-Century British Atlantic* (Charlottesville: University of Virginia Press, 2016).

54. While miscegenation is a frequent motif in criminal confessions, perhaps most famously in that of Joseph Mountain, this may well be the first time such a union between a Black man and a white woman was part of fictive text in the United States.

55. Caroline Karcher has argued that the interracial marriage which produces the young Hobomok symbolizes "both the natural alliance white women and people of color and the natural resolution of America's racial and sexual contradictions." More recently, Cathy Rex has advanced the idea that in crafting this character Child really

moved "to mine the indignity of Native identity in order to write white womanhood—and white female authorship—into existence," and that while so doing she also very carefully did not "write a version of Indian masculinity into existence," not giving it "dominance over Anglo-American women" or "equality with Anglo-American men" (152). See Lydia Maria Child, *Hobomok and Other Writings on Indians*, ed. Carolyn L. Karcher (New Brunswick, NJ: Rutgers University Press, 1986); and Cathy Rex, *Anglo-American Women Writers and Representations of Indianness, 1629–1824* (London: Ashgate Publishing, 2015). For more information on Cooper's crafting *The Last of the Mohicans* as a rebuttal to Child, see Nina Baym, "How Men and Women Wrote Indian Stories," in H. Daniel Peck, *New Essays on Last of the Mohicans* (New Brunswick, NJ: Rutgers University Press, 1992), 67–86.

56. For more information about how these references to Shakespeare function in the text, see the textual notes in the "Just Teach One" edition of *The Black Vampyre* https://jto.americanantiquarian.org/wp-content/uploads/2019/08/Black-Vampyre-for-JTO.pdf

57. For more information on the cultural figurations of the Apollo Belvedere, see Partha Mitter, "Western Theories of Beauty and Non-Western Peoples," in *Artistic Visions and the Promise of Beauty*, ed. K. Higgins, S. Maira, and S. Sikka (New York: Spring, 2017), 79–89.

58. An influential lawyer with a host of political connections, in his role as secretary of the American Academy of Fine Arts, John G Bogert had an outsized role in shaping cultural tastes during this period in New York.

59. The Black Vampyre's facility with language as a seductive tool perversely echoes Shakespeare's depiction of Othello's successful wooing of Desdemona. For more information on Black Atlantic figurations of Othello, see Miles P Grier, *Inkface: Othello and White Authority in the Era of Atlantic Slavery* (Charlottesville: University of Virginia Press, 2023). Grier's book deftly considers the performance history of over two centuries of *Othello* to uncover how the play had a formative role in the Anglo-American project of "producing legible gendered and racialized characters out of the strangers in a far-flung Atlantic economy."

60. The licentiousness of French women is a staple of long-eighteenth-century Anglophone literature, and perhaps finds its most succinct rendition in the fact that Susannah Rowson names the French governess who contributes to Charlotte Temple's ruination "Madam Le Rue." The ways in which the Caribbean only heightened this overt Francophone sexuality is a recurrent theme, for example, in Lenora Sansay's *Secret History* (1808).

61. Bryan Edwards was a Jamaican plantation owner, staunch supporter of the slave trade, and influential British colonial politician. His work on the history of British Caribbean possessions were both popular and influential, beginning with his *History of the British Colonies in the West Indies* which was widely circulated and translated. He later wrote, *An Historical Survey of the French Colony in the Island of St Domingo*, which attempted to describe the, then still unresolved, Haitian Revolution. Part of Edwards's notoriety (and imagined expertise) stemmed from how he attempted to describe Obeah, a group of Creole religious and medical practices associated with enslaved Africans in the British Caribbean.

62. Here Dey directly cites Edwards, by the inclusion of a footnote within the original text, and references Edwards's account (from the fourth chapter of his *Historical Survey of*

St. Domingo) of the capture and execution of Vincent Ogé, a free person of color, who had been accused and convicted for attempting to lead a revolt in Saint Domingue in 1790. For more information on Dey's use of Edwards here, see the introduction and the textual notes to the "Just Teach One" edition of *The Black Vampyre* and: https://jto.americanantiquarian.org/wp-content/uploads/2019/08/Black-Vampyre-for-JTO.pdf

63. Demetrius L. Eudell has compellingly argued that in "Black Metamorphosis," Wynter advances a way to think about "the countercosmogonic conceptual and social systems of the peoples brought from Africa to the Americas, which, she illustrates, can serve as the basis from which to rethink the praxis of being human" (48). In so doing, Wynter details how these conceptual and social systems refused and subverted the insidious Western commodification of Africans through the Middle Passage. Similarly, Katherine McKittrick argues that Wynter's "Black Metamorphosis" discloses "how the plantation slavery system and its postslave expressions produced black non-persons and nonbeings (through brutal acts of racist violence designed to actualize psychic and embodied alienation) just as this system generated black plantation activities that rebelled against the tenets of white supremacy" (81). Again, the presentation of the assembly in the cavern as disinterested or unaware of the value of the precious materials adorning its walls works to differentiate them from their oppressors whose only motivation across the text is to think about value and extraction as the defining tenets of personhood. See Eudell, "From Mode of Production to Mode of Auto-Institution: Sylvia Wynter's Black Metamorphosis of the Labor Question," *Small Axe: A Caribbean Journal of Criticism* 49 (2016): 47–61; and McKittrick, "Rebellion/Invention/Groove," *Small Axe: A Caribbean Journal of Criticism* 49 (2016): 79–97.

64. See *OED*: https://www.oed.com/view/Entry/69003?redirectedFrom=fee-tail#eid

65. Hortense J. Spillers, "Mama's Baby, Papa's Maybe: An American Grammar Book," *Diacritics* 17, no. 2 (1987): 64–81.

66. Spillers, "Mama's Baby, Papa's Maybe," 66.

67. As cited and translated by Laurent Dubois. See Dubois, *Avengers of the New World: The Story of the Haitian Revolution* (Cambridge: Harvard University Press, 2005), 58.

68. Dubois, *Avengers of the New World*, 58.

69. No accounts of Coco's rebellion or his death sentence provide any detailed accounting of his life beyond the brief notation of his connection to Haiti, and it remains difficult to measure (aside from the usual paranoias) what sparked the spread of this information to begin with.

70. As I have noted in earlier chapters, a wide range of historians of (including Alfred Hunt, David Geggus, and Douglass Egerton) have detailed the ways in which rumors about possible connections to Haiti seemed to surface in response to any domestic uprising against enslavement in the United States. In this regard, the rumors about Coco's origins are symptomatic of the larger ways in which fears about Haitian influence were a consistent incipient fever that inflected the American cultural imagination for much of the early nineteenth century.

Coda

1. I am deeply indebted to Stefano Morello for his help in tracing the various ways in which these images circulated across social media platforms, and for his expert

guidance in thinking about how to extrapolate information from these various plat-forms. The original photos and posting by @Noushiex3 can be seen here: https://www.instagram.com/p/CA9UZj7gWjA/

2. In the second photo, @Noushiex3 poses by taking a knee, with her head slightly tilted to the left, holding the sign in her right hand and with her left hand raised in a fist. This image portrays @Noushiex3 as gesturing toward other famous forms of African American social justice protests (echoing the posture of Colin Kapernick and other professional athletes taking a knee during the national anthem, as well as the gestures of sprinters Tommie Smith and John Carlos at the 1968 Olympic Games). Despite the photos being posted together as a series, the second image did not receive the same attention on social media as the first. This may simply be the result of the tendency to privilege the first item in a series in terms of social media behaviors, or it may well result from the fact that it is harder to separate this image from recognizable American gestures of protest against specific American forms of anti-Blackness.

3. See https://m.facebook.com/TheHaitianAmerican/photos/a.181242528594364/3251067391611847/?type=3&p=30

4. Changes to the privacy settings on Facebook and Instagram render it difficult to scrape all the comments from a post in order to use a digital tool designed to enable a more fine-grained textual analysis of all of a post's comments or interactions. Still, even a cursory reading of the comments associated with The Haitian American's sharing of the photo suggests that the majority of users who interacted with this post agreed with message in @Noushiex3's sign. https://m.facebook.com/TheHaitianAmerican/photos/a.181242528594364/3251067391611847/?type=3&p=30

5. See Michelle Alexander, *The New Jim Crow: Mass Incarceration in the Age of Colorblindness* (New York: The New Press, 2010); see also, Aaron Carico, *Black Market: The Slave's Value in National Culture after 1865* (Chapel Hill: The University of North Carolina Press, 2020).

6. While Campt writes here about ethnographic photographs of rural Africans in the Eastern Cape, her injunctions about the necessity of listening to images has been gen-erative for my thinking with @Noushiex3's photos. Campt deftly urges us to look beyond surface readings in order to attune ourselves to the other affective frequencies registered in portraits of Black subjects so that we might "reclaim the black quotidian as a signature idiom of diasporic culture and black futurity" (9). In many ways, @Noushiex3's social media posts are an example of widely felt reactions to the murder of George Floyd, with hundreds of thousands of people posting selfies of their own experiences at public protests all over the globe. At the same time, in this specific instance (again following Camp) we can see how @Noushiex3's "stasis" presents "a state of being and becoming" by linking the U.S. present to the legacies of Haitian free-dom (51). See Campt, *Listening to Images* (Durham: Duke University Press, 2017), 50.

7. In this regard we might think of @Noushiex3's blurring of temporalities as a version of what Elizabeth Freeman defines as the political possibilities of queering "chro-nonormativity," or resisting the imperative to always organize productivity in relation to normative time. In queering normative time, @Noushiex3 and Freeman assert that the past exists in transformative relation with the present. Freeman's work on visual artists who refute the supposedly liberating frames of "postfeminist" and "postgay"

reveals the ways many of these artists insist that past struggles are still unfolding within present temporalities. Freeman's work allows us one way to understand the aims of @Noushiex3's conception of the overlapping and always intersecting temporalities of freedom. See Freeman, *Time Binds: Queer Temporalities, Queer Histories* (Durham: Duke University Press, 2010).

8. For example in one Reddit thread in which alt-right social media users reacted to @ Noushiex3's photos, there were over 2,000 reactions to the photo and over 600 individual comments; extracting these comments and loading them into a data visualization program creates a tabulation of word usage, and the frequency with which "white" appears in proximity to "genocide," or "killing," or "racism," or "violence" is startling. For the original Reddit thread, see https://www.reddit.com/r/iamatotalpieceofshit/comments/hissz0/ in_1804_haiti_massacred_all_white_population/?utm_source=share&utm_ medium=ios_app&utm_name=iossmf And for a visualization of the data in this thread, see https://voyant-tools.org/?corpus=743779a817beb764e8b87d97915a51bc

9. In her recent book, *Hate in the Homeland: The New Global Far Right* (Princeton: Princeton University Press, 2020), Cynthia Miller-Idriss charts how across the last two decades the far right has attempted to mainstream its message through actively rescripting public understanding of contemporary events. In essence, these highly structured and organized propaganda campaigns disseminate misinformation in an effort to make white supremacist ideologies more palpable to a wider public audience. See especially chapter 2 of Miller-Idriss's book entitled "Mainstreaming the Message." Miller-Idriss's work provides us with a way to think about why the alt-right has invested so much attention in building meme generators, so that they can flood the digital town square with their insidious fabrications of contemporary events. Recontextualized versions of @Noushiex3's photos appeared on hundreds of alt-right social media posts and websites, including for example a right wing blog, which posts a variety of memes for easy dissemination from subscribers, called Meme Warfare Blog; see https://memewarfare.blog/2020/06/.

The photo was also posted on 9gag (the largest meme repository currently on the internet, and often the source for users to find memes and generate traffic around them; see https://9gag.com/gag/aEP233x

For a sense of the wide variety of Facebook and Twitter posts which used this photo as evidence of a violent conspiracy, see the results of a reverse Google image search https://www.google.com/search?hl=en&tbs=simg:CAQSsgIJhCV-MMnN3 MkapgILEKjU2AQaAghDDAsQsIynCBpiCmAIAxIorQysDJYEyQyuDIMbhhuKG9 Uetx_1sOrMw0C_1oLqU65DymOuM8rTrPLxow_1CReM_1V_1phUooTLoVDpPF TgTM-rkUR7Ww6JN3nl-Un7mr2s3PJVPPGxf5hb4bW5tIAQMCxCOrv4IGgoKCA gBEgQF263HDAsQne3BCRqTAQoaCgdwcm90ZXN02qWI9gMLCgkvbS8wMW55 kX24KGgoHc3BhbmRleNqliPYDCwoJL20vMDE0Mnk3ChwKCGFjdGl2aX- N02qWI9gMMCgovbS8wal83dmw2ChkKBnN0cmVldNqliPYDCwoJL20vMD- FjOGJyCiAKDWRlbW9uc3RyYXRpb27apYj2AwsKCS9tLzBnbnd6NAw&sxsrf= ALeKk01hmp5kWXyb1CHYyK2gZq8Z2w1_cg:1609786195081&q=haiti+ did+it+in+1804+this+is+just+round+2+we+got+you&tbm=isch&sa=X&ved= 2ahUKEwiBo8ny-ILuAhUIpFkKHUbBCckQ2A4oAXoECBMQMg& biw=1366&bih=625

10. One of the lengthiest of these alt-right diatribes concerning @Noushiex3's photos is a two-part blog post by a self-professed libertarian blogger named Rick Ardito. The caption that Ardito provides for the photo reads "Woman holding sign calling for Haitian style Revolution that resulted in the torture and killing of whites residing in Haiti." Since these blogposts seek to slow-walk readers through what it thinks of as an unveiling of the nefarious international conspiracy supposedly funding #BLM, they are particularly revealing of the rhetorical strategies of the alt-right. Another example appears in the apologetic coverage of the insurrectionary rioting in Washington, DC, on January 6th of 2021 from conservative media outlets. These distorting reports routinely sought to erroneously suggest that BLM protests were to be blamed for this attempted coup (by creating the conditions of possibility for violent public demonstrations), providing another example of the far-right attempting to dismiss structural racism by describing protests against its horrors as representing a danger to the United States. As Ardito's columns make clear, the intent of this alt-right framing of anti-racist protests as un-American is to create the sense that increased policing is necessary for cultural preservation (which is a thinly disguised attempt to reify white supremacist power structures). See https://rickardito.medium.com/part-1-tread-on-thee-but-not-on-me-b91f38792acb for the self-identification of Ardito's political leanings and the first iteration of these linked columns concerning the Black Lives Matter movement. The second column can be found here: https://rickardito.medium.com/if-you-landed-here-but-have-not-yet-read-part-1-of-this-series-i-would-recommend-that-you-go-back-eeb3c0dc9d35

11. This tendency to equate any positive reference to Haiti as foreign intrigue, I think, explains why the alt-right focused on the first of the two images posted by @Noushiex3, since the second photo, as I have noted above, references specifically American forms of social justice protest linked to very public protests by African American athletes.

12. This phenomenon only increased in the waning days of the Trump presidency as his previously favorite party organ Fox News began to concede that he did indeed lose his failed attempt at a second term. This slight corrective on the part of Fox has fueled the rise of even more partisan news organizations like Newsmax and OAN (One America News Network). And once Twitter began to question the validity of Trump's faulty missives after years of spreading lies (and the subsequent temporary ban of his account from the platform), many on the right have begun to cultivate Parlor and Truth Social as an "uncensored" (i.e. right wing) social media platform.

13. In *Imagine Otherwise: On Asian Americanist Critique* (Durham: Duke University Press, 2003), Kandice Chuh theorizes that a field of inquiry should not be defined by its subjects and objects, but rather by its critique. In essence, Chuh asserts that to think otherwise entails a foregrounding of the constructedness of terms (in this case the idea that Haiti represents for white Americans) and a subsequent decision to still use those terms to try and advance a critique of hegemonic constriction.

14. Leslie M. Harris, *In the Shadow of Slavery: African Americans in New York City, 1626–1863* (Chicago: The University of Chicago Press, 2003), 123,122, 122.

15. Robert S. Levine, "Fifth of July: Nathaniel Paul and the Construction of Black Nationalism," in *Genius in Bondage: Literature of the Early Black Atlantic*, ed. Vincent Carretta and Philip Gould (Lexington: University of Kentucky Press, 2001), 242.

16. Kevin Quashie, *The Sovereignty of Quiet: Beyond Resistance in Black* Culture (New Brunswick, NJ: Rutgers University Press, 2012), 3.

17. Quashie, *The Sovereignty of Quiet*, 4.

18. Born to free parents in Delaware, Cornish had lived in Philadelphia prior to moving to New York in 1821. Shortly after his arrival in New York, Cornish helped found the First Colored Presbyterian Church; he would later go on to edit two other periodicals, *The Rights of All* and the *Colored American*, and was also a founding member of American Anti-Slavery Society. Russwurm was born in Port Antonio, Jamaica, the mixed-race son of an English merchant and enslaved mother. At the age of 8, his family sent him to Quebec to begin his education, and he later joined his father in Maine in 1812. After becoming the first African American to graduate from Bowdoin College, Russwurm moved to New York just as the city's Gradual Emancipation Act was coming to its final phase. During his time in New York, he also joined the Haytian Emigration Society. After Corish departed the paper in September of 1827, Russwurm used his position to advocate for voluntary emigration for African Americans to both Haiti and Liberia. After his own migration to Liberia, Russwurm worked as the editor of *Liberia Herald*. For a more detailed account of the influential African Americans in New York who created *Freedom's Journal* and appointed Cornish and Russworm as its inaugural editors, see Harris, *In the Shadow of Slavery*, 120–8.

19. See Ira Berlin, *Many Thousands Gone* (Harvard University Press, 1998), 372.

20. As noted in Chapter 5, Christy Pottroff's work around the prohibitions of non-white people handling U.S. mail underscores the lengths to which the idea of African American participation in the print public sphere (of any kind) was a consistent source of anxiety to white authorities.

21. Gordon Fraser, "Emancipatory Cosmology: Freedom's Journal, The Rights of All, and the Revolutionary Movements of Black Print Culture," *American Quarterly* 68, no. 2 (2016): 263.

22. For more information on how Noah's racist rantings in New York spurred the work of *Freedom's Journal*, see Jacqueline Bacon, "The History of *Freedom's Journal*: A Study in Empowerment and Community," *The Journal of African American History* 88, no. 1 (2003): 1–20.

23. "To Our Patrons," *Freedom's Journal* [New York], March 16, 1827.

24. See Benjamin Fagan, "Chronicling White America," *American Periodicals: A Journal of History and Criticism* 26, no. 1 (2016): 10–13. While Fagan is analyzing a contemporary public humanities project housed at the Library of Congress for its limited attention to African American periodicals in its digitization efforts, the whitewashing of the print public sphere was something that resonates with the intervention intended by the counterformation of *Freedom's Journal*.

25. "To Our Patrons," March 16, 1827.

26. "To Our Patrons," March 16, 1827.

27. "To Our Patrons," March 16, 1827.

28. "To Our Patrons," March 16, 1827.

29. Shane White's indispensable work on the ways in which the acculturation of free Black people was continually compromised in New York offers a deep understanding about these new forms of domination. See White, *Somewhat More Independent: The End of Slavery in New York City, 1770–1810* (Athens: University of Georgia Press, 1991).

30. Chapters three and four of Harris's *In the Shadow of Slavery* provide a wealth of information about the struggles facing emancipated African Americans in New York. As the title of chapter four, "Free but Unequal: The Limits of Emancipation," suggests, the obstacles faced in the struggle for equality were delimited by the resurgent interest of white supremacists in oppressing African Americans.

31. For a brief discussion of the Overton window and racial politics, see Miller-Idriss, *Hate in the Homeland*, 45–7.

32. In his recent book, Aaron Carico deftly exhibits the failures of post-Civil War emancipation efforts by laying out a variety of ways in which "freedom" for formerly enslaved peoples really unfolded as new forms of exploitation and indebtedness; see Carico, *Black Market*. These dates mark Lincoln's signing of the Emancipation Proclamation in 1863, the passage of the 13th Amendment which ended slavery and involuntary servitude (except as punishment for a crime) in 1865, and the passage of the 14th Amendment which granted citizenship to the formerly enslaved people born or naturalized in the United States in 1868.

33. "To Our Patrons," March 16, 1827.

34. "To Our Patrons," March 16, 1827.

35. "To Our Patrons," March 16, 1827.

36. Saidiya Hartman, *Scenes of Subjection: Terror, Slavery, and Self-Making in Nineteenth-Century America* (New York: Oxford University Press, 1997), 6.

37. These fears about diasporic African solidarity, for example, animate the revolutionary rhetoric of the titular Black Vampyre as discussed in Chapter 5.

38. Chapter six, "Redemption, Regeneration, Revolution: Africa and Haiti," of Jacqueline Bacon's indispensable history of *Freedom's Journal* provides the most vigorous and detailed account of the editors' interest in Haiti; see Bacon, *Freedom's Journal: The First African-American Newspaper* (Lanham: Lexington Books, 2007), 147–77.

39. Mary Grace Albanese, "Caribbean Visions: Revolutionary Mysticism in 'Theresa: A Haytien Tale,'" *ESQ: A Journal of Nineteenth-Century American Literature and Culture* 62, no. 4 (2016): 572.

40. Albanese, "Caribbean Visions," 572.

41. See Benjamin Fagan, *The Black Newspaper and the Chosen Nation* (Athens: University of Georgia Press, 2016), especially chapter 1, "Acting Chosen," 20–41.

42. See Jeffrey Sommers, *Race, Reality, and Realpolitik: U.S.-Haiti Relations in the Lead Up to the 1915 Occupation* (Lanham: Lexington Books, 2015), 124.

43. Sara Fanning, *Caribbean Crossing: African Americans and the Haitian Emigration Movement* (New York: NYU Press, 2015), 10.

44. Fanning, *Caribbean Crossing*, 2.

45. Francis Smith Foster, "Forgotten Manuscripts: How Do You Solve a Problem Like Theresa?" *African American Review* 40, no. 3 (2006), 631–45. After her critical introduction, Foster reproduces the text of "Theresa," and thus provides the first modern reprinting of the text. See Foster, "Forgotten Manuscripts," 631–3, 637, and 637.

46. Eric Gardner, *Unexpected Places: Relocating Nineteenth-Century African American Literature* (Jackson: University of Mississippi Press, 2009), 4.

47. I have learned much from Sean Gerrity's work on these literary geographies of freedom, especially his thinking about the mappings of freedom which figured in Harriet Jacobs work. I very much look forward to the forthcoming publication of his sure to

be important book, *A Canada in the South: Maroons in American Literature*. See also, Gerrity, "Harriet Jacobs, Marronage, and Alternative Freedoms in *Incidents in the Life of a Slave Girl*." *Legacy: A Journal of American Women Writers*, vol. 38 no. 1, 2021, pp. 67–89.

48. Foster, "Forgotten Manuscripts," 631.
49. Foster, "Forgotten Manuscripts," 637–9.
50. I am thinking here with Lois Parkinson Zamora's notion of a "usable past," which she frames as the ways in which writers self-consciously work to insert themselves in the construction of an American canon as a means to claim a different version of that canon as foundational; see Zamora, *The Usable Past: The Imagination of History in Recent Fiction of the Americas* (New York: Cambridge University Press, 1997).
51. Foster, "Forgotten Manuscripts," 634.
52. Foster, "Forgotten Manuscripts," 641–62.
53. Foster, "Forgotten Manuscripts," 642.
54. As I argued in Chapter 3, much of the North American interest in promoting maple sugaring (abolitionist or otherwise) was a direct result of the almost total monopoly that the plantocracy in Haiti had on the sugar industry. Sugar harvesting in pre-revolutionary Haiti was almost a monoculture, and thus the ways in which "S" reimagines the agricultural production of the island is a clear instance of the text's fabulist impulses. In a kind of reversal of the ways in which Kara Walker's "A Subtly" sought to conjure a reckoning of the human beings involved in sugar cultivation and production as a means of asking for historical acknowledgement, "S" seeks to dissociate diasporic Africans from sugar production to register their historical attachments to the New World not as forced laboring bodies, but as humans with social, cultural, and political networks that needed to be recognized.
55. Marlene Daut concludes, "it is painfully obvious that the writer of this brief tale had little or no first-hand knowledge or experience of either Haiti or Saint Domingue"; see Daut, *Tropics of Haiti: Race and the Literary History of the Haitian Revolution in the Atlantic World, 1789–1865* (Liverpool: Liverpool University Press, 2015), 309.
56. As early as Foster's recovery of the text, much speculation about the authorship of "Theresa" has suggested that it was written by an African American man, but Marlene Daut has argued otherwise and has convincingly suggested that it may well have been written by Maria W. Stewart or Sarah Forten; see Daut, *Tropics of Haiti*, 290–6.
57. One indication of this notable feature is that any version of the word slave only appears once in the text, in its opening line and in association with the riotous behaviors of the French, and that the Black figures in the text are routinely referred to as "Revolutionists," "Haytiens," or "natives."
58. In "Venus in Two Acts," Saidiya Hartman unfolds both the ubiquitous presence and the impossibility of accurately knowing anything about the suppressed experiences of enslaved peoples given the violences creating the archives of Atlantic slavery. In order to move forward given these impossible obstacles, salutatory Hartman begins to unfold her methodology of critical fabulation that animates much of her work; see Hartman, "Venus in Two Acts," *Small Axe* 12, no. 2 (2008): 1–14.
59. In this regard, I want to assert that "S" returns to the arguments that Russwurm and Cornish made in their "To Our Patrons" column, where they argued that Black writers needed to speak on Black issues because for far too long white writers have circulated denigrating and delusory accounts of Black life.

60. Recently, Marcy J. Dinius and Peter Thompson have explored the ways in which Walker deploys references to Haiti as part of his sustained critique of white America's anti-Blackness; see Dinius, *The Textual Effects of David Walker's "Appeal": Print-Based Activism Against Slavery, Racism, and Discrimination, 1829-1851* (Philadelphia: University of Pennsylvania Press, 2022); and Thompson, "David Walker's Nationalism—and Thomas Jefferson's," *Journal of the Early Republic* 37, no. 1 (2017): 47–80.

61. For more on these figurations of Haiti and Toussaint, see Ivy Wilson, "Entirely Different from Any Likeness I Ever Saw": Aesthetics as Counter-Memory Historiography and the Iconography of Toussaint Louverture," in *The Haitian Revolution and the Early United States Histories, Textualities, Geographies*, ed. Elizabeth Maddock Dillon and Michael Drexler (Philadelphia: University of Pennsylvania Press, 2016), 83.

62. For an in-depth analysis of how Hopkins journalistic and editorial work on Haiti reemerges as a fulcrum in her novel, see Mary Grace Albanese, "Unraveling the Blood Line: Pauline Hopkins's Haitian Genealogies," *J19: The Journal of Nineteenth-Century Americanists* 7, no. 2 (2019): 227–48.

63. In his provocative *Black Mirror: The Cultural Contradictions of American Racism* (Cambridge: Harvard University Press, 2017), Eric Lott traces how what he calls "the black mirror" of the American cultural imagination reflects back an essential representation of the white self, colored by the impossibility of suppressing the blackness so central to the composition of our reality. The black mirror serves, in other words, as the means by which racist Americans find (and still haven't found) what they are looking for.

64. Anthony Bouges, "Two Archives and the Idea of Haiti," in *The Haitian Revolution and the Early United States Histories, Textualities, Geographies*, ed. Elizabeth Maddock Dillon and Michael Drexler (Philadelphia: University of Pennsylvania Press, 2016), 315.

65. In this regard, my project aligns with a range of emergent Americanist works that seek to think beyond the decisiveness embedded in these terms. For example, see works like Robin Bernstein's *Racial Innocence: Performing American Childhood from Slavery to Civil Rights* (New York: NYU Press, 2011), which maps how childhood innocence gains racialized valences in the middle of the nineteenth century; or Cody Marr's *Nineteenth-Century American Literature and the Long Civil War* (New York: Cambridge University Press 2015), which advocates for considering such canonical writers as Herman Melville, Frederick Douglass, Walt Whitman, and Emily Dickinson as "transbellum," since they all continued writing well after the "Renaissance" they are habitually plotted into; or Kyla Wazana Tompkins's *Racial Indigestion: Eating Bodies in the 19th Century* (New York: NYU Press, 2012), which feasts on a range of neglected archives to think about how food production and consumption became a means of consolidating a national mythos around whiteness across the nineteenth century; or many of the important essays published within three recent collections that each disrupt traditional narratives about American literary history: Dana Luciano and Ivy Wilson eds, *Unsettled States: Nineteenth-Century American Literary Studies* (New York: NYU Press 2014); Cody Marrs and Christopher Hager (eds.), *Timelines of American Literature* (Baltimore: Johns Hopkins University Press, 2019); and Justine S. Murison (ed.), *American Literature in Transition, 1820-1860* (Cambridge: Cambridge University Press, 2022).

Works Cited

Adams-Campbell, Melissa. *New World Courtships: Transatlantic Alternatives to Companionate Marriage* (Hanover: Dartmouth College Press, 2015).

Albanese, Mary Grace. "Caribbean Visions: Revolutionary Mysticism in 'Theresa: A Haytien Tale,'" *ESQ: A Journal of Nineteenth-Century American Literature and Culture* 62.4 (2016): 569–609.

Albanese, Mary Grace. "Unraveling the Blood Line: Pauline Hopkins's Haitian Genealogies," *J19: The Journal of Nineteenth-Century Americanists* 7.2 (2019): 227–48.

Alemán, Jesse. "The Age of U.S. Latinidad," in *Timelines of American Literature*, ed. Marrs, Cody and and Christopher Hagee (Baltimore: Johns Hopkins University Press, 2019).

Alexander, Michelle. *The New Jim Crow: Mass Incarceration in the Age of Colorblindness* (New York: The New Press, 2010).

Allewaert, Monique. *Ariel's Ecology: Personhood and Colonialism in the American Tropics, 1760–1820* (Minneapolis: University of Minnesota Press, 2013).

Allewaert, Monique. "Super Fly: François Makandal's Colonial Semiotics," *American Literature* 91.3 (2019): 459–90.

Armstrong, Nancy, and Leonard Tennenhouse, "The Problem of Population and the Form of the American Novel," *American Literary History* 20.4 (2008): 667–85.

Azoulay, Ariella Aïsha. *Potential History: Unlearning Imperialism* (New York: Verso, 2019).

Bacon, Jacqueline Bacon. "The History of Freedom's Journal: A Study in Empowerment and Community," *The Journal of African American History* 88.1 (2003): 1–20.

Bailey, Lauren. "Gothic Economies: Capitalism and Vampirism," in *The Routledge Companion to Literature and Economics*, ed. Matt Seybold and Michelle Chihara (New York: Routledge, 2018), 89–95.

Bannet, Eve Tavor. "The Constantias of the 1790s: Tales of Constancy and Republican Daughters," *Early American Literature* 49.2 (2014): 435–66.

Baucom, Ian. *Specters of the Atlantic: Finance Capital, Slavery, and the Philosophy of History* (Durham: Duke University Press, 2005).

Baym, Nina. "Early Histories of American Literature: A Chapter in the Institution of New England," *American Literary History* 1.3 (1989): 459–88.

Baym, Nina. "How Men and Women Wrote Indian Stories," in *New Essays on Last of the Mohicans*, ed. H. Daniel Peck (New Brunswick: Rutgers University Press, 1992), 67–86.

Beltrán, Cristina. *Cruelty as Citizenship: How Migrant Suffering Sustains White Democracy* (Minneapolis: University of Minnesota Press, 2020).

Bergner, Gwen. "Introduction: The Plantation, the Postplantation, and the Afterlives of Slavery," *American Literature* 91.3 (2019): 447–57.

Berlin, Ira. *Many Thousands Gone* (Cambridge: Harvard University Press, 1998).

Bernstein, Robin. *Racial Innocence: Performing American Childhood from Slavery to Civil Rights* (New York: NYU Press, 2011).

Blackwell, Matthew Ryan. "Creating the Cold War canon: A History of the Center for Editions of American Authors" (Diss. University of Iowa, 2019).

Bouges, Anthony. "Two Archives and the Idea of Haiti," in *The Haitian Revolution and the Early United States: Histories, Textualities, Geographies*, ed. Elizabeth Maddock Dillon and Michael J. Drexler (Philadelphia: University of Pennsylvania Press, 2016), 314–25.

Bray, Katie. "'A Climate…More Prolific…in Sorcery': *The Black Vampyre* and the Hemispheric Gothic," *American Literature* 87.1 (2015): 1–21.

Brickhouse, Anna. "The Indian Slave Trade in Unca Eliza Winkfield's *The Female American*," *The Yearbook of English Studies* 46 (2016): 115–26.

Bruegel, Martin. *Farm, Shop, Landing: The Rise of a Market Society in the Hudson Valley, 1780–1860* (Durham: Duke University Press, 2002).

Burgett, Bruce. "Every Document of Civilization Is a Document of Barbary? Nationalism, Cosmopolitanism, and Spaces between: A Response to Nancy Armstrong and Leonard Tennenhouse," *American Literary History* 20.4 (2008): 686–94.

Butler, Judith "'Is Kinship Always Already Heterosexual?'" *Differences: A Journal of Feminist Cultural Studies* 13.1 (2002): 14–44.

Campt, Tina. *Listening to Images* (Durham: Duke University Press, 2017).

Carico, Aaron. *Black Market: The Slave's Value in National Culture after 1865* (Chapel Hill: The University of North Carolina Press, 2020).

Carso, Kerry Dean. *American Gothic Art and Architecture in the Age of Romantic Literature* (Cardiff: University of Wales Press, 2015).

Castronovo, Russ. *Fathering the Nation: American Genealogies of Slavery and Freedom* (Berkeley: University of California Press, 1995).

Cayton, Andrew. "The Authority of the Imagination in an Age of Wonder," *Journal of the Early Republic* 33.1 (2013): 1–27.

Chatellier, Courtney. "'Not of the Modern French School': Literary Conservatism and the Ancien Régime in Early American Periodicals." *Early American Studies: An Interdisciplinary Journal* 16.3 (2018): 489–513.

Chuh, Kandice. *Imagine Otherwise: On Asian Americanist Critique* (Durham: Duke University Press, 2003).

Cleves, Rachel Hope. *The Reign of Terror in America: Visions of Violence from Anti-Jacobinism to Antislavery* (New York: Cambridge University Press, 2009).

Connolly, Brian. *Domestic Intimacies: Incest and the Liberal Subject in Nineteenth-Century America* (Philadelphia: University of Pennsylvania Press, 2014).

Couch, Daniel Dietz. *American Fragments: The Political Aesthetics of Unfinished Forms in the Early Republic* (Philadelphia: University of Pennsylvania Press, 2022).

Cowie, Alexander. *The Rise of the American Novel* (New York: American Book Company, 1951).

Crane, Jacob. "Barbary(an) Invasions: The North African Figure in Republic Print Culture," *Early American Literature* 50.2 (2015): 331–58.

Dangerfield, George. *The Era of Good Feelings* (New York: Harcourt, Brace and Co., 1952).

Daut, Marlene. *Tropics of Haiti: Race and the Literary History of the Haitian Revolution in the Atlantic World, 1789–1865* (Liverpool: Liverpool University Press, 2015).

Daut, Marlene. "The Wrongful Death of Toussaint Louverture," *History Today* 70.6 (2020). https://www.historytoday.com/archive/feature/wrongful-death-toussaint-louverture

Davidson, Cathy Davidson. *Revolution and the Word: The Rise of the Novel in America* (New York: Oxford University Press, 1986).

Dayan, Colin, *Haiti, History, and the Gods* (Berkeley: University of California Press, 1998).

Derrida, Jacques, *Specters of Marx: The State of the Debt, the Work of Mourning and the New International,* Translated from the French by Peggy Kamuf (New York: Routledge 1994).

Dillon, Elizabeth Maddock. "The Original American Novel, or, The American Origin of the Novel," in *A Companion to the Eighteenth-Century English Novel and Culture*, ed. Paula Backscheider and Catherine Ingrassia (London: Blackwell, 2009), 235–60.

Dillion, Elizabeth Maddock. *New World Drama: The Performative Commons in the Atlantic World, 1649–1849* (Durham: Duke University Press, 2014).

Dillon, Elizabeth Maddock, and Michael Drexler, "Haiti and the Early United States, Entwined," in *The Haitian Revolution and the Early United States: Histories, Textualities, Geographies*, ed. Elizabeth Maddock Dillon and Michael J. Drexler (Philadelphia: University of Pennsylvania Press, 2016), 1–16.

Dillon, Elizabeth Maddock, and Kate Simpkins. "Makandal and Pandemic Knowledge: Literature, Fetish, and Health in the Plantationocene," *American Literature* 92.4 (2020): 723–35.

Dinius, Marcy J. *The Textual Effects of David Walker's "Appeal": Print-Based Activism Against Slavery, Racism, and Discrimination, 1829–1851* (Philadelphia: University of Pennsylvania Press, 2022).

Diouf, Sylviane A. *Servants of Allah: African Muslims Enslaved in the Americas* (New York: NYU Press, 1998).

Diouf, Sylviane A. *Slavery's Exiles* (New York: New York University Press, 2015).

Doolen, Andy. *Territories of Empire: U.S. Writing from the Louisiana Purchase to Mexican Independence* (New York: Oxford University Press, 2014).

Dowling, William C. *Literary Federalism in the Age of Jefferson: Joseph Dennie and The Port Folio, 1801–1811* (Columbia: University of South Carolina Press, 1999).

Doyle, Laura. *Freedom's Empire: Race and the Rise of the Novel in America* (Durham: Duke University Press, 2008).

Drexler, Michael, and Ed White. *The Traumatic Colonel: The Founding Fathers, Slavery, and the Phantasmatic Aaron Burr* (New York: NYU Press, 2014).

Drexler, Michael, and Ed White. "The Constitution of Toussaint: Another Origin of African American Literature," *A Companion to African American Literature* (Oxford: Wiley-Blackwell, 2010), 59–74.

Dubois, Laurent. *Avengers of the New World: The Story of the Haitian Revolution* (Cambridge: Harvard University Press, 2004).

Dubois, Laurent. *A Colony of Citizens: Revolution and Slave Emancipation in the French Caribbean, 1787–1804* (Chapel Hill: The University of North Carolina Press, 2004).

Dubois, Laurent. *Haiti: The Aftershocks of History* (New York: Picador, 2013).

Dubois, Laurent. *The Banjo: America's First African Instrument* (Cambridge: Harvard University Press, 2016).

Dwight, Theodore. *History of the Hartford Convention: With A Review of the Policy of the United States Government which led to the War of 1812* (New York: N. & J. White, 1833).

Egan, Jim. *Oriental Shadows: The Presence of the East in Early American Literature,* (Columbus: Ohio State University Press, 2011).

Egerton, Douglas. *Gabriel's Rebellion: The Virginia Slave Conspiracies of 1800 and 1802* (Chapel Hill: The University of North Carolina Press, 1993).

Eudell, Demetrius L. "From Mode of Production to Mode of Auto-Institution: Sylvia Wynter's Black Metamorphosis of the Labor Question," *Small Axe: A Caribbean Journal of Criticism* 49 (2016): 47–61.

Fagan, Benjamin. *The Black Newspaper and the Chosen Nation* (Athens: The University of Georgia Press, 2016).

Fagan, Benjamin. "Chronicling White America," *American Periodicals: A Journal of History and Criticism* 26.1 (2016): 10–13.

Faherty, Duncan. " 'The Mischief That Awaits Us': Revolution, Rumor, and Serial Unrest in the Early Republic," in *The Haitian Revolution and the Early United States: Histories, Textualities, Geographies*, ed. Elizabeth Maddock Dillon and Michael J. Drexler (Philadelphia: University of Pennsylvania Press, 2016), 58–80.

Faherty, Duncan. " 'Murder, Robbery, Rape, Adultery, and Incest': Martha Meredith Read's *Margaretta* and the Function of Federalist Fiction," *Warring for America: Cultural*

Contests in the Era of 1812 (Chapel Hill: The University of North Carolina Press, 2017), 95–126.

Faherty, Duncan. "On the Hudson River Line: Postrevolutionary Regionalism, Neo-Tory Sympathy, and 'A Lady of the State of New-York,'" *Mapping Region in Early American Writing* (Athens: The University of Georgia Press, 2015), 138–59.

Fanning, Sara. *Caribbean Crossing: African Americans and the Haitian Emigration Movement* (New York: NYU Press, 2015).

Fichtelberg, Joseph. "Friendless in Philadelphia: The Feminist Critique of Martha Meredith Read," *Early American Literature* 32.3 (1997): 205–21.

Fichtelberg, Joseph. "The Sentimental Economy of Isaac Mitchell's 'The Asylum.'" *Early American Literature* 32.1 (1997): 1–19.

Fichtelberg, Joseph. "Heart-Felt Verities: The Feminism of Martha Meredith Read," *Legacy* 15.2 (1998): 125–38.

Fichtelberg, Joseph. *Critical Fictions: Sentiment and the American Market, 1780–1870* (Athens: The University of Georgia Press, 2003).

Fick, Carolyn E. *The Making of Haiti: The Saint Domingue Revolution from Below* (Knoxville: University of Tennessee Press, 1990).

Fielder, Brigitte Fielder. "*The Woman of Colour* and Black Atlantic Movement," *Women's Narratives of the Early Americas and the Formation of Empire*, ed. Mary Balkun and Susan Imbarrato (New York: Palgrave, 2016), 171–85.

Foster, Francis Smith. "Forgotten Manuscripts: How Do You Solve a Problem Like Theresa?," *African American Review* 40.3 (2006), 631–45.

Franklin, Wayne. *James Fenimore Cooper: The Early Years* (New Haven: Yale University Press, 2007).

Fraser, Gordon. "Emancipatory Cosmology: Freedom's Journal, The Rights of All, and the Revolutionary Movements of Black Print Culture," *American Quarterly* 68.2 (2016): 263–86.

Fraser, Gordon. "Review of *The Haitian Revolution and the Early United States: Histories, Textualities, Geographies*, ed. Elizabeth Maddock Dillon and Michael Drexler," *MELUS: Multi-Ethnic Literature of the U.S.* 42.4 (2017): 221–23.

Freeman, Elizabeth. *Time Binds: Queer Temporalities, Queer Histories* (Durham: Duke University Press, 2010).

Frost, Linda. "The Body Politic in Tabitha Tenney's *Female Quixotism*," *Early American Literature* 32.2 (1997): 113–34.

Fuentes, Maria J. *Dispossessed Lives: Enslaved Women, Violence, and the Archive* (Philadelphia: University of Pennsylvania Press, 2016).

Gardner, Eric. *Unexpected Places: Relocating Nineteenth-Century African American Literature* (Jackson: University of Mississippi Press, 2009).

Gardner, Jared. *The Rise and Fall of Early American Magazine Culture* (Urbana: University of Illinois Press, 2012).

Gaul, Theresa S. "Recovering Recovery: Early American Women and *Legacy's* Future," *Legacy* 26.2 (2009): 262–76.

Geggus, David. *Haitian Revolutionary Studies* (Bloomington: Indiana University Press, 2002).

Gellman, David N. *Emancipating New York: The Politics of Slavery and Freedom, 1777–1827* (Baton Rouge: LSU Press, 2008).

Gilmore, Ruth Wilson. "Race and Globalization," in *Geographies of Global Change: Remapping the World*, ed. R. J. Johnston et al. (New York: Wiley-Blackwell, 2002): 261–74.

Ginsburg Rebecca. "Escaping through a Black Landscape," in *Cabin, Quarter, Plantation: Architecture and Landscapes of North America*, ed. Clifton Ellis and Rebecca Ginsburg (New Haven: Yale University Press, 2010), 51–67.

Gordon, Avery. *Ghostly Matters: Haunting and The Sociological Imagination* (Minneapolis: University of Minnesota Press, 1997).

Gordon-Reed, Annette. *Thomas Jefferson and Sally Hemings: An American Controversy* (Charlottesville: University of Virginia Press, 1997).

Goudie, Sean X. *Creole America: The West Indies and the Formation of Literature and Culture in the New Republic* (Philadelphia: University of Pennsylvania Press, 2006).

Greeson, Jennifer. Rae *Our South: Geographic Fantasy and the Rise of National Literature* (Cambridge: Harvard University Press, 2010).

Grier, Miles P. *Inkface: Othello and White Authority in the Era of Atlantic Slavery* (Charlottesville: University of Virginia Press, 2023).

Gustafson, Sandra. "Histories of Democracy and Empire," *American Quarterly* 59.1 (2007): 107–33.

Hamnett, Brian. *The Historical Novel in Nineteenth-Century Europe: Representations in History and Fiction* (Oxford: Oxford University Press, 2011).

Harris, Leslie M. *In the Shadow of Slavery: African Americans in New York City, 1626–1863* (Chicago: University of Chicago Press: 2003).

Hartman, Saidiya. *Scenes of Subjection: Terror, Slavery, and Self-Making in Nineteenth-Century America* (New York: Oxford University Press, 1997).

Hartman, Saidiya. *Lose Your Mother: A Journey Along the Atlantic Slave Route* (New York, Farrar 2007).

Hartman, Saidiya. "Venus in Two Acts," *Small Axe* 12.2 (2008): 1–14.

Hartman, Saidiya. *Wayward Lives, Beautiful Experiments: Intimate Histories of Riotous Black Girls, Troublesome Women, and Queer Radicals* (New York: Norton, 2019).

Hattem, Michael D. "Citizenship and the Memory of the American Revolution in Nineteenth-Century Political Culture," *New York History* 101.1 (2020): 30–53.

Haulman, Clyde A. *Virginia and the Panic of 1819: The First Great Depression and the Commonwealth* (London: Pickering & Chatto, 2008).

Hewitt, Elizabeth. *Speculative Fictions: Explaining the Economy in the Early United States* (New York: Oxford University Press, 2020).

Holt, Keri. *Reading These United States: Federal Literacy in the Early republic, 1176–1830* (Athens: The University of Georgia Press, 2019).

hooks, bell. *Ain't I a Woman? Black Women and Feminism* (Abington: Routledge, 2013).

Horn, James J, Jan Ellen Lewis, and Peter S. Onuf (eds.) *The Revolution of 1800: Democracy, Race, and the New Republic* (Charlottesville: University of Virginia Press, 2002).

Hunt, Alfred. *Haiti's Influence on Antebellum America* (Baton Rouge: Louisiana State University Press, 1988).

Hutchinson, Peter. "A Publisher's History of American Magazines Eighteenth-Century American Magazines" (2008). http://www.themagazinist.com/uploads/Part_One_Birth_of_American_Magazines.pdf

Iannini, Christopher. *Fatal Revolutions: Natural History, West Indian Slavery, and the Routes of American Literature* (Chapel Hill: The University of North Carolina Press, 2012).

Jackson, Zakiyyah Iman. "Animal: New Directions on the Theorization of Race and Posthumanism," *Feminist Studies* 39.3 (2013): 669–85.

James, C.L.R. *The Black Jacobins: Toussaint L'Ouverture and the San Domingo Revolution* (New York: Random House, 1938).

Johnson, Sarah E. *The Fear of French Negroes* (Berkeley: University of California Press, 2012).

Jones, Kelly Houston. "'A Rough, Saucy Set of Hands to Manage': Slave Resistance in Arkansas," *The Arkansas Historical Quarterly* 71.1 (2012): 1–21.

Jones-Rogers, Stephanie E. "Rethinking Sexual Violence and the Marketplace of Slavery," in *Sexuality & Slavery*," in *Reclaiming Intimate Histories in the Americas*, ed. Daina Ramey Berry and Leslie M. Harris (Athens: The University of Georgia Press, 2018), 109–23.

Judy, R.A. *Sentient Flesh: Thinking in Disorder, Poiesis in Black* (Durham: Duke University Press, 2020).

Kaplan, Amy. "'Left Alone in America': The Absence of Empire in the Study of American Culture," in *Cultures of United States Imperialism*, ed. Amy Kaplan and Donald Pease (Durham: Duke University Press 1993), 3–21.

Kammen, Michael. *A Season of Youth: The American Revolution and the Historical Imagination* (New York: Alfred A Knopf, 1978).

King, Stewart. "The Maréchaussée of Saint-Domingue: Balancing the Ancien Régime and Modernity," *Journal of Colonialism and Colonial History* 5.2 (2004) doi:10.1353/cch.2004.0052.

Klein, Lauren. *An Archive of Taste: Race and Eating in the Early United States* (Minneapolis: University of Minnesota Press, 2020).

Knirsch, Christian. "Transcultural Gothic: Isaac Mitchell's *Alonzo and Melissa* as an Early Example of Popular Culture," in *Transnational Gothic: Literary and Social Exchange in the Long Nineteenth Century*, ed. Monika Elbert and Bridget M. Marshall (New York: Routledge, 2016), 35–47.

Koenigs, Tom. *Founded in Fiction: The Uses of Fiction in the Early United States* (Princeton: Princeton University Press, 2021).

LaFleur, Greta. *The Natural History of Sexuality in Early America* (Baltimore: Johns Hopkins University Press, 2018).

Levine, Robert S. "Fifth of July: Nathaniel Paul and the Construction of Black Nationalism," in *Genius in Bondage: Literature of the Early Black Atlantic*, ed. Vincent Carretta and Philip Gould (Lexington: University of Kentucky Press, 2001), 242–60.

Loughran, Trish. *The Republic In Print: Print Culture in the Age of U.S. Nation Building, 1770–1870* (New York: Columbia University Press, 2007).

Loshe, Lillie Deming. *The Early American Novel* (1907).

Lott, Eric. *Black Mirror: The Cultural Contradictions of American Racism* (Cambridge: Harvard University Press, 2017).

Lowe, Lisa. *The Intimacies of Four Continents* (Durham: Duke University Press, 2015).

Lowe, Lisa. "History Hesitant," *Social Text* 33.4 (2015): 85–107.

Luciano, Dana, and Ivy Wilson (eds.) *Unsettled States: Nineteenth-Century American Literary Studies* (New York: NYU Press, 2014).

Luis-Brown, David. *Waves of Decolonization: Discourses of Race and Hemispheric Citizenship in Cuba, Mexico, and the United States* (Durham: Duke University Press, 2008).

Mallipeddi, Ramesh. *Spectacular Suffering: Witnessing Slavery in the Eighteenth-Century British Atlantic* (Charlottesville: University of Virginia Press, 2016).

Malone, Gloria. "What Kara Walker's 'Sugar Baby' Showed Us," *Rewire News*, July 21, 2014. https://rewire.news/article/2014/07/21/kara-walkers-sugar-baby-showed-us/

Manganelli, Kimberly Snyder. *Transatlantic Spectacles of Race: The Tragic Mulatta and the Tragic Muse* (New York: Rutgers University Press, 2012).

Manning, Peter J. "Edmund Kean and Byron's Plays," *Keats-Shelley Journal* 21/2 (1972–3): 188–206.

Marrs, Cody. *Nineteenth-Century American Literature and the Long Civil War* (New York: Cambridge University Press, 2015).

Marrs, Cody, and and Christopher Hagee (eds.) *Timelines of American Literature* (Baltimore: Johns Hopkins University Press, 2019).

McIntosh, Hugh. "Constituting the End of Feeling: Interiority in the Seduction Fiction of the Ratification Era," *Early American Literature* 47.2 (2012): 321–48.

McKean, David. *Suspected of Independence: The Life of Thomas McKean, America's First Power Broker* (New York: Public Affairs, 2016).

McKittrick, Katherine. "Rebellion/Invention/Groove," *Small Axe: A Caribbean Journal of Criticism* 49 (2016): 79–97.

McGill, Meredith. *American Literature and the Culture of Reprinting, 1834–1853* (Philadelphia: The University of Pennsylvania Press, 2007).

Melamad, Jodi. *Represent and Destroy: Rationalizing Violence in the New Racial Capitalism* (Minneapolis: University of Minnesota Press, 2011).

Miller-Idriss, Cynthia. *Hate in the Homeland: The New Global Far Right* (Princeton: Princeton University Press, 2020).

Mintz, Sidney W. *Sweetness and Power: The Place of Sugar in Modern History* (New York: Penguin Books, 1986).

Mitter, Partha. "Western Theories of Beauty and Non-Western Peoples," in *Artistic Visions and the Promise of Beauty*, ed. K. Higgins, S. Maira, and S. Sikka (New York: Spring, 2017), 79–89.

Mohammed, Patricia. "'But Most of All mi Love Me Browning': The Emergence in Eighteenth and Nineteenth-Century Jamaica of the Mulatto Woman as the Desired," *Feminist Review* 65 (2000): 22–48.

Morgan, Jennifer. *Laboring Women: Gender and Reproduction in the Making of New World Slavery* (Philadelphia: University of Pennsylvania Press, 2004).

Morgan, Jennifer. *Reckoning with Slavery: Gender, Kinship and Capitalism in the Early Black Atlantic* (Durham: Duke University Press, 2021).

Mott, Frank. *A History of American Magazines 1741–1850* (Cambridge: Harvard University Press, 1957).

Murison, Justine S. (ed.) *American Literature in Transition, 1820–1860* (Cambridge: Cambridge University Press, 2022).

Murphy, Kieran M., and Kieran M. "What Was Tragedy during the Haitian Revolution?," *Modern Language Quarterly* 82.4 (2021): 417–40.

Ngai, Sianne. *Ugly Feelings* (Cambridge: Harvard University Press, 2007).

Pattee, Fred Lewis. "Call for a Literary Historian," *American Mercury* 2.6 (June 1924): 134–40.

Perez, Louis A., Jr. "Cuba and the United States: Origins and Antecedents of Relations, 1760s–1860s," *Cuban Studies* 21 (1991): 57–82.

Petter, Henri. *The Early American Novel* (Columbus: The Ohio State University Press, 1971).

Pitcher, Edward W.R. *Fiction in American magazines before 1800: An Annotated Catalogue* (Schenectady: Union College Press, 1993).

Polcha, Elizabeth. "Voyeur in the Torrid Zone," *Early American Literature* 54.3 (2019): 673–710.

Polcha, Elizabeth. "Redacting Desire: The Sexual Politics of Colonial Science in the Eighteenth-Century Atlantic World" (PhD diss., Northeastern University, 2019).

Popkin, Jeremy D. *Revolutionary News: The Press in France, 1789–1799* (Durham: Duke University Press, 1990), 19.

Pottroff, Christy L. "Circulation," *Early American Studies* 16.4 (2018): 621–27.

Powers, Nicolas. "Why I Yelled at the Kara Walker Exhibit," *The Indypendent*, June 30, 2014. https://indypendent.org/2014/06/why-i-yelled-at-the-kara-walker-exhibit/

Quashie, Kevin. *The Sovereignty of Quiet: Beyond Resistance in Black Culture* (New Brunswick: Rutgers University Press, 2012).

Read, Martha Meredith. *Monima; or, The Beggar Girl* (New York: T. B. Jansen & Co. Booksellers, 1802).

Rezek, Joseph. *London and the Making of Provincial Literature: Aesthetics and the Transatlantic Book Trade, 1800–1850* (Philadelphia: University of Pennsylvania Press, 2015).

Roberts, Neil. *Freedom as Marronage* (Chicago: The University of Chicago Press, 2015).

Salih, Sara. *Representing Mixed Race in Jamaica and England from the Abolition Era to the Present* (New York: Routledge, 2011).

Schuller, Kyla. *The Biopolitics of Feeling: Race, Sex, and Science in the Nineteenth Century*, (Durham: Duke University Press, 2018), 157.

Scott, David, *Conscripts of Modernity: The Tragedy of Colonial Enlightenment* (Durham: Duke University Press, 2004).

Scott, Julius S. *The Common Wind: Afro-American Currents in the Age of the Haitian Revolution* (London: Verso, 2018).

Scruggs, Dalia. "Photographs to Answer Our Purposes: Representations of the Liberian Landscape in Colonization Print Culture," in *Early African American Print* Culture, ed. Laura Langer Cohen and Jordan Stein (Philadelphia: University of Pennsylvania Press, 2012), 203–30.

Serres, Michel, with Bruno Latour, *Conversations on Science, Culture, and Time*, trans. Roxanne Lapidus (Ann Arbor: The University of Michigan Press, 1995).

Serwer, Adam. "The Fight over the 1619 Project Is Not about the Facts," *The Atlantic*, December 23, 2019. https://www.theatlantic.com/ideas/archive/2019/12/historians-clash-1619-project/604093/

Simpkins, Kate. "The Absent Agronomist and the Lord of Poison: Cultivating Modernity in Transatlantic Literature, 1758–1854" (Diss, Northeastern University 2016). https://repository.library.northeastern.edu/files/neu:cj82nc446/fulltext.pdf

Sitterson, Carlyle. *Sugar Country: The Cane Sugar Industry in the South, 1753–1950* (Lexington: University of Kentucky Press, 1953).

Sokol, Zack. "How Kara Walker Built a 75-Foot-Long Candy Sphinx in the Abandoned Domino Sugar Factory," *Vice*, May 8, 2014. https://www.vice.com/en_us/article/3d5qaj/how-kara-walker-built-a-75-foot-long-candy-sphinx-in-the-abandoned-domino-sugar-factory

Sommers, Jeffrey. *Race, Reality, and Realpolitik: U.S.-Haiti Relations in the Lead Up to the 1915 Occupation* (Lanham: Lexington Books, 2015).

Spillers, Hortense. "Mama's Baby, Papa's Maybe: An American Grammar Book," *Diacritics* 17.2 (1987): 65–81.

Stovall, Tyler. *White Freedom: The Racial History of an* Idea (Princeton: Princeton University Press, 2021).

Sturgess, Mark, "Bleed on, Blest Tree!" Maple Sugar Georgics in the Early American Republic," *Early American Studies* 16.2 (2018): 353–80.

Sublette, Ned, and Constance Sublette. *The American Slave Coast: A History of the Slave-Breeding Industry* (New York: Lawrence Hill Books, 2015).

Sundquist, Eric J. *To Wake the Nations: Race in the Making of American Literature* (Cambridge: Harvard University Press, 1993).

Tawil, Ezra. *Literature, American Style: The Originality of Imitation in the Early Republic* (Philadelphia: The University of Pennsylvania Press, 2018).

Taylor, Alan. *William Cooper's Town: Power and Persuasion on the Frontier of the Early American Republic* (New York: Vintage Books, 1996).

Taylor, Christopher. *Empire of Neglect: The West Indies in the Wake of British Liberalism* (Durham: Duke University Press, 2019).

Tennenhouse, Leonard. "Libertine America," *Differences: A Journal of Feminist Cultural Studies* 11.3 (1999): 1–28.

Tennenhouse, Leonard. *The Importance of Feeling English: American Literature and the British Diaspora, 1750–1850* (Princeton: Princeton University Press, 2007).

Thompson, Peter. "David Walker's Nationalism—and Thomas Jefferson's," *Journal of the Early Republic* 37.1 (2017): 47–80.

Tomba, Massimiliano. *Insurgent Universality: An Alternative Legacy of Modernity* (New York: Oxford University Press, 2019).

Tompkins, Jane. *Sensational Designs: The Cultural Work of American Fiction, 1790–1860* (New York: Oxford University Press, 1986).

Tompkins, Kyla Wazana. *Racial Indigestion: Eating Bodies in the 19th Century* (New York: New York University Press, 2012).

Trouillot, Michel-Rolph. *Silencing the Past: Power and the Production of History* (New York: Beacon Press, 1995).

Tuck, Eve, and C. Ree, "A Glossary of Haunting," *Handbook of Autoethnography*, ed. Stacey Holman Jones, Tony E. Adams, and Carolyn Ellis (New York: Routledge, 2013), 639–58.

Van Bergen, Jennifer. "Reconstructing Leonora Sansay," *Another World Is Possible* 1 (2010), accessed 25 April 2023. http://www.a-w-i-p.com/index.php/2010/01/03/reconstructing-leonora-sansay

Warfel, Henry R. *Charles Brockden Brown: American Gothic Novelist* (Gainesville: University of Florida Press, 1949).

Weheliye, Alexander G. *Habeus Viscus: Racializing Assemblages, Biopolitics, and Black Feminist Theories of the Human* (Durham: Duke University Press, 2014).

White, Ashli. *Encountering Revolution: Haiti and the Making of the Early Republic* (Baltimore: Johns Hopkins University Press, 2010).

White, Ed. "Divided We Stand: Emergent Conservatism in Royall Tyler's *The Algerine Captive*," *Studies in American Fiction* 37.1 (2010): 5–27.

White, Ed. "Trends and Patterns in the US Novel 1800–1820," in *The Oxford History of the Novel in English: The American Novel to 1870*, ed. J. Gerald Kennedy and Leland S. Person (New York: Oxford University Press, 2014), 73–88.

White, Shane. *Somewhat More Independent: The End of Slavery in New York City, 1770–1810* (Athens: The University of Georgia Press, 2012).

Wilkens, Matthew. "The Geographic Imagination of Civil War-Era American Fiction," *American Literary History* 25.4 (2013): 803–40.

Williams, Raymond. "Pastoral and Counter-Pastoral," *Critical Quarterly* (1968): 277–90.

Wilson, Ivy. "Entirely Different from Any Likeness I Ever Saw": Aesthetics as Counter-Memory Historiography and the Iconography of Toussaint Louverture," in *The Haitian Revolution and the Early United States: Histories, Textualities, Geographies*, ed. Elizabeth Maddock Dillon and Michael J. Drexler (Philadelphia: University of Pennsylvania Press, 2016), 80–94.

Wortendyke, Gretchen. "Romance to Novel: A Secret History," *Narrative* 17.3 (2009): 255–73.

Wright, Nazera Sadiq. *Blackgirlhood in the Nineteenth Century* (Urbana: University of Illinois Press, 2016).

Wynter, Sylvia, and Katherine McKittrick (eds.) *Sylvia Wynter: On Being Human as Praxis* (Durham: Duke University Press, 2015), 10.

Young, Elizabeth. *Black Frankenstein: The Making of An American Metaphor* (New York: New York University Press, 2008).

Zamora, Lois Parkinson. *The Usable Past: The Imagination of History in Recent Fiction of the Americas* (New York: Cambridge University Press, 1997).

Zilversmit, Arthur. *The First Emancipation: The Abolition of Slavery in the North* (Chicago: University of Chicago Press: 1967).

Index

For the benefit of digital users, indexed terms that span two pages (e.g., 52–53) may, on occasion, appear on only one of those pages.